Political Conversion

Lexington Studies in Political Communication

Series Editor: Robert E. Denton, Jr., Virginia Tech University

This series encourages focused work examining the role and function of communication in the realm of politics including campaigns and elections, media, and political institutions.

Recent Titles in the Series

Political Conversion: Personal Transformation as Strategic Public Communication
By Don Waisanen

The 2016 American Presidential Campaign and the News: Implications for the American Republic and Democracy
Edited by Jim A. Kuypers

A Rhetoric of Divisive Partisanship: The 2016 American Presidential Campaign Discourse of Bernie Sanders and Donald Trump
By Colleen Elizabeth Kelley

Studies of Communication in the 2016 Presidential Campaign
Edited by Robert E. Denton, Jr.

The Monstrous Discourse in the Donald Trump Campaign: Implications for National Discourse
By Debbie Jay Williams and Kalyn L. Prince

The Political Blame Game in American Democracy
Edited by Larry Powell and Mark Hickson

Political Campaign Communication: Theory, Method, and Practice
Edited by Robert E. Denton, Jr.

Still Paving the Way for Madam President, Revised Edition
By Nichola D. Gutgold

James Farmer Jr.: The Great Debater
By Ben Voth

Political Conversion

Personal Transformation as Strategic Public Communication

Don Waisanen

LEXINGTON BOOKS
Lanham • Boulder • New York • London

Published by Lexington Books
An imprint of The Rowman & Littlefield Publishing Group, Inc.
4501 Forbes Boulevard, Suite 200, Lanham, Maryland 20706
www.rowman.com

Unit A, Whitacre Mews, 26-34 Stannary Street, London SE11 4AB

Copyright © 2018 by The Rowman & Littlefield Publishing Group, Inc.

All rights reserved. No part of this book may be reproduced in any form or by any electronic or mechanical means, including information storage and retrieval systems, without written permission from the publisher, except by a reviewer who may quote passages in a review.

British Library Cataloguing in Publication Information Available

Library of Congress Cataloging-in-Publication Data

Names: Waisanen, Don, author.
Title: Political conversion : personal transformation as strategic public communication / by Don Waisanen.
Description: Lanham, Maryland : Lexington Books, [2018] | Series: Lexington studies in political communication | Includes bibliographical references and index.
Identifiers: LCCN 2018007527 (print) | LCCN 2018014910 (ebook) | ISBN 9781498575737 (Electronic) | ISBN 9781498575720 (cloth : alk. paper)
Subjects: LCSH: Communication in politics--United States. | Religion and politics--United States. | Conversion. | Chambers, Whittaker. Witness. | Podhoretz, Norman. Breaking ranks. | Horowitz, David, 1939- Radical son. | Wills, Garry, 1934- Confessions of a conservative.
Classification: LCC JA85.2.U6 (ebook) | LCC JA85.2.U6 W35 2018 (print) | DDC 320.97301/4--dc23
LC record available at https://lccn.loc.gov/2018007527

∞™ The paper used in this publication meets the minimum requirements of American National Standard for Information Sciences Permanence of Paper for Printed Library Materials, ANSI/NISO Z39.48-1992.

Printed in the United States of America

This project was supported by a Eugene M. Lang Fellowship and a Professional Staff Congress grant from the City University of New York

Table of Contents

Acknowledgments	ix
Introduction: Political Transformation as a Pervasive Strategy	1
1 Political Conversion as Manichaean Deduction: Whittaker Chambers's *Witness*	39
2 Political Conversion as Intellectual Reduction: Norman Podhoretz's *Breaking Ranks*	83
3 Political Conversion as Generational Induction: David Horowitz's *Radical Son*	119
4 Political Conversion as Bypassed Seduction: Garry Wills's *Confessions of a Conservative*	159
5 Political Transformation in U.S. Politics	181
Bibliography	209
Index	235
About the Author	245

Acknowledgments

I'd like to thank Randall Lake for his early encouragement and steadfast feedback throughout the first phase of this project. I'd also like to thank Stephen O'Leary, Tom Goodnight, and Nina Eliasoph for reading and responding to drafts in this book with interest, insights, and care. To Dean David Birdsell, his incredible staff, and all of my colleagues and students at the Baruch College, CUNY Marxe School of Public and International Affairs, I owe immense gratitude for all the support and guidance you have offered me over the last decade. I consider myself fortunate to be part of such a wonderful team. To my parents, thanks for your unconditional support and love; every day I'm trying to pay it forward. Last, all my love goes to my spouse Lauren and sons Joel and Sam, without whom this project would not have been possible. You bring inspiration, wisdom, and joy to my every day.

Introduction

Political Transformation as a Pervasive Strategy

"I once was lost, but now am found, was blind but now I see."[1] This famous verse from John Newton's eighteenth-century hymn "Amazing Grace" shares an experience echoed across the ages—the religious conversion story. Conversion is one of the oldest persuasive practices in Western history. For the last 2,500 years, people have used tales of their fundamental change from one orientation to another to convince themselves and others that their new beliefs, values, and attitudes are superior to their former approaches. Given their history and influence, some even describe conversion stories as "nearly perfect rhetorical devices."[2]

People have publicized their conversion experiences to audiences through autobiographies, such as Augustine's *Confessions*, George Fox's *The Journal of George Fox*, and Thomas Merton's *The Seven Storey Mountain*.[3] Yet many have adapted conversion narratives in contexts outside religion. Jean-Jacques Rousseau wrote his tell-all *The Confessions* to reveal his turn to a deeply individualist, secular lifestyle and philosophy.[4] Thomas De Quincy's *Confessions of an English Opium Eater* documented a struggle with drug addiction.[5] Scientists like René Descartes and Nicolas Copernicus used secular conversion narratives to convey their scientific journeys and findings to the general public.[6] Even Sigmund Freud's psychoanalysis promoted a type of nonreligious change in worldview and identity.[7]

Following these trends, an intriguing phenomenon has developed in the United States, as prominent figures have not only imported the conversion narrative into public affairs but conceived of it as a political, rather than a religious, experience. While religious conversion narratives have a long history, the political version is a more recent development as a strategy aimed at winning the hearts and minds of the public. Walking through any local bookstore, one is struck by the volume of political conversion autobiographies in the marketplace.[8] A broad range of political converts and party switchers exist, both producing and being influenced by networks of rhetoric about personal transformation. Such figures as Ronald Reagan, Hillary Clinton, Arthur Koestler, Irving Kristol, Richard Weaver, and Malcolm X—and, more recently, David Horowitz, Arianna Huffington, James Jeffords, David Brock, Christopher Hitchens, Linda Chavez, Dennis Miller, Thomas Sowell, Rick Perry, Michelle Bachmann, Bruce Bartlett, and Charlie Crist—all have used political conversion stories to gain support for their lives and causes.

These stories act as strategic messages in public affairs. In 2004, for instance, the Republican Party asked former Democratic governor Zell Miller to deliver its keynote address at the Republican National Convention, in order to support President George W. Bush's campaign and policies. Jane Roe, of the landmark Supreme Court abortion case *Roe v. Wade*, renounced her pro-choice views and was embraced by conservative organizations as a model for antiabortion advocacy. Roe even wrote an autobiography documenting her journey as a religious and political convert.[9] From the other side of the political spectrum, former Republican governor of Florida Charlie Crist used the tactic in his book *The Party's Over: How the Extreme Right Hijacked the GOP and I Became a Democrat.*[10] Amid the tumult of Donald Trump's presidency, former National Public Radio CEO Ken Stern even penned *Republican Like Me: How I Left the Liberal Bubble and Learned to Love the Right*, documenting his transformation from a Democrat to an independent.[11] These leaders stand before the public as convincing examples, testifying to a personal change with political relevance.

Political conversion narratives have circulated in other ways. Many volunteers for Barack Obama's 2008 presidential campaign were specially trained not to share their policy views with potential supporters but, instead, to tell "potential voters personal stories of political conversion" to Obamaism.[12] From a different viewpoint, one need only look at former Marxist-turned-conservative David Horowitz's relationship to the Republican Party. Horowitz was among "the refugees from the New Left who . . . turned up on George W. Bush's doorstep," as one of many ex-radicals responsible for Bush administration policies. Converted elites such as Horowitz drew from their former experiences to invent terms such as "compassionate conservative," a symbol intended to appeal to voters on the left and on the right in Bush's presidential campaign.[13] David Brock provides another example. In a past life as a conservative writer, Brock was infamous for his coverage of Anita Hill during the Supreme Court hearings over the nomination of Clarence Thomas and another series of writings that fostered conservative campaigns to impeach President Clinton in the 1990s.[14] Yet years later, President Clinton praised Brock for converting from conservatism.[15]

Overall, in whichever medium they might be presented, conversion narratives are messages with public significance. These "stories of transformation" aim to sway or further reinforce readers' very views of the world.[16] They have influenced leaders at the highest levels of power and have been foundational in the creation of movements such as neoconservatism and ideas like the Cold War domino theory.[17] As this book will detail at greater length, many audiences have also seen these stories as model examples of communication and contributions to public discourse. Readers have described political conversion narratives as produced by some of the "most sophisticated thinkers in the postwar era,"[18] who have possessed "a fearless capacity for self-examination"[19] and exhibited intellectual virtues across their writings.[20] They have been perceived as positively influencing public debate in the United States,[21] promoting an "open, honest contest of ideas in the public square,"[22] and, in a comment that I hope to rebut convincingly, as "surprisingly free from rhetoric."[23]

This project thus explores and evaluates political conversion as strategic public discourse in the last half century of U.S. politics. As they circulate, political conversion stories raise questions about how and why this rhetorical strategy has evolved to meet the needs of contemporary authors and audiences. They straddle the spheres of religion and politics in unexpected ways, acting as atypical public "information and influence campaigns."[24] They show us what kinds of stories are acceptable to tell in public and how such stories draw and redraw the lines of public communication.

This book details the features and functions of these discourses as rhetorical tools and persuasive tactics in postwar politics. The principal focus of this volume is on the communicative qualities and contributions that these modes of storytelling make in public affairs. In contrast to many leaders and other readers who have praised such stories, I conclude—through in-depth, close textual and contextual analyses of four interrelated, touchstone case studies—that political conversion narratives tend to have propagandistic, antideliberative qualities in public communication. What I find most remarkable is that the authors of these stories fashion such problematic messages by fusing the conversion narrative with other rhetorical devices and resources. For example, in *Witness*, author Whittaker Chambers does more than simply tell the tale of his political conversion; he puts "conversion" and "conspiracy" rhetorics in the service of each other, bringing the realism and linear structure of the convert's story (i.e., from an old to a new life) to bear on abstract and random conspiracy claims in a way that creates authority for unsupported assertions. As a rhetorical weapon, the conversion form hence brings certain emphases and pressures to public discourse worth challenging upon close examination.

As a secondary consideration, this book argues that political conversion narratives are civil-religious strategies that negotiate the uneasy lines between church and state in U.S. politics. That is, political conversions benefit from projecting a traditionally resonant religious form in politics without seeming too religious. As Brian Kaylor has observed, "sometimes the political conversion experience on the way to Washington seems even more dramatic than the spiritual conversion of the biblical Paul on the way to Damascus."[25] Kaylor's statement is illustrative of both the religious and political power with which these stories tend to be leveraged. Moreover, these narratives work with expectations for not bringing church and state too closely together by, to varying degrees, using the conversion form and general religious beliefs while downplaying explicit religious content. Many figures have ultimately enlisted the conversion narrative's religious undertones in this way to absolve their public sins, justify a grand change in public affairs, and make their political work more effective.

In support of these arguments, this book covers three types of political conversion narratives that correspond to the book's first three case studies, each of which presents a conversion story in a different guise. Departing from these types, a fourth case study is offered as evidence of how at least one author bypassed the allures of the other political conversion narratives in his work, escaping the rhetorical trajectory established by the first case study.

Before delving into this book's framework, some sense of the environment in which political conversion narratives have developed, and several concepts, key terms, and definitions related to personal and public transformation, are first necessary to understand the strategy. This introductory chapter will then chart the journey that conversion narratives have taken from religious spheres to U.S. politics, spotlighting how and why these kinds of stories are largely unique to the modern era. The chapter then provides examples of religious and secular conversion strategies as a bridge to four intertextual works propagating—and, in one case, bypassing—political conversion, which will be examined in subsequent chapters.

Political conversion stories raise issues related to persuasive political practices, deliberation, and modes of reasoning in public culture. Beyond their history and influence, they speak to projects to understand and develop more "cosmopolitan" forms of communication across societies.[26] In this regard, in surveying both religious and secular tales of transformation, Golden, Berquist, and Coleman summarize a need to analyze this strategy across various times and places: "[C]onversion discourse is with us—'tracking' us. . . . The professional evangelists are here to stay. We need to know about these people—their strategies and habits. We need to consider ethics and the effect these wizards have on our daily existence."[27]

MEDIA, POLITICS, AND RELIGION: REASONING IN CONTEXT

Since 1945, the decline of political parties has fostered an environment where celebrities and personal experience have become increasingly revered in public affairs. The rise of mass media changed how citizens and leaders communicate about public issues, focusing on the individual lives of politicians to an unprecedented extent.[28] Some researchers have argued that U.S. political participation focuses more on entertainment than substance[29] and that the media environment has been too directed toward "the present, the unusual, the dramatic, simplicity, action, personalization, and results."[30] Renowned scholar Jürgen Habermas also believes that the following media forces work against political engagement in contemporary societies:

> [R]eporting facts as human-interest stories, mixing information with entertainment, arranging material episodically, and breaking down complex relationships into smaller fragments—all of this comes together to form a syndrome that works to depoliticize public communication.[31]

These media values undermine the complexity of political situations and promote individual over collective action.

For the past century, the world has further undergone a revolution in communication technologies. Citizens live in such a dense information environment that they have to use shortcuts to make political decisions, relying on simplified narrative structures and cultural symbols as guides to thought and action. Samuel Popkin describes the process as similar to a "drunkard's search."[32] Religious appeals, in particular, provide "cues that Americans use to truncate their information exposure and consideration."[33] Under these conditions, pseudo-political, anti-intellectual norms often trump thoughtful public participation.[34] Overall, modern media bear upon the types of reasoning and expectations for reasonability that have emerged in political life, providing a context well suited to appeals like political conversion.

Over the last sixty years, other trends include a general decline in voting and involvement in elections[35] (with some exceptions, such as the 2008 presidential election) and a number of policies that turned many political behaviors from public to private acts.[36] Some believe that an increasingly irrational climate and declining spaces for civic education have only compounded these problems.[37] At the same time, Americans came out of World War II with a consensus fractured by Communist scares and the unrest of ensuing decades,[38] exemplified by events such as Vietnam and new demands for civil rights. Given the ferment and fragmentation in the postwar climate, the conversion narrative provided a sense of order for various figures, with new commitments creating a linear path for individuals and groups to follow.

Relative to U.S. politics, the extent to which such performances and rituals of citizenship promote or hinder public values has become an important issue.[39] Conversion narratives are a dramatic means of self-disclosure, leveraging one's private encounters toward political purposes. They promote certain visions of public engagement, fitting within the developing political and media ecologies of postwar culture and prompting questions about how they work and what they contribute to democracy.

Political conversion narratives additionally respond to a series of church and state developments creating unique demands for public communicators. The United States is a nation with a distinctive history of church–state relations. In antiquity, and for much of Western history, there simply was no difference between church and state.[40] The United States's founders made a break from their past experiences of religion and politics by calling the connection between these two realms into question, as reflected in a number of the nation's founding documents, such as the First Amendment to the U.S. Constitution.

Yet from the nation's inception, many religionists have sought to influence the public square with their faiths. These tensions between church and state have made it both easy and difficult to argue a religious perspective in U.S. politics. Many leaders have had few qualms about asserting their religious beliefs in politics as a way to gain support from various publics, but there are also clear pressures *not* to have religion in the public arena. When religion intrudes too far into the political realm, it can have a "Pharisee effect"—where audiences react negatively to religious appeals.[41] Some postwar factors accentuated this tension between church and state. Surprisingly, it was not until 1947 that the Supreme Court decided that the government must be neutral toward religion.[42] But in both official and unofficial ways, individuals and groups have stretched—and, in many cases, broken—this neutral stance. During the 1940s and 1950s, "civil-religious" discourses combining religious and secular appeals increased,[43] highlighting the evolving ways in which church and state have come to coexist.

It should therefore come as little surprise that traditionally religious forms such as conversion have found their way into politics. One can negotiate the demands of church–state tensions by subtly drawing upon the power of a religious structure, without explicitly stating religious doctrine. In fact, one need not have any religious beliefs at all to pursue this strategy. Although the content of political conversion narratives may be explicitly nonreligious, advocates can still use the historically resonant religious conversion form— of fundamental change from an old to a new life—to try to influence select audiences. While conversion continues to be an enduring historical pattern, its use in politics is largely uncharted. Many works on rhetoric have alluded to, but left undeveloped, the role that converts play in public campaigns and movements.[44]

Positioned with developments in U.S. media, politics, and church–state relations, conversion narratives complicate traditional notions of public reasoning. They make use of a narrative form in politics that has mostly emerged from past religious contexts, to argue in a way that is intensely personal and public, and propositional yet story-driven. These narratives document and intertwine a mass of empirical experience and abstract philosophical advocacy, often within the bounds of a chronological, autobiographical medium that is appropriated by individuals as well as larger movements in public affairs. To narrow these issues and provide a foundation for understanding the functions of political conversion rhetoric, some consideration must be given to storytelling as a means of public reasoning.

THE PROMISES AND PERILS OF PUBLIC STORYTELLING

Interdisciplinary scholarship raises the issue of what norms, standards, or conceptions of reason are critical for a functioning democracy. Traditionally, public deliberation has been defined as "debate and discussion aimed at producing reasonable, well-informed opinions in which participants are willing to revise preferences in light of discussion, new information, and claims made by fellow participants."[45] It is "an unconstrained exchange of arguments that involves practical reasoning and always potentially leads to a transformation of preferences."[46] Robert Asen argues that "deliberation entails a meta-level of critical reflection that promotes perspective-taking, which is a form of recognizing difference. . . . [D]eliberation unsettles and makes available for examination individual desires and suggests their possible transformation through discourse. It asks participants to judge critically their own claims and the claims of others."[47] Yet not all deliberation is of the same kind; the different communication styles, choice of topics, or values that citizens bring to public discourse can affect a discussion's quality.[48] Researchers differ about whether civility or rowdier forms of deliberation are best for democracy,[49] but questions about deliberation generally examine how "an advocate's discourse implicitly or explicitly widens or narrows discursive space for others."[50] For example, Cass Sunstein worries that many modern forms of communication foster "deliberative enclaves," where citizens interact with like-minded others without coming into contact with or engaging wider publics.[51]

Interactive processes of communication are not the only way of looking at deliberation—actual media content can also affect democratic participation by modeling particular norms or behaviors for audiences.[52] For instance, media content exhibiting "complexity" and the "co-presence of other claims" invites audiences to adopt similar practices, indicating how much authors care about evidence and how open their discourse is to alternative positions.[53] Oppositely, some find that cumulatively formulaic and obscure language, evocative words and twisted syntax, and other criteria can also constrain political ideas and informed decision making.[54] By surveying media messages, critics can closely track, as Daniel Brouwer suggests, how the "qualities and quantities of various [rhetorical] resources delimit the available means of persuasion."[55]

Deliberation scholars have underscored a need to describe why different public discourses should be considered democratic or not in a political environment where citizens can easily miss how such texts operate.[56] Habermas and others pose a more specific question relative to these issues: Which religious forms of communication support or detract from just and useful models of deliberative democracy?[57] Since religious and political conversion experiences are cast in story form, it is critical to examine the content and structure of these tales.

The impact of narrative modes of reasoning upon public affairs has also been widely debated.[58] Some find that narratives are a democratic form of communication. Stories, such as those that groups tell about injustice, can lead citizens to greater participation in public life.[59] On the other hand, narratives can focus too much on "emotional identification and familiar plots rather than on [the] testing or adjudication of truth claims, [and] they are better able than other discursive forms to rule out challenge."[60] As public arguments, the very pattern of stories can have an impact on public decision making by squeezing complex issues into the borders of their constricted, ordered molds.[61] Stories can also exclude and delegitimize alternative voices in political deliberations, privilege elite interpretations of events, and discourage critical reasoning.[62]

As a subset of these narrative issues, the roles that testimonies and personal experience play as evidence for citizens' claims have been of special concern. As argumentation scholar Charles Willard outlines, "the disciplined study of public deliberation may include such questions as: How is technical knowledge translated into testimony or public prose?" and "how do the narrative structures of entertainment media interfere with the rational evaluation of policy consequences?"[63] Feminist scholars have further led the way in discussions about whether experience undercuts or advances good reasoning, with Catherine Palczewski concluding that "we cannot discount the argumentative power of testimony and its ability not only to garner assent, but also to reconfigure [political] history and authority."[64]

During the Reagan presidency, for example, a government commission struggled with the place of citizens' seemingly subjective interpretations of events in public discussions.[65] Reagan's use of a personal "conversation" metaphor, which privileged motives of sincerity, consensus, and civility, ultimately framed a limited participation for others hoping to gain a voice in public policy formation.[66] In the 1990s, too, testimonies of "former welfare recipients" were used strategically in congressional debates to make it appear that low-income populations had a voice in the deliberations, while in effect, only elite interpretations toward the policy were advanced.[67] Similarly, some research contrasts highly individualistic forms of talk in policy discussions, where "the self monopolizes; the individual is central subject, provider of evidence, and solution," with more reasoned forms of public discussion that use an "analysis of data beyond subjective personal narratives and performances of self-identity."[68]

That said, many women activists have successfully used autobiography and personal experience to combat oppressive conditions, "enlarging the rhetorical spaces suitable for a discussion of women's roles and rights by offering their lives as evidence for their claims."[69] Studies of abortion advocacy have shown how personal testimony can transport evidence from the private to the public sphere, bringing relational morals into a realm dominated by strict, rule-based standards, and offering one liberating way of asserting how people know what they know.[70] As such, testimony is not necessarily a singular concept, with various deliberative functions worth teasing out in different contexts. The presence of conversion narratives in politics focuses the same tensions apparent in work on stories, testimonies, and experience as forms of evidence.

In sum, looking at stories in terms of deliberative democracy raises questions about the workings and functions of political conversion narratives. Gerald Peters suggests that, historically, conversion narratives have been all-encompassing forms of communication.[71] Primarily, it is a communicator's claim of fundamental change that is of most concern for public discourse, since "the application of any 'fundamental'—that is, revealed—truth to the political scene, being undebatable, makes impossible the open market place of ideas and powers."[72] Civic engagement relies on an ability to learn, to be corrected, and to work collaboratively with others, but such forms of communication challenge the very basis of this premise.

To understand this communication practice, it is worth examining how conversion arose in particular social and historical contexts—especially in Christianity and Judaism. The background of this traditionally totalizing strategy remains relevant to its current uses in politics.

CONVERSION AS A PERSUASIVE APPEAL

Given the long history of the term "conversion," it is critical to justify my use of it and to construct a definition for "political conversion." Some may question whether stories of political transformation can be called "conversions," since the transcendent elements typically involved in religious conversions are often missing in political accounts. While studied with the history of religion, conversion also had some secular foundations in the pre-Christian era of Greek philosophy.[73] There is a basis for studying secular conversion in both the classical and contemporary periods, although ancient philosophical conversion still retained many of the otherworldly elements characteristic of its religious counterparts. Most important, conversion was virtually unknown to most people in antiquity. Judaism, Christianity, and early Greek philosophy were mostly exclusive in their use of this practice.[74]

As a development emerging from this premodern history, conversion discourse is now prevalent in Western societies.[75] Most scholarship has focused on religious conversion accounts. Yet there are also clear examples of conversion rhetoric operating in less religious settings. In this wider sense, "conversion experiences have been described by feminists, Communists, television-evangelists, alcoholics, psychoanalysts, and scientists, by men, women, atheists, believers, whites, and peoples of color."[76] Wayne Booth called "secular conversion" discourse a "vast neglected area of rhetoric."[77] Kenneth Burke further admonished scholars to track the secular equivalents to religious change, using the term "secular conversion" to describe how the vocabulary of psychoanalysis constitutes conversion rhetoric.[78] Others have even described how the classical meanings of conversion are evident in concepts such as Maslow's self-actualized, healthy-minded individuals.[79]

Conversion has been construed in a variety of ways.[80] There is broad scholarly agreement that A. D. Nock and William James set forth the original definitions of conversion in twentieth-century scholarship. Nock describes conversion as: "The reorientation of the soul of an individual, his deliberate turning from indifference or from an earlier form of piety to another, a turning which implies a consciousness that a great change is involved, that the old was wrong and the new is right. It is seen at its fullest in the positive response of a man to the choice set before him by the prophetic religions."[81] James defines conversion similarly as "gradual or sudden, by which a self hitherto divided or consciously wrong, inferior and unhappy becomes unified and consciously right, superior and happy, by consequence of its firmer hold on religious realities."[82] Religious conversions have been described as "a radical reorganization of identity, meaning, and life,"[83] "the process of changing a sense of root reality," and "a conscious shift in one's sense of grounding."[84] More than a simple modification, each of these definitions involves a deep and total change in one's life.

Drawing closer to the rhetorical dimensions of conversion, and reviewing literatures on the concept from Nock and James to the present, Thomas Finn finds that "conversion in Greco-Roman religion, whether Pagan, Jewish, or Christian, was an extended ritual process that combined teaching and symbolic enactment—the cognitive and performative—and yielded commitment and transformation."[85] Whether religious or secular, conversion is connected to communication processes, involving a radical change in one's language community and available ways of talking about experience.[86] Although conversion typically documents one's fundamental crossing from an old to a new life, many researchers have developed more advanced typologies for the stages described in these journeys.[87] But more intriguing is "not how the [conversion] formula is strictly adhered to and repeated but, rather, how it is renovated, adapted, and deployed."[88]

Most definitions of conversion involve a transformative change in an individual's identity *and* social network. It is change that is fundamental and deep, and less short-term and more constant than other adjustments. Conversion is typically connected to the development of one's life. It can be a complete change of one's most cherished beliefs, values, and attitudes, or a return to one's past that provides a newfound sense of reality. It almost always involves groups, as one joins a group in converting from one paradigm to another (and in-group and out-group boundaries are often reconfigured through the switch), bringing legitimacy and emotional bonding through its ritualistic, communal emphases.

Many terms relate to conversion—for example, confession, mortification, and apologia. But conversion still most captures the sense of transformation constituted by those asserting a public, deep, fundamental change from one state of being, knowing, and acting to another. What, then, is the threshold of political conversion? For this book's purposes, it is enough to define political conversion as one's public assertion of or justification for changing from one political ideology to another.[89] Confessional rhetorics in politics, for instance, may or may not evidence conversion. Individuals might assert that they are sorry for past mistakes, without necessarily turning away from former allegiances and converting into or out of a new political party or worldview. I believe that major policy changes, say, from pro-life to pro-choice on abortion policy, constitute a type of political conversion to particular causes that can occur without party changes. For the moment, these types of political conversions are left outside the scope of this book, in order to focus on accounts where a major shift in party or political paradigm coincides with one's fundamental public reorientation and repositioning.

A Historical Emergence of Political Conversion

As authors such as Craig Martin, Russell McCutcheon, and Mark Noll have written about extensively, many people of faith in the United States efface the historical and social trends in which their faith practices are situated to make individual religious claims appear free from the influence of language communities and particular interpretive choices.[90] So it is critical to position seemingly "personal" narratives of political conversion in certain sociohistorical settings. The conversion pattern grew out of Greek philosophy, Old Testament, Pauline, and Augustinian accounts of public transformation.[91]

Many believe that Augustine's autobiography *Confessions* was the grandest articulation of conversion in the classical period. Indeed, Augustine's touchstone work "devised three autobiographical forms—historical self-recollection, philosophical self-exploration, and poetic self-expression," which most lengthy conversion accounts have followed and adapted.[92] But the genre's popularity took some time to develop; Augustine's work was not copied extensively until the medieval and late classical periods, mainly because of Catholic rituals supplanting a need for these kinds of performances.[93] Later in Western history, public communicators revived the connection between conversion and autobiography. In particular, conversion narratives burgeoned during the Reformation.[94] In this period, autobiography arose and coincided with the increasing value of individual experience and change in Western societies.[95] The medium corresponded with the development of modern conversion forms, providing a means of propagating both the content and form of these transformations.

For this book's purposes, a starting point for conversion narratives in contemporary U.S. politics is with the Puritans in the 1600s. The Puritans are emblematic of church–state tensions that have been present in American society from its beginnings.[96] The conversion narrative became a social requirement for acceptance into the Protestant Puritan faith, and a large number of religious conversion autobiographies appeared in the eighteenth and nineteenth centuries. These conversion testimonies became common during and after the Reformation, providing recognized structures for new religious sects that lacked the formal sacraments of Catholicism, such as the confessional.[97] Autobiographical writing became a means of displaying one's guilt and grace, promoting a conventionalized mode of practice used to rein in spiritual disorder within communities—in effect, becoming "an ideal method of regulating spiritualization."[98]

Puritan conversion narratives differed from their Pauline and Augustinian predecessors, which both focused on one's instantaneous, assured convictions of religious transformation. Since the Puritans' Calvinist doctrine stressed that no person was guaranteed heavenly salvation, conversion became a highly public demonstration. Puritan figures emphasized how they were continually fighting for salvation throughout their lives.[99] Notably, the Puritan conversion narrative was a "literary morphology, a total way of perceiving and talking about experiences rather than a particular, predetermined mold."[100] That is, while conversion narratives and autobiographical writing and speaking were used to regulate religious and political beliefs, these experiences also became highly flexible in the American context.

Over time, people reconfigured the conversion narrative beyond its early Puritan form. Explicit connections between conversion narratives and scientific thinking developed. "Logics of discovery" by scientific rationalists like Descartes corresponded with the patterns of religious conversion narratives, functioning as persuasive acts.[101] Political theorists John Locke and John Rawls used conversion narratives to structure their theoretical writings—so much that Matthew Scherer proposes that "figures traditionally identified with religion, such as 'conversion,' can and should be reactivated in the imagination of contemporary politics"—highlighting how "religious modes of thought persist within secular rationality."[102]

Epistemic shifts between the religious and secular deepened during the Romantic and Victorian periods. Rousseau's *Confessions* marked a turning point in Western autobiographies.[103] Rousseau argued that an individual self can be found only in nature, rather than in a community of others.[104] He created a sense of individuality that "underlies virtually all modern autobiographies," shifting from the transcendent in Christian autobiography to "personal identity" and the "interaction between men and their secular fictions."[105] Autobiographical discourse during the Victorian period made a parallel swing from religion to politics, as writers began to focus on social responsibility, using conversion rhetoric grounded in scientific rationalism to straddle "the paradox between uniqueness and universality that so troubled Rousseau."[106] As one example, John Stuart Mill simultaneously attacked transcendence while employing conversion narratives to structure his advocacy toward concepts such as "progress."[107]

For writers such as women's movement activist Elizabeth Cady Stanton, conversion to the "scientific enlightenment" replaced religious faith—while she simultaneously used the conversion form (a fundamental change from an old to a new life) to describe this very journey. Overall, "she appropriated 'conversion' for a feminist cause."[108] In a similar fashion, feminist Emma Goldman wrote an autobiography about her conversion to "anarchism."[109] More secular conversion narratives hence retained their individual foci while replacing transcendent elements with a new faith in an external realm of objective, scientific truth.

This trend continued and evolved in the twentieth century. Underscoring the connections between conversion, identity, and women's political movements, the Women's Social and Political Union appropriated and modified traditional conversion narratives to create new modes of self-representation about this-worldly change and converts for the suffragist cause. These political conversions differed from religious stories: "Rather than being blinded by the light of truth," suffragist converts testified to the role of "gradual and reasoned" agency, or "reading, thinking, and debating" in their conversions to the political movement. As such, suffragist conversions focused less on personal sin than the social structures impeding feminist progress.[110] Activists reworked formal, religious conversion stories to target political goals, as strategic rhetoric for social campaigns.

African American slave narratives mark an additional, critical point in the development of political conversion autobiographies. Slave narratives often used the conversion form to persuade white audiences to join abolitionist efforts.[111] Authors of these narratives structured their conversions as about a religious "reception of grace" as well as a political goal of "achieving liberation from legal bondage"—effectively targeting public institutions and shifting redemption from individuals to larger social contexts.[112]

As mentioned, when conversion arose, it did so with Greek philosophy, Judaism, and Christianity. It is likely that it could not go into the political realm until modernity because there was less of a sense of politics as demanding choice during these times. In feudalism, politics was still courtly, lacking a civil society. In this respect, there needs to be a modern sense of politics even for talking about overtly political conversions. When human beings moved from the premodern into the modern world, it was a monumental movement "from fate to choice."[113] As Edwin Black notes, Christianity made an individual's "beliefs" primary, and "these changes in Western consciousness crystallized in religious form, but they became archetypal patterns of perception and cognition" and "extended into nonreligious areas, most notably into politics."[114]

Conversion was not as widely available to the ancients in the same way it is to moderns.[115] In fact, the notion of conversion is uniquely tied to what anthropologists have described as the boundary-setting nature of literate religions in the West.[116] The choice to convert also became more of a possibility with the printing press and the broad dissemination of written texts in modernity, which expanded people's options to join different movements or causes. The development of mass communications in the last century likely influenced these events, making the role of transformation and repositioning in both religion and politics more visible and thus more possible, ultimately opening up vistas to alternative thoughts and actions that would have been harder to come by in previous historical periods.

Conversion in Contemporary Politics

In the mid- to late-twentieth century, some key figures used the conversion strategy in politics. Religious conversion narratives have often been placed in the service of election goals. President George W. Bush used his campaign biography, which mirrored a Pauline conversion narrative, to identify with his Christian audience, frame his past transgressions (e.g., alcohol abuse) as beyond public inquiry, and gain the support of religious figures.[117] Related to this book's primary focus on deliberative rhetoric, David Bailey finds that Bush's conversion appeals evidenced a certainty about religion and politics that left little space for argument; hence, "there is much to be learned about how religious elements like the Pauline conversion form inspire public policy initiatives and the rhetoric offered in support of them."[118]

Bush's narrative had precedent. In the 1970s, public conversions became rituals for revitalizing individuals' images in the aftermath of Watergate and the Vietnam War, with politicians from Jimmy Carter to Jerry Brown propagating tales of spiritual change.[119] Combining religious and political appeals in his conversion narrative, former Nixon administration lawyer Charles Colson even downplayed the transgression phase in his religious conversion to Christianity to minimize his culpability in Nixon administration crimes.[120] The very form of conversion as a linear journey from one life stage to another plays a large role in making such accounts seem truthful.[121] The historical conversion pattern has been resonant with many U.S. audiences,[122] and similar religious forms continue to function within a wide range of secular discourses.[123]

Beyond its individual claims to truth, conversion has been a staple form of evidence for modern movements. Conservative abortion documentaries have used converts' stories to provide model paths for multiple audiences, using "secular language for the unconverted" but "spiritual narrative conventions and resonances for intra-movement appeals."[124] Pointing toward the potentially anti-deliberative dimensions of these narratives, these convert tales often describe facts as moving in one direction, and leave little room for allowing or legitimating alternative viewpoints.[125] At an intersection between political identity appeals and movement claims, President Jimmy Carter underwent a type of political transformation from a "dove to a hawk" over the course of his administration.[126] Since conversion accounts often activate confessional rhetorics, confessional language in contemporary presidential and other forms of speech raise parallel concerns. Dave Tell argues that confessional discourses can "naturalize historical events and thereby constitute a master narrative of inevitability in which further rhetorical intervention seems unnecessary."[127] Like conversion, confessional rhetoric may prevent alternative interpretations of events because of its cultural ties to notions of absolute truth and authenticity.[128]

Outside the United States, the conversion form has appeared in other public contexts. Valeria Fabj explored how secular conversion tales have functioned as constructive resources for anti-Mafia advocates in Italian politics. Former Italian Mafia women used collective appeals to describe their secular conversions to a new life outside of the mafia. Ultimately, these conversions legitimized the Italian government's fight against a criminal culture and created invitations for transformation in civil society.[129] These examples spotlight how conversion strategies have moved into a broad base of public settings, often toggling between religious or secular variations.

Political Conversion as a Civil-Religious Strategy

Beyond these stories' emergence and the issues they raise for public discourse, political conversion should be understood as a civil-religious strategy. Since the United States's founding, the relationship between church and state has created many challenges for public communicators. Political conversion narratives should partly be read as attempts to negotiate this territory.

The concept of "civil religion" originated with Rousseau, but Robert Bellah's work initiated inquiry into the ambiguities between political and religious symbolism.[130] Civil religion combines secular politics with religious symbols, rites, and rituals. It attempts to resolve double binds between an individual's or a group's competing allegiances to religious values and political authority. For example, Protestant nationalism has a civil-religious dimension, where political values are made religious and religious values are secularized.[131] Civil religion has been used to support politicians and policies and has been a major factor in deciding some U.S. elections.[132] Relevant to political conversion, as institutionalized religion has diminished in power in industrial societies, "new frameworks have emerged to take over some of the social functions once performed by it."[133] In this regard, state symbols such as memorials, flags, or anthems have received the awe and respect once reserved for religious artifacts,[134] or are blended with religious texts to provide political institutions with a holy halo.

Stark divides between the religious and secular are no longer adequate to describe the evolving, elastic range of faith-based practices in the modern world.[135] Sociologists since Émile Durkheim "have argued that the social is essentially religious, and what counts as 'religion' does not decline, it just keeps transforming."[136] Conceptions of church–state separation have been critical to these developments. Some scholars find that "because of disestablishment, U.S. religious forms have historically been malleable"—especially since the United States is a place where market models of church membership and ecumenical pluralism, adaptation, and switching beliefs have been the norm compared with, for example, European churches.[137] Communication regulates the church–state contract in U.S. society, and the religious content in this rhetoric tends to be global and morphous so that, "at best, the American civil religion is a political version of Unitarianism."[138]

Against generalized appeals to civil religion in contemporary U.S. politics are, of course, vigorous forms of religious activism against the political, or what Jason Bivins identifies as "Christian antiliberalism," where religious advocates attempt to counter the state at every turn, typically with specific faith claims.[139] Most of this activism involves dissent against elites and centralized power, with a high regard for local community identity and morality. Antiliberalism has been prominent since the 1960s in the United States, frequently collapsing the boundaries between religion and politics completely. In characterizing political conversion narratives as civil-religious, I make a distinction between more explicit ways of using religion in the public square (e.g., antiliberalism) and the implicit, subtle ways of crossing religion and politics found in political conversion stories. This understanding of religion fits with Craig Martin's admission that the dominant rhetoric of capitalism in the United States has propelled the development of minimalist forms of religion that expect few obligations of their followers, making maximalist expressions of religion a rarity in the overall political landscape.[140] That the political conversions in my project were all created by elites using layered messages to garner assent from both religious and political, elite and nonelite audiences, works with these current theories about religion.

Moreover, varying uses of faith still remain important to both civil and specific forms of religion. After all, contemporary Christian antiliberalism "exemplifies the polyvocality and the protean nature of political religion in America," as an evolving mode of engagement modified for new contexts—like conversion narratives themselves.[141] And, as Susan Harding amply documents, despite disavowing secularism and postmodernism, Christian leaders such as Jerry Falwell and their followers aggressively merged religious and nonreligious cultural traditions in their practices.[142]

As expressions of civil religion, political conversion narratives give public figures an opportunity to communicate in a resonant evangelical fashion without bearing the costs that explicit religious faith claims can carry in public. This claim is not intended to invoke a framework of legal determinism, where such accounts might be seen as following strictly from founding documents or legal doctrines such as the disestablishment clause. Rather, these narratives are the outgrowth of a whole host of cultural performances in U.S. history (of which founding texts and legal doctrines are certainly a part), where communicators have attempted to meet paradoxical, official and unofficial expectations over religion's role in politics.

LOOKING BACK, STRATEGIZING FORWARD

Looking back, conversion narratives' social and historical influence has been well documented, with individuals and groups adapting the pattern across time and contexts. Although political conversion narratives generally do not use transcendent truth as their revealed fundamentals, they often use "experience" in an evangelical way. As such, this book will draw out and evaluate the standards by which these stories can be assessed as arguments that invite audiences to view public affairs in certain ways.

The selection of this book's four case studies stems from my finding that conversion narratives are nexus points between identities and movements. Conversion narratives exemplify liminal moments in the formation of selves and groups, influencing political parties and coalitions. Yet it's critical to note that, at least in the U.S. context, the playing field has not been level. Many American political conversion narratives describe their authors' turns from the political left to the right. Fewer tell the story of turning from the political right to the left,[143] at least in terms of writings or speeches circulated in public discourse.

Political scientists confirm that the conversion of former Democrats to the Republican Party has been widespread in postwar America; but there appear to be far fewer documented cases of Republican to Democrat converts.[144] Similarly, studies of abortion advocates relate that many pro-lifers are "converts to Catholicism, people who have actively chosen to follow a religious faith, in striking contrast to the pro-choice people, who have actively chosen not to follow any."[145] This project explores why so many conversion narratives in U.S. politics are from the left to the right, following some of the most prominent texts that happen to be mostly conservative, while concluding that the strategy cannot necessarily be reduced to any one ideology. In previous exploratory work examining David Brock's political conversion from the right to the left,[146] I found a mostly propagandistic form of rhetoric, similar to the first three case studies in this larger project. While political conversion strategies have tilted to one side of the political spectrum, this book emphasizes that it is the type of discourse itself rather than any inherent ideological designation that presents problems for deliberative democracy.

Another reason so many conversion narratives have been told among conservatives relates to a historical, performative "print culture" among those on the right. Michael Lee finds that a secular "canon" of works—of which Whittaker Chambers's *Witness* was a part—helped bring together (and into contention) various sects like traditionalists, neoconservatives, and others, establishing certain argumentative commonplaces, patterns, and models of social capital.[147] Emphasizing how amenable the conversion form was to the subculture, this conservative canon "was a sacred force encountered during a sinner's journey," with movement advocates continually highlighting the inspirational force of conservative books and testimonies in their own journeys.[148]

Looking forward, four case studies provide an intertextual, connected body of work for studying political conversion. This book invites a larger confrontation with conversion stories by charting an evolving history, focusing on a group of texts that encapsulate this social trend.[149]

Four Intertextual Political Conversion Autobiographies

Autobiographies tend to emerge during periods of intense political change.[150] As one scholar wrote: "Augustine's *Confessions* coincided with the breakthrough of Christianity in the Roman world; Montaigne studied himself in the midst of civil war; and Jean-Jacques Rousseau was not merely one of the inventors of modern autobiography but a major figure in the buildup to the French Revolution."[151] Autobiographies and social movements often correlate, with abolitionist literatures about the humanity of slaves preceding historical events such as the Emancipation Proclamation—and feminist and black power autobiographies accompanying major movements during the sixties.[152]

More than merely interesting or entertaining invitations to consider a person's life, then, many writings can be described as "social movement autobiographies."[153] In essence, autobiographical writing structures enable "the rhetorical functions of *self-definition* and *social advocacy* to become mutually reinforcing."[154] Activists have used autobiographies to create new audiences for their beliefs, with the medium containing an array of underexplored rhetorical devices employed in public campaigns.[155]

Prior to World War II, several non-American writers and intellectuals began to propagate their "ex-Communist" experiences to the public in exactly this fashion. In the 1940s, figures such as Arthur Koestler compiled ex-Communist stories in *The God That Failed*, which described several authors' conversions from Soviet-style totalitarianism to Western democracy.[156] Following these initial essays, in 1952, Whittaker Chambers published the touchstone political conversion autobiography *Witness*. In the 1960s and 1970s, as self-disclosure and transformation became thematic in American politics, many "ideologically motivated autobiographies" flooded the public square.[157] During this period, ex-liberal intellectuals like Norman Podhoretz used the conversion narrative in works such as *Breaking Ranks* (1979). In the following decades, the trend continued, with conservatives mobilizing political conversion autobiographies, including David Horowitz's *Radical Son* (1997).

The autobiographies of Chambers, Podhoretz, and Horowitz evidence intriguing similarities and differences that merit consideration as a class of left-to-right political conversion accounts. All these autobiographers are journalists or pundits. They all use conversion rhetoric to reflect upon and structure their political transformations. They have all been influential figures in U.S. postwar politics and, in some cases, beyond. These autobiographies also draw upon and cite one another: an intertextual thread and unity to these texts justifies their selection as circulating sites of political persuasion. I trace conversion discourses that influence one another, covering a strategic trail established by these tales across time and in their unique historical moments. Since these texts reference and build on one another, they create a body of work whose sum is greater than its individual parts.

Although these works possess common themes, each author had unique situational demands. Chambers addressed an uncertain postwar environment and the pressing Communist scare enveloping the nation in the 1950s. Podhoretz's political conversion autobiography lamented the 1960s counterculture and the Vietnam War. For Horowitz, political events from the 1960s through the 1990s provided an impetus for his book. While there are clear links between these conversion narratives, contextual changes in each of these authors' lives affected how and why they used these types of stories.

Generally, a decrease in sacred spaces within modern societies has left experience-making in the hands of individuals; as John Lofland and Norman Skonovd suspect, "conversion motifs differ significantly from one historical epoch to another, across societal boundaries, and even across subcultures within a single society."[158] Heilbrunn writes that the difference between the old intellectual rank-breakers (such as Chambers) and their newer counterparts (such as Horowitz) is that there was more at stake in the former cases, both personally and contextually. In the 1990s and 2000s "rank-breaking has become an industry, and a rewarding one at that. . . . [T]he dark night of the soul that Chambers dramatizes in Witness is now more akin to an audition for American Idol."[159] Because the first three texts in this study stretch over nearly fifty years of public discourse, they similarly provide a way of exploring shifts in the rhetorical styles and resources available to those crafting conversion messages.

There are also religious and political differences between these autobiographies. Chambers offers the most explicitly religious account, simultaneously offering the reader proof of his political and faith-based conversion. From the opposite side, Podhoretz occasionally discusses religion, mostly to argue that it should be kept out of politics, while asserting that his political journey was grounded in rationality and reason. I find that these autobiographies are political analogues to what Peter Berger has described as three contemporary modes of religious thought (or ideal types) that each respond to the relativity, choice, and pluralistic demands inherent to modern societies.[160]

The first mode of religious thought, deduction, affirms traditional religious authorities and otherworldly realities in the face of contemporary, pluralistic challenges. Here the strategy is to administer one's faith in a top-down fashion to almost all of life's events, in a way that typically ignores, minimizes, or deflects tensions or contradictions in the tradition or with others. Religious communicators frame knowledge claims in terms of orthodox, fundamentalist certainties. The second, reduction, works with such tensions to intellectualize and secularize religious traditions. In this turn, modern historical scholarship and critical methods substitute for religious authority to foster highly rational forms of religion. The third, induction, focuses on one's own experience or the experiences of human beings within religious traditions as grounds for affirming faith. This last, introspective mode reflects an "empirical attitude" and emotional "experience of inner liberation," emanating from a "nonauthoritarian approach to questions of truth."[161] Although not without overlaps, the respective narratives of Chambers, Podhoretz, and Horowitz generally correspond to these three ways of approaching the world. Loosely speaking, some similarities also exist between these types and what Lofland and Skonovd call mystical, intellectual, and experimental types of conversion, and what Max Weber described as three bases for political authority—traditional, rational, and charismatic.[162]

Following this framework, my first case study begins with Chambers's *Witness*, a foundational text in contemporary conservative politics. By many accounts, "Chambers' odyssey would become the gold standard against which the experience of future generations of rank-breakers would be measured."[163] President Reagan said that reading Chambers's *Witness* was instrumental in his own political conversion from Democrat to Republican,[164] frequently referring to the book as "represent[ing] a generation's disenchantment with statism and its return to eternal truths and fundamental values"[165] —themes exercised in U.S. politics to this day.

In this lengthy autobiography, Chambers tells the story of his former life as a spy for the international Communist Party. He became an employee of the U.S. government, spending years working with other Communist spies to gather and send classified documents to Soviet leaders. Through many twists and turns, Chambers left Communism and testified at the famous Hiss trials (1949–1950) that Alger Hiss, an assistant to the assistant secretary of state, was a Communist. In Chambers's later years, he began writing for conservative publications and became friends with figures such as William F. Buckley. Chambers's political transformation worked hand in hand with becoming a Quaker.[166]

The second case study explores Podhoretz's *Breaking Ranks*, which covers the author's turn from liberalism and radicalism to become one of the founders of the neoconservative movement. Podhoretz's autobiography acknowledges the influence of former ex-leftists like Chambers in his own political conversion. Yet it is a puzzling account. *Breaking Ranks* is highly intellectual, written less with the agonizing personal revelations that many political conversion autobiographies use and instead centering almost exclusively on political ideas. Podhoretz describes his struggles with liberal policies during the Vietnam War and the movements of the 1960s, which, he argues, had little to do with the liberalism that he had always known. When Podhoretz came out as a conservative, he responded to these pressures with his 1979 book and propelled a new conservative movement.

The third case focuses on Horowitz's *Radical Son*, which responds to political events from the 1960s through the 1990s. Horowitz describes his gradual conversion from a former life as a Marxist to a very public, staunch conservative in later decades. He provides extensive details about his family history and the political events that shattered his previous worldview, while providing readers with prescriptions for his country's civic future. Horowitz often cites both Chambers and Podhoretz as his models, illustrating the influence that political converts can wield with prospective movement members.

There is another work with insight into the functions of political conversion strategies, although not so much for what it does as what it doesn't do. Like Podhoretz's and Horowitz's tales, this story follows the same intertextual thread in its reference to Chambers's *Witness*. But unlike the three other case studies, Garry Wills's *Confessions of a Conservative* avoids the types of problems manifest in the other political conversion narratives. As a prominent public figure, Wills could be described as turning from the right to the left in his politics. Yet the book is more remarkable for deferring and deflecting many of the rhetorical practices described in the other cases. Most important, Wills's work provides an understanding of what more deliberative forms of transformation rhetoric could look like.

Examining the strategic resources across the four autobiographies, I analyze the particular vision of deliberation that each author constructs, comparing and contrasting the cases toward a theory and evaluation of these stories in public culture. Each case works toward a cumulative conclusion about the communicative possibilities and limitations of political conversion narratives. With the exception of Wills's case, each chapter builds on the last, both in terms of chronological order and the intertextual connections that each autobiography provides to the previous work(s).

One way I track how each author constructs his political outlook is by looking to what Edwin Black calls the "second persona," or implied audience in each narrative.[167] My goal is not to make hard experimental claims about the effect of these discourses on people's ability to deliberate. Rather, my conclusions will center on the kind of audiences that these messages create in their features and functions. In each chapter, I thread the emergent rhetorical norms from each political conversion narrative together with various interpretations, responses, and controversies that each autobiography has evoked in public affairs. In addition to other scholarly and journalistic coverage of these works, many responses to the autobiographies were collected in the form of major and minor book reviews. The contextual analyses were not limited to book reviews, but they provided one means for exploring some responses to the primary sources. The book reviews build support for my claims about each autobiography's strategic norms as well as provide evidence of how some audiences either confirmed or invalidated the second persona in each. In using these supplementary sources, I am, again, less interested in making any representative claims about audience effects than in simply deepening our understandings of the social and historical milieu of these works and the vision, or what sociologist Charles Taylor has termed the "imaginary,"[168] that each constructs.

Judging Political Conversion

It is the argument of this book that, collectively, the first three case studies illustrate how political conversion narratives tend to be propagandistic, anti-deliberative communication strategies. They combine the conversion form (a public proclamation of fundamental, bifurcated identity change from an old to a new life) with various rhetorical devices and themes to produce a seemingly reflective yet totalizing type of public argument. That is, the deep, underlying structure of the conversion form functions to control several resources in each story, creating an anti-deliberative text whose sum is greater than its parts.

This thesis distinguishes the anti-deliberative dimensions of the conversion narrative from other, less all-encompassing, communication practices. At least in these cases, the conversion narrative tends not to portray a simple experience or change of mind but, instead, a heavily bifurcated, unidirectional experience or change of mind from a fundamental wrong to a right. Burke discusses the dangers of temporality and essentializing rhetoric in narratives, which tend to fix points of origin beyond language, foreclosing the possibility of starting from other places and working in different directions from those implied by a story's structure. In other words, these types of stories fail to recognize that the inevitability implied by their narrative structures is not unavoidable.[169]

Yet public figures have performed this strategy in different, complex ways toward such ends. The first three case studies in this book each present a political conversion narrative in a different anti-deliberative guise—deductive, reductive, and inductive,[170] respectively—in ways that are equally troubling as public communication practices. Collectively, the case studies employ civil-religious rhetoric as a response to their overall postwar context. Individually, however, each autobiography also incarnates its era's ethos by emphasizing religion and secularity in different ways. Chambers's narrative is quasi-religious, while Podhoretz and Horowitz create secular conversion stories with reductive and inductive approaches that are at odds with each other. These religious and secular differences show how contextual shifts within the postwar period called for conversion texts under varying guises.

A key component of this historical argument is that authors of political conversion narratives can submerge religious content in their stories while still drawing from the resonant form of conversion for their lives and causes. They are, in Thomas Luckmann's terms, forms of "invisible religion,"[171] downplaying or even completely discarding religious content while using an enduring historical-religious form to convince audiences that their lives and causes are worth supporting. Much research establishes that U.S. audiences generally favor civil-religious sentiments but not the specific articulation of religious beliefs in politics.[172] Conversion narratives are situated on this religious-political axis, paradoxically supporting and negating religion in public life, like the U.S. disestablishment clause itself.

In the following analysis, chapter 1 examines Chambers's foundational autobiography, *Witness*. My investigation reveals that Chambers engages in an anti-deliberative, interactional form of rhetoric that combines the conversion narrative with conspiracy, anti-intellectualism, dualism, nature, and prefiguring resources. This mutually reinforcing rhetoric creates a potent public argument form tailored to its Cold War context, with Chambers wedding his bifurcated conversion experience to cosmic and worldly binaries between good/evil and Communism/anti-Communism. The anti-deliberative vision ultimately is cast as a fundamentalist, deductive Manichaean odyssey.

Chapter 2 explores Podhoretz's political conversion autobiography, *Breaking Ranks*. I find three major rhetorical resources with bearing on public communication: intellectualism, expression, and accuracy. Each resource corresponds to concerns for reason, restraint, and rightness in public life. At first glance, Podhoretz uses a language of reason and reasonability that may appear to be deliberative. The deep structure of the conversion form works with these resources to create a totalizing public argument, however. Given Podhoretz's criteria for public discourse, several contradictions surface in his performance of the political conversion narrative. As a whole, the strategic political vision is cast in terms of an intellectual, reductive journey responding to the rowdy nature of Podhoretz's political circumstances.

Chapter 3 explores Horowitz's autobiography, *Radical Son*. I find three major resources in *Radical Son*: reflexivity, maturity, and psychological experience. These resources relate to a language of reason, progress, and caring participation that have been part of the political Left's vocabulary. Horowitz draws on these leftist experiences to appeal to assumed virtues such as open-mindedness, creating a generational journey from a socialized, childish naïveté to an individual, adult capacity for reflection on the world's truths. Horowitz's autobiography ultimately puts the conversion form in the service of an experiential, inductive vision that sums to an inherently anti-deliberative discourse.

Departing from these stories, in chapter 4 I turn to Garry Wills's *Confessions of a Conservative*. Wills had been part of many of the same conservative social circles as the other authors in this project and, given his turn from his former alliances, had every reason to fashion a political conversion narrative like the others. Instead, I find that by prioritizing rhetorical processes over products, conceptualizing a politics of human convention over redemption, creating grounds for endless argumentation, and constructing conditions for expansive identity rhetorics, Wills's text bypasses the types of totalizing features exemplified in the other political conversion narratives. Wills's work provides an entry point for discussing how messages of political change can be created in a more deliberative way, providing one path through the thicket of concerns raised by the preceding conversion narratives. In so doing, Wills offers a view of what such rhetorical understandings have to offer our public discourse more generally.

Last, in chapter 5, I summarize the deliberative standards constructed across the conversion narratives, presenting some final implications about the cumulative workings of these case studies (including Wills's divergent case) and what they portend for public discourse. This book concludes with a call to be vigilant about the rhetorical operations of the historical, evolving conversion narrative, whose enduring structure continues to emerge and be applied in as many contexts as citizens can imagine.

NOTES

1. John Newton, "Amazing Grace," in *500 Best-Loved Song Lyrics*, ed. Ronald Herder (Mineola, NY: Dover, 1998), 11.
2. C. Burkhart, "Right Wing Conspiracy . . . ," *Christian Century*, 2002, 60.
3. Augustine, *Confessions*, trans. R. S. Pine-Coffin (New York: Penguin Books, 1961); George Fox, *The Journal of George Fox* (Richmond, IN: Friends United Press, 2006); Thomas Merton, *The Seven Storey Mountain* (New York: Harcourt Brace, 1999).
4. Jean-Jacques Rousseau, *The Confessions*, trans. J. M. Cohen (New York: Penguin Books, 1953).
5. Thomas De Quincy, *Confessions of an English Opium Eater* (New York: Penguin Books, 2003).
6. René Descartes, *Discourse on Method and Meditations*, trans. Lawrence Lafleur (Indianapolis, IN: Bobbs-Merrill, 1960); Nicolas Copernicus, *On the Revolutions [De Revolutionibus]*, ed. Jerzy Dobrzycki, trans. Edward Rosen (London: Macmillan, 1978).
7. See Sigmund Freud, *The Basic Writings of Sigmund Freud*, ed. and trans. A. A. Brill (New York: Random House, 1995).
8. For examples of political conversion autobiographies and related texts, see Herman Badillo, *One Nation, One Standard: An Ex-Liberal on How Hispanics Can Succeed Just Like Other Immigrant Groups* (New York: Sentinel, 2006); David Brock, *Blinded by the Right: The Conscience of an Ex-Conservative* (New York: Three Rivers, 2002); Tammy Bruce, *The New American Revolution: Using the Power of the Individual to Save Our Nation from Extremists* (New York: HarperCollins, 2005); John H. Bunzel, ed., *Political Passages: Journeys of Change through Two Decades* (New York: Free Press, 1988); Linda Chavez, *An Unlikely Conservative: The Transformation of an Ex-Liberal (or How I Became the Most Hated Hispanic in America)* (New York: Basic Books, 2002); Patrick Cormack, ed., *Right Turn: Eight Men Who Changed Their Minds* (London: Leo Cooper, 1978); Nonie Darwish, *Now They Call Me Infidel: Why I Renounced Jihad for America, Israel, and the War on Terror* (New York: Sentinel, 2006); Michael K. Deaver, ed., *Why I Am a Reagan Conservative* (New York: Harper, 2005); Isaac Deutscher, *Heretics and Renegades* (New York: Bobbs-Merrill, 1957/1969); John P. Diggens, *Up from Communism: Conservative Odysseys in American Intellectual Development* (New York: Columbia University Press, 1975/1994); Terence Dooley, *Innisken, 1912–1918: The Political Conversion of Bernard O'Rourke* (Dublin: Four Courts, 2004); Mary Eberstadt, ed., *Why I Turned Right: Leading Baby Boom Conservatives Chronicle Their Political Journeys* (New York: Threshold, 2007); Thomas W. Evans, *The Education of Ronald Reagan: The General Electric Years and the Untold Story of His Conversion to Conservatism* (New York: Columbia University Press, 2006); Bernard Goldberg, *Crazies to the Left of Me, Wimps to the Right: How One Side Lost Its Mind and the Other Lost Its Nerve* (New York: HarperCollins, 2007); David Horowitz, *Radical Son: A Generational Odyssey* (New York: Touchstone, 1997); Joshua Key, *The Deserter's Tale: The Story of an Ordinary Soldier Who Walked Away from the War in Iraq* (New York: Atlantic Monthly Press, 2007); Irving Kristol,

"An Autobiographical Memoir," in *Neoconservatism: The Autobiography of an Idea*, ed. idem (New York: Free Press, 1995), 3–40; Michael Lind, *Up from Conservatism: Why the Right Is Wrong for America* (New York: Free Press, 1996); Norma McCorvey, *Won by Love* (Nashville: Thomas Nelson, 1997); Michael Medved, *Right Turns: Unconventional Lessons from a Controversial Life* (New York: Crown Forum, 2005); Susan Mulcahy, ed., *Why I'm a Democrat* (Sausalito, CA: PoliPointPress, 2008); Steve Olsen, *Why You May Be a Liberal (and Why That's Okay): The Political Conversion of a Utah Mormon Bishop* (Printed by author, 2007); Rick Perry, *Fed Up!: Our Fight to Save America from Washington* (New York: Little, Brown, 2010); Burt Prelutsky, *Conservatives Are from Mars, Liberals Are from San Francisco: 101 Reasons Why I'm Happy I Left the Left* (Nashville: Cumberland House, 2006); Walid Shoebat, *Why I Left Jihad* (Top Executive Media, 2005); Harry Stein, *How I Accidentally Joined the Vast Right-Wing Conspiracy (and Found Inner Peace)* (New York: Perennial, 2000); Keith Thompson, *Leaving the Left: Moments in the News That Made Me Ashamed to Be a Liberal* (New York: Penguin, 2006); Richard M. Weaver, "Up from Liberalism," in *Life without Prejudice and Other Essays*, ed. Richard M. Weaver (Chicago: Regnery, 1965), 129–55; Garry Wills, *Confessions of a Conservative* (Garden City, NY: Doubleday, 1979); Bertram Wolfe, *A Life in Two Centuries* (New York: Stein and Day, 1981). See also Adam Shatz, "About Face," *New York Times*, January 20, 2002, www.nytimes.com/2002/01/20/magazine/about-face.html. Of course, political conversion tales can also be told in other media, such as Thomas Sowell's interview on Fox News detailing his turn from Marxism to conservatism. "The Difference between Liberal and Conservative," March 17, 2010, YouTube, www.youtube.com/watch?v=5KHdhrNhh88

9. McCorvey, *Won by Love*.

10. Charlie Crist and Ellis Henican, *The Party's Over: How the Extreme Right Hijacked the GOP and I Became a Democrat* (New York: Dutton, 2014).

11. Ken Stern, *Republican Like Me: How I Left the Liberal Bubble and Learned to Love the Right* (New York: HarperCollins, 2017).

12. John Hill, "Obama Basic Training," *Sacramento Bee*, January 31, 2008, www.sacbee.com/111/v-print/story/649427 (no longer available), par. 7.

13. Julie Kosterlitz, "Bush's Left Right-Hand Men," *National Journal* (May 5, 2002): 1297.

14. Brock, *Blinded by the Right*, 340. Some of this section's examples (e.g., Zell Miller) are used in an in-depth study of David Brock by Don Waisanen, "Political Conversion as Intrapersonal Argument: Self-Dissociation in David Brock's *Blinded by the Right*," *Argumentation and Advocacy* 47 (2011): 230.

15. . Bill Clinton, *My Life* (New York: Knopf, 2004), 565.

16. Dana Anderson, *Identity's Strategy: Rhetorical Selves in Conversion* (Columbia: University of South Carolina Press, 2007), 57.

17. For instance, the political conversion narrative *Witness* has been described as setting the "intellectual moorings for American conservatives that would last into the twenty-first century." Alfred S. Regnery, *Upstream: The Ascendance of American Conservatism* (New York: Simon & Schuster, 2008), 39.

18. Bruce Bartlett, "Kristol Clear," *National Review*, June 26, 2002, http://old.nationalreview.com/nrof_bartlett/bartlett062602.asp (no longer available), par. 5.

19. Christopher Caldwell, "Renegade," *Commentary*, June 1997, available in ProQuest database, par. 15.

20. Johnny "Uncle Johnny," "Introspective, Insightful & Intellectually Honest," Amazon.com, February 9, 2007, www.amazon.com/Radical-Son-Generational-David-Horowitz/product-reviews/0684840057/ref=dp_top_cm_cr_acr_txt?ie=UTF8&show Viewpoints=1, par. 1.

21. Lee Edwards, "Modern Tomes," *Policy Review* 84 (1997): par. 3, www.hoover.org/research/modern-tomes, under "Breaking Ranks," par. 1.

22. F. Earle Fox, "Witness by Whittaker Chambers," www.theroadtoemmaus.org/RdLb/21PbAr/Hst/US/ChmbrsWitnss.htm, par. 12, 13.

23. This comment is Hugh Kenner's, in William F. Buckley, Jr., foreword to *Witness*, by Whittaker Chambers (Washington, DC: Regnery, 1980), v.

Introduction

24. See Jarol Manheim, *Strategy in Information and Influence Campaigns: How Policy Advocates, Insurgent Groups, Corporations, Governments and Others Get What They Want* (New York: Routledge, 2011).

25. Brian T. Kaylor, "My Take: Don't Be Fooled by Candidates' God Talk," CNN.com, September 14, 2011, http://religion.blogs.cnn.com/2011/09/14/my-take-dont-be-fooled-by-candidates-god-talk, par. 19.

26. See W. Barnett Pearce, *Communication and the Human Condition* (Carbondale: Southern Illinois University Press, 1989), 167–206.

27. James L. Golden, Goodwin F. Berquist, and William E. Coleman, "Secular and Religious Conversion," in *The Rhetoric of Western Thought*, 4th ed., ed. James L. Golden, Goodwin F. Berquist, and William E. Coleman (Dubuque, IA: Kendall/Hunt, 1989), 578.

28. Thomas Hollihan, *Uncivil Wars: Political Campaigns in a Media Age* (New York: Bedford/St. Martin's, 2001). See also Elizabeth Drew, *The Corruption of American Politics: What Went Wrong and Why* (Woodstock, NY: Overlook, 2000).

29. Richard Davis and Diana Owens, *New Media and American Politics* (New York: Oxford University Press, 1998), 5.

30. Dov Shinar, "The Peace Process in Cultural Conflict: The Role of the Media," *Conflict & Communication Online* 2 (2003): 1–10.

31. Jürgen Habermas, *Between Facts and Norms: Contributions to a Discourse Theory of Law and Democracy*, trans. William Rehg (Cambridge, MA: MIT Press, 1996), 377.

32. Samuel Popkin, *The Reasoning Voter: Communication and Persuasion in Presidential Campaigns* (Chicago: University of Chicago Press, 1991), 92.

33. David Domke and Kevin Coe, *The God Strategy: How Religion Became a Weapon in America* (New York: Oxford University Press, 2008), 20.

34. See Richard Hofstadter, *Anti-intellectualism in American Life* (New York: Vintage Books, 1963); Susan Jacoby, *The Age of American Unreason* (New York: Vintage Books, 2009).

35. Thomas Patterson, *The Vanishing Voter: Public Involvement in an Age of Uncertainty* (New York: Alfred A. Knopf, 2002).

36. Michael Schudson, *The Good Citizen: A History of American Civic Life* (Cambridge, MA: Harvard University Press, 1998).

37. Kevin Mattson, "Do Americans Really Want Deliberative Democracy?" *Rhetoric & Public Affairs* 5 (2002): 327–29.

38. See James Darsey, "Joe McCarthy's Fantastic Moment," *Communication Monographs* 62 (1995): 65–86.

39. On discursive performances of citizenship, see Robert Asen, "A Discourse Theory of Citizenship," *Quarterly Journal of Speech* 90 (2004): 189–211. Warner provides a helpful definition for how communication articulates politics, arguing that publics are "scenes of self-activity, or historical rather than timeless belonging, and of active participation rather than ascriptive belonging. . . . Public discourse craves attention like a child. . . . The direction of our glance can constitute our social world." Publics are also continuous spaces, not single texts or acts, but "multigeneric lifeworld[s]" interactively organized with "potentially infinite axes of citation and characterization." Michael Warner, "Publics and Counterpublics," *Public Culture* 14 (2002): 62, 63. This book uses Habermas's perspective that embodied political actors are "caught up in networks of communicative action." Habermas, *Between Facts and Norms*, 324. See also Elisabeth Bruce, *Autobiographical Acts: The Changing Situation of a Literary Genre* (London: Johns Hopkins University Press, 1976); Porter H. Abbot, "Autobiography, Autography, Fiction: Groundwork for a Taxonomy of Textual Categories," *New Literary History* 19 (1988): 597–615.

40. In Greco-Roman contexts, for example, there was no separation between religion and politics. Thomas M. Finn, *From Death to Rebirth: Ritual and Conversion in Antiquity* (Mahwah, NJ: Paulist Press, 1997), 52.

41. The Pharisee effect is drawn from the New Testament's Luke 18:9–14, where Jesus disapproved of a Pharisee for "being too public with his prayers." Larry Powell and Eduardo Neiva, "The Pharisee Effect: When Religious Appeals in Politics Go Too Far," *Journal of Communication and Religion* 29 (2006): 74.

42. Martin Medhurst, "Forging a Civil Religious Construct for the Twenty-First Century," in *The Political Pulpit Revisited*, ed. Roderick Hart and John Pauley (West Lafayette, IN: Purdue University Press, 2004), 143–52.

43. Domke and Coe, *The God Strategy*.

44. Jasinski writes that "participants in a movement are, in effect, converts to a cause; they undergo a process of secular conversion that often involves the adoption of a new identity or a new sense of self." But this "new sense of self is always threatened by the old self." In both secular and religious conversion narratives, a temptation to return to the old self is always a problem (e.g., in the sixties, many new feminists were surrounded by messages that they should return to their old ways of life). Much rhetorical work goes into conversion narratives since, "if a movement fails to satisfy this need, then it runs the risk of having its members backslide and return to their pre-movement identities." James Jasinski, *Sourcebook on Rhetoric* (Thousand Oaks, CA: Sage, 2001), 375–76. Leland Griffin describes movements as moving through stages of inception, negation, and then a turn to the "rhetoric of conversion and catharsis." Leland Griffin, "A Dramatistic Theory of the Rhetoric of Movements," in *Critical Responses to Kenneth Burke 1924–1962*, ed. William M. Rueckert (Minneapolis: University of Minnesota Press, 1969), 464. In an earlier article, Griffin also describes how the "New Left" needed rituals of rebirth to respond to crises that it faced in 1962. The movement's developments were intimately connected to these patterns of identity change. Leland Griffin, "The Rhetorical Structure of the 'New Left Movement': Part I," *Quarterly Journal of Speech* 50 (1964): 113–35. King explores how power was maintained by government elites through strategies such "co-optation" (e.g., the use of seemingly assimilated black people to thwart the goals of the black power movement). He also describes the "official betrayal alibi" strategy, where rank-breaking white dissidents were blamed for helping black organizations in the 1950s. The use of converts in the public square was further underscored by elite strategies of "rebirth and revenge." Andrew King, "The Rhetoric of Power Maintenance: Elites at the Precipice," *Quarterly Journal of Speech* 62 (1976): 127–34. Conversion analyses overlap with what Simons has described as a leader-centered theory of social movements. Herbert Simons, "Requirements, Problems, and Strategies: A Theory of Persuasion for Social Movements," *Quarterly Journal of Speech* 56 (1970): 1–11. In explaining the "ego-function" of black power and women's liberation consciousness-raising rhetoric, Gregg writes that all had to "struggle for a resurrected self." Richard Gregg, "The Ego-Function of the Rhetoric of Protest," *Philosophy & Rhetoric* 4 (1971): 81. Bormann, Cragan, and Shields describe a stage of U.S. Cold War rhetoric as involving the testimonies of new political converts to the anti-Communist cause. Public figures used these converts to buttress their Cold War rhetoric. Ernest G. Bormann, John Cragan, and Donald Shields, "An Expansion of the Rhetorical Vision Component of the Symbolic Convergence Theory: The Cold War Paradigm Case," *Communication Monographs* 63 (1996): 1–28. Maurice Charland argues that constitutive rhetoric in movements is similar to conversion; "the process by which an audience member enters into a new subject position is therefore not one of persuasion. It is akin more to one of conversion that ultimately results in an act of recognition of the 'rightness' of a discourse and of one's identity with its reconfigured subject position." Deepening a question about how such rhetoric might advance or hinder public engagement, he further believes that "narratives are but texts that offer the illusion of agency," demanding totalizing responses and restricting the possibilities for audience action(s). Maurice Charland, "Constitutive Rhetoric: The Case of the Peuple Quebecois," *Quarterly Journal of Speech* 73 (1987): 142.

45. Simone Chambers, "Deliberative Democratic Theory," *Annual Review of Political Science* 6 (2003): 309.

46. Maeve Cooke, "Five Arguments for Deliberative Democracy," *Political Studies* 48 (2000): 948.

47. Robert Asen, "Toward a Normative Conception of Difference in Public Deliberation," in *Readings on Argumentation*, ed. Angela J. Aguayo and Timothy R. Steffensmeier (State College, PA: Strata, 2008), 290.

48. Ibid., 290, 292–93; Don Waisanen, "Toward Robust Public Engagement: The Value of Deliberative Discourse for Civil Communication," *Rhetoric & Public Affairs* 17 (2014): 287–322.

49. See the debate between Forbes Hill and Karlyn Kohrs Campbell: Forbes Hill, "Conventional Wisdom—Traditional Form—the President's Message of November 3, 1969," *Quarterly Journal of Speech* 58 (1972): 373–86; Karlyn K. Campbell, "An Exercise in the Rhetoric of Mythical America," in *Critiques of Contemporary Rhetoric*, ed. idem (Belmont, CA: Wadsworth, 1972), 50–58. For the "rowdy" argument, see Robert L. Ivie, "Rhetorical Deliberation and Democratic Politics in the Here and Now," *Rhetoric & Public Affairs* 5 (2002): 277–85.

50. Robert Asen, "Ideology, Materiality, and Counterpublicity: William E. Simon and the Rise of a Conservative Counterintelligensia," *Quarterly Journal of Speech* 95 (2009): 263.

51. Cass Sunstein, "Deliberative Trouble? Why Groups Go to Extremes," *Yale Law Journal* 110 (2000): 113.

52. Hartmut Wessler, "Investigating Deliberativeness Comparatively," *Political Communication* 25 (2008): 1–22. A further call to examine "communication content" can be found in Jennifer Stromer-Galley and Peter Muhlberger, "Agreement and Disagreement in Group Deliberation: Effects on Deliberation Satisfaction, Future Engagement, and Decision Legitimacy," *Political Communication* 26 (2009): 173–92.

53. Wessler, "Investigating Deliberativeness Comparatively," 12.

54. David S. Birdsell, "George W. Bush's Signing Statements: The Assault on Deliberation," *Rhetoric & Public Affairs* 10 (2007): 338; John Gastil, *Political Communication and Deliberation* (Thousand Oaks, CA: Sage, 2008), 89–92.

55. Daniel C. Brouwer, "Communication as Counterpublic," in *Communication as . . . : Perspectives on Theory*, ed. Gregory J. Shepherd, Jeffrey St. John, and Ted Striphas (Thousand Oaks, CA: Sage, 2006), 201.

56. James Bohman, *Public Deliberation: Pluralism, Complexity, and Democracy* (Cambridge, MA: MIT Press, 2000), 17.

57. As cited in G. Thomas Goodnight, "The Engagements of Communication: Jürgen Habermas on Discourse, Critical Reason, and Controversy," in *Perspectives on Philosophy of Communication*, ed. Pam Arneson (West Lafayette, IN: Purdue University Press, 2007), 103.

58. See, e.g., Jeffrey D. Bass, "The Appeal to Efficiency as Narrative Closure: Lyndon Johnson and the Dominican Crisis, 1965," *Southern Speech Communication Journal* 50 (1985): 103–20; Laura W. Black, "Deliberation, Storytelling, and Dialogic Moments," *Communication Theory* 18 (2008): 93–116; Walter R. Fisher, "Narration as a Human Communication Paradigm: The Case of Public Moral Argument," *Communication Monographs* 51 (1984): 1–22; Lisa M. Gring-Pemble, "'Are We Now Going to Govern by Anecdote?': Rhetorical Constructions of Welfare Recipients in Congressional Hearings, Debates, and Legislation, 1992–1996," *Quarterly Journal of Speech* 87 (2001): 341–65; Kathleen H. Jamieson, *Eloquence in an Electronic Age: The Transformation of Political Speechmaking* (New York: Oxford University Press, 1988); Jasinski, *Sourcebook on Rhetoric*, 160–64; William F. Lewis, "Telling America's Story: Narrative Form and the Reagan Presidency," *Quarterly Journal of Speech* 73 (1987): 280–302; Jennifer A. Peeples, "Arguments for What No One Wants: The Narratives of Waste Storage Proponents," *Environmental Communication* 2 (2008): 40–58; David M. Ryfe, "Narrative and Deliberation in Small Group Forums," *Journal of Applied Communication Research* 34 (2006): 72–93; Michael Salvador, "The Rhetorical Genesis of Ralph Nader: A Functional Exploration of Narrative and Argument in Public Address," *Southern Communication Journal* 59 (1994): 227–39; Iris M. Young, "Communication and the Other," in *Democracy and Difference: Contesting the Boundaries of the Political*, ed. Seyla Benhabib (Princeton, NJ: Princeton University Press, 1996).

59. William A. Gamson, *Talking Politics* (New York: Cambridge University Press, 1992).

60. Francesca Poletta, "'It Was Like a Fever . . .': Narrative and Identity in Social Protest," *Social Problems* 45 (1998): 155.

61. See Robert J. Branham, "The Role of the Convert in *Eclipse of Reason* and *The Silent Scream*," *Quarterly Journal of Speech* 77 (1991): 407–26.

62. Gring-Pemble, "'Are We Now,'" 341–42, 345; Robert C. Rowland, "Narrative: Mode of Discourse or Paradigm?" *Communication Monographs* 56 (1987): 272–73.

63. Charles Willard, "The Creation of Publics: Notes on Goodnight's Historical Relativity," in *Readings on Argumentation*, ed. Angela J. Aguayo and Timothy R. Steffensmeier (State College, PA: Strata, 2008), 272.

64. Catherine H. Palczewski, "Argument in an Off Key: Playing with the Productive Limits of Argument," in *Arguing Communication and Culture*, ed. G. Thomas Goodnight (Washington, DC: National Communication Association, 2002), 15.

65. Catherine Helen Palczewski, "Public Policy Argument and Survivor Testimony: Pro-Ordinance Conservatives, Confession, Mediation and Recuperation," in *Argument and the Postmodern Challenge: Proceedings of the Eighth SCA/AFA Conference on Argumentation*, ed. Raymie E. McKerrow (Annandale, VA: Speech Communication Association, 1993), 465, 462.

66. Windy Y. Lawrence, "Debilitating Public Deliberation: Ronald Reagan's Use of the Conversation Metaphor," *Southern Communication Journal* 72 (2007): 37–54.

67. Gring-Pemble, "'Are We Now,'" 360.

68. Mari Boor Tonn, "Taking Conversation, Dialogue, and Therapy Public," *Rhetoric & Public Affairs* 8 (2005): 409, 421.

69. Martha Watson, *Lives of Their Own: Rhetorical Dimensions in Autobiographies of Women Activists* (Columbia: University of South Carolina Press, 1999), vii, 118. See also Joan W. Scott, "The Evidence of Experience," *Critical Inquiry* 17 (1991): 773–97.

70. Barbara Pickering, "Women's Voices as Evidence: Personal Testimony Is Pro-Choice Films," *Argumentation and Advocacy* 40 (2003): 1, 2, 17.

71. Gerald Peters, *The Mutilating God: Authorship and Authority in the Narrative of Conversion* (Amherst: University of Massachusetts Press, 1993).

72. Seymour Lipset and Earl Raab, *The Politics of Unreason: Right-Wing Extremism in America, 1790–1977* (Chicago: University of Chicago Press, 1978), 12. Lipset and Raab explain that the Right invests in preservationism, while the Left pursues innovation. They note that conservatives can develop a "quondam complex," where one has a greater investment in the past than in the present. The pitfalls of monism can, however, be as great on the political left as on the right—particularly in how the Left tends to focus on economic problems, rather than the past. Ibid., 507.

73. Nock finds that "the only context in which we find [conversion] in ancient paganism is that of philosophy, which held a clear concept of two types of life, a higher and a lower, and which exhorted men to turn from the one to the other." A. D. Nock, *Conversion: The Old and the New in Religion from Alexander the Great to Augustine of Hippo* (Baltimore: Johns Hopkins University Press, 1933/1998), 14. Reviewing earlier studies, Finn finds:

> [T]o enter a philosophical school required conversion. The language of conversion studded the language of philosophy. For Plato, its purpose was to turn the soul around (*epistrophe*); for Cicero, to turn people from carelessness to piety (*conversio*); for Seneca, to discover the truth about things divine and human (*verum invenire*); for the author of *Polmandres*, to summon to repentance those who follow the path of error and ignorance (*metanoia*). . . . As a result, philosophers wrote missionary propaganda, which acquired a technical name, protreptic, a tradition that started with Aristotle, whose early work, *Protreptikos*, extols the supreme value of contemplation as a way of life. Protreptics were exhortations that appealed to people to cast off their old ways and adopt philosophy as the true way of life.

While "radical change" is a common quality in all definitions of conversion, Finn also finds that ancient Greco-Roman communicators shaped one definition of conversion as "a change in the way a person understood, valued, and lived in her or his world. The emphasis was on the cognitive—a change of mind, a new way of seeing—and led to a religious world of contemplation and mysticism." On the other hand, "the biblical world of ancient Israel and Judaism shaped the other. Conversion meant a person's change from a life of infidelity to one of fidelity to God which involved repentance, return, and reconciliation." Finn, *From Death to Rebirth*, 85, 239–40.

74. Nock, *Conversion*, 7, 164–86.

75. See Jasinski, *Sourcebook on Rhetoric*; Thomas W. Benson, "Rhetoric and Autobiography: The Case of Malcolm X," *Quarterly Journal of Speech* 60 (1974): 1–13; Patricia Caldwell, *The Puritan Conversion Narrative* (Cambridge, MA: Harvard University Press, 1983);

Charles Griffin, "The Rhetoric of Form in Conversion Narratives," *Quarterly Journal of Speech* 76 (1990): 152–63; Brian R. McGee, "Witnessing and *Ethos*: The Evangelical Conversion of David Duke," *Western Journal of Communication* 62 (1998): 217–43; Kimberly K. Smith, *The Dominion of Voice: Riot, Reason, and Romance in Antebellum America* (Lawrence: University Press of Kansas, 1999).

76. Peter A. Dorsey, *Sacred Estrangement: The Rhetoric of Conversion in Modern American Autobiography* (University Park: Pennsylvania State University Press, 1993), 2.

77. Wayne Booth, "The Scope of Rhetoric Today," in *The Prospect of Rhetoric: Report on the National Development Project*, ed. Lloyd F. Bitzer and Edwin Black (Englewood Cliffs, NJ: Prentice Hall, 1971), 102. In other fields, there have also been calls to study conversion outside of religion. In a review of the sociological literature on conversion, Gooren writes that "if conversion is to remain a useful concept for scholars, it has to be carefully distinguished from its original religious—Christian—context and meanings. In other words, conversion needs to be thoroughly reconceptualized to move it beyond the Pauline idea of a unique and once-in-a-lifetime experience." Henri Gooren, "Reassessing Conventional Approaches to Conversion: Toward a New Synthesis," *Journal for the Scientific Study of Religion* 46 (2007): 349–50. Commenting on the shortcomings of modern conversion theories, Dorsey suggests that "neither literary theory nor contemporary psychology gives us an adequate framework for understanding conversion. . . . [M]uch work remains to be done on this phenomenon, which continues to structure many aspects of American life." Dorsey, *Sacred Estrangement*, 196.

78. Kenneth Burke, *Permanence and Change* (Berkeley: University of California Press, 1984).

79. Wayne E. Oates, "Conversion: Sacred or Secular?" in *Conversion: Perspectives on Personal and Social Transformation*, ed. Walter E. Conn (Staten Island, NY: Alba House, 1978), 165.

80. Barth says that conversion is "not a question of a reformed or ennobled life, but a new one." This distinguishes conversion from confessional discourse (while still incorporating the latter concept). Karl Barth, "The Awakening to Conversion," in *Conversion*, ed. Conn, 36. Smith finds that conversion derives from the root term "to turn around." It has a spatial orientation, where the turning describes one's transfer between different realities. The term "convert" can be used as a noun, describing a person who has converted to a new way of thinking. It can also be used as a verb, as in the phrase, "he was trying to convert me." Underscoring its communicative nature, conversion "can be brought about by speaking, arguing, [and] persuading on the part of another person." John Smith, "The Concept of Conversion," in *Conversion*, ed. Conn, 51, 53–54.

81. Nock, *Conversion*, 7. Nock also seems aware of the symbiotic, rhetorical relationship between communicators and audiences in conversion tales: "the originality of a prophet lies in his ability to fuse into a white heat combustible material which is there, to express and to appear to meet the half-formed prayers of some at least of his contemporaries." Ibid., 10.

82. William James, *The Varieties of Religious Experience* (New York: Longmans, Green, 1902), 189.

83. Richard Travisano, "Alternation and Conversion as Qualitatively Different Transformations," in *Social Psychology through Symbolic Interaction*, ed. G. P. Stone and H. Faberman (Waltham, MA: Ginn-Blaisdell, 1970), 600.

84. Max Heirich, "Change of Heart: A Test of Some Widely Held Theories about Religious Conversion," *American Sociology Review* 83 (1977): 674.

85. Finn, *From Death to Rebirth*, 9.

86. David A. Snow and Richard Machalek, "The Convert as a Social Type," *Sociological Theory* 1 (1983): 265.

87. Transgression, transformation, and commissioning phases are all present in the Pauline conversion narrative, as well as the situational factors of an existential crisis, suddenness, and a specific time and place that "serves to lend ethos to the story." David C. Bailey, "Enacting Transformation: George W. Bush and the Pauline Conversion Narrative in *A Charge to Keep*," *Rhetoric & Public Affairs* 11 (2008): 222, 236. Spencer argues that stages of contact, confrontation, conflict, commitment, and communion occur in a gradual religious conversion. Gregory Spencer, "The Rhetoric of Malcolm Muggeridge's Gradual Christian Conversion," *Journal of*

Communication and Religion 18 (1995): 55–64. Caldwell defines the path as one of "sin, preparation, and assurance; conviction, compunction, and submission; fear, sorrow, and faith." P. Caldwell, *The Puritan Conversion Narrative*, 2. Branham describes stages of ignorance, confrontation, recantation, and the embrace of a new order. Branham, "The Role of the Convert," 413.

88. Peters, *The Mutilating God*, 6.
89. This definition was constructed in Waisanen, "Political Conversion as Intrapersonal Argument," 230.
90. Craig Martin and Russell T. McCutcheon, eds., *Religious Experience: A Reader* (New York: Routledge, 2012); Mark A. Noll, *The Scandal of the Evangelical Mind* (Grand Rapids, MI: Wm. B. Eerdmans, 1994).
91. Finn, *From Death to Rebirth*, 15.
92. William C. Spengemann, *The Forms of Autobiography: Episodes in the History of a Literary Genre* (New Haven, CT: Yale University Press, 1980), 32.
93. Dorsey, *Sacred Estrangement*, 23.
94. Ibid., 24.
95. Ibid.
96. See John F. Wilson and Donald L. Drakeman, *Church and State in American History* (New York: MJF Books, 2003).
97. Paul Delany, *British Autobiography in the Seventeenth Century* (New York: Columbia University Press, 1969).
98. Sacvan Bercovitch, *The Puritan Origins of the American Self* (New Haven, CT: Yale University Press, 1975), 36.
99. Edmund Morgan, *Visible Saints: The History of a Puritan Idea* (New York: New York University Press, 1963), 70. Weber notes a similar historical development. Max Weber, *The Protestant Ethic and the Spirit of Capitalism*, trans. Talcott Parsons (New York: Scribners, 1930).
100. P. Caldwell, *The Puritan Conversion Narrative*, 178.
101. Richard Harvey Brown, *Toward a Democratic Science: Scientific Narration and Civic Communication* (New Haven, CT: Yale University Press, 1998). Brown finds that discourses about key scientific discoveries and classical ethnographies were based upon "logics of discovery [or invention] as narratives of conversion." He finds that classical ethnographies "are narratives that convert the reader and the topic from strangeness to familiarity . . . deployed to induce readers into new ways of thinking and experiencing in a variety of fields. . . . Narratives of conversion are ways of moving from outside to inside, from the Other to the self—ways of transforming the unknown into the familiar." Similarly, in science, far from following the logico-deductive method proposed in his *Discourse*, Descartes presents readers with "a travel story, an autobiographical journey of discovery of this method." Descartes overcomes the problem of describing his method to unfamiliar readers by "a narrative of his own conversion to the new worldview." Copernicus used his own conversion narrative, the *Narratio Prima*, to incline the public toward his radical heliocentric theories. Most important, Brown finds that historically, "the narrative justified the theory." Richard Harvey Brown, "Logics of Discovery as Narratives of Conversion: Rhetorics of Invention in Ethnography, Philosophy, and Astronomy," *Philosophy and Rhetoric* 27 (1994): 3–4, 11–12, 19.
102. See Matthew Scherer, "The Politics of Persuasion: Habit, Creativity, Conversion" (PhD diss., Johns Hopkins University, 2006), iv. Scherer finds that Locke and Rawls denounced religion and conversion tropes to some distant past, while extending their own liberal conversion narratives to establish their authority as political theorists. He demonstrates how the public ironically came to care about Rawls as a "saintly persona," who evaded demonstrations of his principles in favor of convincing character displays (e.g., by arguing how much he rejected moral perfectionism), deferrals of reason, and conversational gestures. In the end, "everything for Rawls depends upon one's willingness to be reasonable," and "the rhetorical genius of Rawls's conversational prose [is] to incline *our* discussion" by "mobilizing disavowed and largely unrecognized rhetorical modes." As globalization shrinks social space, Scherer thinks that "the pressures of conversion are likely to intensify," raising the need to track conversion discourses. Ibid., 52, 76, 207; emphasis in original. Other examples of this religious mode of

thought in secular rationality include Walsh, who studies the conversion rhetoric of radical, insurgent social movements, finding that converts garner new plausibility structures through enactments of hate, guilt, fear, affective identification with others, and self-criticism sessions to purge ideological impurities. Critically, "the moment of conversion occurs when candidates use revolutionary language to describe their breakdowns." James F. Walsh, Jr., "Rhetoric in the Conversion of Maoist Insurgency Cadres and the Emotional Component of Conversion in Radical Social Movements: III," *World Communication* 19 (1990): 12. Combining the religious and the political, Jensen and Hammerback argue that Eldridge Cleaver had "dizzying shifts in associations, actions, and words," between his membership in the Black Panther movement and eventual conversion to Mormonism over the course of his public career. They find, however, "a strand of consistency tied together Cleaver's shifts," as "he found new organizations and ideologies to reach his goals" of liberating blacks from oppressive social structures. Richard J. Jensen and John C. Hammerback, "From Muslim to Mormon: Eldridge Cleaver's Rhetorical Crusade," *Communication Quarterly* 34 (1986): 24, 38–39. Kellett invites communication researchers to look at conversion accounts from an interpretive, phenomenological perspective. Peter M. Kellett, "Communication in Accounts of Religious Conversion: An Interpretive Phenomenological Account," *Journal of Communication and Religion* 16 (1993): 71–81. Studying religious and secular conversion, communication scholars Golden, Berquist, and Coleman discover a blend of religious and secular arguments in Jim Jones's rhetoric of "exigency marking." See Golden, Berquist, and Coleman, "Secular and Religious Conversion," 581. Bond examines the transformation of Friedrich von Gentz, finding that "his reading contributed towards his political conversion." M. A. Bond, "The Political Conversion of Friedrich von Gentz," *European History Quarterly* 3 (1973): 11.

103. See Martin Loschnigg, "Autobiography," in *Routledge Encyclopedia of Narrative Theory*, ed. David Herman, Manfred Jahn, and Marie-Laure Ryan (New York: Routledge, 2008); Rousseau, *The Confessions*.

104. Dorsey, *Sacred Estrangement*, 48.

105. Huntington Williams, *Rousseau and Romantic Autobiography* (London: Oxford University Press, 1983), 3. The development of modern autobiography in the eighteenth and nineteenth centuries secularized the religious conversion form, and continued to act as a means of socialization—but with some authors, also "estrangement" and "antisocialization." Dorsey, *Sacred Estrangement*, 9–10. Loschnigg clarifies that autobiography became a literary genre only in the late eighteenth century, despite its public presence since Augustine's *Confessions*. There is wide scholarly agreement that during the eighteenth century, confessional religious discourses gave way to new emphases on individual development and (secular and worldly) subjectivity in autobiography, since "individuals felt the need to ascertain their identities in the face of a rapidly changing environment" (as evident in works such as Rousseau's *Confessions* and Benjamin Franklin's *Autobiography*). In the 1970s, deconstructionist theories eliminated notions of a "self" and "subject" in autobiography. Since the late 1980s, however, "the concept of autobiographical reference has reappeared. But now the referent is no longer a pre-existing self, but rather a time-bound human experience corresponding with the temporality of narrative." In this "narrativist turn . . . the self is the product of his or her stories, and is therefore a psychological process of creating an identity rather than a literary form per se." Loschnigg, "Autobiography," 35–36. I would add that, rather than reducing identity to psychological processes, we should view the self as constituted by rhetorical/communicative strategies. In such writing, Bruner finds that "there is something curious about autobiography. . . . [T]he larger story reveals a strong rhetorical strand. . . . The Self as narrator not only recounts but justifies. And the Self as protagonist is always, as it were, pointing toward the future. When somebody says, as if summing up a childhood, 'I was a pretty rebellious kid,' it can usually be taken as a prophecy as much as a summary." Jerome Bruner, *Acts of Meaning* (Cambridge, MA: Harvard University Press, 1990), 121.

106. Dorsey, *Sacred Estrangement*, 59.

107. Ibid., 35.

108. Ibid., 69, 71.

109. Watson, *Lives of Their Own*, 31–46.

110. See Kabi Hartman, "'What Made Me a Suffragette': The New Woman and the New (?) Conversion Narrative," *Women's History Review* 12 (2003): 39, 40. See also Roxanne Harde, "'I Consoled My Heart': Conversion Rhetoric and Female Subjectivity in the Personal Narratives of Elizabeth Ashbridge and Abigail Bailey," *Legacy* 21 (2004): 156–71.

111. Henry Louis Gates, "Frederick Douglass and the Language of the Self," in *Figures in Black: Words, Signs, and the 'Racial' Self*, ed. idem (New York: Oxford University Press, 1987): 98–124.

112. Dorsey, *Sacred Estrangement*, 81. In sum, Dorsey says that "the intellectual and political life of the eighteenth and nineteenth centuries was permeated by the ideas of revolution, freedom, and reform; and these concepts, when applied to the self, presuppose the necessity of personal change, which, when universalized, becomes the basis for social transformation." Ibid., 84.

113. Peter Berger, *The Heretical Imperative: Contemporary Possibilities of Religious Affirmation* (New York: Anchor/Doubleday, 1979), 10.

114. Edwin Black, *Rhetorical Questions* (Chicago: University of Chicago Press, 1992), 183.

115. In Carlyle's *Sartor Resartus*, the character Teufelsdrockh comments on the possibility that choice has been a progressive achievement in human history: "Blame not the word; . . . rejoice rather that such a word signifying such a thing, has come to light in our modern Era, though hidden from the wisest Ancients. The old World knew nothing of Conversion: instead of an *Ecce Homo*, they had only a choice of Hercules." Thomas Carlyle, *Sartor Resartus and Selected Prose* (New York: Holt, Rinehart and Winston, 1970), 189.

116. Goody describes how, in an oral society, religion is much different now than in previous eras because of the impermanence of the spoken word. On the other hand, literate religions "are generally religions of *conversion*, not simply religions of birth." Cultures with writing demarcate boundaries, making concepts like apostasy more tenable. Literate churches practice a dogmatism and rigidity unknown to their oral counterparts, as people herald ideals that correspond to a "text, not a context." Jack Goody, *The Logic of Writing and the Organization of Society* (New York: Cambridge University Press, 1986; emphasis added), 5, 21. Peters similarly finds: "[T]he fact that the concept of conversion may have come to fruition first in the philosophical schools may seem somewhat surprising to many who have claimed the term for religion alone. But if we consider that conversion presupposes a unity of consciousness only possible with the advent of an integrated and systematic form of expression . . . [t]he hieratic form of writing makes ideology possible insofar as it produces a structured system of belief which 'compels assent' and polarizes human behavior." Peters, *The Mutilating God*, 31. Graham further probes the question of how orality and literacy affect conversion: "[W]e can also ask if there may not be a correlation between highly oral use of scripture and religious reform movements. . . . We need to know more about the ways in which memorization and recitation of scriptural texts are related to movements of revival and reform. . . . For example, the 'internalizing' of important texts through memorization and recitation can serve as an effective educational or indoctrinational discipline." Shared texts are influential devices for group cohesion, "and especially with a minority group at odds with and bent on reforming or converting the larger society around it. Such issues . . . all deserve attention." William Graham, *Beyond the Written Word: Oral Aspects of Scripture in the History of Tradition* (New York: Cambridge University Press, 1987), 161.

117. Bailey, "Enacting Transformation," 215. At the same time, Bush recast the Pauline form to suit his own political needs, omitting important details about having had two religious conversions, and softening his past transgressions, effectively bypassing confession while "he plunged headlong into the rhetoric of transformation." Ibid., 226.

118. Ibid., 232.

119. David B. McLennan, "Rhetoric and the Legitimation Process: The Rebirth of Charles Colson," *Journal of Communication and Religion* 19 (1996): 5.

120. Ibid., 8. Similar to Colson, former Ku Klux Klan leader David Duke's viability as a mainstream political candidate in Louisiana was accomplished by his witnessing to (and having others witness to) a Christian religious conversion narrative. Duke overcame his Klan association problem by persuasively coupling religious and political themes, so that his motives and sincerity were hard to question. McGee, "Witnessing and *Ethos*."

121. Ch. Griffin, "The Rhetoric of Form," 161.

122. The conversion form is also similar to what Lake describes as the persuasive "descent-ascent" pattern in American antiabortion discourse. Randall Lake, "Order and Disorder in Antiabortion Rhetoric: A Logological View," *Quarterly Journal of Speech* 70 (1984): 425–43.

123. As an example, O'Leary demonstrates how "just as religious arguers have found apocalyptic [rhetorical] forms useful for frightening audiences into conversion, earthquake predictions served a normative purpose by promoting public awareness of the necessity for disaster preparation." Stephen O'Leary, "Apocalyptic Argument and the Anticipation of Catastrophe: The Prediction of Risk and the Risks of Prediction," *Argumentation* 11 (1997): 309.

124. Branham, "The Role of the Convert," 418.

125. Ibid.

126. Yael S. Aronoff, "In Like a Lamb, Out Like a Lion: The Political Conversion of Jimmy Carter," *Political Science Quarterly* 121 (2006): 425.

127. Dave Tell, "The 'Shocking Story' of Emmett Till and the Politics of Public Confession," *Quarterly Journal of Speech* 94 (2008): 156.

128. This confessional form developed between the eighteenth and twentieth centuries in the United States and ultimately severs links between speakers and accountability for their actions. Ibid., 160. Tell finds that "the power of the expressive form lies in its claim to transcend the political," as abstract, naturalized self-expression replaces rhetorical action. Ibid., 172. Burke explores the deliberative implications of certain kinds of experiential discourse, arguing that "a thoroughly 'confessional' art may enact a kind of 'individual salvation at the expense of the group,'" which has a "sinister function, from the standpoint of overall social necessities." Kenneth Burke, *The Philosophy of Literary Form*, 3rd ed. (Berkeley: University of California Press, 1973), 116–17.

129. Valeria Fabj, "Intolerance, Forgiveness, and Promise in the Rhetoric of Conversion: Italian Women Defy the Mafia," *Quarterly Journal of Speech,* 84 (1998): 190–208.

130. Robert Bellah, "Civil Religion in America," *Daedalus* 1 (1967): 1–21. See also Jean-Jacques Rousseau, *The Social Contract, Book IV*, trans. Donald A. Cress (Indianapolis, IN: Hackett, 1987). There is an interesting connection between Rousseau being a progenitor of modern autobiography and the term "civil religion"—as the turn to self and subjectivity concerns the former, while the stripping of religious details and the praising of abstract Unitarian sentiments informs the latter. Both qualities are features of contemporary political conversion narratives.

131. Richard K. Fenn, "The Relevance of Bellah's 'Civil Religion' Thesis to a Theory of Secularization," *Social Science History* 1 (1977): 502–17.

132. Ronald C. Wimberley and William H. Swatos, Jr., "Civil Religion," in *Encyclopedia of Religion and Social Science*, ed. William H. Swatos, Jr. (Walnut Creek, CA: Altamira, 1998), 95. The authors mention that there has been little effort to look at the civil-religious dimensions of politics across large periods of time. Empirical evidence also suggests that many Americans find civil religion compatible with the doctrine of church–state separation. Ronald C. Wimberley and James A. Christiansen, "Civil Religion and Church and State," *Sociological Quarterly* 21 (1980): 35–40.

133. Allan G. Johnson, *The Blackwell Dictionary of Sociology*, 2nd ed. (Oxford: Blackwell, 2000), 39.

134. Ibid.

135. Thomas Luckmann, *The Invisible Religion* (New York: Macmillan, 1967).

136. In Nicholas Abercrombie, Stephen Hill, and Bryan S. Turner, *The Penguin Dictionary of Sociology*, 5th ed. (New York: Penguin Books, 2006), 341–42.

137. R. Stephen Warner, "Work in Progress toward a New Paradigm for the Sociological Study of Religion in the United States," *American Journal of Sociology* 98 (1993): 1064.

138. Hart and Pauley, *The Political Pulpit Revisited*, 38.

139. Jason C. Bivins, *The Fracture of Good Order: Christian Antiliberalism and the Challenge to American Politics* (Chapel Hill: University of North Carolina Press, 2003).

140. Craig Martin, "Williams James in Late Capitalism: Our Religion in the Status Quo," in *Religious Experience: A Reader*, ed. idem and Russell T. McCutcheon (New York: Routledge, 2012), 190.

141. Bivins, *The Fracture of Good Order*, 158, 171.

142. . Susan F. Harding, *The Book of Jerry Falwell: Fundamentalist Language and Politics* (Princeton, NJ: Princeton University Press, 2000), 3–18, 270, 272.

143. Jacob Heilbrunn, "Rank-Breakers: The Anatomy of an Industry," *World Affairs* (Spring 2008), www.worldaffairsjournal.org/2008%20-%20Spring/full-breaking-ranks.html, par. 9. Heilbrunn does, however, find that there were a number of other prominent conservatives-turned-liberals such as Garry Wills (covered in this book), John Leonard, Arlene Croce, Joan Didion, Damon Linker, Kevin Phillips, Lawrence J. Korb, Andrew Sullivan (to a certain extent), and Jim Sleeper. Heilbrunn thinks that Wills set the path that others, such as Michael Lind, would later follow in their right-to-left conversions. Ibid., par. 20, 24, 29. Cashill also writes that "indeed, there is a whole literature of conversion from the left, even the very hard left, to the principled right. For inspiration, I would recommend Chambers's 'Witness' or Horowitz's 'Radical Son.' There is no comparable literature on the left." Jack Cashill, "Conservatism for Dummies," *WorldNetDaily*, July 21, 2009, www.wnd.com/index.php?fa=PAGE.printable&pageId=102080, par. 6. These observations comport with my own research on the topic, which finds that the majority of these narratives are conservative texts. See n. 8 above for a list of autobiographical- and conversion-related texts.

144. John A. Clark et al., "I'd Rather Switch than Fight: Lifelong Democrats and Converts to Republicanism among Campaign Activists," *American Journal of Political Science* 35 (1991): 577–97. See also Kyle L. Saunders and Alan I. Abramowitz, "Ideological Realignment and Active Partisans in the American Electorate," *American Politics Research* 32 (2004): 285–309. Killian and Wilcox argue that pro-life Democrats are much more likely to become Republicans than pro-choice Republicans are to become Democrats. Mitchell Killian and Clyde Wilcox, "Party Switching: The Effect of Abortion Attitudes" (paper presented at the annual conference of the Midwest Political Science Association, Chicago, April 15–18, 2004). Martin Medhurst has also called for more inquiry into conservative movements from a rhetorical perspective: "Scholars must become better versed in conservative political philosophy. . . . [T]heorists must [also] seek to distinguish what is unique to political conservatism from that which is common to all resistance efforts." Martin Medhurst, "Resistance, Conservatism, and Theory Building: A Cautionary Note," *Western Journal of Speech Communication* 49 (1985): 112.

145. Kristin Luker, *Abortion and the Politics of Motherhood* (Berkeley: University of California Press, 1984), 196.

146. Waisanen, "Political Conversion as Intrapersonal Argument," 228–45.

147. Michael J. Lee, "The Conservative Canon and Its Uses," *Rhetoric & Public Affairs* 15 (2012): 1.

148. Ibid., 16.

149. Calls for this type of work in rhetoric studies can be found in Roderick P. Hart and Suzanne Daughton, *Modern Rhetorical Criticism*, 3rd ed. (Boston: Pearson, 2005), 23–28.

150. James M. Cox, *Recovering Literature's Lost Ground: Essays in American Autobiography* (Baton Rouge: Louisiana State University Press, 1989).

151. Matti Hyvarinen, "Rhetoric and Conversion in Student Politics," in *Interpreting the Political: New Methodologies*, ed. Terrell Carver and Matti Hyvarinen (New York: Routledge, 1997), 21.

152. Ibid.

153. Martha M. Solomon, "Autobiographies as Rhetorical Narratives: Elizabeth Cady Stanton and Anna Howard Shaw as 'New Women,'" *Communication Studies* 42 (1991): 354–70; Watson, *Lives of Their Own*; Charles Griffin, "'Movement as Motive': Self-Definition and Social Advocacy in Social Movement Autobiographies," *Western Journal of Communication* 64 (2000): 148–64.

154. Ch. Griffin, "'Movement as Motive,'" 148; emphasis added.

155. Watson, *Lives of Their Own*, 5. Although it's beyond the scope of this project, it's worth mentioning the potential connections between other media and conversion stories. Film is now a defining medium for our time, and the narrative structure of many commercial films can be seen as also following a conversion logic of changes from old to new ways of being, thinking, and acting. Part of a film's very appeal may have to do with this resonant structuring. My thanks go to one of this book's anonymous reviewers for providing these additional insights.

156. Arthur Koestler et al., *The God That Failed*, ed. David H. Crossman (New York: Columbia University Press, 2001).
157. Loschnigg, "Autobiography," 36; McLennan, "Rhetoric and the Legitimation Process," 5.
158. John Lofland and Norman Skonovd, "Patterns of Conversion," in *Of Gods and Men*, ed. E. Barker (Macon, GA: Mercer University Press, 1983), 19.
159. Heilbrunn, "Rank-Breakers," par. 23.
160. P. Berger, *The Heretical Imperative*, xi.
161. Ibid., 58–59.
162. Lofland and Skonovd, "Patterns of Conversion," 5–19; Max Weber, *Max Weber: The Theory of Social and Economic Organization*, trans. A. M. Henderson and Talcott Parsons (New York: Free Press, 1947).
163. Heilbrunn, "Rank-Breakers," par. 23.
164. Ronald Reagan and Richard Gibson Hubler, *Where's the Rest of Me?* (New York: Duell, Sloan and Pearce, 1965).
165. Doug Linder, "The Trials of Alger Hiss," 2003, under "Trial Aftermath," http://law2.umkc.edu/faculty/PROJECTS/FTRIALS/hiss/hissaccount.html, par. 3. Underscoring my project's foci, if "eternal truths and fundamental values" are at stake, conversion narratives often straddle a dialectic between "otherworldly" and "this-worldly" forms of deliberative reasoning that may forgo public argument.
166. Religious associations are the most common form of membership in the United States, so it is little surprise that the religious and political overlap in this and many other cases of conversion. See Robert Putnam, *Bowling Alone: America's Declining Social Capital* (New York: Simon & Schuster, 1995), 69.
167. Edwin Black, "The Second Persona," *Quarterly Journal of Speech* 56 (1970): 109–19.
168. Taylor clarifies that "by social imaginary, I mean . . . the way ordinary people 'imagine' their social surroundings, and this is often not expressed in theoretical terms, but is carried in images, stories, and legends. . . . [T]he social imaginary is that common understanding that makes possible common practices and a widely shared sense of legitimacy." Charles Taylor, *Modern Social Imaginaries* (Durham, NC: Duke University Press, 2004), 20.
169. Kenneth Burke, *The Rhetoric of Religion* (Berkeley: University of California Press, 1970).
170. P. Berger, *The Heretical Imperative*, 51.
171. Luckmann, *The Invisible Religion*.
172. See, e.g., Hart and Pauley, *The Political Pulpit Revisited*, 91.

Chapter One

Political Conversion as Manichaean Deduction

Whittaker Chambers's Witness

Few books have shaken a generation, divided a country, and created a trajectory of influence and critique many years beyond their inception. On May 21, 1952, Whittaker Chambers published one such book, his nearly 800-page opus, *Witness*. The autobiography details Chambers's former life as a Communist agent and his religious-political conversion from Communism to Christianity and the political Right. Michael Kimmage writes: "*Witness* helped to create a modern conservatism in America,"[1] while others find that it "has remained something of a bible among conservatives."[2] Michael Lee relates that *Witness* was one display of "a style of verbal combat that became essential to the public performance of the conservative political language."[3] Many scholars and journalists agree that *Witness* has been one of the most impactful books in U.S. political history,[4] spurring generations of Republican candidates and party leaders to engage in anti-Communist advocacy during the Cold War.[5]

Richard Nixon often turned to *Witness*'s domino theory of Communist influence.[6] In a series of congressional hearings in 1948, Chambers's testimony that Communists existed in the federal government put Congressman Nixon in the public spotlight and launched his career.[7] Ronald Reagan considered himself Chambers's disciple and described his own political conversion from liberal to conservative in similar terms.[8] Some believe that the Reagan revolution would not have been possible without *Witness*.[9] Reagan memorized and inserted entire sections of *Witness* into his political speeches, and even awarded Chambers a posthumous Presidential Medal of Freedom in

1984.[10] In a controversial act, Reagan's secretary of the interior even turned Chambers's farm in Maryland into a national historic landmark.[11] Years later, former members of President George W. Bush's administration followed these acts by holding public events to celebrate the iconic book and figure.[12]

Beyond presidential politics, *Witness* influenced *National Review* publisher William Rusher and *Time* magazine journalist John Chamberlain, as well as William F. Buckley and Senator Bob Kerrey.[13] Robert Novak wrote that in the U.S. Army in 1953, "I read the newly published *Witness*. It changed my worldview, my philosophical perceptions, and, without exaggeration, my life."[14] George Will called *Witness* one of the most indispensable books of the twentieth century,[15] Ann Coulter declared it her favorite book,[16] and conservative actor Jon Voight, a fan of *Witness*, has dreamed of one day creating and starring in a movie version of the story.[17] Leaders continue to revive Chambers's narrative to address current issues. *New York Times* writer David Brooks said that images of Iraqis lining up to vote in their 2005 elections reminded him of Chambers's toil for freedom.[18] Chambers's writings have also been leveraged against President Clinton,[19] while Don Imus compared Chambers's court case to the O. J. Simpson trial.[20]

Given *Witness*'s enduring role in politics and contrary to the lavish praise that Chambers has found with many political figures, this chapter details how *Witness* fashions a largely propagandistic form of public discourse. Chambers creates a Manichaean, deductive conversion narrative, whose structure works hand in hand with five rhetorical resources: conspiracy, anti-intellectualism, dualism, nature, and prefiguring. In the end, the very form of conversion interacts with these themes to generate rhetoric with anti-deliberative features. To provide a background for these issues, some sense of Chambers's experiences is first worth exploring.

CHAMBERS'S LIFE AND TIMES

Chambers was born in Philadelphia on April 1, 1901, and grew up in a middle-class family in New York. He attended Columbia University but dropped out and joined the Communist Party in the 1920s. Chambers became a Communist Party writer and underground agent in New York and Washington, DC.[21] He worked with a group interested in infiltrating the U.S. State Department, but eventually became disillusioned with factions in the American Communist Party and the news of atrocities emerging from Stalinist purges in the former Soviet Union. He also read several books on Communism that influenced his eventual turn.[22] Chambers and his wife, whom he met in the Communist Party, defected from the organization and went into hiding.

Chambers finally emerged in the late 1930s, confronted some of his former Communist colleagues, and told Assistant Secretary of State Adolf Berle about Communists in the U.S. government. Little followed from these revelations, so Chambers went on with a life as a writer and editor of *Time* magazine over the following decade. Chambers and his wife moved to a farm in Maryland, where they had two children. During this time, Chambers joined the Quakers and converted to Christianity.

Several events in 1948 drew the nation's attention, such as former Communist Party member Elizabeth Bentley's congressional testimony about Communist espionage in the government. Chambers testified in a series of congressional hearings about his former life, naming several Communist Party members from the 1930s, which included a high-ranking U.S. State Department official, Alger Hiss. The infamous House Un-American Activities Committee examined Hiss's and Chambers's claims in front of the nation. Hiss repeatedly denied Chambers's allegations, attacked the *Time* editor's credibility, and brought two Supreme Court Justices (Reed and Frankfurter) to testify on his behalf.[23]

In events widely regarded as setting in motion McCarthyism and the Red Scare of the 1950s, two public trials emerged from the dramatic hearings to determine if Hiss had perjured himself in statements denying that he was a Communist. In the second trial, jurors unanimously convicted Hiss of perjury, sentencing him to five years in prison. After the trials, as a new anti-Communist champion of the Right, Chambers went back to his farm in Maryland and spent several years writing the story of his life. After the success of *Witness*, Chambers wrote briefly for new conservative publications such as William F. Buckley's *National Review*, which embraced Chambers as the pioneer for a new conservative movement. Yet Chambers's years with *National Review* were filled with contention with Buckley and others; Chambers did not approve of Senator McCarthy and called for more compromises and political tact than was offered by his colleagues.[24] Following *Witness*'s publication, Chambers's tenure at *National Review* and remaining years as a writer were short-lived. After a rapid decline in health, he died at his home in Maryland on July 11, 1961.

With each passing decade, political actors revive the controversy over *Witness* and the Hiss trials. Commentators have dissected every detail of the Hiss-Chambers case. Many think that Allen Weinstein's 1978 book, *Perjury*, was decisive in proving Chambers's claims against Hiss.[25] Weinstein began his project intending to prove Hiss innocent but came to the opposite conclusion. Hiss's son-in-law had the same experience.[26] The controversy arose again in a debate between Nixon, Hiss, and the general public in the *New York Times* in the 1980s.[27] In the 1990s, the Central Intelligence Agency and the National Security Agency released a series of decoded cables between U.S. agents and Moscow from 1939 to 1957, which appeared to implicate

Hiss as a Communist spy.[28] Despite these developments, many people, including his son and stepson,[29] maintain Hiss's innocence. A conference at New York University pursued the topic as recently as 2007.[30]

Chambers's grandson runs a comprehensive website devoted to research on his grandfather.[31] Hiss's son similarly maintains a website dedicated to literature on his father.[32] There are even Facebook and other social media pages devoted to Whittaker Chambers.[33] Susan Jacoby writes that Chambers's life and the events of the Alger Hiss case continue to be relevant today: "[F]or the left and the right, the story remains an emblem of their values," dividing those who support New Deal–type government interventions from those who believe in aggressive forms of market activism.[34]

Other personal and contextual factors prompted Chambers's book. The financial rewards for *Witness* were great: Chambers earned over a quarter of a million dollars for his manuscript, a huge sum in 1952.[35] Chambers had been a divisive symbol in politics for many years and needed to establish his credibility and humanize himself with the public.[36] Against an opposition that framed him as pathological, he wanted to model a unique, difficult path worth emulating.[37] Chambers said that he became an informer from feeling alone and having a need to speak out,[38] feeling a dual obligation to break the silence and fight Communist evils. Chambers also faced recurring public questions, such as how it was that he became a Communist.[39] Above all, he wanted to give his life a grander meaning.[40] Chambers thus hoped to address debates about his motives and create awareness of what he perceived to be a colossal conspiracy.

Chambers further needed to show the public how well he could remember his life in the past,[41] since he made a number of costly mistakes in his testimony during the public trials and did not realize how much precision was required.[42] Moreover, Chambers perjured himself in front of the grand jury during one of the Hiss trials, arguing that he made this decision so that Hiss would not be implicated in government espionage—a decision he later regretted.[43]

Last, *Witness*'s rhetoric relates to its 1950s context. With World War II as a backdrop, U.S. politicians continued to push a pro-military foreign policy. The 1940s had put the country into the atomic age, and the 1950s marked a boom in the development of big scientific industries.[44] Spectacles such as McCarthyism and containment policies propelled general anxieties about the Cold War, fueling "a decade of tension as annihilation by ever-more-powerful weapons seemed always possible and too-often imminent."[45] At the same time, many citizens explored new artistic cultural forms such as rock and roll, while others remained concerned that such developments undermined traditional values.[46] *Witness* can partially be read as a response to some of these societal developments.

WITNESS AS DELIBERATION

Previous writings about *Witness* maintain an overriding concern for the truth or falsity of the book's material and the forensic questions raised in the Hiss-Chambers trials. Less considered is how the book acts as a forward-looking policy document and type of rhetoric with certain deliberative norms.[47] *Witness* could be described as a conversion narrative, an autobiography, a confessional, a mystery thriller, a posttrial testimony, and a philosophical treatise and manifesto. It has been called "the greatest memoir of any man of the right. Possibly the greatest memoir ever,"[48] "not unlike an epic poem,"[49] and a "many-dimensioned apologia, which is also a spy drama, a Quaker testament, and spiritual autobiography."[50] Further highlighting the text's many facets, John Judis writes: "*Witness* was part of a tradition of Christian confessional literature and part of an entirely modern postwar genre that blended together journalism, autobiography, and political commentary."[51]

Witness can also be viewed as a type of deliberation. Communication theorists have argued for moving beyond narrow conceptions of deliberation that reduce the subject to a rational argument system, instead capturing a broader picture of the means by which people deliberate or assert particular visions of public discourse.[52] Some examples of the many forms that deliberation can assume include "testimony, performance, gossip, and jokes."[53] Darrin Hicks finds that narratives and "poetic speech are not simply different forms of expression, but rather each of these genres of communication is constituted by different forms, functions, and effects," such that biographical narratives can also be seen as sites of deliberation that move beyond formal, unemotional, and heady types of argument.[54] Deliberation involves many types of rhetoric, making the styles and genres employed in *Witness* a compelling site for investigation.

Rather than assuming the deliberative norms of this type of text in advance, I track each author's own deliberative criteria as they emerge across each work. In other words, while traditional tests of public reasoning will be applied where appropriate, this and subsequent chapters will move through each case study by primarily looking to each author's own standards for reasoning and reasonability. Additional contextual support for these criteria is provided by the public responses that *Witness* provoked. These responses highlight how many readers confirmed,[55] provided mixed reviews,[56] or negated the second persona of *Witness*.[57]

As a communication strategy, *Witness* is a deductive, quasi-religious conversion narrative, proclaiming the authority of a general, otherworldly reality in the face of Chambers's historical situation. Using modern Christian Protestantism as a case, Peter Berger argues that a central figure representing deductive religious thought was Swiss theologian Karl Barth, who affirmed an orthodox certainty in almost all matters of faith.[58] As an analogue to this religious mode of thought, Chambers approaches politics from a fundamentalist, deductive perspective. As a deliberative form, Chambers's conversion narrative combines with the mutually reinforcing resources of conspiracy, anti-intellectualism, dualism, nature, and prefiguring, forming an interactional, civil-religious rhetoric greater than the sum of its parts.

SETTING A PRECEDENT: CHAMBERS'S RHETORICAL RESOURCES

Dark and Sinister Forces Are Out There: Conspiracy

One of *Witness*'s striking features is its combination of conspiracy and conversion messages. Through Chambers's story, conspiracy and conversion become mutually reinforcing elements. By launching an onslaught of life details at his readers, Chambers overclaims his findings about Communist espionage in the U.S. government, in a way that seems as though the evidence for the existence of conspiracies mostly stacks up in his favor. A deductive conversion form reinforces Chambers's conspiracy arguments by connecting seemingly unconnected bits of information into a coherent whole—giving direction and force to the evidence of his experience, however inadequate these details are in supporting the conspiracy claims. The conversion story equally answers objections to Chambers's conspiracy arguments. Chambers becomes a model of authority for readers in explaining that, because he is someone who has entered and exited Communism firsthand, he has an experience-based, insider vantage point that precludes further investigation.

Conspiracy messages have a long history.[59] They are difficult to disprove and hence "self-sealing," tend to forward polarizing rhetorical dichotomies, and ask their auditors to deductively connect scattered evidence toward their conclusions.[60] As a response to "evil" and many imagined societal problems,[61] the very form, rather than content, of conspiracy arguments proves harmful for public discourse.[62] Audiences often experience psychological satisfaction from conspiracies, which tend to be open texts offering an aura of realism and a community with which to identify, but also much "oversimplification" in their use of evidence and lack of reasoning.[63] Scholars note that conspiracy rhetoric can foster an environment of suspicion,[64] particularly as a "paranoid style" has moved from the "ideological extremes to the mainstream of political life."[65] By using the conspiracy device in the convert's narrative, Chambers creates a potent form of communication.

Chambers makes his Communist conspiracy claims directly: "Those who insist plaintively on evidence against a force whose first concern is that there shall be no evidence against it must draw what inferences they please."[66] Conspiracy arguments like this are self-referential, with a circularity and disjunction between claims and evidence that prevent falsification. John Strachey similarly finds that the authors of ex-Communist literatures have one aspect in common: "[T]he men who wrote these books regarded themselves as agonized, half-strangled outcries against an advancing, and almost certainly invincible tyranny."[67] Similarly, Chambers leaves little room for readers to draw what inferences they please. Testifying in front of the House Un-American Activities Committee, he hoped that "my testimony helps to make Americans recognize at last that they are at grips with a secret, sinister and enormously powerful force whose tireless purpose is their enslavement."[68]

The Communist conspiracy is called a "hidden power," a "hidden history," and a "Fifth Column," with a "much greater power that lurks behind it" lending a secrecy to these forces.[69] As the narrative unfolds and more is learned about Chambers's conversion to Christianity and conservatism, these word choices slip back and forth between the evil, unseen, dark forces of the spiritual world and his past life as a Communist, fusing religion with politics. The "charge of conspiracy" was also at the center of Hiss's defense against Chambers,[70] providing an additional motivation to co-opt this language in the service of a perceived Communist threat.

Witness connects converts to conspiracy claims. Chambers projects authority by implying that his conversion gave him a special knowledge unavailable to others: "[N]o one knows so well as the ex-Communist the character of the conflict, and of the enemy . . . [f]or no other has seen so deeply into the total nature of the evil with which Communism threatens mankind."[71] The author relates that his deep and overpowering experience as a convert should translate directly into an authority claim for the existence of sinister motives and secret forces lurking just beyond the sight of every U.S. citizen. But the convert's experience asks readers to make inferences about horrific forces that go beyond the idiosyncratic evidence presented. This is not to discount Chambers's real experience as a Communist. Nor is it to discount Hiss's potential guilt, given the weight of historical evidence now accumulated about the legal case. But as a matter of degree, Chambers's experiences establish claims for which there is little or no support, combining conspiracy and conversion devices in a way that oversteps their reach.

Within the conversion narrative structure, conspiracy claims are positioned in a crowd of details about Chambers's personal life. He joins the American Communist Party before going into underground work. Yet for secrecy's sake, this underground work was set up in a way that Chambers admits did not let him know the extent of its influence.[72] Chambers remarks that "[I]t is certain that, between the years 1930 and 1948, a group of almost unknown men and women, Communists or close fellow travelers, or their dupes, working in the United States Government, or in some singular unofficial relationship to it . . . affected the future of every American now alive.[73] In the first sentence, Chambers asks readers to believe "certain" knowledge about "unknown men and women." In comments like these, *Witness* merges Chambers's structured conversion experience with conspiratorial randomness. Chambers leverages the dangers of his old life and the foresight of his new life toward the claim that nonverifiable, secret Communist cabals not only existed while he was a Communist (prior to 1939), but in the following years when he was no longer in the Communist Party. Although Chambers fled the Communist Party in 1938 (so he did know about the influence of *some* Communists in government prior to that period), he overstates his knowledge by implying that between 1938 and 1948, all sorts of deeply threatening activities continued in the United States.[74] Other critics also find that Chambers greatly exaggerated Hiss's and his own influence throughout *Witness*.[75]

Chambers twice provides lists of Communists in the U.S. government.[76] He asserts that any sane person looking at the notes that Assistant Secretary of State Adolf Berle took in his 1938 conversation with Chambers should conclude that "the essential framework of the conspiracy is here. . . . It is equally clear that I am describing not a Marxist study group, but a Communist conspiracy. The Communists are described as such."[77] Yet the list is replete with question marks, aliases instead of real names, fragmented words, and redundant references appearing in the rest of *Witness*. Aside from the list's truth or falsity, when looked at in total, Chambers names a rather small group of people. Over the course of *Witness*, it may be felt that Chambers cumulatively establishes a list of names of those in Washington, DC, involved in espionage. When looked at comparatively throughout the book, however, we find a repetition of the same names over and over. For example, Chambers lists the Ware group committee and the jobs that led them through the federal government from pages 344 through 346,[78] but repeats the same names later on pages 466–69.

Through recurrent lists, Chambers strings together bits of information throughout the autobiography that collectively compile scattered grounds for his conspiracy claims. In addition to the catalog of Communist agents, he includes a long list of underground techniques used by Soviet spies.[79] Chambers records those killed under Stalin's purges and lists people he knew who were killed by Communists.[80] Dispersed between simple life details and world news events, these compilations are made to bear a direct connection to the claim that the conspiracy is widespread and influential.

In toggling between old and new lives, conspiracy claims appear within a mass of concrete personal details.[81] This volume of detail and cataloging in the book led Reinhold Niebuhr to remark that "only a man who has deeply suffered could have written it."[82] Yet the same details led Hiss's son to conclude: "Chambers got enough details right, or half right, to sound informed."[83] One review further notes that "hammer blows of facts rain down about us," which "not only has failed to induce a religious experience in us but has been unable to authenticate [Chambers's] own."[84] More so, *Witness*'s scattered details—reinforced by the testimonial authority and linearity of the conversion form—are used to give weight to the idea that Chambers has a global vantage point on conspiracy.

Aside from *Witness*'s quantity of details, Chambers uses vivid, singular examples to claim a larger conspiracy. During the Hiss trials and in *Witness*, much effort goes into describing a car that Hiss possessed and gave to another presumed Communist agent in the 1930s.[85] Similarly, describing his experience in an underground Communist group at length, Chambers speculates about the existence of a Communist "sleeper apparatus"—or a Communist Party cell that "exists not to act. It waits for the future. It is a reserve unit which will be brought into play only when those who control it see fit, when events dictate, or when it has matured."[86] These claims are generalized from his limited experience in the underground to note that much similar criminal activity is widespread throughout the United States. In this sense, conversion and conspiracy claims align through what Ernest Bormann calls "fantasy themes," or vivid symbols that evoke a network of associations, essentially offering one or more key facts toward which audiences contribute additional information or fill in the gaps.[87]

The important point for public deliberation is that Chambers fashions a form of rhetoric in which many such activities cannot be confirmed or argued against. He writes that at least one of these sleeper apparatuses is in the United States,[88] and speculates about how every publication in the United States likely has a Communist in it.[89] In another part of the book, Chambers even calls upon an "unnamed" agent to come forward and speak about Communist espionage.[90] The author's experiences as a Communist were limited to relatively sequestered operations in New York and Washington, DC. Yet within the deductive mold of his conversion framework, Chambers claims an authority to speak in an all-encompassing manner about hidden people, places, and motives.

Sometimes Chambers's commitment to maintain the details of his life experience challenge the more grandiose, generalized conspiracy arguments. In a telling moment, he reflects that "conspiracy itself is dull work. . . . Its object is never to provide excitement, but to avoid it."[91] He describes a Communist meeting where the members seemed more like a group of deli workers than revolutionaries.[92] On the other hand, *Witness* leads the reader toward a conclusion that "it's hard to believe that a more highly placed, devoted and dangerous espionage group existed anywhere."[93] Chambers's host of life details hence presents a deliberative difficulty for the conversion narrative—it is hard to maintain a directional, deductive consistency when making conspiracy claims across the course of a life story that also evades such linearity.

To be clear, this is not to discount the genuine political and ethical problems raised in Chambers's life. In the face of the Soviet Union's human rights abuses, Chambers asserts that he could not simply desert the Communist Party and stay quiet about his experiences.[94] While some sources that Chambers cites about Communist murders in the United States and abroad are likely true, they do not establish sufficient links between the claims and evidence provided.

Throughout the autobiography, the language of conversion and the language of conspiracy combine. Chambers argues that he was on truth's side in his battle against the Communist conspiracy.[95] Note how conspiracy is related to being on truth's "side." In the conversion divide, the notion of being on the "right" side (both propositionally and politically) establishes the enemy's schemes. The double meaning of "truth" makes the conspiracy claims in *Witness* more than political matters: they are grounded in the progress of Chambers's conversion and eventual alignment with transcendent forces, weaving a concern about society's secretive and sinister forces with the author's new theological allegiance. Clarifying his relationship with Hiss, Chambers says that he "represents the concealed enemy against which we are all fighting . . . but in a moment of history in which this Nation now stands, so help me God, I could not do otherwise."[96] Drawing upon one of the Martin Luther's most famous lines from the Protestant Reformation,[97] Chambers ties his new Christian convictions to the political conspiracy claim about "concealed" enemies. In doing so, the conversion form tidies up the narrative's miscellaneous details, propelling Chambers's authority and philosophy forward.

Most important, the conversion and conspiracy devices in *Witness* found audiences ready and willing to accept Chambers's rhetoric.[98] For Sidney Hook, "the evidence of this book is so overwhelmingly detailed and cumulative, it rings with such authenticity, that it is extremely unlikely any reasonable person will remain unconvinced by it.[99] One blogger writes that *Witness* "certainly establishes beyond a shadow of doubt that Alger Hiss, Harry Dexter White, and company were active Communists dealing with very important matters in the upper reaches of the U.S. government."[100] Even a legal analysis states that "this book bears evidences of sincerity and truth which do not confirm the hypothesis that Chambers' accusations against Hiss were part of a vast psychopathic lie."[101]

Other reviews critiqued Chambers's conspiracy claims. A *Life* magazine editorial comments on *Witness*'s "deep but narrow conspiratorial experience."[102] John Kenneth Galbraith argues that Chambers "exaggerates the role of the Party and the associated conspiracy,"[103] just as Rebecca West finds that "there must be a series of events which arouse the suspicion that a crime has been committed, and at the same time so tangled that it is hard to verify or disprove that suspicion."[104] Despite general praise for *Witness*, Arthur

Schlesinger argues that the book exemplifies "the hazard of founding dogmatic generalizations on experience so narrow and fragmentary."[105] One critic says that Chambers "seem[s] able to persuade some people who were not there that [his] aberration was an all but universal aberration. . . . [A] small army can look like a large army to a man who is in the midst of it."[106] To John Judis, too, Chambers simply "overestimate[d] his role in life."[107]

Although many of *Witness*'s conspiracy claims have been contested, more remarkable is how conversion and conspiracy function together.[108] Conspiracy rhetoric can be problematic for deliberation when communicators fail to establish evidence for their claims, but more so when combined with the conversion narrative's emphases. This is not the only problematic aspect of Chambers's discourse, as the author uses another rhetorical resource in a similar way.

Let Unreason Reign: Anti-intellectualism

Chambers combines a political conversion narrative with an attack upon the Enlightenment, modernism, rationalism, and intellectualism. I sum up this focus as "anti-intellectualism." As Chambers castigates reason and reasonability, he downplays the power of human communication to create social changes. Toward this end, the conversion form and anti-intellectual rhetoric are enlisted as mutually reinforcing resources across the narrative.

Throughout *Witness*, Chambers minimizes the role of reason while elevating a discourse of the private and transcendent in human affairs. *Witness* equates belief in the capacity of human beings to change their world with a crude materialism,[109] which partly emerges from World War II's savagery, and the atomic and hydrogen bombs that illustrate how "man without God is a beast."[110] Chambers hopes to return to a premodern existence uncluttered by Enlightenment thought, and laments the loss of religious faith, family, community, farming, and other traditions as devastating for the human race.[111] He names reason and science as regressive and relegates rationality to a subordinate place in his newly acquired religious conception of the universe. Chambers repeatedly chastises modernity's developments for causing horrific historical events such as the Holocaust.[112] Through such emphases, *Witness* connects the rise of science with totalitarianism.[113]

Conversion rhetoric augments arguments for anti-intellectualism by comparing human reason to a false religion. Chambers says that Communism is a secular religion that requires discipline and piety.[114] The analogy channels intellectualism through the conversion framework so that the political philosophy becomes a false religion of the past, compared with the true religion of Chambers's present. This bipolar structure admits little middle ground, dividing reason from religion. Chambers conflates Communism and reason to combat man's replacing God's mind with human intelligence.[115] Under the conversion form's veil, Chambers poses a choice between humanity and God in the most polarized terms, concluding that only one story or viewpoint should gain the public's adherence.

By framing intellectualism as a false religion, Chambers maps theology onto politics. He associates modernism and Enlightenment intellectualism with a faith-free government, arguing that citizens should join a true politics with a true religion. A false politics engages policy without divine guidance; hence, from a deductive perspective, politics necessitates metaphysics. The author makes a case for this relationship by referencing how many intellectuals do not believe in God anymore and have replaced faith with politics, and how religion and politics cannot and should not be separated, forcing humanity into one of two categories—those who believe in or reject God.[116] Because of such passages, some consider Chambers one of the key figures in bringing religion into the modern conservative movement.[117] The point of politics is not for humans to communicate and figure out how they will live together but for those who worship God to battle with those who reject God. Struggles to deliberate about humanity's future are placed within a framework where all minor conflicts can and should be related to cosmic issues.

Civic issues become adjunct to a grander, deductive faith narrative. This deliberative vision has not been lost on other critics who have called into question Chambers's belief that faith is an answer to the crises of history, rather than any ongoing, experimental political efforts.[118] Chambers applies conversion to politics, so that intellectuals and intellectualism must be rejected as signs of a past life. As he continually reminds readers, his experience has led him to conclude that people need spiritual connections.[119]

The truths of a conversion experience are accessible only to those who abandon rationality. Despite the Communist Party's stance against intellectuals, at one point in his career Chambers claims that he was too naïve to realize that the Communist Party was run by intellectuals.[120] Communists and intellectuals are lumped together, and the author's beliefs about the dangers of intellectualism are further confirmed by scores of MAs and PhDs who were to call for his demise in the Hiss case and during his tenure at *Time* magazine.[121] When joined with conversion's spiritual emphases, this type of anti-intellectual position may track back to interpretations of the biblical book of Genesis locating the origin of sin in the temptations of knowledge.[122]

Resisting knowledge is given a populist twist, with Chambers asserting that the jury could sense what intellectuals could not.[123] In this scheme, Chambers disempowers citizens from using reason, ironically turning a populist strategy on its head. By connecting an aversion toward intellectuals with a distaste for the intellect, reason and deliberation are placed beyond citizens' reach. Instead, the inward soul becomes the deductive locus of decision making.[124]

In essence, Chambers provides us with a theory of persuasion in these comments—that, like two tuning forks resonating to the vibrations of each other, influence works best when the instantly recognizable intuitions of the soul confirm or disconfirm knowledge, over and above the engagement of two or more minds in reason and deliberation. Describing an original relationship with Hiss that was once quite amiable, Chambers says that his friendship was based on "character" rather than "mind,"[125] positioning communication as about a priori soul-work rather than reasoning between two or more interlocutors. This theory of persuasion bears a similarity to research finding that advocacy groups often have an overarching commitment to "intuition" as a "unique moral sense" that cannot be refuted.[126] Historically, Protestant religious movements in the United States have downplayed learning and rationality in favor of inner, emotional validity.[127] These trends continue in the present, as anti-intellectual religionists often bypass public standards for evidence, inflicting social and scientific costs upon the body politic.[128] Chambers's deliberative vision also reduces reason to an individual resonance that represents transcendence, bypassing communication as a source of knowledge in favor of populist appeals to mind-abandonment.[129]

The life experiences that prompt a conversion further underscore the narrative's deductive, anti-intellectual features. Chambers draws divides between the mind and one's inward and external experiences. In the first chapter, he writes a letter to his children, urging them to consider that the knowledge they needed would be gained from living in nature, not by reading books or believing in the power of their minds.[130] Chambers locates inward life and external nature as points from which to coordinate actions. The story draws a distinct line between reverence for personal experience and the external world and the brain's creative capacities. Experience and nature are endowed with fixed and positive qualities, while a negative flexibility characterizes innovation, reason, and human agency.

When Chambers therefore says that "an inward experience itself, beyond any power of the mind, had reached me,"[131] he links internal experience with external, transcendent forces. *Witness* constructs the political-religious conversion experience as deep within the individual and also driven from without, blocking human reason from two directions simultaneously. Drawing divides between intellectual texts and life experience, the author recalls that in an early trip to study socialism in Europe when he was younger, theories and books replaced real living.[132] Here Chambers promotes an individualistic, autobiographical epistemology, where an inward search and an externalized agency become the sole routes to knowledge.

Through this vision, narrative and autobiographical texts bypass human minds to simply channel divine guidance. Chambers favors books such as *Les Misérables* and *The Journal of George Fox* by linking their grounded stories with transcendent work.[133] Such texts are more than books;[134] they are vehicles for truths that make the human intellect look inadequate for accomplishing much in this world. His book's title, *Witness*, has multiple meanings relevant to these earthly and divine revelations. Chambers states that "*such [a] witness completes a greater witness.*"[135] Under the conversion form, Chambers codes the word "witness" ambiguously, in terms of a political obligation to testify to an old and new life from Communism to capitalism, as well as a religious testimony of a journey from Communism to Christianity. Each use of "witness" thus becomes civil-religious in alternating between faith and civic meanings.

Part of the very conversion experience involves a loss of faith in rhetorical action. Chambers reflects on his decade-long tenure as an editor at *Time* magazine, writing that only acts rather than words could win these battles.[136] Moreover, testifying before the congressional committee about Communists in the government, Chambers asserts that a time for words had ended, only his acts could now save the day.[137] As a witness to a conversion experience internally and externally separated from his own agency, Chambers argues that words have little role to play in human affairs. In the political conversion, an "act" is not found in language but in experiences that necessarily form and mold the trajectory of one's life.

Admittedly, there is one point in the book where Chambers indicates that reason and knowledge may have some value: that faith comes into play where reason fails.[138] But there are no other places in *Witness* where humankind progresses through reason, and no threshold is provided for when or where the use of one's intellect might be appropriate throughout the rest of the narrative. Only personal experience and transcendent faith appear as viable directors of human action.[139]

Overall, the conversion narrative fuels anti-intellectual rhetoric. Chambers says that a saying by Quaker Robert Barclay explains what he went through in his conversion: that the truth of his witness had nothing to do with arguments.[140] The reference, as well as Chambers's deliberative vision, follows from Quakerism's two essential principles, which involve "the possibility of direct, unmediated communion with the Divine" and "a commitment to living lives that outwardly attest to this inward experience."[141] Human arguments are merely a nuisance in this scheme. Knowledge is not gained by individual reflection or social talk but through "direct" truth reaching an individual. The conversion uses the power of an experience deep within and beyond oneself to reinforce a point that reason, being so mediated and limited, should play little part in personal or public affairs.

As with the other rhetorical resources, various critics affirmed and denied the anti-intellectual vision. Ralph de Toledano writes that if it had not been for Chambers, "the Hiss case would have been one more dreary process of the law, a police assault on treason. Through [Chambers] it became a contest of faith, a confrontation of God and Man,"[142] affirming the narrative's grand, cosmic level of interpretation. John Sheerin says: "Chambers has given a salutary warning to a prodigal generation to leave the arid wastes of atheistic humanism and return to God."[143] Decades later, Marvin Olasky writes: "Chambers noted that 'the enlightened and the powerful,' the leaders of media and academia, fell hard for the man-centered approach of Alger Hiss."[144] John Weidner, too, finds that *Witness* taught him that "there is only one struggle. Only one story. . . . The story, the battle, just takes different forms from one century to the next"—a battle of secularism as opposed to religious faith.[145]

On the other hand, critics such as Henry Roberts argue against Chambers's use of experience and transcendence: "[T]he reader may be less convinced by this impressive and tortured demonstration that the life of Mr. Chambers is a mirror to the crisis of our times."[146] Daniel Mahoney finds that "at the heart of Chambers' moral vision is a rejection of the fundamental conceit of the Enlightenment: the self-sovereignty of 'autonomous' man."[147] Russell Nieli comments that Chambers "stood within a common mystic-prophetic line of protest that sought to judge man and his world *sub specie aeternitatis.*"[148] Finally, Merle Miller finds that "in the most fundamental sense, *Witness* is an appeal to un-reason," with Chambers lacking a perspective that "the whole history of western progress is based on the belief . . . that, by reason, man can reduce the chaos of nature."[149]

Overall, fusing conversion with anti-intellectualism undermines deliberation. *Witness* asks readers to affirm a persona where one must choose between the intellect or an internal intuition guided by external, transcendent forces. The conversion narrative's either/or structure advances this anti-intellectualism but also continually divides, interprets, and reduces the world's phenomena into a choice between two options at each juncture. This dualistic, Manichaean strategy illustrates further problems for public discourse.

A TWO-SIDED UNIVERSE: DUALISM

Political conversion narratives can be fused with Manichaean dualism, which sees the universe as a battle between good and evil forces. As rhetorical resources, the conversion form and a dualistic philosophy share binary structures that reinforce each other. This rhetorical move allows an author to construct a paradoxical, complex dichotomy—where a mass of life details fosters the impression that simple, dichotomous divides are not being drawn in the narrative. As a result, in Chambers's case many black and white arguments are made in a way that does not seem as though he is making black and white arguments. Chambers writes about the polar choices that converts face—for example, "a Communist breaks because he must choose at last between irreconcilable opposites—God or Man, Soul or Mind, Freedom or Communism."[150] Being "irreconcilable," *Witness* asks readers to find little nuance in these rhetorical dichotomies. Chambers uses the authority of his conversion from Communism to reinforce a twofold choice that human beings face in their political and religious allegiances. Embedded within so much narrative detail, Chambers makes these Manichaean points complex— as final judgments proceeding from a long, torturous journey.

Toward *Witness*'s end, Chambers invokes a dualistic theological claim in describing the Hiss trial. The fight between himself and Hiss indicates a grander point, that "a struggle between two men—was precisely what it was not. It was the struggle between the force of two irreconcilable faiths— Communism and Christianity—embodied in two men."[151] Chambers's conversion is described as more than a journey between his past life as a Communist and new life as a conservative Christian. He believes that these very categories reflect an external, universal struggle between good and evil forces, aligning the deliberations of the court case with cosmic considerations. Humans personify this transcendent battle in comments about men and women exemplifying evil.[152] Human arguments are already determined in advance; as Chambers relates to a colleague at *Time* magazine, "I cannot really be beaten because on my side is a Power."[153]

Across the text, the political conversion fuses with an abstract, philosophical dualism vacillating between the local and the universal. The personal details of the author's conversion experience mirror arguments about dualistic, universal realities to which all human beings are accountable. Infusing local life details with universal force, Chambers writes that the two men in the trial personified a grand universal battle between faiths.[154] Seemingly minor human events are subsumed under an absolute dichotomy reinforced by the conversion form's divisions between old and new. This division gains traction as the reader continues through 800 pages of writing, which repeatedly highlights how personal conversion and cosmic dualism go together.

This dualistic rhetoric informed Cold War discourses for the next forty years. *Witness* constructs an individual's actions in terms of a larger, dichotomous political battle between nations—which represents an ultimate battle between good and evil on a celestial level. Chambers writes in the letter to his children that the Second World War reduced the world to two options.[155] All events are reduced to a binary old and new life, two political superpowers, and two celestial forces. Politics and religion become intertwined, but religion is given a superior, subsuming status in these divisions. This vision is evident in Chambers's remark that leaving Communism is a faith experience,[156] relegating political experience to the fate of an external, spiritual dimension. By implication, Chambers suggests that political debate is unnecessary, as politics simply represents an ultimate battle between the forces of good or evil. The good or evil sides could need to be argued for—but downplaying human agency under the terms of a Manichaean battle urges readers to devalue the role that communication could play in creating societal changes.

At points in the narrative where it seems as though Chambers might drop this approach, he ends up reinforcing the polarizing structure of the conversion form. Many journalists made unfounded, ad hominem charges against Chambers, with some claiming that he was a drunkard and had once been a patient in a mental institution during the Hiss trial.[157] Chambers laments the scandal focused nature of the media and tabloids.[158] He also notes how media such as television can trivialize public discussion, noting that by making the Hiss Case into a drama between two people, the larger issue of the battle between faith and political systems had been obscured.[159] Chambers argues against the simplistic, dramatizing norms of modern media, but only in the sense that they are not hyperbolic enough about the larger issues at play—i.e., that the two men are dualistic representations of a larger universal battle. Ironically, his concerns about media norms are undermined by *Witness*'s dramatic and simplified narrative dualism.

By reducing the universe to two options, the text forecloses courses of action that do not fit within the parameters of the dualistic mold. In crossing conversion and dualism, the author additionally fails to admit matters of degree that might expand opinions or the possibility for incremental forms of change. For instance, many reviewers took issue with *Witness*'s relentless clustering of groups under the label Communist and thus Manichaean evil, as when Chambers notes how all the people he knew who believed in the New Deal had been Communists, or close to it.[160]

More so, conversion and dualism appear to promote a polarizing form of consciousness applied to other events. Chambers says that FDR's New Deal substituted business for politics.[161] Chambers's polarizing discourse admits little space for intersections between politics and business. As one critic objects, Chambers's distinction between the New Deal and business "obscures the fact that 'business' is still very much alive and still a powerful and active force in the political arena."[162]

Dualism constitutes another way that political conversion narratives are civil-religious rhetorical strategies. Chambers's conversion is assertively Christian, but he also characterizes faith at a general level. At two different points in *Witness*, the author details the pressures he felt to not be too religious in the public square.[163] The text describes Chambers's conversion to "Christianity" but tends not to cover faith specifics—negotiating expectations for not bringing church and state too closely together by mostly using the conversion form and general religious beliefs while downplaying explicit religious content. This lack of specificity may simply reflect that Christianity is the only "true religion" and hence the only one worth mentioning. But more notable is the absence of specific faith references—for example, the name "Jesus" is used only once in the book.

Witness provided U.S. conservatism with a new religiosity in World War II's aftermath. Joseph Salemi finds that Chambers was instrumental in subordinating Ayn Rand's libertarian objectivism within the movement (which had little place for religion). As a broad appeal, "because Chambers's religion seems non-doctrinal . . . his book could strike a chord in conservatives of every religious persuasion. As Chambers once said to William Buckley, 'You stand within a religious orthodoxy. I stand within no religious orthodoxy.'"[164] In these appeals, conversion and dualism work together as an inclusivist, civil-religious way to get religion into the public square. Chambers argues for a general Christianity that implicates divisions between Manichaean good and evil, Communism and freedom, but not Jesus and Satan.

Overall, many audiences found the fusion of conversion and dualism persuasive. President Reagan remarked in a speech:

> Chambers, the man whose own religious conversion made him a witness to one of the terrible traumas of our time, the Hiss-Chambers case, wrote that the crisis of the Western world exists to the degree in which the West is indifferent to God, the degree to which it collaborates in Communism's attempt to make man stand alone without God. And then he said, for Marxism-Leninism is actually the second oldest faith, first proclaimed in the Garden of Eden with the words of temptation, "Ye shall be as gods."[165]

In this remark, we find Chambers's conversion, the dualistic world-historical crisis of political East versus West, and the grand universal battle that they reflect all wrapped into one statement. The passage also summons the conversion narrative's anti-intellectual resource (the temptation of "ye shall be as gods"). These techniques and the emphasis upon "evil" had an impact on Reagan, whose "Evil Empire" speech cited parts of *Witness* dealing with this theme.[166] Other recent responses confirm this deliberative vision, particularly comments affirming Chambers's lumping together of liberals with Communists. *Witness* convinced Bishop Williamson that "communism is a religious problem, and all liberals are virtual communists."[167] Chambers's idea that Communism is an evil religion was even taken up almost fifty years later by Craige McMillan, who cites *Witness* in attacking "the liberal's cozy secular faith—faith in man."[168]

Yet Chambers's dualism has also been opposed in important ways. Hannah Arendt took issue with Chambers and the "ex-Communists see[ing] the whole texture of our time in terms of one great dichotomy ending in a final battle. There is no plurality of forces in the world, there are only two. . . . Ultimately, others don't count."[169] Some argue that Chambers was receptive to "overly melodramatic world systems."[170] With deliberative implications,

> if an evil, and not merely undesirable, policy is the issue, what room is there for compromise or maneuver. . . . Chambers sought to teach American conser-

vatives the art of political compromise. In *Witness*, however, he provided them with an ideal that brooked no compromise. . . . [This] condemned America's conservatives to wander between theology and pragmatism, between dreams of redemption and the intractable complexities of politics and diplomacy.[171]

Similarly, Arthur Schlesinger thinks that Chambers errs in his philosophical diagnosis, finding that *Witness*'s "conviction of infallibility" bypasses "concrete facts," giving absolutism precedence over pragmatism.[172] Indeed, the fragile relations between Chambers and many conservatives in the years after *Witness*'s release may have followed from this tension between his lived need for expediency and his manifesto's call for dogmatism.

Other reviewers have been even less sparing about *Witness*'s dualism. Kingsley Martin critiques the dichotomy between a barbaric Communism and a liberating faith by arguing that very religious countries such as Spain have been brutally intolerant in the past. He takes issue with the world being "divided into Good and Evil" and the characterization of "reason" as necessarily leading people "logically step by step through liberalism to Communism."[173] Another reviewer remarks that in *Witness*, "things become either black or white, with no intermediate ground. . . . As a result, the reader is haunted by a sense of insincerity" and "too neat definitions."[174] One citizen writes that Chambers "puts the Spirit of God and the mind of man in opposing camps. . . . Plenty of good Americans can oppose communism without embracing mysticism, even if Whittaker Chambers can't."[175] Others note that Chambers simply needs to consider that many Democrats do not serve Communism.[176]

Irving Howe reflects that "if you believe that the two great camps of the world prepare for battle under the banners, Faith in Man and Faith in God, what is the point of close study and fine distinctions? You need only sound the trumpets."[177] Tony Judt portrays Chambers's "account of human history since the Renaissance as a hubristic assertion of the centrality of man for which a price must now be paid: all this is a one-dimensional version of the Manichaean creed."[178] Chambers's polarized view of the world also makes it appear unreformable.[179] In each case, Chambers's divisions are perceived as bringing an unwarranted fanaticism into public life.

Some even critique Chambers's substitution of one totalitarian system for another. Philip Rahv objects that "Chambers eliminates from his account anything that might be conceivably taken as ambiguous and incongruous." *Witness* has a "lack of humor" and "a failure of sensibility" that proceeds from converting to and from dogmatic systems—"first History, now God."[180] A letter to *Time* magazine opines that Chambers "has substituted one faith for the other and in his processing has disregarded rationality."[181]

These reviews highlight some of the democratic problems that dualistic communication strategies pose. While many chastise Chambers's penchant for dichotomies and lack of nuance, they miss the underlying operations of his conversion narrative that reinforce these simplistic binaries with their emphases on bifurcated experience. If conversion is by definition dualistic, it likely generates these very binaries. The conversion narrative advances a form of consciousness in which communicators divide their lives between "old" and "new" identities. Binary rhetoric proceeds from this form, fusing the autobiography's structure with Manichaean content.

In sum, *Witness* maintains a marginal role for human communication. Chambers's political-religious conversion and the battle between good and evil that it indicates are wrought from above. In Chambers's worldview, communication is a tool for propagating preordained truths, a means of converting humankind to one of two options at personal, political, and universal levels. Each of these realms infuses the other, but the personal and political remain subordinate to and reflective of universal religious truths. One's personal and political choices are either in or out, meaning that further reflection, doubt, struggle, or interaction beyond this dualism remain unnecessary. Communication is not a driver of human experience but a means of aligning with or diverting from cosmic realities that care little for human effort or will.

Bypassing Human Action: Nature

Conversion narratives can be written with an eye toward nature. In *Witness*, "nature" is used in a specific sense. Similar to Chambers's use of dualism, the world of nature is merely a transfiguration of the spiritual realm and its deductive demands. *Witness* positions nature's scenes or environments as guiding human action.[182] But the nature appeals are also a way of supplementing the conversion narrative. The author not only documents his extensive life experiences but provides the reader with a swath of information about the natural world to reinforce the narrative's authenticity. Since the natural world is a phenomenon shared by all human beings, Chambers makes his conversion and political theories more relatable by continually dropping details about the natural world in front of the reader, grounding his abstract, deductive dualism.

Although some may consider the contemporary conservative movement antienvironmental, previous generations of conservatives were highly agrarian and reverential toward nature.[183] Many iconic conservative figures were environmental advocates[184] —but in a precise sense. Illustrative of the trend, Richard Weaver asserted that nature is "given and something that is finally inscrutable. . . . [It is] the creation of a Creator. There follows from this attitude an important deduction, which is that man has a duty of veneration toward nature and the natural."[185] Nature is a reflection of the transcendent, or a transfigurative representation of the ultimate order of things.[186] Weaver's experience with nature is, in essence, told in terms of a "conversion" from liberalism and scientism to a new life of spiritual restoration, a conscious turn from public and commercial events to the enduring external world.[187]

Chambers uses nature in exactly this way. The Christian conversion and political dualism are reinforced by the book's focus on the transfigured, external world. Chambers says that he wants his son to look to external reality as a "standard" for his life.[188] Conversion and nature work together, with the environment acting as a prompt to truth. Chambers explains that his religious conversion was influenced by nature, particularly in seeing the design at work in his children's growth.[189] In breaking with Communism and entering into a new Christian, conservative life, Chambers writes that he had offered himself "to the murderous mountain" but was entering a new period of "sinking roots and fostering growth."[190] He fashions the conversion through nature metaphors to make his individual transformation—as well as the external, immovable transcendent realm to which it refers—more concrete.

In joining conversion and nature, the author makes his post-Communist life a natural progression. In one passage, Chambers explains: "I returned to the land and undertook that second life."[191] Looking to nature is made a part of the born-again "second life." Nature not only describes the conversion but reflects a universal division between truth and falsity. Connecting nature to conversion, Chambers thus relates the conversion's stages to the building shocks of an earthquake, and his transformation to a river whose stream had now found its true channel.[192] Chambers further links his childhood memories of the sea on Long Island's south shore with the transcendent realm.[193] *Witness* fuses the "beyond" of religious faith, which cannot be seen, with the common human experience of nature.

To buttress the conversion story, Chambers uses themes of darkness and light throughout the book. Michael Osborn finds that light and dark are archetypal metaphors, which appeal to people across times and places as "prominent features of experience . . . which are inescapably salient in the human consciousness."[194] Overlapping with conversion, these terms correspond with Chambers's "dark" past life, in contrast with the "light" of his new faith. Nature infuses both natural and social worlds with a sense of good and evil, supplementing *Witness*'s philosophical dualism.

Chambers tells his children that his book was written to give them a path through the woods and up through dark, rocky paths.[195] Following this trope, the story concludes with a line from Dante's *Inferno* and Marx's *Capital* about emerging to view the stars.[196] The autobiography's structure begins in darkness and ends in light, with dark and light metaphors generating a teleological frame for Chambers's life and the universe's progression. The emphases on steep and lonely paths traveled underscores an exceptional pilgrim's progress through this world guided by the light of a higher power.

A network of associations is built between darkness and light and death and life metaphors. The birth of Chambers's first child led "us out of that darkness, which we could not even realize, toward that light, which we could not even see."[197] Light and dark, death and life: these constitute two classic metaphors for religious transformation.[198] Yet this language also generates the political conversion, as the "seen" is reflective of the "unseen," Chambers not only emphasizes religious responsibilities to unseen realms but deepens his political conspiracy rhetoric, which uses the "unseen" as an evidentiary standard. The religious and political issues both become indisputable matters of life and death.

Nature rhetoric makes the abstract claims to religious realities and hidden, conspiratorial political threats tangible for audiences. When Chambers was told by the Communist Party that he was not allowed to see his future wife while a party member, he recalls sensing that a cold and serpent-like force existed behind such efforts.[199] By framing Communism as an underground, shadowy force, Chambers's nature metaphors reinforce his conspiracy claims, positioning such machinations as part of a relatable, material realm.

The life and death emphases of this rhetoric relate to nature's inflexible characteristics. Chambers explains to his wife that her choice was not between being a Communist or adhering to a different belief system but between death and life.[200] Like conversion rhetoric, nature limits human choices to only two options at each juncture. Human action becomes a part of nature's processes, but these processes are anything but diverse. For example, nature could be conceived differently—not as light or dark but of varying colors and shades. Similarly, life and death could be understood less as stark opposites than as about patterns of growth and entropy, or as rhizomic and recursive.[201] Each of these rhetorical choices contributes to a picture of public deliberation where humans submit to the external world rather than try to engage with or change it.

To draw distinctions between old and new lives, nature appeals additionally transfigure youth in terms of natural innocence and goodness. Chambers describes how he lacked friends as a child, and withdrew to nature and books in his innocence.[202] In a Rousseauian construction,[203] Chambers locates purity with the innocent individual in nature rather than in corrupted society. He takes this premise further by transfiguring these experiences in transcendent terms; his withdrawal into nature is no simple escape but, rather, a forced alignment with God and all that is good. Conservatives often use deep appeals to childhood innocence and what Randall Lake calls "presymbolicity" to limit the role of choice in public decision making.[204] Chambers's combination of conversion and nature similarly minimizes human freedoms and deliberative possibilities through youthful terms.

Like writers such as Weaver, Chambers in *Witness* fuses conversion and nature rhetorics through a romantic, agrarian focus on city evils as contrasted with country virtues. Chambers explains that he took a job writing poetry in New York early in his career because he wanted to retain Long Island's beauty before the city destroyed it.[205] Chambers's conversion from Communism to Christianity/conservatism comport with a retreat from city life.[206] The author's post-conversion purchase of a farm symbolizes a past life among humans as distinct from a new spiritual withdrawal into a transfigured nature. Rahv, too, notes how Chambers's farm "is at once a real place and a piece of ideology pure and simple."[207]

Relevant to deliberation, the nature resource elevates a deductive version of "experience" as a form of reasoning. Chambers remarks that he and one colleague "understood one another at once with a birdlike intuition in which common experience took the place of explanation."[208] In this situation, "intuition" and "common experience" trump "explanation" and, as Chambers implies, "reasoning." The "birdlike" term reinforces this view by juxtaposing intuitive, animalistic communication with reflective human reasoning. In other words, Chambers infers that interlocutors best communicate by using signs rather than symbols. Birdlike also connotes that Chambers has a wide perspective on the public realm. Like a bird in the sky, the convert maintains a broad, weathered view of the world.

Nature's order contrasts with humankind's disorder. Chambers states: "I never found the loneliness of the woods at night as disturbing as people by daylight."[209] He also attributes certain characteristics to other people through bird metaphors. In the Hiss trial's aftermath, he runs through an extensive scheme comparing intellectuals in the Hiss trial to birds such as skimmers and boobies.[210] Just as Chambers saw his own actions as "birdlike," his enemies are characterized in animal form. Their communication is reduced to screeching at best. The bird names generate metaphorical images of his enemies huffing and puffing, as "boobies" or fools. The "skimmers" merely skim along surfaces, connoting that Chambers's enemies are superficial. Unlike Chambers, the seabirds stay within their own myopic realm, so that their thinking and actions are literally out to sea. As a site of innocence and purity, nature-as-transcendence confirms the author's blamelessness. His converted life links with a pure nature reflecting an unchanging deity. With such rhetoric on his side, the author atones from the past and legitimates his actions in the present.

Witness elevates what Kenneth Burke calls a "scene" as a determining guide in human affairs, with the nature rhetoric underscoring the importance of civic withdrawal rather than engagement. A stress upon "scene" connects with a materialistic philosophy that reduces human communication to physical processes.[211] That is, human "acts" flow from external environments. Burke looks at how this perspective played out in Baruch Spinoza's philosophy—whose "word for 'God' might well be translated 'total context.'" [212] Of interest is how contexts can forward the same kind of determinism that religious rhetorics use. Chambers's nature is also transfigured—highlighting what Burke calls a purpose-scene ratio, where an overarching belief conclusively drives how one views a context.[213] This ratio reverses the line about Spinoza, so that in Chambers's vision, the context could be translated God. Ultimately, the political-religious conversion to this purpose-scene viewpoint declares that fate, rather than choice, drives human action.

Some critics resonated with *Witness*'s use of nature. John Dos Passos was affected by the "landscape" that Chambers detailed, reflecting that "a society or nation has some aspects of a living organism."[214] Murray Hausknecht writes: "Chambers skillfully manages to depict himself as both an intellectual and man of the soil who earns a living by the sweat of his brow."[215] Rebecca West finds that the sense of nature in Chambers's account "reveals that he belongs to a certain well-recognized order of man. . . . He is, in fact, a Christian mystic of the pantheist school."[216] Robert Genter asserts that Chambers followed Kierkegaard's teachings of "the movement from the aesthetic sphere to the ethical sphere, that is, from a world of immediacy and possibility to a world of requirement and necessity."[217] Before covering some implications of this rhetoric, there is a final strategy that contributes to *Witness*'s propagandistic communication.

It Shall Pass . . . : Prefiguring

Prefiguring is a time-based rhetorical strategy describing an author's shifts between past, present, and future. Chambers creates a god's-eye view of his life, continually shifting his story back and forth in time, and prefiguring what will happen in the future when referring to the major and minor details of his life. This move endows Chambers with authority and establishes an impression that his life has been guided by a progressive and determined revelation.

Witness takes readers on a journey where, with truth on his side and in a predetermined fashion, Chambers is destined to come out a winner. When prefiguring is combined with a religious conversion, the writing implies that much about the future can be known. In this vision, communication propagates certainties. Chambers's rhetoric prefigures the future, using the conversion as evidence that the seeds of one's new life can be found in the old. External forces have already determined the past, present, and future. As such, conversion and prefiguring create a type of apocalyptic rhetoric in which human deliberation can do little.[218]

The story heaps deterministic terms on current events. During the Hiss trial, Chambers asserts that his strength lay in the trial being a faith conflict.[219] Rather than being a forum for forensic inquiry, the court case is seen as a place where fixed convictions were already playing out their roles. Within this verbal framework, humans simply act out history's scripts.

Chambers uses prefiguring and conversion by arguing that, paradoxically, he has kept his motives consistent over the course of his life. For example, despite his grand life transformation, the author maintains that he has always cared for the poor.[220] The author inoculates audiences from the objection that his life has been inconsistent, showing that his conversion was already prefigured in many past actions from his Communist life. This paradox invites a double-pardon communicating: "I have come to a new life that absolves my prior mistakes" while maintaining that "the seeds of my goodness were also prefigured in my prior life." Chambers states that as an ex-Communist, he was operating from many of the same motives from his previous life.[221] In another section, Chambers says that he once treated a caretaker with a lot of dignity, acting as a Communist and unconsciously as a Christian.[222] Chambers retrospectively cleans up the details of his life, framing past behaviors in terms of future beliefs. While maintaining the distinction between his old and new lives, he prefigures the latter in the former.

Conversion and prefiguring ultimately create a discourse of fulfillment, so that Chambers sees purpose everywhere. When he was a child, Chambers saw a group of boys urinate on a lollipop and then hand it off to another unsuspecting boy. He compares the shock of this experience with how he was treated by the Hiss lawyers during his trial.[223] Reflecting upon his brother's suicide, Chambers writes that "there is some purpose in my life which I feel but do not understand. I must go on living until it is fulfilled."[224] Under these terms, past events prefigure future episodes.

The stories from Genesis through Revelation in the Old and New Testaments are largely about progressive revelation. The coming of Christ and the end of time were prefigured in the Old Testament. In a similar fashion, Chambers shifts between past, present, and future, putting each in terms of a fulfilling destiny that has shaped his life. In the very act of writing, the end is already written at the beginning. Humanly created symbols like words or images exist solely to be aligned with "true" or "correct" courses of action, rather than as variable tools. These religious connections with the prefiguring terms of Old and New Testaments further reinforce the bifurcating emphases between the "old" and "new" in the conversion narrative itself.

More than an isolated strategy, prefiguring can gain momentum through repetitive flash-forwarding. Chambers reflects on a time when his failing sight saved his life later.[225] These details contain future purposes, highlighting the author's foreshadowing consciousness. He meets an individual named Arvid Jacobsen, and then forecasts how this person would be arrested in the future.[226] Numerous characters that Chambers introduces are cast in these terms, whether notaries or associates who corroborate Chambers's testimony later in life;[227] each plays a meaningful part that prefigures the ultimate victory and vindication that Chambers repeatedly claims by the story's end.

One key term describes how the author interprets such life events: "providential."[228] With a divine plan guiding humanity, Chambers urges readers to see that there is little point in struggling to communicate with others in other than prophetic ways. Logically, this is a time-based version of reasoning from definition, or deductivism. Burke argues that a rhetoric of "essences" (or of set natures or characteristics) can be joined with rhetorics about time when communicators describe points of origin as beyond human language use.[229] In other words, authors are always selective in where they begin their stories and in the words that they choose to talk about those beginnings, since other starting points could have been chosen. A story's form may create the impression that events are inevitable, precluding considerations of alternative starting points or directions. With deliberative implications, choosing particular starting points as natural can prevent human beings from being led to new conclusions.[230] *Witness*'s prefiguring rhetoric eludes choice or innovation but under the terms of a conversion to a "new" life. Thus, paradoxically, readers are presented with a prefigured rhetoric of new choices.

Cold War events lent credibility to Chambers's prefiguring rhetoric, particularly the fall of the USSR and of many Communist countries around the world. One critic in 2004 found the writing prescient: "Chambers was a prophet for our times."[231] Philip Yancey thinks that Chambers "served as a forerunner of what has transpired on a global scale."[232] These responses partly suggest that Chambers's prefiguring rhetoric was affirmed by some, but also that audiences have metonymically used *Witness* to interpret the Cold War in prefigured terms.

Many have been unconvinced by Chambers's determinism, however, arguing that the unpredictability of human behavior prevents us from knowing about future givens: "[I]t is the reason why politics as human activity was deemed (since Plato and Aristotle) to be inferior in quality to other forms of human activity."[233] More so, as Arendt says, "it belongs to totalitarian thinking to conceive of a final conflict at all. There is no finality in history—the story told by it is a story with many beginnings but no end."[234] Hyrum Lewis finds, too, that "a religiously-based historical determinism" informs much of Chambers's thought.[235] In a way, "Marxism never left him"—as Chambers creates a Christian eschatology with "historical directionality."[236] Reed Whittemore writes that in *Witness*, "recollected details appear to have been put through some sort of strainer so that only the significant details, the details useful in illustrating a point, get into the text."[237] These reviewers point toward the determinism, directionality, and definitive sense of the past, present, and future evidenced in *Witness*, adding to the book's cumulative picture another reason that conversion can be so propagandistic.

CONCLUSION

Chambers shares part of his motivation for writing *Witness* about a third of the way into his book: that he could influence policy by writing a story that people would want to read, rather than polemics that would not be popular.[238] Indeed, as scholars have found, stories are powerful because they "do more than just relay a series of events. They make arguments."[239] *Witness* shows that conversion narratives can interact with various persuasive resources to produce a propagandistic type of story.

Witness combines the conversion form with a quasi-religious, deductive form of Manichaean rhetoric that, in sum, portends poorly for public engagement and political possibilities. The autobiography's totalizing tendencies are demonstrated through each theme, with the deep structure of the conversion form functioning to generate and amplify its anti-deliberative emphases. Many features of traditional argument theory are present in Chambers's narrative (such as the role of reason in public discourse), but each is reconfigured under the conversion form. Chambers presents readers with a detailed, complex autobiography that, on its surface, makes a contribution to public discourse. But when the rhetoric's subtle operations are examined, a different picture emerges. A number of implications follow from this analysis.

First, interactions between rhetorical resources like conspiracy and the conversion form demonstrate how anti-political messages can be advanced by certain rhetorical patterns. In the autobiography, conversion reinforces conspiracy rhetoric, with Chambers putting his political conversion and the vast context of his life experience in the service of unsupported assertions. The story's sheer length allows him to gloss over a wealth of needed detail in support of the conspiracy claims. The realism and authority of the convert's tale are brought to bear on these conspiracy arguments, as are recurrent lists and vivid, singular examples, so that, in the end, the structured conversion experience directs the book's conspiratorial randomness. The conspiracy arguments' circularity combines with the conversion experience's directionality to produce a rhetorical form undermining reasoning and reasonability. Conversion and conspiracy fashion the convert as an authority in a way that cannot be confirmed or argued against.

Second, Chambers's combination of anti-intellectualism with the conversion form further functions to weaken reason's place in the political sphere. *Witness* undercuts deliberation by elevating the private and transcendent at the expense of human communication. The authority of a conversion experience is simply made to fill in whichever intellectual or knowledge gaps that one might possess. The conversion form separates all political issues into religious or nonreligious bins. *Witness* forms a fateful political vision by constituting the autobiography as part of a divine master plan and by presenting one's inner soul and outer spiritual validations as the central points from which decisions should be made. The linear structure of a conversion hence lends a hand to the message that rational human faculties should be abandoned in favor of, colloquially speaking, "getting with the program."

Third, dualism and conversion can form what I term a "complex dichotomy," where dogmatic arguments appear more complex than warranted. *Witness*'s depth and breadth of experiential evidence make many of its black and white arguments appear a lot less like black and white arguments. Dualistic rhetoric places absolute and irreconcilable demands upon the public realm, locating all personal and political events under the canopy of deductive, rule-bound divides. Chambers asserts that his long journey reinforces his final polarized judgments about politics and religion, that life's events are mere reflections of an external battle, and thus that public actions are already known in advance by good and evil forces. By reducing the universe to two options, Chambers blocks agency, invention, and compromises that do not fit within the dualistic mold. The dualism leaves little room for matters of degree, promoting a bifurcated consciousness from which binary rhetoric proceeds. Ultimately, one's choices are either in or out, meaning that reflections, interactions, or communication beyond this dualism remain unnecessary.

Fourth, *Witness* pictures nature as a transfigurative reflection of a Manichaean universe, following a long line of conservative, agrarian discourse that also undermines a role for rhetoric in human affairs. Nature reinforces Chambers's conversion, as an earthly instantiation of a deductive religious reality. *Witness*'s swath of nature rhetoric reinforces the authenticity of the conversion narrative, grounding Chambers's abstract religious-political dualism in concrete detail and functioning to make the conversion journey appear part of the natural progression of a transfigured universe. At the same time, since nature is a relatable experience common to all people, Chambers uses metaphors such as dark and light to generate the ends-driven conversion framework. Each of these choices contributes to an image of public deliberation in which little malleability or hope is available for the development of future policies.

Last, shifting between past, present, and future, the political conversion narrative persistently prefigures what will happen in *Witness*, progressively revealing to readers that the future is determined. Communication propagates certainties under such emphases, with people simply acting out history's scripts above and beyond possible choices. A teleological rhetoric permeates the narrative, merging the conversion with transcendence. Flash-forwarding and other techniques create a sense that providence is at work and that human actions are foreordained—but under the subtle terms of conversion to a "new" life—evidencing a complex, prefigured discourse of new choices.

In all these ways, *Witness*'s rhetoric constructs a propagandistic worldview greater than the sum of its parts. Tracing the cumulative interactions between the conversion form and these rhetorical resources, readers are left with an anti-political outlook. Despite how the autobiography is driven by a number of pressing ethical issues, such as a concern about human rights violations and how television may harm civic engagement, Chambers's very discourse works against rhetorical interventions that might address these abuses.

Ultimately, the structure of the conversion form creates a tragic vision of civic resignation in the face of determining forces. Lee has also noted that an "oracular melancholia" of mortification rather than redemption informs Chambers's tale.[240] Prefigured under transcendent realities, Chambers implies that only one's self-sealing experience can make any difference in the world. This deliberative vision would be less worrying had *Witness* not gone on to influence figures at the highest echelons of U.S. power. And beyond being a Cold War manifesto, *Witness* is still being used by many hoping to dismantle New Deal policies and advance theocratic political designs.[241]

It may be objected that one should not overlook how *Witness* has prompted much public discussion. Some may believe that talk about the book and its contents highlights a lively, ongoing civic discussion worth some deliberative weight. A *Time* magazine review of *Witness*'s book reviews finds, for instance, that "few books in a dozen years have provoked such a burst of prompt, wide and heart-searching reviews."[242] With debates about the book ensuing through the present,[243] the text can certainly play a role in the overall marketplace of ideas.

Yet there is a critical difference between deliberation as a forum and deliberation as a mode of communication. *Witness* constitutes a contribution to deliberative forums as a text circulating in the public realm. In its mode of operation, however, the political conversion narrative is as much a contribution to public discourse as propaganda, modeling a certain kind of communicative behavior for audiences. *Witness*'s communication form is equivalent to talk-show guests sticking their fingers in their ears while others try to have a discussion. This is *not* to exclude passionate advocacy as a rhetorical option in public life but is to recognize that *Witness*'s conversion form does such a comprehensive job of narrowing discursive space and human agency that its qualities sum to an anti-deliberative text.

It is remarkable how public debates about the book, in turn, affected Chambers's post-*Witness* life. Conservatism has been a contested and controversial political philosophy in the postwar period,[244] and Chambers's own political views in the later 1950s underwent some strain and amendment.[245] After leaving the conservative magazine *National Review*, Sam Tanenhaus found that the end of Chambers's life demonstrated an "evolving humanism" and a new opposition to "a rigid and unrealistic conservatism. Having allied himself to the right, he seemed bent on challenging, rebuking, and even outraging its axioms."[246]

Chambers's post-*Witness* shifts spotlight a tension between the stringent positions in his book (e.g., dualism) and experienced disagreements within his own movement. These changes show how there is always a potential to be too fanatical or to misconstrue one's opponents or issues. Overall, the conversion experience that *Witness* calls for is ultimately insufficient for a viable politics. It does not always guarantee the right outcomes and, as Chambers's own life evidenced, is not necessarily *the* way toward political progress.

In the U.S. postwar period, *Witness* influenced other political conversion narratives that have made their own mark on public culture. While support for Chambers's story continues unabated within and outside conservative circles, similar texts have appeared as responses to the personal and political crises of their respective times. I next explore the conversion narrative of another touchstone work that shows the variety of ways in which these tales may be told.

NOTES

1. Michael Kimmage, "Whittaker Chambers's *Witness* and the Dilemma of Modern Conservatism," *Literature Compass* 3 (2006): 941.

2. "Whittaker Chambers, American Journalist, Witness in the Alger Hiss Spy Case," in *The Cold War, 1945–1991*, ed. Benjamin Frankel (Farmington Hills, MI: Gale, 1992), under "The Hiss-Chambers Affair," reproduced in *Biography Resource Center* (Farmington Hills, MI: Gale, 2009), http://galenet.galegroup.com/servlet/BioRC, par. 3. Moreover, conservatives have drawn upon the book's religious and political symbolism in continuing to ask questions like: "What Would Whittaker Chambers Do?" Cliff Kincaid, "AIM Report: What Would Whittaker Chambers Do?—August A," *Accuracy in Media*, August 2, 2007, www.aim.org/aim-report/aim-report-what-would-whittaker-chambers-do-august-a.

3. Michael J. Lee, *Creating Conservatism: Postwar Words That Made a Movement* (East Lansing: Michigan State University Press, 2014), 16; idem, "The Conservative Canon and Its Uses."

4. Eric J. Sundquist, "*Witness* Recalled," *Commentary*, December 1988, 57–63. Kimmage further finds that *Witness* was part of "a literary genre that would flourish after World War II . . . the 'literature of witness.'" The book was "part of a new American genre, the ex-communist memoir." Kimmage, "Whittaker Chambers," 948, 962. Genter calls *Witness* "the most successful entry in a new genre of autobiography—the confessional tale of a former member of the Communist party who had recently abandoned political radicalism and had come forth to testify about the dangerous appeal of authoritarian ideologies." Robert Genter, "Witnessing Whittaker Chambers: Communism, McCarthyism and the Confessional Self," *Intellectual History Review* 18 (2008): 243. Hausknecht, too, names *Witness* "the archetype" of "a new genre [of] autobiographical writing, the literature of political confession." Murray Hausknecht, "Confession and Return," *Antioch Review* 14 (1954): 76.

5. Patrick Swan, "Preface," in *Alger Hiss, Whittaker Chambers, and the Schism in the American Soul*, ed. idem (Wilmington, DE: ISI Books, 2003), xxii.

6. See Richard M. Nixon, "Plea for an Anti-Communist Faith," *Saturday Review*, May 24, 1952, 12–13. In 1986, Nixon wrote: "Chambers . . . had a profound effect in shaping my attitude about the war in Vietnam." Richard Nixon, "Lessons of the Alger Hiss Case," *New York Times*, January 8, 1986, www.nytimes.com/1986/01/08/opinion/lessons-of-the-alger-hiss-case.html, par. 10.

7. Thomas B. Allen, *Declassified: 50 Top-Secret Documents That Changed History* (New York: Random House, 2008), 124, 125.
8. For more on Reagan's conversion, see Evans, *The Education of Ronald Reagan*, 51.
9. Matthew Spalding and A. Beichman, "The Cold War's Magnificent Seven," *Policy Review* 59 (1992): 44–55.
10. Paul Kengor, "The Intellectual Origins of Ronald Reagan's Faith," Heritage Lectures, February 25, 2004, www.heritage.org/political-process/report/the-intellectual-origins-ronald-reagans-faith, 1–6.
11. See John J. Miller, "The House of Chambers," *National Review*, August 27, 2007, 31–32. The History Division of the National Park System Advisory Board voted against landmark status (using the guideline that historic sites need to be landmarks for at least fifty years), which was overturned by Reagan's secretary of the interior. Bruce Craig, "Politics in the Pumpkin Patch," *Public Historian* 12 (1990): 9–24; Barry Mackintosh, "'Politics in the Pumpkin Patch': A Response," *Public Historian* 12 (1990): 53–56; "Site in Hiss-Chambers Case Now a Landmark," *New York Times*, May 18, 1988, http://query.nytimes.com/gst/fullpage.html?sec=travel&res=940DEEDA1339F93BA25756C0A96E948260, par. 4.
12. Elaine Sciolino, "G.O.P. Devotees Pay Honor to Whittaker Chambers," *New York Times*, July 10, 2001, www.nytimes.com/2001/07/10/us/gop-devotees-pay-honor-to-whittaker-chambers.html.
13. Lee Edwards, "Whittaker Chambers: Man of Courage and Faith," Heritage.org, April 2, 2001, www.heritage.org/political-process/report/whittaker-chambers-man-courage-and-faith.
14. Robert D. Novak, foreword to *Witness*, by Whittaker Chambers (Washington, DC: Regnery, 1980), xiii.
15. George F. Will, "Whittaker Chambers: Up a Winding Staircase," *National Review*, December 31, 1985, 65.
16. Ann Coulter, "Snuggle Up With Ann Coulter's Top 10 Favorite Books," *Human Events*, November 29, 2005, http://humanevents.com/2005/11/29/snuggle-up-with-ann-coulters-top-10-favorite-books/.
17. Fred Barnes, "Jon Voight, Whittaker Chambers Fan," *Weekly Standard*, September 3, 2007, www.weeklystandard.com/Content/Public/Articles/000/000/014/018hyldo.asp.
18. David Brooks, "Stepping Out of the Tar Pit," *New York Times*, February 1, 2005, 19.
19. See ReleaseTheHounds, "Whittaker Chambers Bears 'Witness' to Bill Clinton's Protestations," *Free Republic*, October 3, 2006, www.freerepublic.com/focus/f-news/1712902/posts.
20. Imus compared the rhetoric of Hiss's defenders to "that bull—that Johnnie Cochran came up with for O. J. Simpson." Matthew Carolan, "Chambers in the Morning," *National Review*, January 26, 1998, 14.
21. Whittaker Chambers, *Witness* (Washington, DC: Regnery, 1980), 276, 279.
22. Chambers describes how Eugene Lyons's book *Assignment in Utopia* and the ex-Communist narrative *I Speak for the Silent*, by Vladimir Tchernavin, contributed to his break. Ibid., 241, 80, 79.
23. Newton Minow, "Some Legal Aspects of the Hiss Case," *Journal of Criminal Law and Criminology (1931–1951)* 40 (1949): 346. See also Chambers, *Witness*, 741.
24. "Whittaker Chambers, American Journalist," under "The Hiss-Chambers Case," par. 10. See also Niels Bjerre-Poulsen, *Right Face: Organizing the American Conservative Movement 1945–65* (Copenhagen: Museum Tusculanum Press, 2002), 59; Sam Tanenhaus, *Whittaker Chambers: A Biography* (New York: Random House, 1997), 452–83.
25. Allen Weinstein, *Perjury: The Hiss-Chambers Case* (New York: Alfred A. Knopf, 1978); Ronald Radosh, review of *Perjury: The Hiss-Chambers Case*, by Allen Weinstein, *American Historical Review* 84 (1979): 586–87. Weinstein notes some of Chambers's deceptive omissions in *Witness*, such as his confession to the FBI that he had engaged in homosexual behavior as a young man. Weinstein, *Perjury*, 358. Another researcher says that in *Witness*, "we find out very little about [Chambers's] several romantic affairs and nothing of substance about the illicit 'party marriage' to Ida Dales that ended with the abortion of their child." Sundquist, "*Witness* Recalled," 60.
26. See G. Edward White, *Alger Hiss's Looking-Glass Wars* (New York: Oxford University Press, 2004), xviii.

27. Hiss writes that "my case has often been trotted out to justify reactionary policies far removed from the issues of the case itself, and Mr. Nixon once again tries to make it a connecting thread for his views on a number of world and domestic events. . . . Once more, I assert that I did not engage in espionage. . . . My case seems to be a barometer of the Cold War." Alger Hiss, "The Lessons of the Richard Nixon Case," *New York Times*, January 9, 1986, www.nytimes.com/books/97/03/09/reviews/chambers-letters-nixon.html, par. 2, 7. One citizen argues that Nixon's op-ed was deceptive, as "Mr. Hiss was convicted not of espionage but perjury" in the "anti-Communist hysteria" of the period. Sol Stember, "The Lessons of the Richard Nixon Case," *New York Times*, January 21, 1986, www.nytimes.com/books/97/03/09/reviews/chambers-letters-nixon.html, par. 1, 4.

28. James Thomas Gay, "1948: The Alger Hiss Spy Case," *American History* 33 (1993): 26–35. See also John Haynes, *In Denial: Historians, Communism and Espionage* (San Francisco: Encounter Books, 2003), 143; Harvey E. Klehr, *Secret World of American Communism: Documents from the Soviet Archives* (New Haven, CT: Yale University Press, 1998), 129; Maria Schmidt, "The Hiss Dossier," *New Republic*, November 8, 1993, 17–19. For a brief but comprehensive overview of Alger Hiss's life, see Janny Scott, "Alger Hiss, 92, Central Figure in Long-Running Cold War Controversy," *New York Times*, November 16, 1996, www.nytimes.com/books/97/03/09/reviews/hiss-obit.html.

29. Anthony Hiss, *View from Alger's Window: A Son's Memoir* (Westminster, MD: Vintage Books, 2000). See also Victor Navasky, "Hiss in History," *Nation*, April 30, 2007, 8. For an opposite perspective, see Sam Tanenhaus, "Witness for the Truth," *National Review*, February 15, 1993, 42–46.

30. Richard Pyle, "Author Suggests Alger Hiss Wasn't a Spy," *Washington Post*, April 6, 2007, www.washingtonpost.com/wp-dyn/content/article/2007/04/06/AR2007040600304.html; "Alger Hiss & History" (conference, New York University, April 5, 2007).

31. David Chambers, "Whittaker Chambers," www.whittakerchambers.org.

32. Jeff Kisseloff, "The Alger Hiss Story," http://algerhiss.com/alger-hiss/we-remember-alger/working-for-and-with-alger-hiss-by-jeff-kisseloff/. Richer finds that this website, "designed by Tony Hiss," is "mendacious in the extreme and ignores most of the damaging evidence against Alger Hiss." Matthew Richer, "The Ongoing Campaign of Alger Hiss: The Sins of the Father," *Modern Age* 46 (2004): 314.

33. Additionally, the Facebook site claims that "more books have been published on the Case in the 2000s than in the 1950s." "Whittaker Chambers Today," www.facebook.com/group.php?gid=30271279599&ref=mf (no longer available). Chambers's Myspace page asserts: "My name pops up in the American press every third or fourth day. The Left vilifies me; the right beatifies me. Both use my name for their own ends." "Whittaker Chambers," www.myspace.com/whittakerchambers.

34. Susan Jacoby, "Alger Hiss—a Case for Our Time," *Los Angeles Times*, March 22, 2009, http://articles.latimes.com/2009/mar/22/opinion/oe-jacoby22.

35. Anthony Hiss, *View from Alger's Window*, 182. Whitfield finds that Chambers was well paid for his efforts: "[T]he *Saturday Evening Post* paid $75,000 for the serial rights to *Witness*. . . . *Witness* was a Book-of-the-Month Club selection as well as the number nine best seller in 1952." Stephen Whitfield, *The Culture of the Cold War* (Baltimore: Johns Hopkins University Press, 1991), 18.

36. Chambers, *Witness*, 362, 70, 73, 481.

37. Ibid., 450, 533.

38. Ibid., 46, 47.

39. Ibid., 191.

40. Ibid., 735.

41. See also ibid., 270, 512, 529.

42. Ibid., 545–46. For example, Chambers said in the hearings that he had joined the Communist Party in 1924, when it was actually 1925. He had also gone to Washington in 1934, not 1935, as he outlined in his testimony.

43. Ibid., 726, 512.

44. Judith S. Baughman et al., eds., "Introduction," vol. 6 of *American Decades* (Detroit: Gale, 2001), vii.

45. Ibid., viii.
46. Ibid.
47. There are some exceptions. Exploring broad conservative trends in the postwar period, Lee finds that "conversion narratives and quasi-religious rituals and testimonies are scattered throughout the print culture of conservatism." In various ways, "these conversion stories constitute a beleaguered, righteous political identity certain of its own conclusions" and "testify both to the existence of a rhetorical form rehearsed and remembered in conservative literature since the postwar period." In particular, Chambers's convert tale "taught conservatives to approach politics with religious fervor." Michael Lee, "Creating Conservatism: Postwar Words That Made a Movement" (PhD diss., University of Minnesota, 2008), 130–64; idem, *Creating Conservatism*. Many years ago, one author also undertook a psychological reading of Chambers's conversion. Hugh J. Schwartzberg, "Philosophy of Whittaker Chambers: A Study in Political Conversion" (B.A. thesis, Harvard University, 1953).

48. Hunter Baker, "A Conservative-Libertarian Booklist for Spectator Readers," *The American Spectator*, December 29, 2008, https://spectator.org/17061_conservative-libertarian-booklist-spectator-readers/, par. 4.

49. William Mcgurn, "The Witness of Whittaker Chambers: A Bitter Hope," *Modern Age* 28 (1984): 203.

50. "Whittaker Chambers," *Booklist* 48 (1952): 319.

51. John B. Judis, "Two Faces of Whittaker Chambers," *New Republic*, April 16, 1984, 27. Judis writes that conservatism in the 1940s and early 1950s was a relatively inchoate movement but that Chambers imparted to the right "a focus through the apocalyptic anticommunism of *Witness*." Ibid., 28.

52. Gerard A. Hauser and Chantal Benoit-Barne, "Reflections on Rhetoric, Deliberative Democracy, Civil Society, and Trust," *Rhetoric & Public Affairs* 5 (2002): 261–75. In another call to read public deliberation rhetorically, see Erik W. Doxtader, "The Entwinement of Argument and Rhetoric: A Dialectical Reading of Habermas' Theory of Communicative Action," in *Readings on Argumentation*, ed. Angela J. Aguayo and Timothy R. Steffensmeier (State College, PA: Strata, 2008), 297–309.

53. John S. Dryzek, "Deliberative Democracy in Divided Societies: Alternatives to Agonism and Analgesia," *Political Theory* 33 (2005): 224.

54. Darrin Hicks, "The Promise of Deliberative Democracy," *Rhetoric & Public Affairs* 5 (2002): 238–40; see also Carolyn M. Hendriks, "Integrate Deliberation: Reconciling Civil Society's Dual Role in Deliberative Democracy," *Political Studies* 54 (2006): 486.

55. See Paul Hutchinson, "The Works of God?" *Christian Century*, June 11, 1952, 700–701. One review notes that *Witness* was the most important ex-Communist book. "*Witness*," *Current History*, July 1952, 61. Downing argues that Chambers was able to "flood his writing with the streaming light of high intelligence" in his "long obscure night of the soul." Francis Downing, "Man Is the Measure of All History," *Commonweal*, February 29, 1952, 515. Schlesinger finds Chambers's love of his children, knowledge of evil, and understanding of Communism unparalleled in modern literature, calling it "one of the really significant American autobiographies" and "an extraordinary personal document" that is "precise, poignant, and wonderfully evocative." Arthur Schlesinger, Jr., "Whittaker Chambers & His *Witness*," *Saturday Review*, May 24, 1952, 8–9. Edwards describes *Witness* as "a memorable autobiography, merciless in self-revelation, the outpouring of a soul, long-tortured, which eventually won peace." Willard Edwards, "*Witness*," *Chicago Daily Tribune*, May 25, 1952, C1. Another reviewer says of Chambers that "the man can write. His prose is swift, powerful at times, deft always. He has written an autobiography the like of which has not been seen." Marcus Duffield, "Amazing Autobiography of a Famous Ex-Communist," *New York Herald Tribune*, May 25, 1952, sec. 6. One writer says that Chambers's descriptions of totalitarian brutality provide generational lessons in how freedom can be destroyed by governmental force. Kathleen Parker, "What They Don't Know Can Hurt Them," *Jewish World Review*, March 17, 2005, www.jewishworldreview.com/kathleen/parker1.asp, par. 15–18. Phillips believes that "[t]here have been other revelations, but they are more fragmentary and less probing than the book by Chambers." William Phillips, "In and Out of the Underground: The Confessions of Whittaker Chambers," *American Mercury*, June 1952, 92–99. To Weinberger, *Witness* is "unbelievably

compelling. . . . [I]t is a deeply felt and at times a deeply moving work." Caspar Willard Weinberger, "*Witness,*" *San Francisco Chronicle*, May 18, 1952, 25. Prescott argues that Chambers symbolized the two truths that the conflicts of the times were "total" and that people are "irrational" and "unstable"; it is "a deeply sincere and passionately earnest testament." Orville Prescott, "Books of the Times," *New York Times*, May 22, 1952, 25. One reviewer says that *Witness* "reads like *The Lord of the Rings* only in real time." F. E. Fox, "*Witness* by Whittaker Chambers," par. 10. One *Time* reader comments that "never did any man write with such righteous lucidity. Fie on those who would measure his abasement in dollars & cents." Perry Carriel, letter to the editor, *Time*, June 16, 1952. Shaidle says: "Chambers' masterpiece teaches us not just why we should fight, but how one man fought: as a lonely, despised herald to the painful truth that eventually set millions free." Kathy Shaidle, "*Witness*, Part Two," RelapsedCatholic.blogspot.com, September 18, 2005, http://relapsedcatholic.blogspot.com/2005/09/witness-part-two.html (no longer available), par. 15. More recently, Neuhaus claims that *Witness* is "one of the most important books of the century." Richard John Neuhaus, "At the Origins of the Culture War," *First Things*, April 1, 2000, 81. In 2006, another reviewer says that it is "a must read conversion story. . . . This should be required reading in public high schools." Brian J. Byrne, "Whittaker Chambers—*Witness*—Must Read," *Catholic Online Forum*, May 24, 2006, http://forum.catholic.org/viewtopic.php?f=35&t=39598&sid=5d49a55fbeaa7463f88dadcd8e09a751&p=532875 (no longer available), par. 1, par. 4. A letter to the editor of *Time* magazine thinks that *Witness* should be used as a school textbook to teach young people about Chambers and Communism. Casper Brendan, letter to the editor, *Time*, June 16, 1952. Griffin finds *Witness* "worth my time. I was especially taken by Chambers's eloquent forward [sic] that he framed as a letter to his children." Robert S. Griffin, "Political Paleontology," *Occidental Quarterly* 5 (2005), www.toqonline.com/archives/v5n2/TOQv5n2Griffin.pdf, par. 12. Evidence of the way in which contemporary audiences still extol Chambers's narrative, almost sixty years later, is found throughout the internet. To a blogger, *Witness* is "the best autobiography I have ever encountered. . . . It seems to have the lugubrious tone appropriate to this election season." Jeff Burton, "*Witness,*" *Burtonia Blogs*, September 29, 2008, www.burtonia.com/blog/labels/Witness.html (no longer available). Another blogger argues that *Witness* "is a modern classic and should be required reading in college level American history curricula." "True Whit," *Jeremayakovka*, April 1, 2007, http://jeremayakovka.typepad.com/jeremayakovka/2007/04/true_whit_part_.html (no longer available), par. 2. Out of 202 reviews of *Witness* on Amazon.com, 85 percent of reviewers give the book a five-star rating. "Customer Reviews: *Witness,*" Amazon.com, www.amazon.com/Witness-Cold-Classics-Whittaker-Chambers/dp/162157296X/ref=sr_1_2?ie=UTF8&qid=1516070151&sr=8-2&keywords=witness. A sample of comments and titles from this review section prove instructive. Huffman titles a review of *Witness* "The Best Autobiography I've Ever Read." Corden calls it the "most influential book, I have ever read." Dietrich thinks that Chambers is "Redeemed by History," and Neulander says that "the witness is gone, but the testimony will stand." Durendal poses the question, "what made Chambers's life so compelling? Two things: courage and redemption. . . . Chambers was one of the special few born with the ability to communicate what his soul says to him." For one person, "Chambers' unique voice, unmatched in credibility, speaks for itself." Berger calls Chambers "a hero for any age." St. John believes that *Witness* is "A Window into the Struggle of the 20th Century." Fantina similarly argues that "many of Chambers' observations are as suitable to the early 21st century as they were in the 1940s. [For example] a cavalier attitude toward abortion permeated communists." Averky finds that "this book is difficult to categorize [but] . . . it is difficult to doubt Hiss guilty after reading this." For Covington, "any open minded reader who observes the facts of this firsthand account cannot help but see the severity of the threat posed by communists in the mid 20th century." Affirming the complex persona asserted in *Witness*, Sum remarks that "many people have said this: Whittaker Chambers was a complex person. Indeed he was." Confirming Chambers's conspiracy rhetoric, a reviewer argues that "it is kind of eerie to read about these hidden cells of terrorists in light of US recent history." Wilson reviews the book under the title "The Essential Struggle of the 20th Century," finding that "as I read this work I realized that the struggle, as Chambers saw it, was Modernity vs. Christianity." Monte says that this is the "most important autobiography of the 20th Century" and that it "personified the Cold War battle." One customer argues that it is "A

Winning Story of a Hapless Unfortunate." The book makes Whiting exclaim, "Yes Virginia, there really were communist spies." Walsh says that Chambers was "truly an American hero as well as a prophet" who "paints a dark picture of the materialistic nihilism that animates the West." Another customer writes that "at some points, I was literally sitting on the edge of my seat," given the "Good vs. Evil on the Battlefield of Political Ideology." Yet another argues that "the historical data found within the book is well worth the price, but Chambers's descriptions of his personal crises and their resolutions are priceless." On the other side, a customer says that "if you read Chambers you might as well read Stalin because there isn't a lot of difference between their thinking." Another customer writes that the book is a "waste of time." Still another writes that Chambers is a "Master of Deceit." Lowenthal cites Charles Alan Wright's 1952 review that *Witness* is "A Long Work of Fiction." Finally, denying the dualistic rhetorical resource created in the book, a customer writes that "yikes. . . . Whittaker Chambers' self-aggrandizing, self-indulgent . . . Manichaean and simplistic ideology . . . is boring and uninteresting. . . . It definitely doesn't lead to a particularly nuanced or satisfying account." In total, very few of these reviews gave mid-range reviews of two to four stars. Most were either one or five stars, spotlighting the polarizing nature of the narrative itself. Olasky writes that "for three reasons, parents of today's children should be aware of *Witness* and the issues it raises. . . . First, Chambers powerfully explains what lay behind the rise of communism (and some other leading isms): the vision of man displacing God. Second, Chambers displays moving concerns for his children. . . . Third, those who pick up *Witness* will discover writing as profound and powerful as anything the 20th century produced." Marvin Olasky, "A Witness for the Ages," *Boundless*, 2000, www.boundless.org/2000/departments/pages/a0000363.html (no longer available), par. 6. Demonstrating that *Witness* had an impact beyond U.S. audiences, British reviewer Szamuely argues that "it is a refusal to look seriously at Whittaker Chambers's (and Bill Buckley's) ideas that keeps conservatism in Britain mostly in the milk-and-water state." Helen Szamuely, "Reputations—21: Whittaker Chambers," *Salisbury Review*, n.d., http://salisburyreview.co.uk/index.php?option=com_content&view=article&id=680:reputations-21-whittaker-chambersamp;catid=47:autumn2008&Itemid=28 (no longer available), par. 12.

56. Stokes finds that *Witness* omits important details about the Hiss trials and sometimes reaches unwarranted conclusions, but says that it is an eloquent and moving book—and "dealing with the raw stuff of history and the mounting crises of our times," sees it as providing a better political vision than Communism. Harold Phelps Stokes, "Whittaker Chambers's Story," *Yale Review* (Autumn 1952): 126. One reviewer says that despite Chambers's "unexpurgated emotionalism," *Witness* "still sustains its driven, dedicated fervor through close to 800 pages." "Witness," *Bull Virginia Kirkus' Bookshop Service*, April 1, 1952, 243. Hook argues that it is "one of the most significant autobiographies of the twentieth century" but refuses to accept Chambers's religious vision. Sidney Hook, "The Faiths of Whittaker Chambers," *New York Times*, May 12, 1952, BR1. One reviewer remarks of Chambers that "his posturing, emotional wallowing, and self-pity may estrange some readers; his narrative power will drive others through 800 pages." "Whittaker Chambers," *Booklist*, 320. A *Time* magazine reviewer relates that Chambers is overly emotional but that "its depth and penetration make Witness the best book about Communism ever written on this continent . . . with the tremendous eloquence of humility ("History and Tragedy," par. 1–2). "Publican & Pharisee," *Time*, May 26, 1952, www.time.com/time/printout/0,8816,859675,00.html. Chambers's biographer addresses *Witness*'s deliberative vision in ambivalent terms: "Chambers champions American democracy but seems wholly inured to its practical operations—the give-and-take, the bargaining, the pragmatic adjustments, the constant dialogue." Tanenhaus, *Whittaker Chambers*, 466. Some say that Tanenhaus's biography "constantly reports as unchallenged fact events and interpretations for which the only or main authority is Chambers. Tanenhaus seems to give Chambers an unmerited moral superiority." David Levin, "The Authority of *Witness* in 'Whittaker Chambers: A Biography,'" *Sewanee Review* 105 (1997): 600–608. Williamson writes that "it is possible to conclude from reading *Witness* that its author is a slightly hysterical monomaniac under the spell of the noisiest Romantic composers and of Quaker piety" but that "it is nearly impossible for a fair reader to doubt, in the end, that Whittaker Chambers did what he said he did, knew whom he said he knew, and saw what he said he saw." Chilton Williamson, Jr., *The Conservative Bookshelf* (New York: Citadel, 2005), 105.

57. Some find it "often an unbelievable book, frequently a boring book, vastly overwritten and sometimes sickening." Merle Miller, "Memoirs from Sanctuary," *New Republic*, May 26, 1952, 19. Wright thinks that "Mr. Chambers is the author of one of the longest works of fiction of the year. . . . [I]t is too persuasive. . . . [T]he author is not a detached teller of truth but rather a pitchman seeking to put across a bill of goods. It is a too well-scrubbed Chambers who is depicted here." Charles Alan Wright, "A Long Work of Fiction," *Saturday Review*, May 24, 1952, 11. Davis finds that ex-Communists such as Chambers appeal to "the lucrative home market for exposures and revelations." Elmer Davis, "History in Doublethink," *Saturday Review*, June 28, 1952, 8–9, 30–32. Countering *Witness*'s deliberative vision, Davis writes that "experimental thinking . . . has played a great part in American history, from Benjamin Franklin down to John Dewey; and it has worked. But the Communists about whom I was writing had no use for it, nor have most of them now that they are ex-Communists" (ibid., 32). Taking Chambers as a representative example of the ex-Communist experience, Arendt argues that many former Communists are made to look "less decent, less honest, less convinced of the dangers of Communism" in comparison with ex-Communists, who are compensated by their public "conversion" and "spectacular confession[s]." Hannah Arendt, "The Ex-Communists," *Commonweal*, March 20, 1953, 595–99. Since Chambers was a white male in a prestigious profession at the time, there is also evidence that other ex-Communists who testified against Communist influence did not receive the same commendation for their efforts. As Olmsted finds, ex-Communists such as Elizabeth Bentley also testified before HUAC, but with little reward; "From Elizabeth's perspective . . . the U.S. government was failing to recognize her sacrifices on its behalf. After her years of service, she was unemployed and nearly penniless. Yet male ex-Communists were profiting nicely: Louis Budenz was 'wealthy,' and Whittaker Chambers was about to make a 'small fortune out of his writings.' She could not understand why she was an object of ridicule while they were heroes." Kathryn S. Olmsted, *Red Spy Queen: A Biography of Elizabeth Bentley* (Chapel Hill: University of North Carolina Press, 2002), 176. Cogley states that Chambers writes a "prelude to Armageddon," presenting himself as a "Christlike figure," in the "unyielding regality of the absolute." John Cogley, "*Witness*: Whittaker Chambers," *Commonweal*, May 23, 1952, 176–77. These authors all share concerns about the impact of *Witness*'s content, methods, and effect on politics. Some argue that these type of narratives are simply an opportunistic means to fortune and fame. Kingsley Martin, "The Witness," *New Statesman and Nation*, July 19, 1952, 60–61. Martin also finds that Chambers's "picture of himself as a lonely and persecuted figure is scarcely consistent with his backing by one of America's greatest publishing houses." Chambers is not "a police witness in a trial, but a witness in the sense of a martyr—one who is prepared to die for a principle. Ibid., 60.

58. Berger says that Barth gained much international credibility for this line of religious thought by standing up to Nazism prior to and during World War II, which created an "aura of heroism" for his movement, undermining the theological liberalism that had flourished in the previous century. P. Berger, *The Heretical Imperative*, 66–67, 85.

59. Daniel Pipes, *Conspiracy: How the Paranoid Style Flourishes and Where It Comes From* (New York: Free Press, 1997).

60. David Zarefsky, "Conspiracy Argument in the Lincoln-Douglass Debates," *Journal of the American Forensic Association* 21 (1984): 63–75; Marilyn J. Young, Michael K. Launer, and Curtis C. Austin, "The Need for Evaluative Criteria: Conspiracy Argument Revisited," *Argumentation and Advocacy* 26 (1990): 89–107; Stephanie Kelley-Romano, "Trust No One: The Conspiracy Genre on American Television," *Southern Communication Journal* 73 (2008): 115.

61. Earl G. Creps, "The Conspiracy Argument as Rhetorical Genre" (PhD diss., Northwestern University, 1980); Mark Fenster, *Conspiracy Theories: Secrecy and Power in American Cultures* (Minneapolis: University of Minnesota Press, 1999), xiv. Fenster further notes that the conspiracy narrative puts "forth a particular narrative logic that organizes disparate events within a mechanistic, tragic framework." Fenster, *Conspiracy Theories*, 111.

62. James Darsey, "A Conspiracy of Science," *Western Journal of Communication* 66 (2002): 469–91.

63. Kelley-Romano, "Trust No One," 115, 117–18.

64. Richard Hofstadter, *The Paranoid Style in American Politics and Other Essays* (Chicago: University of Chicago Press, 1979). Hofstadter notes that "what is felt to be needed to defeat [the conspiracy] is not the usual methods of political give-and-take but an all-out crusade." Ibid., 29.

65. G. Thomas Goodnight and John Poulakos, "Conspiracy Rhetoric: From Pragmatism to Fantasy in Public Discourse," *Western Journal of Communication* 45 (1981): 299. See also Peter Knight, *Conspiracy Culture: From the Kennedy Assassination to the "X-Files"* (New York: Routledge, 2000), 45.

66. Chambers, *Witness*, 789.

67. As referenced in Steven Hayward, "Desperately Seeking David," *Reason*, March 1997, www.reason.com/news/printer/30159.html, par. 10.

68. Chambers, *Witness*, 542.

69. Ibid., 34, 78, 627.

70. Tanenhaus, *Whittaker Chambers*, 516.

71. Chambers, *Witness*, 462. Chambers tells readers earlier in the book that ex-Communist is a title exclusively reserved for converts, involving a total previous commitment and an unconditional break with the paradigm. Ibid., 12.

72. See, e.g., ibid., 309–18.

73. Ibid., 331. In other sections, Chambers claims that the Communist Party had a staggering power in the day-to-day decisions of U.S. policy, and the effects of this work—and not the number of people involved—should be the criterion from which to judge its efforts. He also admits that he had only a small view of the total operation, but could tell how great the number of communists in government were. This claim is indicted by the remainder of the book, where Chambers mostly asserts without reservation that the conspiracy is unrelenting, evil, and vast. Ibid., 427, 32.

74. Morris finds that Chambers does not have proof for his assertion that U.S. policy was influenced by Hiss or at least evidence that postdates 1938. Richard B. Morris, "Chambers's Litmus Paper Test," *Saturday Review*, May 24, 1952, 13.

75. See K. Martin, "The Witness," 60. One reviewer writes that

> the warnings against the "underground" are, I believe, justified; there are the cases of Klaus Fuchs and the British scientists. But these are not in the book. Chambers' belief that there is a causal connection between Hiss and the Communist triumph in China will not be historically proved (or disproved) in this generation; he himself offers only an assertion, not proof. . . . [I]t does not make clear enough what Hiss and all the others named as Communist agents—including Chambers himself—actually *did* to make the various underground "apparatuses" worth much to the Russians or the horrifying danger we are told they were to this country. (Hutchinson, "The Works of God?" 700)

One review opines that "the little conspiracy in which Chambers and Hiss were collaborators is presented as though by itself it actually 'changed the world.' The emphasis is false and misleading to the last degree. . . . A good editor, we believe, would have returned Chambers's manuscript, told him to cut it by 90 per cent, and in revising what was left, urged him to 'stick to the facts.' "Editors' Shop Talk," *Antioch Review* 12 (1952): 130.

76. Chambers, *Witness*, 344–46, 466–69.

77. Ibid., 469.

78. Ibid., 344.

79. Ibid., 286.

80. Ibid., 35, 72, 77, 80.

81. Ibid., 443.

82. In ibid., 507.

83. Anthony Hiss, *View from Alger's Window*, 50. Hiss argues that as Chambers accurately reported, Alger had beautiful manners and loved birds (although he also claimed that the Hisses "gave up bird watching in 1934"). Prossy called Alger "Hill" and "Hilly." Then again, he never once, as Chambers claimed, called her "Dill" or "Dilly," nor was Alger deaf in one ear. And so

what? Misremembering a few facts needn't cloud or compromise an otherwise comprehensive depiction of a person. But manners, birds, and Hill are about the only points of overlap I can find between Chambers's Alger and my Alger. (Ibid., 50).

84. The reviewer writes that "everything is either/or. . . . This is simplification with a vengeance." Brendan Gill, "Either/Or," *New Yorker*, May 24, 1952, 133–34. Nelson finds that "if this book had more of Chambers' ideas and less endless narration of every irrelevant detail of his life, it could have been one of the better books of the twentieth century." T. J. Nelson, "*Witness*," August 16, 2003, http://brneurosci.org/reviews/witness.html (no longer available).

85. Chambers, *Witness*, 637, 669.

86. Ibid., 405.

87. Ernest G. Bormann, *The Force of Fantasy: Restoring the American Dream*, 2nd ed. (Carbondale: Southern Illinois University Press, 2001).

88. Chambers, *Witness*, 405.

89. Ibid., 475.

90. Ibid., 434. This point led Wright to remark that Chambers "displays a remarkable attitude toward evidence. . . . [H]e is fond of referring to mysterious unnamed witnesses, who have confirmed his story, although, regrettably, they have never given their testimony in public." See Wright, "A Long Work of Fiction," 11–12. Wright finds that other items of evidence in *Witness* are also problematic: "Chambers's claim that he hired his colored maid on the suggestion of his landlady looks ridiculous in the light of the recent affidavit by a relative of the landlady that Chambers had no maid when he was living in the apartment in question." Ibid.

91. Chambers, *Witness*, 321.

92. Ibid., 203.

93. Ibid., 30.

94. Ibid., 64.

95. Ibid., 758.

96. Ibid., 695.

97. "Here I stand! I can no other! God help me. Amen." Cited in James Atkinson, *The Trial of Luther* (New York: Stein and Day, 1971), 161–62.

98. In response to *Witness*, Dos Passos writes: "[W]hat shall we say of the right-thinking men and women, of the men and women of position and education who repeat these slanders without investigating their origins and who refuse, in the light of all the evidence, to recognize the existence of a conspiracy of assassins bent on the destruction of the right-thinking liberals, as much as on the destruction of the rest of us?" John Dos Passos, "Mr. Chambers's Descent into Hell," *Saturday Review*, May 24, 1952, 11. Hook finds that *Witness* "throws more light on the conspiratorial and religious character of communism . . . than all of the hundred great books of the past combined." Hook, "The Faiths of Whittaker Chambers," BR1. One reviewer says that *Witness* provides a lens for understanding modern politics: "[E]verything he predicted sixty years ago is being fulfilled. If there were so many Communists and fellow travelers in our government then, we can only imagine how many are now in positions of high authority in our country." Me364459, "Re: Most Overlooked Essential," *WorldNetDaily*, December 27, 2008, http://forums.wnd.com/index.php?pageId=262&pageNo=4 (no longer available), par. 2.

99. Hook, "The Faiths of Whittaker Chambers," BR1.

100. DC Dave, "PBS Lies for FDR over Allegations by Whittaker Chambers," DCDave.com, January 1, 2006, www.dcdave.com/article4/060129.htm, par. 2.

101. James G. Miller and Jessie L. Miller, "*Witness*," *University of Chicago Law Review* 20 (1953): 599.

102. "Chambers and His Critics," *Life*, June 9, 1952, 36.

103. John Kenneth Galbraith, "A Revisionist View," *New Republic*, March 28, 1970, 18.

104. Rebecca West, "Whittaker Chambers," *Atlantic Monthly*, June 1952, 33.

105. Schlesinger thinks that little came of the espionage that Chambers describes, that there is little proof that those on the Nye Committee (of which Hiss was a part) affected political policy, and no evidence that they accomplished anything within the domestic realm. Chambers thus "commits the fallacy of excess interpretation and thereby does the Communists altogether too much credit. The one striking fact about the Communists in the Thirties and Forties was not their success, but their failure." Schlesinger, "Whittaker Chambers," 10, 39.

106. E. Davis, "History in Doublethink," 8.
107. Judis, "Two Faces of Whittaker Chambers," 27.
108. One review affirms the conspiracy persona in asserting that "although these autobiographical details are given in somewhat incidental fashion, cumulatively they reveal much of the cause of the Chambers tragedy," highlighting "a Christian faith that is both moving and persuasive" and "one of the most absorbing and instructive testaments of the present generation." "Chambers, Whittaker," *United States Quarterly Book Review* 8 (1952): 232.
109. Chambers, *Witness*, 10. Chambers critiques the belief that changing the world is necessary and attacks modernity in other sections, too. Ibid., 9, 82.
110. Ibid., 10, 13.
111. Ibid., 33. Chambers says that *The Journal of George Fox*, which was instrumental in his religious conversion, beckoned him to live like a first-century Christian. Ibid., 483.
112. See ibid., 13, 83, 220, 769.
113. Genter, "Witnessing Whittaker Chambers," 246. One scholar argues that Chambers poses his own version of secularization theory by describing how the increase of science and technologies in modern societies leads to a general decline in faith and religious beliefs. Hyrum Lewis, "Sacralizing the Right: William F. Buckley, Jr., Whittaker Chambers, Will Herberg and the Transformation of Intellectual Conservatism, 1945–1964" (PhD diss., University of Southern California, 2009), 81. One irony is that, after writing *Witness* and at the urging of his friend Arthur Koestler, Chambers returns to college to study science at the very end of his life. See Buckley, foreword to *Witness*, x, xi.
114. Chambers, *Witness*, 232.
115. Ibid., 9.
116. Ibid., 449.
117. Lewis finds that Chambers was one of three postwar figures (the others were William F. Buckley and Will Herberg) who did the most to connect conservative thought with religious belief. H. Lewis, "Sacralizing the Right."
118. John Strachey, "The Absolutists," *Nation*, October 4, 1952, 291–93.
119. Chambers, *Witness*, 83. In another chapter, Chambers puts the human brain and mystery in opposition. Ibid., 517. Chambers's claim that this is the first century where man has been without mysticism is also not true. At the very least, many ancient Greeks, Egyptians, and more would be surprised to hear this.
120. Ibid., 209.
121. Ibid., 476.
122. I once heard this point during a lecture: Randall Lake (lecture, University of Southern California Annenberg School for Communication, Los Angeles, April 12, 2006).
123. Chambers, *Witness*, 507, 763. There are many other places in *Witness* where Chambers also draws a dichotomy between the common person and intellectuals. See ibid., 63, 673, 793, 794.
124. In another section Chambers argues that the soul and intutition stand in opposition to reason and the mind. Ibid., 83.
125. Ibid., 360.
126. Randall A. Lake, "The Metaethical Framework of Anti-abortion Rhetoric," *Signs* 11 (1986): 494.
127. Hofstadter, *Anti-intellectualism in American Life*, 1–2.
128. Jacoby, *The Age of American Unreason*.
129. To be fair, there are a few places in *Witness* where Chambers objects to limitations on dissent. He mentions that one of his biggest problems with Stalin was the suppression of free speech under his regime. Chambers, *Witness*, 250. Chambers also says that many claimed Hiss's innocence without considering what Chambers actually said. Ibid., 473, 793. Over 800 pages, however, these thoughts are countered by an overriding anti-intellectualism.
130. Ibid., 19.
131. Ibid., 484.
132. Ibid., 194.
133. Ibid., 134–35.
134. Ibid., 483.

135. Ibid., 763; emphasis added.
136. Ibid., 500.
137. Ibid., 525.
138. Ibid., 83.
139. This last point has been made about conservative rhetoric in general by G. Thomas Goodnight, "The Liberal and the Conservative Presumptions: On Political Philosophy and the Foundation of Public Argument," in *Proceedings of the [First] Summer Conference on Argumentation*, ed. Jack Rhodes and Sara Newell (Annandale, VA: Speech Communication Association, 1980), 323–24.
140. Chambers, *Witness*, 484.
141. "What Do Quakers Believe?" Quaker Information Center, November 4, 2009, www.quakerinfo.org/quakerism/beliefs.html, par. 3–4.
142. Ralph de Toledano, "The Imperatives of the Heart: A Friend Remembers Whittaker Chambers," *National Review*, August 1, 1986, www.nationalreview.com/article/219901/imperatives-heart-williumrex, par. 4.
143. John B. Sheerin, "Chambers Provokes the Reviewers," *Catholic World*, July 1952, 245. See also idem, "Chambers Again," *Catholic World*, December 1952, 164.
144. Olasky, "A Witness for the Ages," 13.
145. John Weidner, "For When You Understand What You See, You Will No Longer Be Children," *Random Jottings*, February 11, 2007, www.randomjottings.net/archives/002713.html, par. 5.
146. Henry L. Roberts, "Recent Books on International Relations," *Foreign Affairs* 31 (1952): 156.
147. Daniel J. Mahoney, "Whittaker Chambers: Witness to the Crisis of the Modern Soul," *Intercollegiate Review* 37 (2002): 42.
148. Russell Nieli, "The Cry against Nineveh: Whittaker Chambers and Eric Voegelin on the Crisis of Western Modernity," *Modern Age* 31 (1987): 267.
149. M. Miller, "Memoirs from Sanctuary," 20.
150. Chambers, *Witness*, 16. In another part of the book, Chambers highlights his deterministic, dualistic vision further. Ibid., 420.
151. Chambers, *Witness*, 699. At the beginning of *Witness*, Chambers also alludes to the Hiss case in this fashion, arguing that two religions were on trial. Ibid., 4.
152. Ibid., 491.
153. Ibid., 479.
154. Ibid., 4. Confirming this asserted persona, Thompson finds Chambers's emphasis on God's work in the court case quite convincing. Craig Thompson, "The Whittaker Chambers I Know," *Saturday Evening Post*, November 15, 1952, 24–25, 116–20.
155. Chambers, *Witness*, 7.
156. Ibid., 16, 17.
157. Ibid., 547, 692.
158. Ibid., 627.
159. Ibid., 576; see also 630.
160. Ibid., 471.
161. Ibid., 472.
162. Hausknecht, "Confession and Return," 85.
163. Chambers, *Witness*, 724–25, 763.
164. Joseph S. Salemi, "The Witness Revisited: Whittaker Chambers and American Conservatism," *University Bookman* 46 (2008), www.kirkcenter.org/index.php/bookman/article/the-witness-revisited, par. 3, 8.
165. Ronald Reagan, "Remarks at the Annual Convention of the National Association of Evangelicals in Orlando, Florida," March 8, 1983, in *Conservatism in America since 1930: A Reader*, ed. Gregory L. Schneider (New York: New York University Press, 2003), 361.
166. Kengor, "The Intellectual Origins of Ronald Reagan's Faith," 5. See Ronald Reagan, "Remarks at the Annual Convention of the National Association of Evangelicals," Columbus, OH, March 6, 1984.

167. Bishop Williamson, "Liberalism Is a Killer," July 7, 2003, www.leofec.com/bishop-williamson/288.html.

168. Craige McMillan, "Fanatical Secular Faith," *WorldNetDaily*, June 24, 1999, www.worldnetdaily.com/index.php?fa=PAGE.printable&pageId=5909.

169. Arendt, "The Ex-Communists," 596. Arendt continues: "[S]ince they have divided the world into two, they can account for the disturbing variety and plurality of the world we all live in only by either discounting it as irrelevant altogether or by stating that it is due to lack of consistency and character." Ibid., 596.

170. Judis, "Two Faces of Whittaker Chambers," 27. Horner, too, emphasizes that "Chambers's way of looking at things" is grounded in "mega-concepts," which "do not stand up very well to the relentless reality of America which somehow always manages to whittle them down." Charles Horner, "Why Whittaker Chambers Was Wrong," *Commentary*, April 1990, 58.

171. Judis, "Two Faces of Whittaker Chambers," 30, 32.

172. Schlesinger, "Whittaker Chambers," 40–41. Echoing each of these themes, while generally praising Chambers's narrative, Hook finds that *Witness*'s faith emphases are too reductionist for a pragmatic politics—"the disjunction" that Chambers draws in saying that "man must worship either God or Stalin" is "neither exhaustive or exclusive." Additionally, "he recklessly lumps Socialists, progressives, liberals and men of goodwill together with the Communists." Hook notes the irony in Chambers's positions, as many of his "fellow-Quakers are appeasers of Stalin while others are valiant fighters in the cause of freedom," which is "enough to establish the irreverence of his theology to his politics." Chambers's boundaries between faith in God and intelligence is a "monstrous piece of dogmatism," which appears to result from "an intellectual impatience, a hunger for absolutes" that "does not offer us an intelligent guide to victory or even survival." Hook, "The Faiths of Whittaker Chambers," BR1.

173. K. Martin, "The Witness," 61. Phillips says that "similarly, Chambers confuses the issue and falls into the Communist trap when he lumps all liberal and progressive opinion with Communism." Phillips, "In and Out of the Underground," 97, 98; emphasis in original. After an interview with Chambers, Breit also took issue with Chambers's dualistic thinking. Harvey Breit, "Talk with Mr. Chambers," *New York Times*, May 25, 1952, BR18.

174. R. S. Taylor, "*Witness*," *Library Journal*, May 15, 1952, 888. Davis also argues that "they used to tell us that black was white, and damn us for doubting them. Now they admit it is black; but then and now they insist that there is no such thing as gray. . . . [O]ne of the most protuberant facts of the history of the past twenty years is that there is a middle ground." E. Davis, "History in Doublethink," 9.

175. E. Scott Pattison, letter to the editor, *Time*, June 16, 1952.

176. M. Miller, "Memoirs from Sanctuary," 20.

177. Irving Howe, "God, Man, and Stalin," *Nation*, May 24, 1952, 503.

178. Tony Judt, "The Dualist," *New Republic*, April 14, 1997, 44.

179. Strachey considers Chambers an "absolutist" who "see[s] the world in terms of one all-embracing antithesis: communism and the West; the Devil and God. . . . Everything is seen in the starkest black and white. Every catastrophic conclusion follows with remorseless inevitability." Strachey, "The Absolutists," 291–93. Miller and Miller find, too, that in *Witness*, "truth is dichotomous in nature," and "his position basically . . . is anti-intellectual. . . . [O]ne philosophy that Chambers does not consider, probably because he cannot, is a positive liberalism based upon a solid defense of the right of man to think as he pleases, to study all points of view, and to advocate orderly change in his own government. A prevailing attitude of fear of mass infiltration and internal threat inevitably leads to defensiveness." See J. G. Miller and J. L. Miller, "Witness," 602, 603.

180. Philip Rahv, "The Sense and Nonsense of Whittaker Chambers," *Partisan Review* (July–August 1952): 474–75. Rahv argues that Chambers's writing is Dostoevskian but bypasses Dostoevsky's insight that even religion can oppress. Ibid., 476.

181. Charles Reis, letter to the editor, *Time*, June 16, 1952.

182. Using Burke's pentadic terms, a "scene" can act as an overriding frame that determines human "acts" and "agency." Kenneth Burke, *A Grammar of Motives* (Berkeley: University of California Press, 1969).

183. John R. E. Bliese, "Richard Weaver and Piety towards Nature," *Modern Age* 47 (2007): 102–10.
184. See John Crowe Ransom, "Reconstructed but Unregenerate," in *I'll Take My Stand: The South and the Agrarian Tradition*, ed. Louis D. Rubin (Baton Rouge: Louisiana State University Press, 2006), 1–27 (orig. pub. 1930); T. S. Eliot, *Christianity and Culture* (New York: Harcourt, Brace and World, 1949), 48–49; Russell Kirk, *The Conservative Mind: From Burke to Eliot*, 7th ed. (Washington, DC: Regnery, 2001).
185. Richard M. Weaver, "The Southern Tradition," in *The Southern Essays of Richard M. Weaver*, ed. George M. Curtis, III, and James J. Thompson, Jr. (Indianapolis, IN: Liberty Fund, 1987), 220–21.
186. Richard M. Weaver, *Ideas Have Consequences* (Chicago: University of Chicago Press, 1948), 174–75.
187. Bliese, "Richard Weaver," 105; Weaver, "Up from Liberalism," 144; Weaver, *Ideas Have Consequences,* 112.
188. Chambers, *Witness*, 797.
189. Ibid., 16, 117.
190. Ibid., 456, 59.
191. Ibid., 88.
192. Ibid., 81, 83.
193. Ibid., 94.
194. Michael Osborn, "Archetypal Metaphor in Rhetoric: The Light-Dark Family," *Quarterly Journal of Speech* 53 (1967): 116.
195. Chambers, *Witness*, 21–22.
196. Ibid., 787.
197. Ibid., 327.
198. Finn, *From Death to Rebirth*.
199. Chambers, *Witness*, 267.
200. Ibid., 267.
201. For an explanation of rhizomic rhetoric, see Andrew Leslie and Stephen O'Leary, "Rhizomic Rhetoric: Toward an Ecology of Institutional Argument," in *Argument in Controversy: Proceedings of the Seventh SCA/AFA Conference on Argumentation*, ed. Donn W. Parson (Annandale, VA: Speech Communication Association, 1991), 64–72. For recursivity, see Jasinski, *Sourcebook on Rhetoric*, 482.
202. Chambers, *Witness*, 114–15.
203. See Jean-Jacques Rousseau, *Émile*, trans. Barbara Foxley (London: Everyman, 2000).
204. R. Lake, "Order and Disorder in Anti-abortion Rhetoric."
205. Chambers, *Witness*, 165.
206. Ibid., 277.
207. Rahv, "The Sense and Nonsense," 472.
208. Chambers, *Witness*, 391.
209. Ibid., 147.
210. Ibid., 789.
211. Burke, *A Grammar of Motives*, 128, 131.
212. Ibid., 143.
213. Ibid.
214. Dos Passos, "Mr. Chambers's Descent into Hell," 11.
215. Hausknecht, "Confession and Return," 81.
216. West, "Whittaker Chambers," 36.
217. Genter, "Witnessing Whittaker Chambers," 251. Genter believes that this was partly accomplished by Chambers's framing of himself as a biblical Jonah, "the hesitant prophet instructed by God to bring his message to the people of Nineveh. Ibid., 251. See also Matthew Richer, "The Cry against Nineveh: A Centennial Tribute to Whittaker Chambers," *Modern Age* 43 (2001): 195–201. Chambers describes his fight with Communism as comparable to Jonah in his posthumous book *Cold Friday*. Whittaker Chambers, *Cold Friday* (New York: Random House, 1964), 265–68.

218. On apocalyptic rhetoric, see Stephen O'Leary, *Arguing the Apocalypse: A Theory of Millennial Rhetoric* (New York: Oxford University Press, 1994).
219. Chambers, *Witness*, 699.
220. Ibid., 160.
221. Ibid., 459; emphasis added.
222. Ibid., 358.
223. Ibid., 5.
224. Ibid., 183.
225. Ibid., 607.
226. Ibid., 295.
227. Ibid., 672, 311.
228. Ibid., 63.
229. Burke, *The Rhetoric of Religion*.
230. R. Lake, "The Metaethical Framework."
231. Tom Donelson, "Whittaker Chambers: A Witness for a New Era," *Blogcritics Magazine*, September 10, 2004, http://blogcritics.org/archives/2004/09/10/124634.php (no longer available), par. 1.
232. Philip Yancey, "The Death of a Red and the Birth of a Soul," *Christianity Today*, March 11, 1991, 104.
233. Arendt, "The Ex-Communists," 598.
234. Ibid.
235. H. Lewis, "Sacralizing the Right," 68.
236. Ibid., 71.
237. Reed Whittemore, "*Witness*," *Furioso*, Summer 1952, 77.
238. Chambers, *Witness*, 261.
239. Katherine Cramer Walsh, *Talking about Race: Community Dialogues and the Politics of Difference* (Chicago: University of Chicago Press, 2007), 143.
240. Lee, *Creating Conservatism*, 130, 167.
241. See, e.g., Michael A. Hiltzik, "Undoing the New Deal," *Los Angeles Times*, June 26, 2005, www.latimes.com/business/investing/la-tm-hiltzik26jun26,1,7141492.story
242. "On the Witness Stand," *Time*, June 9, 1952, http://content.time.com/time/magazine/article/0,9171,806492,00.html, par. 1.
243. The editor of the *Saturday Review* said that *Witness* is "at the core of one of the most important public debates in American history. Far from ending a celebrated controversy, this book may reopen and enlarge it, coming as it does in the middle of a Presidential Campaign." This editor, in turn, devoted a nine-page forum to the subject of the book, where hostile and friendly critics engaged the book's merits. *Saturday Review*, May 24, 1952, 8.
244. Bruce Frohnen, Jeremy Beer, and Jeffrey O. Nelson, eds., *American Conservatism: An Encyclopedia* (Wilmington, DE: ISI Books, 2006).
245. Bjerre-Poulsen finds that when William F. Buckley, Jr. and Willi Schlamm founded the leading right-wing magazine *National Review* in 1955, Chambers ranked highest on the list of potential editors to whom they catered. Chambers, however, declined the offer to join the magazine due to the important differences he saw between Buckley's reactionary positions and his own Disraelian visions of an organic pro-limited social reform conservatism. (Chambers did eventually join the staff of *National Review* in 1957.) In a letter to Buckley and Schlamm, he explained that his differing views on the social needs and political instincts of "the common man" had been crucial for his decision. . . . Chambers' explanation highlights the inherent tension between elitist and populist strains within American conservatism. This tension would persist, and from time to time it would break out in the open, as in the conflict between "neoconservatives" and "paleoconservatives" in the 1990s. (Bjerre-Poulsen, *Right Face*, 36–37).
246. Tanenhaus, *Whittaker Chambers*, 487, 500–501.

Chapter Two

Political Conversion as Intellectual Reduction

Norman Podhoretz's Breaking Ranks

If there was ever a figure who could challenge F. Scott Fitzgerald's statement that "there are no second acts in American lives,"[1] it would be Norman Podhoretz. Podhoretz has spent a good portion of his public career writing about his political transformation from a 1950s liberal and 1960s radical to a staunch neoconservative in the 1970s and beyond. He is considered one of the intellectual "founding fathers of neoconservatism."[2] Indeed, the very meaning of neoconservatism is tied to political conversion, as a movement whose originators all had previous lives on the political left. As Podhoretz explains, "neo-conservative means new conservative. We neo-conservatives were new in the sense that we had all begun somewhere on the left—radical, liberal, whatever—but somewhere on the left. So we were new to conservatism."[3] Neoconservatives became dissatisfied with political developments in the 1960s, including the New Left's rejection of the Vietnam War. In time, Podhoretz and many others gradually drifted from the political left to the right.

No stranger to public revelation, Podhoretz has written four autobiographies telling and retelling the story of his life from various angles.[4] Yet his second autobiography, *Breaking Ranks* (hereafter *BR*), most uses a political conversion narrative. The book was released in 1979, situated between U.S. conservatism's fragile post-Watergate alliance and the presidential election victory of Ronald Reagan. It is considered a foundational work in advancing political conservatism in recent decades, redirecting its intellectual climate, factions, and leaders[5] and documenting "one of the most momentous switches in American Jewish intellectual history, as well as that of American political discourse."[6]

By Podhoretz's own admission, we should look at texts such as his own as persuasive communication. As he relates, "the rhetoric mattered, as rhetoric in politics always does, because it sets the terms and defines the goals by which actions and policies are judged."[7] *BR*'s rhetoric is quite different from the other political conversion narratives in this volume, however. Three major rhetorical resources bear upon this story's particular guise: intellectualism, expression, and accuracy, each corresponding to respective concerns for reason, restraint, and rightness in public life. At first glance, Podhoretz uses a language of reason and reasonability that may appear to be deliberative. But the conversion narrative's features work with the autobiography's devices to create a totalizing type of public argument. Several rhetorical contradictions surface in the performance of the political conversion narrative, given Podhoretz's own criteria for public discourse. The story ultimately is cast in terms of a highly intellectual journey responding to the period in which Podhoretz is writing, highlighting the subtle ways conversions can be used for political purposes.

PODHORETZ'S LIFE AND TIMES

As one of the United States's most prominent public intellectuals, Podhoretz has provided a model for conservatism. In his controversial book, *Making It*, Podhoretz told a story of his rise from poverty to become one of the most sought-after writers in the New York publishing industry,[8] describing his assimilation into U.S. culture as a "conversion."[9] He joined a famous group of New York intellectuals, whose members included Lionel Trilling and Hannah Arendt.[10] Although Podhoretz was first trained as a literary critic, his work became increasingly political.[11]

Podhoretz attended Columbia and Cambridge Universities and joined the army for two years. His literary reviews for *Commentary* magazine landed him a job with the publication in 1955.[12] In 1960, at the age of thirty, Podhoretz became the editor of *Commentary* and continued in this position for the next thirty-five years, broadening the magazine's scope and influence beyond Jewish interests.[13] *Commentary*'s development from a voice for the political Left to a forum for conservative thought followed Podhoretz's political conversion.[14] By the mid-1960s, the magazine's circulation had tripled under his leadership,[15] becoming "one of the most influential magazines in the United States."[16]

During his tenure at *Commentary*, Podhoretz informed politicians and policy making at the highest levels of government. He attempted to revise Americans' views on Vietnam and "helped create the conditions that elevated Ronald Reagan to the White House."[17] The magazine was so influential that an article criticizing President Reagan's soft approach toward the Soviet Union prompted the president to call Podhoretz to discuss the piece.[18]

Podhoretz has written and edited twelve books, including *Making It, Why We Were in Vietnam, Ex-Friends, My Love Affair with America: The Cautionary Tale of a Cheerful Conservative, World War IV: The Long Struggle against Islamofascism,* and *Why Are Jews Liberals?*, in addition to countless political articles. In 2004, President George W. Bush awarded Podhoretz the Presidential Medal of Freedom.[19] Podhoretz was an adviser to Rudolph Giuliani's campaign for president in 2008 and has been a fellow at the Hudson Institute.[20] His writings have established conservative positions on many issues, including affirmative action and "political correctness," especially in academia.[21] Podhoretz is married to another writer, Midge Decter, who also underwent a political conversion to the right.[22]

Podhoretz offers many reasons for his political conversion and the writing of *BR*. As a former radical, he became disillusioned with the countercultural movements of the 1960s, especially with what he describes as the nihilism of groups like the Weather Underground and the drug culture that developed among many youth.[23] Youth become a key concern throughout *BR*,[24] which begins and ends with "A Letter to My Son"—a device that Chambers and Horowitz also use. Podhoretz argues that the United States is inherently good, that all forms of centralized power should be regarded with suspicion,[25] and that the United States's effort in Vietnam was morally sound but politically misguided.[26] He became a conservative to defend Israel in international politics, to condemn American universities that he believes capitulated to the anti-intellectual forces of the New Left, and to target other institutions and publications sympathetic to the 1960s, such as the *New York Review of Books*.[27] Podhoretz asserts that *Making It* and a highly controversial essay in *Commentary*, "My Negro Problem—and Ours," earned him public scorn, also prompting him to write *BR* and defend his previous work.[28] The author describes how alienated he felt after these writings, with many people considering him a "turncoat."[29]

Podhoretz's book can be viewed partly as a product of his decade (e.g., conservatism's lost legitimacy after Watergate), as a response to demands for change wrought by the 1960s, and as a way to reaffirm U.S. foreign policy from the 1950s. *BR* can further be viewed as part of the 1970s efforts to retreat from activism and respect experts in the management of public affairs.[30] Under these circumstances, the author draws on a language of rational intellectualism to advance his political vision, rather than the type of quasi-religious fundamentalism seen in the previous chapter.

BREAKING RANKS AS DELIBERATION

Podhoretz draws inspiration from former political converts, such as Whittaker Chambers, in his turn to the right.[31] While Podhoretz, Chambers, and Horowitz share the common conversion form, Podhoretz's political conversion narrative takes a different approach by avoiding the kinds of religious appeals that mark Chambers's story. Podhoretz writes a more qualified and idea-focused tale, charting a gradual, intellectual journey taken over the course of nearly two decades. *BR* is also more optimistic than Chambers's tragic, fatalistic vision of politics. Where Chambers establishes a place for religion in modern conservatism, Podhoretz instead focuses on bringing a type of intellectualism into the movement.

BR is a rational odyssey, as Podhoretz states: "I experienced a special happiness that comes from breaking out of a false position and giving free rein to previously inhibited *ideas*."[32] The book begins and ends with a personal message about his political conversion to his son, John,[33] but much of the text reads like a history lesson or series of opinion articles, threading discussions of policy through the transformation narrative. Others have also noted this outward focus in *BR* and subsequent Podhoretz works.[34] Amid these intellectual details, Podhoretz laces together a narrative describing his long journey from the political left to the right. Similar to *Witness*, *BR* has evoked a variety of responses, many of which center on Podhoretz's conversion motif. Some of these reactions affirm the second persona (or implied audience) in the text.[35] Many reviews are more ambivalent,[36] while others reject the book.[37]

Examining both the book and these responses for clues about how Podhoretz's rhetoric works, I find that *BR* is a reductive political conversion narrative. Using modern Protestantism as a case study, Peter Berger compares the deductive mind that denies or evades the cognitive difficulties of contemporary life with a reductive form of reasoning, which works with the intellectual demands of modern social contexts.[38] A model example is German Protestant theologian Rudolph Bultmann, whose rationalist program of "demythologization" stripped the supernatural from much of the New Testament, i.e., as unsupportable in an age of science and reason.[39] As a political analogue to this type of religious thinking, Podhoretz approaches public affairs from a reductive perspective, asserting the centrality of the mind and a particular, narrow version of reason in his writing.

Interacting with the conversion form, intellectualism, expression, and accuracy constitute Podhoretz's three major rhetorical resources in *BR*. These resources work with conversion in different ways from the other cases; for instance, the device of "intellectualism" is opposite to Chambers's use of "anti-intellectualism." The subject of deliberation actually emerges as a major concern in the book, with the three resources acting as deliberative criteria that Podhoretz asserts are vital to the future of political discourse. Using a technique with past precedent in rhetoric studies,[40] I apply the author's very criteria to the text itself to see if Podhoretz's political conversion narrative holds up to its own deliberative standards. In other words, as Robert Asen argues, rhetorical scholarship can subject "the values espoused by a text to a process of immanent critique to see whether the text upholds or betrays its values."[41] Several deliberative contradictions surface in the performance of the conversion narrative. Podhoretz advocates for public argument and intellectual testing in the narrative.[42] But *BR*'s conversion form overrides the intellectualism that the story asserts to create an anti-deliberative vision greater than the sum of its parts.

NEW INFLECTIONS: PODHORETZ'S RHETORICAL RESOURCES

The March of Reason: Intellectualism

Political conversion narratives can emphasize the importance of being an "intellectual" and centering one's life on "ideas" and "reason." Along with figures such as William F. Buckley and Irving Kristol, Podhoretz has been one of the primary advocates for intellectualism in modern conservatism, and the repetition of the words "intellectual" and "ideas" throughout *BR* bombards readers with a sense that reason and authority are firmly in the author's hands.[43]

Conversion can be thought of as an irrational process, as simply faith dropping down from the heavens to reach an individual or a group. From this perspective, intellectualism and reason are correctives to conversion, with Podhoretz committed to rationality and a belief in the mind's powers,[44] while maintaining a fundamental identity change from an old to a new life between the political Left and the Right. Unlike Chambers, Podhoretz uses his conversion narrative to praise the Enlightenment and intellectual pragmatism.[45] In essence, the conversion is framed as a hard-won journey to the truth, since in his former political life, he thought Republicans stood for stupidity, the status quo, and anti-intellectualism.[46]

Fashioning a political conversion as a painstakingly gradual process (in the author's case, over two decades) plays a major role in blending intellectualism and traditional standards of reason with the conversion narrative. A common expectation for argument is that advocates accumulate and evaluate evidence. An instantaneous, dramatic, mystical, and emotional Pauline conversion story is at odds with this approach.[47] From the perspective of traditional reason, this might be seen as jumping wildly to a conclusion. When a writer uses two decades of life experience to come to a conclusion, however, he or she may be perceived as following more reasonable standards, allowing the conversion experience and intellectualism to become mutually reinforcing rhetorical elements.

For example, before his conversion to neoconservatism, Podhoretz emphasizes his reasonability in a first turn to radicalism years earlier, which took years of reflection, reading, and turmoil.[48] In this reflection, no deus ex machina saves the day. The political journey involves only contemplation, soul-searching, and considered analysis. The author portrays himself as an expert who has tested political theory against experience, and he underscores the constancy of this reasoned, arduous process in explaining to his son that

> *it was on these attitudes toward Communism on the one side and America on the other that I cut my teeth as a young intellectual. It was from here that my odyssey to radicalism began, and it was back to a remarkably similar set of attitudes that my gradual revision from radicalism eventually took me. . . . [T]here is no way I can truly explain the differences both gross and subtle, both large and small, without telling the whole story of how and why I went from being a liberal to being a radical and then finally to being an enemy of radicalism in all its forms and varieties.*[49]

The conversion narrative justifies a new philosophy, with the "whole" language connoting that the book is a committed conclusion drawn from a logical process. By signaling that this was an extended journey, Podhoretz implies that any changes resulted from complex thought rather than ill-informed or knee-jerk reactions to his environment. Critically, by fusing intellectualism and conversion, "reason" is made a bifurcated, directional concept. Podhoretz says that *BR* and some of his other autobiographies employ a method called "autocase history,"[50] where the author uses his personal experience as a standard, representative case for judging the political environment. Political arguments are endowed with direction, embedded within a narrative framework that is at once a personal story and a universalizing journey toward the right.

Another traditional standard of reason functions in this scheme: that one maintains some personal distance from others in examining ideas. This standard is exemplified in traditional fallacies such as the ad hominem argument, where an arguer inappropriately attacks a person rather than the person's ideas. Relative to this concern, the conversion in *BR* is more subtle than overt. Specific details about Podhoretz's political transformation appear infrequently, as a way to bring order to the mass of intellectual testing. This distance partly explains the outward focus in much of the book and why Podhoretz only lightly applies the conversion narrative framework: to create an impression that the writer has enough distance from his claims while still focusing two decades worth of arguments.

Under the conversion narrative's pressures, high intellectual standards take on an immutable cast. In *The Neoconservative Vision*, Mark Gerson establishes that one of neoconservatism's philosophical underpinnings is the belief that the world is controlled by ideas,[51] a point repeated by Podhoretz.[52] Ideas are given a life of their own, existing independently from political considerations or human choices. In this sense, ideas possess a fixity that makes argumentation less a means of seeking interactive, imaginative courses of action than looking for a priori political truths. In Kenneth Burke's terms, emphasizing ideas and the autocase method position the author as "agent" centered, a philosophy that views the universe mostly in terms of the self.[53] Positioning such ideas under the conversion framework further raises a question about revisability—as argumentation is set within a lengthy, storied framework, the possibility for public amendment appears diminished.

Podhoretz underscores his deliberative vision in copious discussions of the contempt that 1960s movements had for intellectualism and reason. These movements' radical loyalties betrayed a commitment to intellectual standards and values, "whereas I was choosing to break political ranks rather than betray what I regarded as my responsibilities to the intellectual community and the intellectual vocation."[54] The repetition of the word "intellectual" spotlights the concept's axiomatic qualities. While it may be true that *BR* attests to a lifetime of nuanced reasoning, the repetition of "loyalty" language throughout the narrative also tends to reduce political choices to a binary opposition. To be clear, this is not to denigrate the championing of intellectual values, truth-seeking, nuance, and mindful responsibility in the public arena. My point is that Podhoretz positions these terms under a uniform rhetoric. In doing so, he gets to have his cake and eat it, ascribing a solidity ("standards") and flexibility ("I was choosing") to himself that are not equally offered to others without the convert tale.

The dividing line for a reductive political conversion is whether a person can be characterized as an intellectual or not,[55] with a special place reserved for intellectual converts. Podhoretz draws upon the intertextual authority of other political converts such as Chambers to justify a turn to the right. He links these conversions with reason by telling his son that they were largely intellectuals.[56] By presenting the story in this fashion, Podhoretz brings another kind of intellectual standard into the picture: peer review. He argues that this journey has not been a solitary excursion but one considered by other scholars and intellectuals who, after sifting through the weight of lived evidence, came to the same conclusion. On one side of the conversion divide lie unthinking, utopian leftists, while political converts to the right are reasoned and reasonable.[57]

Medical metaphors reinforce the intellectual conversion. Podhoretz describes the New Left and 1960s movements in terms of epidemics and illness.[58] He argues that by being in the intellectual community, he sought "a *healthy* political activity."[59] Just as doctors go through the arduous process of medical school training, Podhoretz uses his two-decade-long conversion as a testament to his ability to prescribe a sound politics. Furthermore, the conversion structure both grounds and is generated by Podhoretz's medical claims. Podhoretz compares the nation's health to the "*fevers and plagues of the two decades just past*," a story that he can now explain.[60] The conversion story works with the medical language to purge the intellectual sicknesses of the past. More troubling are the metaphorical entailments—"fevers" and "plagues" are, after all, forces to be extinguished rather than deliberated with.

These medical associations sometimes emphasize divides between youth and adulthood, which correspond with the old and new lives underscored in the conversion form. Podhoretz argues that 1960s radicalism was an "*infection*" and "*epidemic*" that affected vulnerable young people.[61] Claiming authority as an intellectual, adult convert, Podhoretz views the young as helpless and vulnerable to the viral ideas of the 1960s. Leftists in the 1960s have not had the experience of an old life from which to draw. This language fashions intellectual agency as beyond the reach of the young, since they have not been around long enough to make political judgments, and remain helpless in the face of the era's antirational illnesses.

In addition to this medical language, Podhoretz grounds the intellectual theme in civil-religious rhetoric. Reductive modes of religious thought downplay traditionalist fundamentalism or mystical and emotional experience in favor of the cognitive; similarly, Podhoretz characterizes himself as a deep thinker and his opponents as religious rather than reasoned. Yet the author also feels an obligation to religion now that he is on the right, giving general nods toward faith while calling the political Left a "religion." A central passage in the book explains Podhoretz's exigency "in the form of a rumor that my new political turn had come about as a result of some kind of religious experience," to which he explains there was some truth; after his turn he thought more about first and last things, but not with the kind of zealotry that only took place on the left.[62] A traditional religious conversion narrative is turned on its head as Podhoretz uses his political transformation as a tool to undermine religious fanaticisms.[63] The author characterizes leftists as disingenuous and simply beyond reason in their faith-filled advocacy. The convert leverages the authority of his fundamental change to exclude motives such as social change and reform from opponents, framing all their motives and behaviors within the false orientations of an old life. Podhoretz maintains the conversion form in his "new political turn," but the civil-religious rhetoric goes no further than an abstract description of faith in terms of first and last things. Straddling this civil-religious nexus, the author is both for and against religion—adhering to what Jean-Jacques Rousseau termed pious "sentiments of sociability" in the public square,[64] while meeting intellectual expectations about the need to separate faith from the civic realm.[65] Like those excising but retaining various elements from faith traditions, Podhoretz uses intellectual expectations about religion in public to characterize his new conservatism as reasoned, while casting others as zealots who cannot use their rational capacities.

This reductive conversion can be distinguished from those of conservatives such as Chambers and Buckley, who both thought that godlessness constituted the chief difference between Communist countries and the West. In *BR*, the difference is intellectual, between totalitarian and democratic societies as ideas rather than as symbolic of battles between noumenal, transcendent powers.[66] This religious difference of opinion would create many tensions within the conservative movement in the following decades.[67]

Ironically, despite the intellectual theme, the civil-religious conversion form can divert attention from an author's lack of support, focusing more on an individual's ethos (and opponents' lack thereof) than reasons. The religious framing of Podhoretz's enemies continues throughout the book in this regard. He argues that the nation's universities and major media outlets became "sanctuaries" for the New Left,[68] describing several leftist activists as "born-again radical[s]."[69] Many radicals worship at the altar of a "liberal faith," just as John F. Kennedy is accused of treating a political scientist's book as a bible.[70]

This civil-religious rhetoric contrasting the new intellectual convert from old religious lunacies narrows room for others' reasons. The author argues against environmentalist agendas, for example, less by inviting reasoning than by simply unmasking others' unthinking, apocalyptic attitudes—such as scientists who treated their projections as equivalent to prophecy and scripture.[71] Little discussion of environmental points takes place within these pages, however, with *BR* simply reducing environmentalism and its advocates' scientific claims to fanatical faith beliefs. The religious and secular can certainly overlap in discourses of catastrophe, as rhetoricians have shown how technical experts may speak in inaccessible, irreparable terms.[72] But *BR* is more concerned with reducing scientific, political positions to an anti-intellectual status through the religious label than with pursuing the details of environmental claims.

At the same time, by lumping socialists, Communists, and those in the New Left together under religion,[73] Podhoretz circumvents important dissimilarities between different people, groups, and historical periods, attributing a singular fanatical motive to them all. The author even pushes the term "conversion" onto others in a pejorative sense, leading to a curious double standard. He describes anti–Vietnam War advocate Ramsey Clark as someone who went through a "genuine and lasting *political conversion*" as a new proponent of radicalism; Clark is hence a "fanatical zealot."[74] By this standard, an incongruity develops between the political conversions of others as negative and anti-intellectual and Podhoretz's own "genuine" political conversion. By directing such arguments outward, the text suggests that a complex intellectualism shields one's own political conversion story from similar critique.

Crossing intellectual rhetoric with the conversion form, authors can equate conversion with complexity while still structuring their texts with binary distinctions. No Manichaean tale, Podhoretz repeatedly argues that his approach is nuanced, in contrast with opponents who trade in hyberbolic, cosmic categories divorced from reality, speaking "in the largest terms one could imagine: of Life and Death, of God and the Devil, of Good and Evil."[75] Podhoretz explains that his conversion story gives him the authority to shirk such grand labels and abstractions.[76] But there are tensions between the claims to nuance and the underlying narrative form, with contradictions emerging between Podhoretz's simultaneous rebukes and the use of abstractions throughout *BR* in appeals to, for example, "freedom" and "*liberty*."[77]

The conversion form ultimately forgoes the complexity that the narrative upholds on its surface. Podhoretz makes the rational human mind the sine qua non of civic engagement, contending that an intellectual, rather than a faith-based, politics is best. But when his opponents work on a human level, Podhoretz denies them their intellectual capacities. He says that 1960s radicalism falsely put its hopes in idealistic policies and rulers to amend problems.[78] *BR* makes systemic political engagement through such means both a human and transcendent phenomenon, putting his opponents in a deliberative bind: whatever individual, normative actions are taken in the public realm are either hopelessly utopian or unreliably faith driven. In other words, following the conversion form's bifurcating rhetoric, Podhoretz categorizes any agency that the Left may evince as blindness or ignorance.

Given how *BR* constructs a reductive political conversion, the scope of intellectualism in the book deserves comment. Podhoretz portrays human reason in highly narrow terms.[79] Partly, he equates reason with high literary culture, excluding all but the most rationalistic forms from public deliberation. He attacks Susan Sontag, for instance, for abandoning commendable forms of literary criticism for less rationalistic forms of communication such as movies and popular music.[80] Podhoretz further chides Marshall McLuhan for doing scholarship on television and Leslie Fiedler for her work on comic books.[81] Reason is restricted to high culture and seemingly timeless literary texts, yet the intellectual guise leads to a performative contradiction at the very center of these objections: *BR*'s rationalistic discussions of public policy are subsumed within a political conversion narrative. The author experiments with a type of communication that he denigrates others for using by writing an autobiography. *BR* tells a story, uses vivid, experiential imagery, and pursues authentic personal representation—standards that expand reason's capacity to include more than propositional criticism—but a stark dichotomy between high and low culture draws binary lines that are not adhered to in the book's writing.

Overall, *BR* is a tricky conversion story. An intellectual language that would seem to fit with traditional understandings of deliberation appears throughout—such as Podhoretz's desire for prudence in policy making, a reflective willingness to outline some of the major debates of his life, and warnings about the dangers of reductionism and support for complexity.[82] Yet the conversion form creates tensions with these intellectual themes, a feature that went unexamined by many supportive reviewers. One critic argues that the "climate of fear" generated by the hostile intellectual environment of the 1960s is undermined by the "battle of ideas" in Podhoretz's analysis.[83] To Ernest Van Den Haag, *BR* is a model intellectual tale, breaching "the never-ending battle of fact and fashion" in politics.[84] Jane Craig embraced Podhoretz's language by affirming that "the book is most completely characterized by a breathtakingly serious enthusiasm for ideas."[85] One critic surveying Podhoretz's books confirms the implied intellectual persona of "nuanced, careful judgments; he time and again laments the anti-intellectualism of at least a major element of the left, and the prevailing tone of his writing is anything but simplistic."[86]

A related consideration informs Podhoretz's rhetoric: the expressions or attitudes that advocates use in public. Podhoretz says that 1960s radicalism should be thought of more of as unserious ideology that serious ideas.[87] That is, *BR* draws a distinction between intellectualism and the means by which public speech occurs.

Civility at All Costs: Expression

A second rhetorical resource informing Podhoretz's deliberative vision is expression. *BR* obsesses over the attitudes, manner, and tone of public communicators, with the author admitting that "I have never succeeded in disciplining myself to overlook or remain unaffected by the tone in which an argument is presented"—mostly to undermine 1960s movements engaging in "rhetorical violence" and negative "tactics."[88] Podhoretz became upset by the overall tone and lack of free speech in the New Left.[89] While the author focuses on intellectualism as an *end* in public affairs, expression centers on the *means* of political communication.[90] Calls for civility further establish the reductive intellectual guise, with the discourse working in demonstrably propagandistic ways. Like the other resources, performative contradictions emerge when the very standard of expression invoked in Podhoretz's theory is applied to *BR* itself.

Literature on confrontational movement rhetoric is relevant to this theme, since *BR* indicts many communication practices emerging from 1960s activism. Podhoretz is disgusted, for example, by the "hirsute and foul-mouthed youths [in U.S. universities] waving Vietcong flags—[who] put off a great many people who might otherwise have been persuaded."[91] Discussing race relations, he hopes to limit such tonal emphases to the civil and decorous when difficult issues are being discussed, and questions why debased language would even be allowed in such important conversations.[92]

Robert Scott and Donald Smith complicate such statements by pointing out how "a rhetorical theory suitable to our age must take into account the charge that civility and decorum serve as masks for the preservation for injustice, that they condemn the disposed to non-being . . . [and] become the instrumentalities of power for those who 'have.'"[93] Because Podhoretz was an elite, powerful writer of a top public affairs magazine, his calls for civility gloss over claims of injustice raised by those on the left. While Podhoretz argues for a minimum standard of civility and candor, there is also, by implication, a tonal threshold that he hopes to uphold. One problem is that this is never quite spelled out.

Just as he did with intellectualism, Podhoretz associates conversion and expression with complexity. Podhoretz uses complexity to divide those who are capable of mannered expression from those who are simple.[94] In the New Left, ideas are "stripped of all complexity, qualification, and nuance and expressed in callow and derivative language."[95] In essence, a communicator's means of expression acts as a sign of the worthiness of his or her ideas. Under the conversion form, expression becomes a dividing line between Podhoretz's old and new political associations, framing advocates in the old paradigm as untamed and those in his new life as civil.

There is more going on with the expression theme than a mere dislike for the level of others' civility, though. The conversion form connects one's means of communication to his or her development as a human being. In other words, Podhoretz uses conversion to link expression with one's intellectual and biological maturity as a person. Podhoretz writes that radical 1960s movements were all about avoiding adulthood.[96] Podhoretz asserts that too much freedom of speech and ideological rhetoric signifies a lack of human development. People's types of expression are an indicator of their life's journey, so much that a lack of restraint rhetorically equates with a lack of biological development. Unrestrained, wholly expressive communicators are hence reduced to espousing meaningless speech divorced from intellectual content.

Under the conversion narrative, paradoxically, opponents become recklessly expressive—as well as muted. Because of their wild expression, leftists have nothing of substance to contribute to public discourse, while 1960s youth are characterized as debilitated advocates.[97] Podhoretz implies that those who have failed to turn rightward are stunted, in a state of arrested development intellectually, expressively, and physically. Associating opponents' expressive modes with human development reduces their speech to simple biological and determined impulses rather than thoughtful claims or choices.[98] While Podhoretz frames his enemies in the former terms, he makes the latter option available to himself by claiming that he could choose to turn in the other direction.[99]

Further reducing antiwar protesters' motives to impulses rather than reasons, Podhoretz fuses "dissent" with "pride." Writers taking a stand against the Vietnam War are crafted as unwilling to meet the decorous communicative standards that should occur between a government and its citizens. Support for the Vietnam War is associated with humble, proper expression before the American pantheon, and antiwar advocacy with maniacal, arrogant speech. Podhoretz assigns tones of self-congratulation to the 99 percent of literary writers in New York who, he says, enjoyed thinking of themselves as heroic "dissenters."[100] Under the conversion framework, then, Podhoretz positions dissent as merely egotistical, glandular expression.

Little purpose is found within a democracy for communication involving tactics such as the use of manifestos, loudness, clichés, and slogans, limiting all public speech to polite decorum at best.[101] As Podhoretz explains, the Students for a Democratic Society had shifted from rational arguments to shouting at speakers who differed in their viewpoints.[102] The author sees protest rhetoric as anti-communicative and violent, an assault on reasoning and reasonability.[103] On its face, *BR* claims a concern for speech and the need for open debate in the public square, but the book itself reduces the university students' critical options to only the most decorous under a civil or uncivil dichotomy. Ultimately, Podhoretz spends so much of his narrative criticizing the students' type of communication that he rarely addresses their actual complaints. He subsequently consigns student rhetoric to a private domain occluding, for instance, a possibility that the student and civil rights movements were related, while implying that student concerns can have little to do with larger political concerns.[104]

The conversion structure drives ambiguities between rhetorical and actual violence to relegate Podhoretz's former colleagues, of all stripes, to a violent, criminal past life. Moreover, the author's web of violent associations forms a cumulative, connotative excess in these designations, incorporating not just the SDS but academics, writers, and others on the left supporting 1960s causes. For example, the author associates the liberal-leaning Ford Foundation with "black nationalists" who "resemble[d] guerillas in their use of violence and the threat of violence."[105]

Speaking about public expression in this way would appear to be deliberative, but the narrative is a wolf in sheep's clothing. Podhoretz cares about the insulated rhetorics of leftist writers who remained aloof from difference, "Where they lived and worked, opposition to the war was universal and dogmatic, and the only arguments were over degrees of zealotry or about tactics for getting out [of Vietnam]."[106] This concern bears similarities to what Cass Sunstein has termed "deliberative enclaves," or imitative, self-reinforcing types of group communication.[107] In his attributions, Podhoretz makes the risk involved in making an antiwar argument more important than the arguments themselves, however. One's "degrees of zealotry" and "tactics" become the primary considerations, so much that the *how* of expression overrides the *why* of content. This subordination of content and the focus on style, tone, and mannerisms also become evident in Podhoretz's analysis of specific intellectuals and groups. Even those who might be expected to advance nuanced, complex arguments—such as many academic supporters of the 1960s movements—are framed as disingenuous and aggressive bullies, at best.

Rather than employing ad hominem argumentation, Podhoretz exhibits what I term *ad expressivism* arguments, where one attacks opponents' tones while avoiding their messages. Describing the playwright Lillian Hellman, the author maintains that her political beliefs were only an attitude or position lacking in content.[108] Each step of the way, others' motives are characterized primarily in terms of their attitudes. And sometimes, one expression simply masks another. Podhoretz says that black activist Stokely Carmichael used nonviolent tactics and a nice demeanor as fronts for his violent and militaristic beliefs.[109] Polar terms describe leftists who were "unattractive people who could be as violent in character and savage in argument as they were pacific in ideology."[110] The conversion narrative implies that, in breaking ranks, Podhoretz was separating himself from these attitudinal postures toward a new, substantive political position. Yet *BR* narrows deliberative space for others through double binds, underscoring that attitude without content is bad and that dissenters who think they know the truth are also bad.

Combined with the expression theme, the conversion narrative dissociates "mere" from "real" expression in a way that relieves Podhoretz from providing support for his claims.[111] For the author, many "*looked*" at first as though they were rational persuaders, such as Noam Chomsky, whose academic background created an "*impression*" of rationality.[112] Large scholarly works become false "impressions" distanced from true reason, so that "*on the surface*" Chomsky's work signaled scholarly reasoning through features such as many footnotes, but actually did a disservice to real intellectualism.[113] In Podhoretz's construction, a consideration of others' civility trumps their claims. An epistemological question arises: How does Podhoretz know that the appearance of scrupulous reasoning isn't real? There is nothing inherently wrong with dissociative reasoning, but Podhoretz's persona and authority as a civil political convert work to avoid addressing this issue. The conversion tale allows Podhoretz to bypass the content of Chomsky's footnotes, assuming that the convert's credibility as a former agent of the radical Left is enough to know the difference between rationality and irrationality, appearance and reality. Concurrently, there is a complete absence of footnotes in *BR* itself.

The conversion narrative fails to abide by expressive standards. Podhoretz indicts Chomsky for using shocking, overstated language comparing U.S. politicians to "Nazi war criminals."[114] Yet in one *BR* section, Podhoretz associates 1960s radicals with the Third Reich to explain to his son how art was suppressed in Nazi Germany.[115] Throughout the book, Podhoretz expects his opponents to follow a deliberative norm—don't use shocking analogies—to which *BR* does not even adhere.

The concept of the "comic frame" in the communication literature on social movements applies to *BR*'s expressive concerns.[116] In a comic frame, people are not evil but mistaken,[117] to be approached with civil attitudes rather than complete rejection. *BR* asserts a comic deliberative vision, urging a civil tone and manner in public affairs. But the conversion form works against this comic content. Podhoretz argues that melodramatic, revolutionary strategies were unnecessary at places like the University of California at Berkeley, where social change could take place without forceful rhetoric and tactics.[118] Calling for restraint amid these types of "irresponsible persuasion"[119] distinguishes the author's comically framed perspective from liberal and radical movements' melodrama. In this way, *BR* uses inclusive language to exclude others' dramatic messages from public discussion. My point here is less about the adequacy of the comic frame than how the author forgoes others' messages, contradicting the open deliberative standards that he raises for movement communication. Podhoretz's strategy constitutes one way that "civility and decorum [can] serve as masks for the preservation for injustice," in Scott and Smith's terms.[120]

Podhoretz's use of expression relates to other movement issues as well. Franklyn Haiman challenges the assumption that protest rhetoric needs to include rational discourse, arguing that opportunities are not always available for peaceful discourse.[121] Theodore Windt further finds that evocative communication forms used during the Vietnam War, such as the diatribe, are effective and morally purposeful since "people seldom become concerned about problems until they are shocked."[122] The expression theme, like intellectualism, asserts a narrow conception of human reason, crafting civility as the only means of persuasion in public affairs. Although Podhoretz admits that leftist activists had some disagreements, he still attributes uniformity to their rhetoric each step of the way.[123] Movements are far from static entities,[124] but the pressure to tell a totalizing conversion story counteracts such fluid attributions. Similarly, one reviewer objects that "Mr. Podhoretz's talent for synthesis serves his book ill. For one thing, it leaves no room for, and pays no respect to, the passionate advocacy of single causes."[125] Ultimately, *BR* is itself a passionate case for a cause, engaging in the kind of advocacy for which it critiques others.

A number of reviewers affirmed the "expressive" second persona. Hilton Kramer resonates with Podhoretz's description of the "militant mode of conformism" in 1960s movements and their intolerance for other viewpoints.[126] For Paul Johnson, Podhoretz maintains "a rational belief in the ability of America to stand for civilised ends and honourable methods of achieving them."[127] And Richard John Neuhaus believes that Podhoretz's depiction of the New Left's forms of expression is on target, since "the rituals of excommunication are immediate and relentless."[128]

Other reviewers were more ambivalent about this theme. Paul Hollander affirms Podhoretz's "spirit of moderation" and the idea that the Left's political efforts were based more on religious fervor than political engagement, but says that Podhoretz's sustained attacks on other intellectuals was less than venerable.[129] Noel Annan finds persuasive "how numbers of the intelligentsia allowed themselves to be conned into tolerating violence as an acceptable way of settling disputes," "turn[ing] a blind eye to shoddy reasoning."[130] He lists a number of reservations about the book, however, including Podhoretz's abandonment of sociable methods of criticism.

Many of the less supportive reviews critiqued this issue. Christopher Hitchens finds *BR* to be written in an "insulting manner" that is anything but reasonable and moderate, particularly in its attacks upon sexual minority movements.[131] One review notes that *BR* "is not generous, particularly to those who . . . have been both righteous and wrong-headed."[132] Robert Lekachman finds the tone of *BR* "unrelievedly vindictive."[133] Reflecting on one of Podhoretz's later works, Bruce Clayton further writes that "the problem for Podhoretz is that he tends to confuse liberal social criticism with hating America."[134] As another reviewer argues, Podhoretz suppresses the validity of questioning dogma and creeds (a process that is a part of the U.S. civic tradition), failing in his "capacity to acknowledge the justness of competing claims in an open democratic field."[135]

Describing sociologist C. Wright Mills, Podhoretz writes that he disliked his approach and attitude, since his books "drew what seemed to me a wildly exaggerated picture of the control exercised by a small number of corporations over the American political system, and . . . gave an equally overdrawn and even hysterical account of the dissatisfactions of middle-class life."[136] A rhetoric about both the "hysterical" and "overdrawn" pivots between concerns for expression and a final resource interacting with Podhoretz's political conversion: accuracy.

Grasping the Truth: Accuracy

Much of the conversion narrative centers on a need for accuracy in public affairs. Dictionary definitions identify accuracy as "the condition or quality of being true, correct, or exact; freedom from error or defect; precision or exactness; correctness."[137] Along these lines, Podhoretz expresses concerns for the fair, precise, proportionate, valid, and correct portrayal of people and events, to stress the rightness of turning rightward. As with the other themes, Podhoretz combines the conversion form with accuracy's terms to create the impression that he has grasped the truth and grasped it better than others. Accuracy is a key concern in literature on deliberation and argument,[138] so it may come as some surprise to see that the term can be wielded in an anti-deliberative fashion. Asserting that his opponents are inaccurate in their intentions and rhetoric because of his experience in and out of the political Left, the author limits deliberative space for others by making the authority of a conversion a means of separating the accurate from the inaccurate.

Central to how the conversion narrative structures the discourse, Podhoretz positions accuracy with the previously mentioned "autocase method," extrapolating from his personal experience to the wider political environment. He states that in his previous book, *Making It*, "my entire purpose was to expose an order of feeling in myself that could be assumed to be representative," through "the use of my own experience as a narrative thread and a focus for describing the larger context in which my personal experience takes shape."[139] In an interview, Podhoretz further said of his books, *Making It* and *Breaking Ranks*, "I think I invented this form. . . . The form consists of using one's own experience as a means of exploring a larger theme," meaning, "I am the case history on the basis of which whatever theme it is I am trying to illuminate, whatever segment of our intellectual or cultural or political history I am exploring, takes place."[140] Note the wording and emphases in these quotations; the conversion story highlights a particular type of precision in public matters, with the radical to neoconservative turn symbolizing an accurate, generalizable chronicle from individual experience as a central evidentiary standard for public reasoning.

What follows is that political conversion and accuracy together establish that converts have a special, more exact, way of knowing, being, and acting in political life than others. Podhoretz explains that *Commentary*'s editorial stances maintained their accuracy and authority by drawing from such distinctive past experiences, since it had been associated with the radical movements and thus had "the authority of an insider"; publications such as the *National Review* and *The Public Interest* could only "sometimes analyze them accurately" or were too nerdy to get a "full accurate measure" of the political movement.[141] Podhoretz's old political life generates an insider status. Like Chambers, Podhoretz sees political converts as guides to the times, using his political change as evidence for the accuracy with which present conditions can be gauged. That conservative publications such as *National Review* and the *Public Interest* are off-base shows how exactness is associated with the rightward turn. *BR* associates accuracy with a special access to the truth that other individuals and groups do not possess. Based on past experience, the conversion generates an ethos of precision, a special ability that only converts can claim.

Conversion gives one an ability to represent other people with accuracy. Podhoretz's totalizing claim to know the 1960s in all its dimensions puts the convert in a privileged position to know opponents' motives, qualities, and interests, with little qualification. The conversion journey constitutes a new possession of comprehensive truth and accuracy, as opposed to the Left's "hysterically overdrawn characterizations of American life"[142] and its inaccurate portrayal of others, such as some writers' hyperbolic attributions of and praise for student protestors.[143] Because the 1960s were a time of economic and social good fortune for intellectuals, the rise of radicalism was more about intellectuals' desire for influence than anything else.[144] It is important to note how Podhoretz's empirical ability to sum up his political environment slips seamlessly into attributions of others' motives. Accuracy gives the convert an authority to speak to the reality of outside events but also to know what others are up to on the inside. Readers are not treated to any insight on how Podhoretz knows others' chief motives beyond the point that, because he was a liberal and radical once and knew some liberals and radicals once, he has the authority to divine present interests.

There is a self-referential solipsism in Podhoretz's use of his own experience as a representative sign of the times, or the degree to which his experience is made to extrapolate to his context, as a kind of indicator or barometer of the public climate. Podhoretz covers issues such as Vietnam, race relations, and the student protests in the 1960s (although curiously, there is little talk of Nixon and Watergate to be found anywhere in the book). But the author's idiosyncratic experience frames these issues in a way that excludes the pluralism of and evidence from others' experiences. Critics examining Podhoretz's autobiographies find that *BR* frequently appropriates large passages out of the author's other works, often without attribution, as a self-plagiarizing form of writing.[145] This practice demonstrates how the autocase writing form puts one at the center of political inquiry. The conversion narrative reinforces such emphases, so that the very gradual turn from an old to a new life makes the author's political generalizations appear less like generalizations, and more like accurate, natural judgments that anyone would come to with the right time and experience.

In this reasoning, the convert even has a precise and proportionate sense of where particular policies or political issues hit the mark or go awry. This strategy pertains most notably to Podhoretz's controversial views on race relations in his 1963 *Commentary* article "My Negro Problem—and Ours" and his earlier book, *Making It*. Drawing from the two previous texts, *BR* repeats a point that creating geographical proximity between black and white people will not necessarily lead to common ground and action, based on Podhoretz's experience growing up in a Brooklyn ghetto and belief that living in the same vicinity promoted hatred rather than cooperation.[146] True to the autocase method and the convert's outlook, Podhoretz generalizes from his own experience to characterize broader political conditions. His previous experience is used as evidence to establish that full integration is too chimerical to apply to present conditions.

The exacting language invites a belief that the gradual political convert measures politics; that his or her incremental journey translates directly into a professional ability to see the degrees by which others are on target. From experience, liberal views about integration are seen as too idealistic and inaccurate, with white and black attitudes as barriers that are too great to achieve such goals soon.[147] Podhoretz does not deny the South's rampant racism, but for him, the situation in the North was different enough that legal efforts on behalf of blacks inaccurately went too far beyond their needed aims.[148] The author thinks that these inaccuracies have led to harmful social programs, which were designed to correct the racial abuses of the past but pressed too far beyond their initial reach (through the implementation of affirmative action programs).[149]

While Podhoretz attacks the Left for inaccuracies and for lacking support for its political claims (e.g., the antiwar movement's apocalyptic thinking about Vietnam), *BR* itself has few citations and no bibliography for many of his most overt conclusions. The author argues against the assumption that being a black person in the United States necessarily meant being poor, because two-thirds of those in poverty in the United States both in the past and now are white.[150] Importantly, there is no evidence provided for such assertions; the convert's authority more than establishes the need to do so. Podhoretz's statement also misleads in ignoring the degree of poverty between whites and blacks in the United States in terms of their ratios with the total population. The U.S. Census confirms that "the poverty rate for Blacks was 32 percent in 1980, about three times the rate for Whites (10 percent). Although Blacks accounted for only 12 percent of the total population, they made up 29 percent of the poverty population."[151] *BR* indicts others for sourcing but fails to provide even minimal, accurate evidence for crucial arguments. This rhetorical move relates to *BR*'s solipsism: the political conversion is used as a self-justifying source of authority.

The conversion narrative testifies to empirical, lived opinions that speak for themselves, as immutable lines between the outdated and current that the author sifts through personal testing. Podhoretz puts concerns for accuracy, Communism, and praise for U.S. foreign policy together in arguing that support for the North Vienamese was "a new form of the old illusions about Communism."[152] Merging political transformation with the accuracy resource, Podhoretz urges others to cast off old inaccurate illusions and see the light, rather than simply perpetuate new forms of the old.

The author's Jewish identity and experience are relevant to the accuracy theme. In particular, the themes of accuracy and hyperbolic speech connect with Podhoretz's concerns about Vietnam, where he says that the *New York*

Review of Books published an inaccurate and hyperbolic portrayal of the United States as ethically comparable to Nazi Germany.[153] In what he views as an inaccuracy from the political Left writ large, Vietnam was not simply evidence of the United States's mistakes, but unethical nature.[154] Much writing by Jews in the postwar era has focused on the accuracy with which the events of World War II are portrayed, including Nazi Germany and the Holocaust.[155] Podhoretz reserves this authority for realistic, sober applications, such as when Senator Patrick Moynihan spoke with "accuracy" in calling people like Idi Amin in Uganda a "racist murderer."[156] Podhoretz says that a government commission created to explore the unrest on university campuses during the Vietnam War "exaggerated wildly in comparing the campus uprisings of the late sixties to the Civil War."[157] Podhoretz also directs his accuracy language toward ideas about anti-Semitism and support for the State of Israel. He rebukes many leftists' anti-Israel positions, especially in their support of Arab and Soviet propaganda that literally characterized Israelis as Nazis in the aftermath of the Six-Day War of 1967.[158]

Ultimately, these discourses show how a conversion experience can be related to identity as a way of accurately drawing lines between good and evil. One's experiences and background can certainly play an important part in public advocacy, but the author makes his discourse totalizing by joining the conversion form with his cultural background in order to argue that others outside his own experiences almost always miss the mark when they use moral terms. Podhoretz says that part of his breaking ranks with the Left and all its institutions involved rejecting the U.S. and Nazi Germany analogy, and the idea that the United States was evil to any degree; rather, the war was being fought out of an "excess of idealism."[159] Good and evil are reserved for the non-fanatical convert, who can accurately sum up situations given his or her *own* background. A curious part of this paragraph concerns the "excess of idealism." Up to this point, Podhoretz has argued against the idealism of 1960s movements, tying leftist organizations to inaccurate, utopian fantasies. The sudden admission that an "excess of idealism" is reasonable in supporting the Vietnam War but not other causes is a deliberative contradiction. The communicative standards of excess and idealism are not offered to others on the left in the same way that Podhoretz is now performing these criteria for the Right.

The use of accuracy as a deliberative criterion calls others to be accountable for their statements and actions, to be as precise as possible in formulating policies and prescriptions and in using evidence to back up their claims. But it is not a standard by which the conversion narrative abides. This is an important consideration, since Podhoretz's political conversion and focus on others' inaccuracies may draw the reader's attention away from these textual moves. In particular, *BR* is rife with a specific type of straw man fallacy, setting up easy targets to knock down in a way that avoids dealing with the scope of opponents' claims. Robert Talisse and Scott Aikin find two prominent forms of the straw man fallacy: "representation" and "selection." The former is the most common, where an advocate (A) misrepresents what another (B) actually says. The latter, trickier approach is a way of "refuting only her weakest opponents."[160] That is, B's objection is not misrepresented; rather, a "straw man is erected by *selecting* a relatively weak version of, or inept spokesman for, the opposition to her view."[161] A could not, of course, represent all of B's views. But a qualitative problem emerges when the opposition's better arguments are not addressed. The weaker version is presented as the best and most relevant example, and hence is "a misrepresentation of the variety and relative quality of one's opposition," with the advocate playing upon audience ignorance of better arguers and arguments. The selection form of the straw man fallacy has been used in a lot of political publishing to present "what is in fact a more-or-less accurate depiction of what some of the weakest opponents have said" to easily dismantle all opposing views.[162]

In the same way, the conversion narrative uses the selection form of the straw man fallacy. Podhoretz finds accuracy lacking in the texts of leftist writers such as Norman Mailer, who, for example, wrote an article advocating that two robbers who had killed a storekeeper had also murdered private property as a pernicious institution and idea.[163] Although Podhoretz represents Mailer's ideas—and hence is not committing the standard form of the fallacy—his implicit strategy is to select an outlandish, weak argument to characterize the entire Left's supposed lunacy. The strategy can also be seen in comments about others' Nazi analogies. Because avoiding the straw man is Podhoretz's own deliberative criterion, this is especially problematic; he thinks that others have not only misrepresented his ideas (particularly regarding "My Negro Problem") but have forgotten about his better arguments, as indicated by the incomplete, out-of-context charges of racism and other angry responses he received for particular lines and passages in previous writings.[164]

The accuracy theme additionally raises a question about the extent to which moral advocacy should be eliminated for not matching existing realities. Podhoretz's argument about whites and blacks not being ready for integration (putting aside whether this is an accurate claim) does not necessarily eliminate the need to continue striving toward integration. Podhoretz draws a strict division between the "is" and "should" of U.S. race relations that, in the name of accurately describing the political context, excludes normative advocacy from deliberative contexts. This "is/should" division results in another contradiction when applied to *BR*, as the text presents readers with a great deal of moral argument that goes beyond existing circumstances to forge a neoconservative vision for the country's future. As Podhoretz says, the making of "aesthetic judgments" is the primary purpose of social criticism[165]—so deliberatively speaking, it is unfair to suggest that such judgments are available only to one part of the political spectrum.

A number of reviewers affirmed *BR*'s accuracy persona. Paul Johnson says that Podhoretz has an "accurate and hard-headed assessment of just what is good and bad about America—leading to the sensible conclusion that the good outweighs the bad by a margin so enormous that only a fanatic, or an intellectual crook, will deny it."[166] Some reviews also reflect Podhoretz's seemingly "accurate" portrayals of others. Van Den Haag says that Podhoretz "does not caricature those who did not applaud him, or aggrandize those who did. Indeed . . . there is no malice in this book, which if anything, is too judicious. There are, however, some deft, even moving, portraits of semipublic figures."[167] Restraint and representation become mutually implicated values, as "does not caricature" is associated with "no malice."

Many more reviews were less sparing in their comments, echoing some of the deliberative concerns already raised. John Romano believes that Podhoretz draws a "clumsy cartoon of liberalism."[168] Paul Hollander remains "dubious about a linking of environmental concerns and conservation movements with political radicalism"[169]—a critique of Podhoretz's lumping of many different groups and factions under the leftist label. John Leonard questions Podhoretz's characterizations of the political Left with a detailed counterargument worth highlighting:

> Rereading *Breaking Ranks*, one becomes indignant . . . because almost everything he has to say about the sixties and the counterculture is at best innocent of nuance and at worst meretricious. Having served my time at Pacifica Radio, at civil rights protests, in the War on Poverty, among migrant workers and in the antiwar movement, before hopping onto the pogo stick of a New York career, I know for a fact that there were white liberals who felt some personal responsibility for the plight of black people even though the Pod insists that "I have rarely met a single one who really did experience a sense of guilt over this issue." . . . I also know that the antiwar movement consisted of a whole lot more than Vietcong flags and "scions of . . . the First Families of American Stalinism"—and what's more, opposition to the war was created by the war itself, not by highbrows in whatever periodical or tank.[170]

Similarly, commenting on a theme running through much of Podhoretz's writing career (before and after *BR*), Glenn Diamond berates the author for reducing the Beat philosophy to nothing but a "death wish."[171] From another perspective, Christopher Lehmann-Haupt thinks that Podhoretz overstates the critical response to his earlier book *Making It* and that the "relentless synthesizing" of Podhoretz's "conversion" also presents an inaccurate picture of the vigor with which he ever advocated support for radical causes.[172] Seymour Krim finds that Podhoretz "exaggerates his slight involvement with 'radicalism,' which was strictly of the safe armchair variety."[173] Murray

Rothbard asks, "[W]hat are we to make of a man whose concept of 'terror' is getting a bad write-up in *Partisan Review*?" and notes that Podhoretz often dismisses others' explanations for their actions in an unfair manner.[174] Some reviewers partly corroborate my findings, claiming that *BR* itself is often a dogmatic book in attacking an abstract, unrealistic political Left.[175] One book review similarly asks, tongue in cheek, "[W]asn't it nice when the Left made such overtly stupid, refutable statements?"[176]

Hitchens says that Podhoretz presents "a series of ungenerous and inaccurate sketches" of characters such as Noam Chomsky, so much that "he is incapable of representing an opposing viewpoint."[177] Annan thinks that Podhoretz "underestimates the enormities of the Vietnam war," both in terms of the country's pillaging and the difficulties faced by soldiers coming home. He also writes that Podhoretz might have admitted that the student movements had "some reasonable pleas" against the colleges and universities.[178]

As a whole, Podhoretz's story combines the conversion form with rhetorics of intellectualism, expression, and accuracy to create an intellectual guise for a type of discourse with dogmatic features. It is a testament to the manifold, subtle ways in which political conversion can be rhetorically activated for strategic public purposes, summing to a deliberative vision that is, by the book's own standards, anti-deliberative.

CONCLUSION

Neil Postman once asserted that "the distinction between language that says 'Believe this' and language that says 'Consider this' is, in my opinion, certainly worth making, and especially because the variety of ways of saying 'Believe this' are so various and sophisticated."[179] In Podhoretz's tale, we find one very sophisticated way that a political conversion story, under a guise of reason and reasonability, can forward propagandistic discourse. A number of points can be gleaned from the reductive political conversion story.

First, intellectualism can be used as a rhetorical resource to create an impression that a gradual conversion narrative comports with traditional standards of reason. Through the intellectual theme, Podhoretz communicates "I'm a complex thinker" by telling the reader that his political conversion was an extended journey rather than a quick decision. These time-based and linear emphases build an intellectual ethos for the author and make his arguments a foregone conclusion, one in which the deep, fundamental identity change moves from a wrong to a right in public affairs. Here the conversion's time-based metaphors (change from an *old* to a *new* life) crosses with the directional metaphors of politics (change from *left* to *right*) to reinforce an invariable public rhetoric. In positioning intellectualism under the conversion form, a question of revisability arises—as argumentation is set within a lengthy, storied framework, the possibility for public amendment appears diminished.

The problem from a deliberative viewpoint is that high intellectual standards take on a totalizing, axiomatic cast under the conversion form. Podhoretz presents readers with a rhetorical theory that is more about independently finding one's way from wrong to right universal criteria than collaboratively creating standards for the public good. *BR* ties reason to the authenticity of one's confession, often so much that displays of genuineness become more important than, or simply gloss over, reasons altogether. Podhoretz is more interested in labeling advocates as apocalyptic than in reasoning with them, with the conversion form skirting much of the intellectual reasoning that the story invokes.

These problems arise from a political transformation that begins and ends with the self. Podhoretz calls this agent-centered form of reasoning "autocase history," drawing conclusions about the political environment from the evidence of personal experience and endowing this experience with an authority to know more than others. Relating to Podhoretz's concern that others are thinking and acting unreasonably, Adam Curtis finds that the "irrational, self-seeking individual" tends to be a major target in neoconservative thought.[180] Yet Podhoretz engages in a self-referential rhetoric throughout the conversion narrative. He claims that his political conversion was like that of other intellectuals who, after sifting through their lived evidence, became political converts, too. Given other features such as the narrative's medical metaphors, however, Podhoretz largely turns himself into an independent expert unmoored from a need to consider others' histories.

Following the conversion form's contours, whatever beliefs or agency that the political Left may exhibit can simply be dealt with as blindness and ignorance. *BR*'s civil-religious rhetoric further allows Podhoretz to claim a minimal threshold of religiosity to appeal to religious audiences but also to frame his opponents as religious fanatics, casting all their motives and behaviors within the false orientation of an old life. Under the intellectual guise, *BR* equates conversion with complexity, but the book's textual moves evidence tensions between claims to nuanced content made within a simplifying narrative form.

An attack upon rhetorics outside a high intellectual and cultural rationalism leads to another deliberative contradiction at the center of these objections: Podhoretz subsumes his rationalistic discussions of public policy within a political conversion narrative—but moreover, he reserves an exclusive right to make appealing, artful judgments in the public sphere.[181] As others have also found, Podhoretz is not an "intellectual as citizen of the world," with narrow formulations in *BR* forgoing a broader political outlook.[182] In the conversion literature, Wayne Booth raises a question about the extent to which converts who have engaged in hard thought about their change can still be considered fundamentalist.[183] Given how the gradual conversion and intellectualism rhetoric work in *BR*, this analysis suggests that such approaches can still exhibit fundamentalist qualities.

Second, the rhetorical resource of expression can support a reductive conversion by dividing those capable of mannered expression from those who are not. In calling for civility, Podhoretz recognizes a need for communication norms and practices best suited to civic engagement, but the narrative engages in performative contradictions, such as the belief that others should not use shocking analogies while Podhoretz uses his own. As a persistent, passionate case for a cause, *BR* also engages in the very kind of advocacy for which it critiques others, and it crafts space for only the most decorous forms of human reasoning.

In the author's vision, the how of expression ends up overriding the why of content—advancing *ad expressivist* arguments. So much of the narrative is spent criticizing opponents' types of communication that their actual complaints are rarely addressed. Simply put, the conversion narrative creates a civil first persona that relieves Podhoretz of the necessity of providing support for his claims. Podhoretz's being a civil political convert also works to avoid addressing the issue of how he can know that the appearance of scrupulous reasoning by intellectual leftist advocates is not real. Recognizing the deliberative features of this kind of rhetoric is important: Judith Albert and Stewart Albert find that "the 1960s were much more than an emotional outburst. So many documents were authored, articles were written, and positions were debated. The 1960s was a time when truly new ideas were articulated, and everything in our country was up for debate."[184]

The reductive conversion form functions to reduce opponents' messages to two paradoxical forms of public expression: either recklessly expressive or mute. In so doing, Podhoretz diminishes others' speech from what Burke calls symbolic "action" to biological "motion,"[185] portraying others as rhetorically incapacitated, undeveloped persons, so that dissent becomes merely egotistical, glandular expressions without value in public discourse.

Third, the conversion story interacts with a rhetoric of accuracy. Accuracy allows the political convert to make precise attributions of others' motives, such as other intellectuals' desire for attention and influence, above and beyond other factors. Podhoretz uses the autocase method to extrapolate from personal experience to accurate views on the wider political environment, and the conversion narrative reinforces that the journey to the right is also about "rightness." The conversion generates an insider status that, like Chambers's story, fashions political converts as representative guides to the times. In these rhetorical constructions, conversion is not just a noun, an experience that one had, but a verb or way of approaching public affairs that allows one to survey and know one's political environment better than others.

The convert's language of accuracy further asserts that singular experience constitutes the best way to judge specific policies and others' motives. Podhoretz's travels from the political left to the right diagnose public problems with a type of accuracy, inviting readers to perceive that fundamental identity change equals an ability to scrutinize wrong from right on major political concerns. But the focus on policies and others' motives raises an epistemological issue for Podhoretz: the conversion narrative claims to know more than he can know. Beyond possessing the convert's authority, readers are rarely treated to any insight on how Podhoretz knows others' motivations.

The selection form of the straw-man fallacy further gives readers easy arguments to knock down in characterizing all leftist demands as unworthy of engaging. But Podhoretz's own accuracy is at stake in leaving out the contestation of and diverse people within the New Left and other 1960s movements.[186] The fairness of the author's metaphorical choices is also questionable. The medical metaphors, particularly language characterizing those on the left as part of a plague, might themselves be viewed as ill-suited, hyperbolic choices lacking the accurate nuance that Podhoretz so often asserts as an essential deliberative criterion. Morality and idealism are not offered to leftists in the same way that Podhoretz now performs these criteria for the Right, drawing exclusive political boundaries for the convert.

By tracing the cumulative interactions between *BR*'s rhetorical resources and the conversion form, the author constructs an anti-rhetorical text. Bruce Bartlett argues that "the [conservative] movement's most sophisticated thinkers in the postwar era . . . came to the right from the far left."[187] Yet Podhoretz's tale asserts a rhetoric that is problematic for public thought. In the next chapter, I explore a political conversion narrative that, in many ways, integrated aspects of Chambers's and Podhoretz's discourses. It, too, illustrates another guise in which these tales may be told.

NOTES

1. Thomas B. Byers, "Hollywood," in *American Icons: An Encyclopedia of the People, Places, and Things That Have Shaped Our Culture*, ed. Dennis R. Hall and Susan G. Hall (Santa Barbara, CA: Greenwood, 2006), 347.

2. Michiko Kakutani, "Of the Words of War and the War of Ideas," *New York Times*, October 26, 2007, E37. Others have also called Podhoretz "godfather of the neoconservative movement." Nicole Gaouette, "Middle East Peace," *CQ Researcher*, January 21, 2005, 60. Crosston says of Podhoretz and Irving Kristol: "[I]t was largely their most famous works which provided a foundational blueprint for contemporary neoconservatives," finding that they played a part in the emergence of President Bush's post-9/11 "war on terror." Matthew Crosston, "Neoconservative Democratization in Theory and Practice: Developing Democrats or Raising Radical Islamists," *International Politics* 46 (2009): 301–2.

3. Harry Kreisler, "The Battle over Ideas: Conversation with Norman Podhoretz, Former Editor, *Commentary*," Institute of International Studies, University of California at Berkeley, http://globetrotter.berkeley.edu/conversations/Podhoretz/podhoretz-con2.html, 4. Neoconservatism's other founder, Irving Kristol, says that the concept and movement "aims to infuse American bourgeois orthodoxy with a new self-conscious intellectual vigor while dispelling the feverish mélange of gnostic humors that, for more than a century now, has suffused our political beliefs and has tended to convert them into political religions." Irving Kristol, *Reflections of a Neoconservative* (New York: Basic Books, 1983), xiv–xv. Tomes writes that "although neoconservatism took several years to develop its full identity, the direction it assumed at the end of the Vietnam War was roughly an inversion of what the democratic socialists were doing. Neoconservatives tended to turn away from the internal agenda, feeling that welfare statism had run its course, and that laissez-faire capitalism was preferable to planned economies. It also sought to reestablish effective control of foreign policy after the war in Vietnam ended." Robert R. Tomes, *Apocalypse Then: American Intellectuals and the Vietnam War* (New York: New York University Press, 1998), 227. It is important not to equate " 'neo' as a synonym for 'ultra.'. . . [N]eoconservatives for a long time occupied a place on the spectrum clearly to the left of the average Republican." David Greenberg, "Zealots of Our Time," *American Prospect* 19 (2008): 39. Others involved in the formation of U.S. neoconservatism included Daniel Bell, Daniel Patrick Moynihan, Midge Decter, Michael Novak, Gertrude Himmelfarb, and Peter Berger. Stefan Halper and Jonathan Clarke, *America Alone: The Neo-Conservatives and the Global Order* (New York: Cambridge University Press, 2004), 41. Harvard professors Edward Banfield, Nathan Glazer, Seymour Martin Lipset, and UCLA scholar James Q. Wilson were also critical players in the movement's development. Carol A. Horton, *Race and the Making of American Liberalism* (New York: Oxford University Press, 2005), 201. See also Lawson H. Bowling, "The New Party of Memory: Intellectual Origins of Neoconservatism, 1945–1960" (PhD diss., Columbia University, 1990). While neoconservatives have greatly influenced presidential administrations over the last few decades, they have also been responsible for the development of a number of prominent think tanks instrumental in developing approaches to issues such as national education policy. Lauren E. McDonald, "The Rise of Conservative Think Tanks: The Debate over Ideas, Research and Strategy in Public Education Policy" (PhD diss., City University of New York, 2008).

4. Some critics rebuke Podhoretz for this fact: "Podhoretz has kept demanding vindication of his claims so obsessively that he's nearly made himself the Rodney Dangerfield of public intellectuals." Jim Sleeper, "Yankee Doodle Dandy: Making It in America while Breaking Ranks and Settling Scores," *Los Angeles Times*, July 2, 2000, 1. "After more than 30 years at *Commentary*'s helm one would think that Podhoretz had long ago consigned his former life as a man on the left to the memory bin, but this is hardly the case." Sanford Pinsker, review of *Ex-Friends*, *Virginia Review Quarterly* 76 (2000): 184. Reviewing one of Podhoretz's later autobiographies, *Ex-Friends*, Leonard finds that "we've also heard it all, twice before. . . . Thrice told, this Pilgrim's Progress . . . somehow coarsens." John Leonard, review of *Ex-Friends*, by Norman Podhoretz, *Nation*, March 22, 1999, par. 13–14.

5. L. Edwards, "Modern Tomes," par. 3.

6. Jonathan Tobin, "The Children of *Commentary*, *Jewish World Review*, February 24, 2004, under "Breaking Ranks," www.jewishworldreview.com/0204/tobin_2004_02_24.php3?printer_friendly, par. 2.

7. Norman Podhoretz, *Breaking Ranks* (New York: Harper & Row, 1979), 109.

8. Podhoretz describes his first book as a "confessional work." Ibid., 223.

9. Norman Podhoretz, *Making It* (New York: Harper & Row, 1967), 19–25. Podhoretz says that he is interested in using the "metaphor of 'conversions,'" to explain his upward rise among New York's intellectuals. Having grown up in a parochial Jewish community, he writes that "wearing a suit from de Pinna would for me have been something like the social equivalent of a conversion to Christianity." Of his college years, he writes: "I suppose one might speak of a conversion in describing what happened to me at Columbia" and calls it "my conversion to 'culture.'" Ibid., 8, 30, 42, 47, 105. Different than *Breaking Ranks*, Podhoretz clarifies that when he wrote *Making It* he was still a leader and member of the radical movement. Podhoretz, *Breaking Ranks*, 224.

10. See Alexander Bloom, *Prodigal Sons: The New York Intellectuals and Their World* (New York: Oxford University Press, 1986).

11. Podhoretz, *Breaking Ranks*, 27. See also Jonah Raskin, *American Scream: Allen Ginsberg* (Berkeley: University of California Press, 2004), 202.

12. Benjamin Frankel, ed., "Norman Podhoretz, American Editor, *Commentary*, 1960–," in *The Cold War, 1945–1991* (Farmington Hills, MI: Gale, 2009).

13. Podhoretz, *Breaking Ranks*, 78. See also Ruth R. Wisse, "The Jewishness of *Commentary*," in *Commentary in American Life*, ed. Murray Friedman (Philadelphia: Temple University Press, 2005), 59.

14. Podhoretz, *Breaking Ranks*, 29.

15. William L. O'Neill and Kenneth T. Jackson, eds., "Podhoretz, Norman Harold," in *The Scribner Encyclopedia of American Lives Thematic Series: The 1960s* (Farmington Hills, MI: Gale, 2009), par. 9. See also George Nash, "Joining the Ranks: Commentary and American Conservatism," in *Commentary in American Life*, ed. Murray Friedman (Philadelphia: Temple University Press, 2005), 152.

16. Ruth R. Wisse, "The Maturing of *Commentary* and of the Jewish Intellectual," *Jewish Social Studies* 3 (1997): 33.

17. Andrew J. Bacevich, review of *The Norman Podhoretz Reader*, by Thomas L. Jeffers, ed., *Wilson Quarterly* 28 (2004): 127–28. *Commentary*'s writers were also hired by the Reagan administration. An article in *Commentary* on the dangers of appeasing totalitarians led to the appointment of author Daniel Patrick Moynihan as U.S. ambassador to the United Nations by President Gerald Ford. Less than a decade later, a similar piece in *Commentary* propelled Jeane Kirkpatrick from academia into the same post. Tobin, "The Children," under "Founding a Movement," par. 3. "Podhoretz and other new revisionists attempted to shift guilt for the war from those who instigated and pursued it to those who opposed it." Keith Beattie, *The Scar That Binds: American Culture and the Vietnam War* (New York: New York University Press, 1998), 21.

18. Arnold Beichman, "Ex-Friends," *Policy Review* 94 (1999): 82–88.

19. "Awards: Presidential Medal of Freedom," *Facts on File World News Digest*, July 8, 2004, *World News Digest*.

20. Matthew Duss, "Giuliani's War Cabinet," *American Prospect*, September 25, 2007, www.prospect.org/cs/articles?article=giulianis_war_cabinet.

21. Mark Gerson, "Norman's Conquest," *Policy Review* 74 (1995), under "The Implosion of Liberalism," www.hoover.org/publications/policyreview/3564402.html (no longer available), par. 4–5. Kesler finds "Podhoretz turned *Commentary* into . . . a crucible in which Reaganite arguments, especially on foreign policy, were annealed and honed." Charles R. Kesler, "An American Original," *National Review*, March 8, 2004, www.nationalreview.com/books/kesler200403251147.asp (no longer available), par. 13. See also Stephen Steinberg, "Nathan Glazer and the Assassination of Affirmative Action," *New Politics* 9 (2003), http://nova.wpunj.edu/newpolitics/issue35/Steinberg35.htm.

22. James C. Roberts, "2002: A Banner Year for Conservative Books," *Human Events*, November 18, 2002, 26.

23. Podhoretz, *Breaking Ranks*, 321.

24. During an interview, Podhoretz states one reason for writing *BR*: "because of the children . . . not only of my own children, but of children and young people all around." "Norman Podhoretz," *Biography Resource Center* (Farmington Hills, MI: Gale, 2009), par. 26.

25. Podhoretz, *Breaking Ranks*, 112.

26. Ibid., 180–88, 256.

27. Podhoretz says that his book is meant to be a message to intellectual as well as Jewish communities on this matter. Ibid., 329.

28. Ibid., 221, 124. For more discussion of the controversy that "My Negro Problem" generated and in relation to Podhoretz's texts in general, see Thomas L. Jeffers, "Norman Podhoretz's Discourses on America," *Hudson Review* 54 (2001): 202–28. See also Jerry Watts, *Amiri Baraka* (New York: New York University, 2001), 42–43; Thandeka, "The Cost of Whiteness," *Afrocentric News*, 1999, www.afrocentricnews.com/html/cost_of_whiteness.html, par. 24, 30; Stanford M. Lyman, "Gunnar Myrdal's *An American Dilemma* after a Half Centu-

ry: Critics and Anticritics," *International Journal of Politics, Culture and Society* 12 (1998): 337.

29. Podhoretz, *Breaking Ranks*, 315. Podhoretz details other critics such as Philip Rahv, who turned "polemical guns on us for having moved to the Right." Ibid., 305.

30. See Baughman et al., eds., "Introduction."

31. Podhoretz, *Breaking Ranks*, 6.

32. Ibid., 320; emphasis added.

33. Ibid., 3.

34. Marcus Klein, review of *Ex-Friends*, by Norman Podhoretz, *New Leader*, December 14, 1998, 20; Rick Perlstein, "Second Read," *Columbia Journalism Review* 6 (2004), http://cjrarchives.org/issues/2004/6/perlstein-tribe.asp (no longer available), par. 23.

35. Kramer says that Podhoretz's political predictions have been historically accurate and convincing and that Podhoretz is right about the "opportunism and cowardice" that the radical movements of the 1960s fostered among the intelligentsia. Hilton Kramer, *"Breaking Ranks: A Political Memoir* by Norman Podhoretz," *New Republic*, November 17, 1979, 34. Johnson, too, praises Podhoretz for not being "vengeful." He "is a witness of truth," whose battle against the *New York Review of Books* has been accurate and illuminating. Paul Johnson, "Shock Troops," *Spectator* (February 9, 1980), 17. Hollander finds *BR* persuasive, citing that in Podhoretz's conversion from radicalism to neoconservatism, "no crude personal interest was involved; he gained little in any objective sense, and suffered much abuse, the loss of friendships, and ostracism without any apparent compensating gain in status, power, or material wealth." Paul Hollander, *"Breaking Ranks: A Political Memoir," Contemporary Sociology* 10 (1981): 440–41. Diamond states that Podhoretz writes with a "refreshing voice" and "unrelenting iconoclasm" in *BR*. Glenn Diamond, "Norman Podhoretz and Jack Kerouac," *Los Angeles Times*, January 24, 1987, 2. Van Den Haag believes *BR* is an intriguing, educational, candid look at a life in politics. Ernest Van Den Haag, "Breaking Bones," *National Review*, February 8, 1980, 163. Freedman says that "it takes guts to do what Norman Podhoretz did. He looked at Reality and saw that the liberal left political and social views of all his friends were mistaken. . . . [H]e waged a War of Ideas." Shalom Freedman, "He Heard the Sound of His Own Drummer," Amazon.com, www.amazon.com/Breaking-Ranks-Political-Memoir-Colophon/dp/0060908165. Edwards believes that *BR* has been most effective in "destroying the automatic equation of liberalism with intelligence and of 'progressivism' with progress." L. Edwards, "Modern Tomes," under "Breaking Ranks," par. 1.

36. *Time* magazine's Edwin Warner says that *BR* has "sometimes powerful and sometimes sluggish prose" but has "a sweeping theme. At a time of testing, the Commentary group upheld standards of civilized discourse and thereby earned an honorable place in the history of American letters. They behaved as intellectuals are supposed to." Edwin Warner, "Radical Retreat," *Time*, October 29, 1979, www.time.com/time/printout/0,8816,917005,00.html. An *Atlantic Monthly* review states that "the book has an odd tone, as if Podhoretz knew perfectly well that the 'letter to my son' motif was a charade," demonstrating the author's "specialty of high-risk memoirs," yet is still "a courageous and thoughtful piece of work." *"Breaking Ranks," Atlantic Monthly*, November 1979, 94. Epstein opines that *BR* is far better than Podhoretz's previous book: "[I]t is more candid, more courageous, written with a better humor and a larger heart" but engages in too much "preening" and "elements of self-glorification." Joseph Epstein, "Remaking It," *New York Times*, October 21, 1979, www.nytimes.com/books/99/02/21/specials/podhoretz-breaking.html, par. 13, 21. Another review states that "although less startling and certainly less entertaining than his 1967 *Making It*, this current work does show us the transformation of a radical who moved to the right," but warns that it is riddled with "heavy and sententious prose. It is an uninspiring life history. . . . Podhoretz and the neo-conservatives are struggling in their moralistic ways to understand the connection between tradition and liberty. What does one keep from the old, what does one expect from the new?" Robert S. Fogarty, "Editorial: Liberty and Security," *Antioch Review* 38 (1980): 3–4. Annan, while generally positive about the book, finds that Podhoretz focuses too much on culture, neglecting a great deal of relevant, historical political theory (from Aristotle through Montesquieu) grounded in concepts such as consent, liberty, and justice. Noel Annan, "An Editor and His Odyssey," *Times Literary Supplement*, April 25, 1980, 473.

37. Romano calls Norman Podhoretz a "Sixtomaniac" for his 1960s obsessions: "the sufferer . . . understands the '50s or '70s only in relation to the Sixties," has "nostalgia for the polarization of '60s politics" and "is 'for' an America that does not vitiate its strength by criticizing itself." John Romano, "Making Politics Simple," *New Leader*, November 5, 1979, 16–17. Lehmann-Haupt thinks that Podhoretz spends far too long defending his previous book, *Making It* (in nearly eighty pages of *BR*) and presents too coherent an account, where the author is too "eager to explain absolutely everything." Christopher Lehmann-Haupt, "Books of the Times," *New York Times*, October 24, 1979, C27. Rothbard chastises Podhoretz for being an intellectual "whose sole literary output is a series of autobiographies celebrating his own life and thought. . . . [A] central purpose shines through: to show how many important people Podhoretz has known, how he has rubbed elbows with people he, at least, considers great." Murray N. Rothbard, "The Evil of Banality," *Inquiry*, December 10, 1979, 26. Levin writes that the book "evokes mainly boredom," "does not succeed in demonstrating his intellectual rigor," and has a "condescending tone and numerous snide remarks about other writers and politicians." James Levin, *"Breaking Ranks: A Political Memoir," Library Journal*, January 1, 1980, 96. Lekachman finds it a worse book than *Making It*. Robert Lekachman, "Mean to Me," *Nation*, November 10, 1979, 469–70. Krim thinks that *BR* suffers from a "lack of humor" and other qualities like the "fierceness, the wholeheartedness, with which he has rushed into the straitlaced clothes waiting for him and the way he has defiantly torched all those bridges to his past." Seymour Krim, "Commentary on Podhoretz," *Book World*, November 4, 1979, 7. Ingwerson finds that "unfortunately, Mr. Podhoretz's keen mind is more that of editor than writer. As a result, this book reads like an extended magazine editorial, without even chapter titles to help focus the reader's attention," and "it never steps from the plane of the purely political interplay of ideas," except for his "personal appearance in the postscript." Marshall Ingwerson, "A Radical Speaks Out," *Christian Science Monitor*, December 3, 1979, B7. Hitchens, perhaps the least sparing of all, calls Podhoretz a "Born-Again Conformist" who has a habit of "martyrdom." Christopher Hitchens, "Born-Again Conformist," *New Statesman*, March 21, 1980, 437.

38. Berger says that within Protestantism, these demands have involved a "cognitive bargaining," where, for instance, the Apostle Paul may now be viewed as wrong about his views of women but right about sinners and repentance. P. Berger, *The Heretical Imperative*, 89, 91–92.

39. Ibid., 93–99.

40. See, e.g., the critique of President Nixon's speech in K. Campbell, "An Exercise in the Rhetoric of Mythical America."

41. Asen, "Ideology, Materiality, and Counterpublicity," 270.

42. Podhoretz, *Breaking Ranks*, 175–78.

43. The examples are too numerous to list completely, but can be found in Podhoretz's descriptions of others, e.g., that intellectuals conduct superb analyses, that Lyndon Johnson was defeated by intellectual ideas, that leftist movements no longer felt responsible to the mind and culture, and more. Ibid., 60, 139, 140, 251, 328.

44. Ibid., 326.

45. Podhoretz complains about *Time* magazine too often blaming the United States's problems on the Enlightenment, an assertion that may hearken back to Chambers's work with the magazine. Podhoretz also positions opposition to rationality and the Enlightenment as a quality of the political Left. Ibid., 89, 311.

46. Ibid., 95.

47. Bormann calls the *"Pauline conversion fantasy"* a historical archetype of the West involving "a worldly sinful man struck by a shattering moment when he was visited by a miraculous experience of the supernatural." It is an "emotional and mystical experience. The more dramatic that experience, the more likely it was to be creditable." Bormann, *The Force of Fantasy*, 7, 31, 86–87; emphasis in original.

48. Podhoretz, *Breaking Ranks*, 54.

49. Ibid., 16; emphasis in original.

50. Kreisler, "The Battle over Ideas," 2.

51. Cited in James Neuchterlein, "This Time: Neoconservative Redux," *First Things* 66 (1996): 7.

52. Podhoretz, *Breaking Ranks*, 93.

53. Burke, *A Grammar of Motives*, 171–72.
54. Podhoretz, *Breaking Ranks*, 209–10.
55. For example, Podhoretz talks about the respect that figures such as Humphrey and Stevenson deserved from the intellectual community. Both John F. Kennedy and Robert Kennedy are targeted for not being interested in ideas. In particular, Podhoretz feels intellectually compromised in the presence of RFK. Ibid., 97–98, 103, 258.
56. Podhoretz also lists James Burnham, Will Herberg, John Dos Passos, and Max Eastman. Ibid., 6; emphasis in original. In other parts of *BR*, Podhoretz draws inspiration from political converts such as R. H. S. Crossman, William Phillips, and Nathan Glazer. Ibid., 138, 286.
57. Ibid., 195, 198.
58. As a result, Podhoretz describes some vulnerable populations such as black youth, who he says inaccurately attributed their problems to whites. The author uses terms of health, plagues, illness, and cures to characterize these beliefs. Ibid., 362.
59. Ibid., 329; emphasis added.
60. Ibid., 17; emphasis in original. Craig's positive review of *BR* affirms this vision; "as only someone who has so deeply lived 'the fevers and plagues of the last two decades' could, Podhoretz defines and explores life on that plane where intellectual abstractions and human personalities interact to create culture. . . . Podhoretz stands as a force for sanity among the intellectuals and beyond." Jane Larkin Craig, "*Breaking Ranks: A Political Memoir*," *Saturday Review*, October 27, 1979, 41.
61. Ibid., 361; emphasis in original.
62. Podhoretz, *Breaking Ranks*, 321.
63. Yet Podhoretz has also taken a more relaxed stance toward religion and politics in later life, especially in his book *The Prophets: Who They Were, What They Are*, where he applies biblical exegeses to contemporary political issues. Norman Podhoretz, *The Prophets: Who They Were, What They Are* (New York: Free Press, 2002). See also Judith Shulevitz, "Norman Podhoretz's Old-Time Religion," *New York Times Book Review*, November 3, 2002, 31. According to Nash, in the 1990s Podhoretz became more interested in religious issues after the end of the Cold War, as "perceived barriers between 'secular' neoconservatives and 'religious' traditional conservatives were fading away. In no respect was this rapprochement more remarkable than in the willingness of Commentary in the 1990s to defend another crucial part of the conservative coalition: the religious Right." This development dovetailed with the Christian Right's increasing support for the State of Israel. Nash, "Joining the Ranks," 167–68.
64. Rousseau, *The Social Contract, Book IV*, 102.
65. Podhoretz, *Breaking Ranks*, 321.
66. Ibid., 27.
67. U.S. conservatism incorporates many competing voices. The acceptance of the welfare state and a general antipathy toward religion in politics would present problems for neoconservatives within a loose Republican coalition. In particular, the traditionalist "paleoconservatives" have often attacked neoconservatives, "who despite their recent rightward journey remained essentially secular, Wilsonian, and welfare-statist in their philosophy." Nash, "Joining the Ranks," 162.
68. Podhoretz, *Breaking Ranks*, 283.
69. Philip Rahv and Mary McCarthy are described in this way. Ibid., 274, 306.
70. Ibid., 111.
71. Ibid., 342.
72. See O'Leary, "Apocalyptic Argument and the Anticipation of Catastrophe."
73. Podhoretz, *Breaking Ranks*, 63–65.
74. Ibid., 311–12; emphasis added.
75. Ibid., 49.
76. Ibid., 16.
77. Ibid., 329, 364–65; emphasis in original.
78. Ibid., 322.
79. On reason as a subset of broader human symbol use, see Susanne K. Langer, *Philosophy in a New Key*, 3rd ed. (1942; repr., Cambridge, MA: Harvard University Press, 1996).
80. Podhoretz, *Breaking Ranks*, 268.

81. Ibid., 269.
82. See also ibid., 202–3.
83. Kramer, "Breaking Ranks," 34–35.
84. Van Den Haag, "Breaking Bones," 164.
85. J. Craig, "Breaking Ranks," 41.
86. Albert S. Lindemann, "Podhoretz in Retirement: A Report on the Morality of Friendship," www.writing.upenn.edu/~afilreis/50s/podhoretz-review.html.
87. Podhoretz, *Breaking Ranks*, 45.
88. Ibid., 175–76.
89. Ibid., 224, 329.
90. Podhoretz's other autobiographies establish similar concerns, particularly *Ex-Friends*. See Norman Podhoretz, *Ex-Friends: Falling Out with Allen Ginsberg, Lionel and Diana Trilling, Lillian Hellman, Hannah Arendt, and Norman Mailer* (New York: Free Press, 1999), 7.
91. Podhoretz, *Breaking Ranks*, 249.
92. Ibid., 142, 262.
93. Robert L. Scott and Donald K. Smith, "The Rhetoric of Confrontation," *Quarterly Journal of Speech* 56 (1969): 8.
94. Podhoretz, *Breaking Ranks*, 229.
95. Ibid., 198.
96. Ibid., 28.
97. Ibid., 29, 310.
98. I draw this point from Burke's explanation of "motion" versus "action," and Karlyn Kohrs Campbell's distinction between behavioristic and symbolic theories of communication. Kenneth Burke, "(Nonsymbolic) Motion/(Symbolic) Action," *Critical Inquiry* 4 (1978): 809–38; Karlyn Kohrs Campbell, "The Ontological Foundations of Rhetorical Theory," *Philosophy and Rhetoric* 3 (1970): 97–108.
99. Podhoretz, *Breaking Ranks*, 28.
100. Ibid., 155.
101. Ibid., 197–98.
102. Ibid., 201.
103. See also ibid., 208–9, 230, 233–34, 327–28.
104. Ibid., 208–9.
105. Ibid., 248.
106. Ibid., 155. *BR* also lists a number of other ways that deliberation turned awry during the 1960s. See Ibid., 215.
107. Sunstein, "Deliberative Trouble?," 113.
108. Podhoretz, *Breaking Ranks*, 44.
109. Ibid., 141–42.
110. Ibid., 177.
111. For more on dissociative argumentation in conversion accounts, see Waisanen, "Political Conversion as Intrapersonal Argument."
112. Podhoretz, *Breaking Ranks*, 234; emphases added.
113. Ibid.; emphasis added.
114. Ibid.
115. Ibid., 9.
116. On the comic frame, see Burke, *Attitudes toward History*, 106. For communication studies examining the adequacy of the comic frame in social movement contexts, see A. Cheree Carlson, "Gandhi and the Comic Frame: 'Ad Bellum Purificandum,'" *Quarterly Journal of Speech* 74 (1986): 310–22; A. Cheree Carlson, "Limitations on the Comic Frame: Some Witty American Women of the Nineteenth Century," *Quarterly Journal of Speech* 78 (1988): 16–32; Adrienne Christiansen and Jeremy Hanson, "Comedy as Cure for Tragedy: ACT UP and the Rhetoric of AIDS," *Quarterly Journal of Speech* 82 (1996): 157–70; Kimberly A. Powell, "The Association of Southern Women for the Prevention of Lynching: Strategies of a Movement in the Comic Frame," *Communication Quarterly* 43 (1995): 86–99; Steven Schwarze, "Environmental Melodrama," *Quarterly Journal of Speech* 92 (2006): 239–61.
117. Burke, *Attitudes toward History*.

118. Podhoretz, *Breaking Ranks*, 213.
119. Ibid., 216.
120. R. Scott and D. Smith, "The Rhetoric of Confrontation," 8.
121. Franklyn S. Haiman, "The Rhetoric of the Streets: Some Legal and Ethical Considerations," *Quarterly Journal of Speech* 53 (1967): 99–114.
122. Theodore Otto Windt, Jr., "The Diatribe: Last Resort for Protest," *Quarterly Journal of Speech* 58 (1972): 8. A host of other studies have debated the merits of communication practices developed during this era. See Karlyn Kohrs Campbell, "The Rhetoric of Radical Black Nationalism: A Case Study in Self-Conscious Criticism," *Central States Speech Journal* 22 (1971): 151–60; Robert Cathcart, "Movements: Confrontation as Rhetorical Form," *Southern Speech Journal* 43 (1978): 233–47; John Cragen, "Rhetorical Strategy, A Dramatistic Interpretation and Application," *Central States Speech Journal* 26 (1975): 4–11; Justin Gustainis and Dan Hahn, "While the Whole World Watched: Rhetorical Failures of the Anti-war Protest," *Communication Quarterly* 36 (1988): 203–16; King, "The Rhetoric of Power Maintenance"; Randall Lake, "Enacting Red Power: The Consummatory Function in Native American Protest Rhetoric," *Quarterly Journal of Speech* 69 (1983): 127–42; John Murphy, "Domesticating Dissent: The Kennedys and the Freedom Rides," *Communication Monographs* 59 (1992): 61–78; Brant Short, "Earth First! and the Rhetoric of Moral Confrontation," *Communication Studies* 42 (1991): 172–88; Theodore Otto Windt, Jr., "Administrative Rhetoric: An Undemocratic Response to Protest," *Communication Quarterly* 30 (1982): 245–50; David Zarefsky, "Civil Rights and Civil Conflict: Presidential Communication in Crisis," *Central States Speech Journal* 34 (1983): 59–66.
123. Podhoretz says that lots of parties and groups existed in the 1960s movement, but that it still managed to establish its influence over many people despite this decentralization. Podhoretz, *Breaking Ranks*, 211.
124. Alberto Melucci, *Challenging Codes: Collective Action in the Information Age* (New York: Cambridge University Press, 1996).
125. Lehmann-Haupt, "Books of the Times," C27.
126. Kramer, "*Breaking Ranks*," 33.
127. P. Johnson, "Shock Troops," 18.
128. Richard John Neuhaus, "Liberalism without a Left, Conservatism without Delusions," *First Things* (December 1999), under "While We're at It," www.firstthings.com/article.php3?id_article=3242, par. 10.
129. Hollander, "*Breaking Ranks*," 441.
130. Annan, "An Editor and His Odyssey," 473.
131. Hitchens, "Born-Again Radical," 437, 438.
132. "*Breaking Ranks*," *Atlantic Monthly*, 94.
133. Lekachman, "Mean to Me," 469.
134. Bruce Clayton, "Memoir as Social Criticism Rings with Passion," *Atlanta Journal-Constitution*, August 6, 2000, L6.
135. Romano, "Making Politics Simple," 17.
136. Podhoretz, *Breaking Ranks*, 192.
137. "Accuracy," Dictionary.com, 2018, http://dictionary.reference.com/browse/accuracy, par. 1.
138. See, e.g., Stephen E. Toulmin, *The Uses of Argument* (New York: Cambridge University Press, 2003); Wayne Brockriede and Douglas Ehninger, "Toulmin on Argument: An Interpretation and Application," *Quarterly Journal of Speech* 46 (1960): 44–53.
139. "Norman Podhoretz," under "Sidelights," par. 24, 47. In *Making It*, Podhoretz says that it was his purpose "to assert without apology that *my* experience, however unrepresentative or peripheral or exotic it might seem, was a valid sample of life in America which could be used to illuminate even the most centrally significant of American problems." Podhoretz, *Making It*, 345; emphasis in original. Rosin says: "Norman Podhoretz's gift—or curse, depending on how you look at it—is to see himself at the center of history . . . as the paragon of an age." Hanna Rosin, "Oedipus & Podhoretz," *New York Magazine*, December 29, 1997, http://nymag.com/nymetro/news/media/features/1968/, par. 14.
140. Kreisler, "The Battle over Ideas," 2.

116   *Chapter 2*

141. Podhoretz, *Breaking Ranks*, 307.
142. Ibid., 195.
143. Ibid., 210.
144. Ibid., 85.
145. See, e.g., George Packer, "Sir Vidia's Shadow," *Dissent* 46 (1999): 99–104; Christopher Hitchens, review of *Ex-Friends*, by Norman Podhoretz, *Harper's*, June 1999, 73–76; Nicholas Lemann, review of *Ex-Friends*, by Norman Podhoretz, *Washington Monthly*, January/February 1999, 37–40.
146. Podhoretz, *Breaking Ranks*, 125.
147. Ibid., 125.
148. Ibid., 167–69.
149. Ibid., 71–72.
150. Ibid., 77.
151. U.S. Bureau of the Census, Current Population Reports, Series P-60, No. 133, *Characteristics of the Population below the Poverty Level: 1980* (Washington, DC: U.S. Government Printing Office, 1982), 1.
152. Podhoretz, *Breaking Ranks*, 190.
153. Ibid., 216.
154. Ibid., 336.
155. See Lawrence L. Langer, *Holocaust Testimonies: The Ruins of Memory* (New Haven, CT: Yale University Press, 1991).
156. Podhoretz, *Breaking Ranks*, 352.
157. Ibid., 287.
158. Ibid., 329. Another exigency that Podhoretz responds to (regarding writings by Truman Capote, Gore Vidal, and others) is inaccurate anti-Semitic claims about the overrepresentation of Jews in universities, business, and other professions. Ibid., 333.
159. Ibid., 219.
160. Robert Talisse and Scott F. Aikin, "Two Forms of the Straw Man," *Argumentation* 20 (2006): 345–52. For more on the straw man, see George Y. Bizer, Shirel M. Kozak, and Leigh Ann Holterman, "The Persuasiveness of the Straw Man Rhetorical Technique," *Social Influence* 4 (2009): 216–30.
161. Talisse and Aikin, "Two Forms of the Straw Man," 350; emphasis in original.
162. Ibid., 350.
163. Podhoretz, *Breaking Ranks*, 46.
164. Ibid., 127–28.
165. Ibid., 23.
166. P. Johnson, "Shock Troops," 18.
167. Van Den Haag, "Breaking Bones," 163.
168. Romano, "Making Politics Simple," 17.
169. Hollander, "Breaking Ranks," 441.
170. Leonard, review of *Ex-Friends*, par. 18–19.
171. Diamond, "Norman Podhoretz and Jack Kerouac," 2.
172. Lehmann-Haupt, "Books of the Times," C27.
173. Krim, "Commentary on Podhoretz," 7.
174. Rothbard, "The Evil of Banality," 27.
175. Perlstein, "Second Read," par. 23–24.
176. Romano, "Making Politics Simple," 16.
177. Hitchens, "Born-Again Conformist," 436. Reviewing Podhoretz's later book *Ex-Friends*, Abrams takes issue with the author's opportunistic choice of covering six ex-friends who were widely known, over and above the choice of less famous others. Abrams writes that "those, like me, too young to have directly experienced many of the events in question would have to do a vast amount of work to validate his claims," and with the exception of one ex-friend, each is dead and thus unable to answer Podhoretz's assertions. Nathan Abrams, "Stormin' Norman Strikes Back," *H-Net Reviews*, January 2001, www.h-net.org/reviews/showrev.php?id=4856. In another review of *Ex-Friends*, Lindemann writes that Podhoretz's characterizations of his former friends denies the diverse range of views between them; they are not all

"moral nihilists," and "his language suggests more than mere tactical differences or normal political jabs and punches—he refers to pollution, sewers and cesspools." Lindemann, "Podhoretz in Retirement," par. 13.

178. Annan, "An Editor and His Odyssey," 473.

179. Neil Postman, *Crazy Talk, Stupid Talk: How We Defeat Ourselves by the Way We Talk, and What to Do about It* (New York: Delacorte, 1976), 170–71.

180. In Robert Koehler, "Neo-Fantasies and Ancient Myths: Adam Curtis on *The Power of Nightmares*," *Cinema Scope* 23 (n.d.), www.cinema-scope.com/cs23/contents.htm (no longer available).

181. Podhoretz, *Breaking Ranks*, 23.

182. This problem echoes another concern—that Podhoretz's pitches for self-interest and ambition-as-virtue are narcissistic "whopping non-sequitur[s]" given the demands of a pluralistic society. Rothbard, "The Evil of Banality," 27–28.

183. Wayne C. Booth, "The Rhetoric of Fundamentalist Conversion Stories," in *Fundamentalisms Comprehended*, ed. Martin E. Marty and R. Scott Appleby (Chicago: University of Chicago Press, 1995), 374.

184. Judith Clavir Albert and Stewart Edward Albert, eds., *The Sixties Papers: Documents of a Rebellious Decade* (New York: Praeger, 1984), xv.

185. See Burke, "(Nonsymbolic) Motion," 809–38.

186. See Melucci, *Challenging Codes*; Simons, "Requirements, Problems, and Strategies."

187. Bartlett, "Kristol Clear," par. 5.

Chapter Three

Political Conversion as Generational Induction

David Horowitz's Radical Son

No observer of U.S. politics over the last few decades could survey the period without running into writer and activist David Horowitz. Once an avid Marxist, Horowitz drew the political Right's ire. Now a conservative, Horowitz leverages his past experience toward Republican causes. Perhaps more than any other American advocate, Horowitz traffics in political conversion, marketing the concept as an industry. Horowitz created the term "second thoughts" to represent his move from the left to the right. He has frequently assembled former radicals and liberals to recount their experiences and underscore lessons learned in public gatherings, once even amassing 25 ex-radicals and 200 attendees at a "Second Thoughts Conference" in Washington, DC.[1] Political conversions to conservatism are further promoted through his publishing imprint, Second Thoughts Books.[2]

This chapter analyzes Horowitz's autobiography *Radical Son* (hereafter, *RS*), which details his political conversion. Like the works of Chambers and Podhoretz, *RS* has influenced leaders at the highest levels of government. When George W. Bush was a presidential contender, Horowitz's work constituted a third of the writings that Karl Rove made him read, especially as a foundation for associating the 1960s with modern social ills.[3] After reading *RS*, Bush remarked that "there was just a lot of history I remember from my early 20s come to life. . . . And here was somebody who blew the whistle."[4] Like the previous authors surveyed in this volume, Horowitz has been a major resource in the Republican Party.[5] Describing the Republican takeover of Congress in 1994, Horowitz stated that many of the elected party's "manifestos resonated with the second thoughts we had arrived at after leaving the radical cause."[6] Even President Reagan once joked with him, "I had second thoughts before you."[7]

Horowitz models his conversion on past leaders of the "second thoughts generation," such as Norman Podhoretz.[8] He characterizes himself as the Whittaker Chambers of his generation, due to the hate directed toward him as an ex-radical in a leftist culture.[9] These intertextual comparisons have also been reflected in audience reactions to the book; one *RS* reviewer asserts that "Horowitz is the Whittaker Chambers of our generation,"[10] and another confirms that "Horowitz's tale can easily be compared with Whittaker Chambers' Witness."[11]

Horowitz's rhetoric is foreshadowed in the book's title, *Radical Son: A Generational Odyssey*. Where Chambers's political conversion narrative is about a deductive, Manichaean political-religious odyssey, and Podhoretz enacts a reductive intellectual story, Horowitz uses an experiential, generation-focused journey to frame his transformation. In *RS*, the conversion form works with three rhetorical features: reflexivity, maturity, and psychological experience. Some sense of Horowitz's life and times is first necessary to understand these rhetorical moves.

HOROWITZ'S LIFE AND TIMES

Horowitz was born in New York City in 1939. The son of Communist activists, he spent some thirty years as a devoted Marxist. After completing an A.B. from Columbia University, an M.A. in English literature from the University of California at Berkeley, and further graduate study at the London School of Economics,[12] Horowitz has spent much of his career as a political writer and activist. He was the former director of publications and research at the Bertrand Russell Peace Foundation, and at the age of twenty-three wrote *The Free World Colossus*, a Marxist manifesto.[13] He was the former editor of the New Left's *Ramparts* magazine from 1969 to 1974, but after his political conversion founded and codirected the Second Thoughts Project in Washington, DC. He is also the founder, president, and codirector of the Center for the Study of Popular Culture, in Los Angeles, "whose purpose is to make inroads for conservatism in notoriously liberal Hollywood."[14]

Horowitz received a Teach Freedom Award from President Reagan and was an alternate delegate at the Republican Party National Convention in 1996.[15] In addition to writing many books,[16] Horowitz has conducted hundreds of interviews on television and radio stations across the United States. Of relevance to themes in this chapter, he has spent a good portion of his career attacking the university system. As a Marxist, he condemned universities as symbols of capitalist imperialism and for their adherence to the status quo during the 1960s. As a conservative, Horowitz now believes that universities are centers for socialist indoctrination. In books like *The Professors*, he has argued for an academic bill of rights to fight against campus speech codes.[17] His anti-university campaigns have often run into problems by relying on anecdotal evidence and questionable assumptions, however.[18] The author has initiated similarly controversial campaigns to oppose reparations to African Americans.[19] After September 11, 2001, Horowitz formed Discover the Networks, a website that identifies individuals and groups supporting leftist causes.[20] The site aims to show how "the political left has forged an 'unholy alliance' with terrorists"[21] and thus invites political conversions to the right. Horowitz states that "the events of 9/11 and their aftermath have produced a whole new generation of second thoughters in various stages of reassessment," as the Left switched from supporting oppressive regimes to "passivity in regard to the defense of America."[22]

Horowitz's earlier book *Destructive Generation*,[23] which he coauthored with Peter Collier, set in motion a series of "autobiographical wars over the Sixties" during the 1990s, putting the decade's legacies into question.[24] Nicolaus Mills argues that Horowitz's autobiography was part of a general attack on the 1960s aligned with movies such as *Forrest Gump* that are filled with clichés about the decade's movements.[25] *RS* sought to revise the claims of historians who found that 1960s discourse centered on demands for "equality," "personal empowerment," and "community as a locus for meaningful engagement in life and politics,"[26] using certain characterizations of the decade to undermine the 1990s Clinton administration and Democrats' policies.[27] Horowitz departs from typical Republican positions on a number of issues, though; he is pro-gay rights, pro-choice, and anti-censorship, and he often criticizes religious conservatives such as Jerry Falwell.[28]

As in *Breaking Ranks*, Vietnam and the 1960s counterculture figure prominently across the narrative. Horowitz attempts to set the record straight about the Black Panthers, with whom he worked for many years while a member of the New Left. A central turning point in the book (and hence in Horowitz's conversion) is when he comes to believe that the Panthers were responsible for a close friend's death.[29] He says that one of *RS*'s purposes is therefore to "name the murderers who are still at large, not just at large, but are celebrated in liberal culture."[30]

RS responds to some other political developments. After the fall of the Soviet Union in 1990, the United States became the planet's only affluent superpower, but regional conflicts occurred around the world in countries such as the former Yugoslavia.[31] President Clinton's two terms in office steered a moderate agenda through the period, despite his impeachment by the House of Representatives and subsequent acquittal by the Senate. Several other relevant events made national headlines in the 1990s, such as the Rodney King beating and Los Angeles riots, the O. J. Simpson trial, the Oklahoma City bombing, and the Columbine school shootings.

The 1990s further brought a new level of celebrity advocacy into the mainstream. An increasing individualism could be observed in U.S. culture, even in different religious faiths, where "Americans turned to religion more often to 'meet their spiritual needs' than out of a sense that worship and service was something they ought to do. Traditional Protestant—and some Catholic and Jewish—congregations became increasingly entertainment oriented."[32] Rather than using traditional or rational appeals as bases for faith, these religious shifts toward "inductive" and self-focused experiences play a role in Horowitz's analogous political conversion rhetoric.

RADICAL SON AS DELIBERATION

Generational rhetoric can be a powerful resource in public affairs. Scholars from Aristotle to Mannheim have engaged the topic.[33] Linking generational discourse to deliberation, G. Thomas Goodnight writes that "to study how reason enters into history . . . the generational potentialities of argumentation itself must be discussed."[34] Generational appeals can position historical experiences as arguments relevant to and limiting present choices.[35] Glenn Wallach finds that a discourse of "generations" has developed within U.S. public life over the last 300 years, especially relative to the concept of "youth."[36] American religionists in the past used the biblical figure of David to evoke a sense of generational responsibility among their audiences,[37] a meaning not lost in (David) Horowitz's autobiography. Horowitz writes that his book is intended to influence youth about to enter into politics and who stood to learn the most from its teachings.[38] In early American public discourse, communicators emphasized generations and youth by bringing together both traditional "conservative motivations" and more progressive "promise[s] of growth."[39] The development of the popular press fueled this trend and forwarded a gendered rhetoric in public culture, since the terms of generations and youth were both associated with masculinity.[40]

Fathers and sons have played an influential role in these messages. In biblical terms, "generation had always been linked to *fathers*."[41] Antebellum speakers went beyond biblical allusions by relating the concept of generations to the nation's "heroic" founding fathers, joining these notions with a conservative rhetoric underscoring how obedient their audiences should be to such models.[42] Over time, public figures delinked a language of generational posterity from its religious foundations and used it in more secular spheres to highlight allegiance to one's kin and the nation.[43] Following these historical developments, Horowitz intertwines a narrative about his conversion to nationalist, political conservatism with the tale of his family struggles—a generational rhetoric of the personal and political.

Beyond its generational focus, *RS* is an inductive political conversion narrative. Using modern Protestantism as a case, Peter Berger relates that inductive religious modes of thought find authority in inward turns and an open-minded "arguing from empirical evidence" that "tak[es] human experience as the starting point of religious reflection."[44] The liberal theologian Friedrich Schleiermacher exemplified this orientation, as he "oppose[d] the two predominant forms of religious thought in his day—a rigid Protestant orthodoxy, on the one hand, and Enlightenment rationalism, on the other hand," instead aiming for a faith of personal experience and feeling.[45]

The authors of *Habits of the Heart* similarly reveal that "through the peculiarly American phenomenon of revivalism, the emphasis on personal experience would eventually override all efforts at church discipline" in different faith congregations, coming to dominate religious understandings in the United States[46] This "radically individualist religion" may appear different from fundamentalist faith performances. In the former, "God is simply the self-magnified," and in the latter, "God confronts man from outside the universe"; the authors find that shifts between these two poles are not at all uncommon, as both orientations tend to use personal experience as a means to knowledge.[47] Horowitz uses personal experience in a fundamentalist way, crafting an inductive rhetoric of reflective ability, growth, and psychological experience to convince readers of his cause.

Many reviewers largely affirmed *RS*'s deliberative vision.[48] Others have been less sparing in their assessments.[49] Some critics found *RS* inaccurate on a number of historical details,[50] while some make a point that, unlike Chambers, Horowitz converted to conservatism at a time when he stood to gain much from the switch.[51] One of the most frequent objections to the book is that Horowitz maintains the same disposition as a conservative that he once had as a Marxist.[52]

With bearing upon public deliberation, the three resources of reflexivity, maturity, and psychological experience correspond with a rhetoric of reason, progress, and caring participation that have also been part of the Left's vocabulary. The three resources create an inductive generational vision, drawing from Horowitz's leftist experiences and acting as conservative appeals to open-mindedness, intellectual maturity, vindication for past actions, and a type of countercultural status. Like Chambers and Podhoretz, the conversion narrative in *RS* works in tandem with several rhetorical resources to create a totalizing, propagandistic discourse.

PERFECTING THE FORM: HOROWITZ'S RHETORICAL RESOURCES

A New Reflective Ability: Reflexivity

Conversion narratives typically characterize change through metaphors of rebirth,[53] with converts proceeding from one state of being to another. On the other hand, *RS* is less an ontological tale of being "born again" than an epistemological story, where Horowitz has "the ability to think again," in contrast with those who do not have this ability. In other words, Horowitz emphasizes *knowing* in his political conversion, using terms of "I reflected again"[54] rather than "I am born again" as a persuasive appeal. Moving beyond ontological understandings of conversion, Horowitz's autobiography shows how political conversions can be grounded in a form of epistemological authority.

Horowitz provides a key difference between other, more religious accounts of conversion and his own less religious, political conversion. While the former presumes an actor (typically God) who initiates change from outside a person, the latter, which may lack an external motivator, is located within the individual. This fits with current definitions of the term "reflexivity" as "the way in which, particularly in modern societies, people constantly examine their own practices and, in the light of that examination, alter them."[55] For example, Horowitz contrasts his own revisable, self-referential orientation with his father's inability to change.[56] To Horowitz, reflexivity is a resource for asserting one's linear path to self-validated truth rather than a collaborative way to test arguments with others.

The reflexivity strategy relates to the book's emphases on generations, youth, and maturity. Horowitz characterizes the inductive conversion as about one's journey from a condition of non-reflexivity (childish naïveté) to a redemptive condition of reflexivity (adult reflection). Epistemological words and images do much work in the account through the redemptive capacities of what he terms "second thoughts." This reflexivity theme is similar to Podhoretz's use of "intellectualism," but under Horowitz's terms, the resource is far less about "being" an intellectual than the special ability to "self-reflect" about one's experience. There are numerous ways to characterize reflexivity as a concept (although all involve a sense of "turning back"),[57] but I define reflexivity in Horowitz's account as *one's special ability or orientation for self-reflection and change*. This definition is partly constructed from Michael Lynch's insights into how academic reflexivity, despite its benefits, can be used as a privileging, epistemological "virtue and source of superior insight," or type of "critical weapon" in claims to understanding the social world.[58] Similarly, Horowitz's reflexivity implies a special, tolerant ability to see into the true, real nature of things.

Biographical work tends to mask its rhetorical moves by proceeding in realist form.[59] This narrative realism associates with what Orrin Judd describes as an "implication that liberalism, as a belief of the young, is a function of being uninformed and emotional, while conservatism, as a belief of the old, comes only with realistic experience."[60] Conservative values can be proposed as worthy simply because an author has taken the time to "think again" in this manner. If, as I have maintained throughout this book, the conversion form tends to have traditionally dogmatic attributes, reflexivity's connections with being "open-minded" give communicators using conversion a way to appear less than dogmatic in their rhetoric.[61] Such a move may be more difficult in strictly religious forms of conversion but is also less needed because in religious spheres, dogmatism is often expected, even celebrated. Given the pluralistic expectations of U.S. politics and the changing nature of public affairs, dogmatism is a difficult strategy to pursue. For example, Horowitz tells readers that he is against "those most certain in their conviction[s], [and] least impressed by ambiguity."[62] Unlike rigid leftists, the author uses the reflexive device to fashion himself as adaptable and reasonable. Reflexivity thus constitutes a civil-religious rhetorical strategy to meet a pluralistic exigency, maintaining the resonant conversion form while reconfiguring it in terms of a tolerant reflexivity more suited to modern political discourse.

Following the pattern of the conversion form, reflexivity is connected with an old and new political life.[63] Horowitz intensifies his newfound reflexivity: "[M]y second thoughts had led me through a night of the soul that involved the condemnation of my own life."[64] These penitent, confessionary terms (e.g., "soul") reproduce the historically sacred bases of the conversion narrative. At the same time, the text reflects more modern demands for rationality and flexibility in discourse. Once he makes his rightward turn, Horowitz explains to one of his former mentors on the left, "I did not turn my back on the struggle we once shared for trivial or *unreflected* reasons."[65] He establishes a new condition as a freethinker capable of revision—for example: "[Y]ears later, I saw that if I had been able to reflect rationally at the time, I would have recognized the truth."[66]

The political Left is cast as religious (as in Chambers's and Podhoretz's tales) but also irreflexive. Horowitz says that in fostering second thoughts, he came to see the leftist complaints as apocalyptic.[67] The author uses reflexivity to describe radicals/liberals as intolerant and lacking in an ability to think about their politics again, like obedient religionists who give little thought to their actions. When growing up, he feared seeing the local Communist Party frequently expel members for having second thoughts.[68] A fundamentalist religiosity and lack of reflexivity were exhibited by the inquisitions with which the Communist Party convicted its members of "thought crimes" and deviance.[69] The conversion story brings dichotomizing pressures to such explanations. The "thought crimes" framing reinforces the Left's inability to have second thoughts. It also underpins Horowitz's fight against censorship in university classrooms, associating totalitarian efforts against alternative thinking with leftist activism. In the face of Black Panther crimes, Horowitz proposes, for example, that "no radical leader proposed any second thoughts."[70] Only the choiceless "first thoughts" of Horowitz's old life are available to the Left, whose members cannot think a second time about new possibilities. On the other hand, Horowitz makes conservative second thoughts an act of volition, praising his and others' desire to even have second thoughts.[71]

The reflexivity device also promotes a network of reflexive advocates who have traveled from the left to the right. The author's conference on second thoughts, *Second Thoughts* radio show, and overall Second Thoughts Project[72] all testify to the proselytizing aim of reflexivity rhetoric. In Horowitz's campaigns to make Hollywood more hospitable to conservatives, he hired a documentary filmmaker who himself was previously a Democrat prompted to generate second thoughts by the movement for political correctness.[73] He hires a corporate lawyer and a Vietnam veteran who had gone through similar experiences as "second-thoughter[s]" to propagate such messages.[74] Second thoughts rhetoric becomes both about an individual's capacity for reflexivity and a signifier for the larger conservative movement's worth. Horowitz has others supplement this theme at every opportunity, including a former wife, who wrote a poem explaining that she had learned from him that "*second thoughts are best.*"[75]

As an example of generational deliberation, the experiential, time-based emphases of the conversion narrative merge with reflexivity to endow converts with a special authority about temporal matters. Horowitz argues that "the Left could not look inward and it could not look back," as it was unable to learn from experience and examine and question its commitments.[76] Horowitz states that his former colleagues' minds were so fixated on the future that they were unable to think again.[77] Unable to turn to the past because of its lack of reflexivity, the Left becomes an ahistorical, unreasoning, and inconvertible entity. Not only does the Left not know how to think again about its commitments, but it has little sense for the long-standing authority that this faculty provides conservatives. *RS* creates a rhetorical equation in which being able to reflect upon the experiences of the past equals generational expertise. As such, the Left did not understand crime because it didn't fit into its redemptive hopes for an idealistic world.[78] Horowitz implies that a reflexive orientation to the past is simply unavailable to leftists whose forward-looking, utopian hopes ignore past lessons.

This time-based rhetoric links with a certain perspective on human knowledge. Argumentation is grounded in a tension between "conserving old knowledge and accepting new knowledge."[79] Yet some research finds that many conservatives have "pessimistic expectations for the likelihood of great new insights in a single generation. The individual should seek to perfect himself, to be inner directed."[80] Fitting with a gradual conversion framework (like Podhoretz), the author makes instantaneous knowledge bad, compared with knowledge that took nearly three decades to arrive at.

This reflexivity also propagates an inner-directed rhetoric with deliberative implications. Horowitz finds that radicals, and liberals, inability to engage in reflection comes about from being out of touch with their very nature and interior lives.[81] Horowitz urges readers to turn inward for insights, rather than engage in public reasoning to discover or create new knowledge.

Similar to *Witness*'s rhetorical pressures, *RS*'s focus on reflexivity as an ability bears a resemblance to conservatism's metaethical commitment to "intuition" as an epistemological basis for political action.[82] Randall Lake finds that in antiabortion rhetoric, "right and wrong are apprehended by a unique moral sense somewhat similar to other human senses" and that this is an intuition that "cannot be refuted."[83] Horowitz uses a comparable sense of reflexivity as a solipsistic, intuitive guide for self-awareness and change. Persuasion emanates from an individual's personal, nonsocial experience, fashioning conversion as a new intuitive ability to judge politics in a way that is free from the burden of others.

Reflexive rhetoric goes beyond simply characterizing others as unthinking. With the conversion form, it becomes a deeply embedded, fixed ability, condition, or faculty that eradicates the deliberative capacities of others. Horowitz argues that his parents were unable to knowingly entertain other alternatives to their entrenched Marxist dreams, since they were "incapable of real self-reflection."[84] This is not to discount his parents' potential ignorance or failure to acknowledge certain political issues. Indeed, Horowitz relates that his obstinate father would not even turn away from some of his beliefs after the unveiling of the Khrushchev report, which detailed the abuses of Stalinism and led many Communist followers to see that their long-standing commitments to Communism were broken.[85] The point is that the rhetoric centers less on his parents' reasons for their political beliefs than on their epistemological, mental faculties.

Determinism and reflexivity correspond with old and new political lives. Horowitz makes his father an embodiment of an old, dogmatic, and fateful worldview, as opposed to the author's new, tolerant, and chosen paradigm. The author's father was incapable of taking ownership for his fate or changing his character in the slightest.[86] Horowitz states that the "arc" of his own life had been different in escaping such "ghettos."[87] The emphases on a directed journey and "ghettos" fashion Horowitz as a broad thinker and cosmopolitan communicator.[88] Wedding geographical range with time-based expansion, the "arc" of life signals that Horowitz considers his experience a directional structure from old to new. Making these connections explicit, he writes: "[W]hat was my own choice? In the beginning, I hardly had one. . . . I would make my choices only later."[89]

In this way, an appetite for self-examination and conversion operate as an organizing principle to bring about what Michael Wallace calls a "retrospective tidying up of the past" across the discourse.[90] Traveling a tenuous, civil-religious path between a convert's fervent devotion and the demands of tolerance in a pluralistic democracy, this retrospective ability, in turn, gives Horowitz what Walter Fisher further terms the "characterological coherence"[91] to deal with possible charges of a self-interested political switch. "Reversals of political opinion" can easily be attributed as "acts of enlightenment or 'flip-flops'" in public affairs.[92] Horowitz promotes the former interpretation by using a lengthy conversion narrative to demonstrate that his life has been coherently reflective. Associating reflexivity with flexibility, Horowitz recalls that being inflexible would be wrong, given the rethinking he had practiced in his own life.[93] Like Podhoretz, Horowitz constructs the journey as a complex, rather than a simple, political conversion. By laying out a life project over approximately 450 pages, Horowitz vindicates himself as having gone through a justified soul-searching over and above more expedient considerations.

In a move echoing Chambers and Podhoretz, Horowitz sometimes entertains a notion that despite the grand change in his life, he also never changed—in this case, that he has almost always been reflexive. He contends that during his years as a radical, he had many doubts about political developments in Vietnam and Cuba but, similar to Podhoretz, thought that his central politics essentially embodied classical liberalism; when asked to justify his political turn, he further advocates for the "continuity of my second thoughts."[94] This discourse has it both ways by communicating that the author is both greatly transformed and stable.

Reflexivity and conversion additionally associate with terms of unique and marginal authority. According to Horowitz, his tome *Destructive Generation* was one of the only books critical of 1960s radicalism—others who wrote similar accounts of the same era had "no real second thoughts."[95] In more colloquial terms, since Horowitz has been there, done that, readers are invited to view the author and his beliefs as exceptional, with an epistemological faculty that simply sweeps away generational nonsense. Horowitz creates the impression that he is a conservative pariah for this faculty. Blaming the *New York Times* for its attack upon his and Peter Collier's biography on the Ford dynasty (and the book's poor sales), Horowitz recounts that it was a penalty they received for their "second thoughts."[96] He even started a journal called *Heterodoxy* to argue that conservatives had become the "counterculture,"[97] appropriating the language of 1960s activism.[98] John Reilly notes that despite *RS*'s approaches, "the fact is that people like Horowitz are still swimming upstream in the major institutions of American life. The upshot is, as under his parents' roof, he can once again think of himself as countercultural."[99] As Oneida Meranto further explains, Horowitz co-opts a language of "inclusivity" and victimhood in his public efforts, seeking to make conservatism a type of "protected class."[100]

It is critical to note how Horowitz joins terms of conversion and flexibility with marginality to communicate that he is both at the center *and* the periphery of societal influence. Horowitz double-codes his rhetoric to appeal to as wide an audience as possible, being everything to everyone. While Horowitz and others speak a language that resounds with many Americans, a history scholar argues that their appeals often hide how they end up leading to cuts in spending for various social programs.[101] Horowitz sees himself as oppressed, in contrast to women, blacks, and other groups historically understood as marginalized. In a sense, his rhetoric of reflexivity appropriates standpoint language by claiming a special vantage point with which to see politics with greater clarity than others.[102] Standpoint theory consists of three central claims: "(1) Knowledge is socially situated. (2) Marginalized groups are socially situated in ways that make it more possible for them to be aware of things and ask questions than it is for the non-marginalized. (3) Research, particularly that focused on power relations, should begin with the lives of the marginalized."[103] Similarly, Horowitz perceives himself an exile, an outsider who has traveled a difficult, forlorn path, but has committed himself to a standard of self-aware, unfettered revision nonetheless.

Critics have affirmed and negated the reflexive persona. Christopher Caldwell writes: "As the gripping pages of Radical Son make clear, Horowitz possesses a fearless capacity for self-examination—hardly a noted virtue of the radical Left. . . . [I]t is this capacity which may have rescued him from an association with murderers. It certainly enabled him to reinvent himself, and to forge a new career as the kind of person his parents had no doubt warned him against."[104] In this passage, a special ability to be self-aware and think again highlights the resonance of Horowitz's epistemological emphases, with the active verbs "rescue," "reinvent," and "forge" each underscoring the author's agency. Sanford Pinsker reflects on how the New Left "lacked . . . a capacity for self-criticism," claiming that *RS*'s "painful narrative is more honest—and to my mind, more important—than other memoirs of those times, places."[105] James Bowman asserts: "Horowitz does have something of Chambers's quality of soul" in the "tremendous political honesty and sincerity" that "he is able to bring to his self-examination."[106] Another reviewer writes: "I had always been disappointed by the memoirs of political figures on the left because of their inability to reflect on themselves. . . . [I]t wasn't surprising that radicals could not confront their interior lives."[107] Frank Monaldo says that he is also persuaded by *BR*'s points about "the *inability* of the Left to address or even admit the brutality" of Communist countries.[108]

John Walker praises Horowitz's "great deal of painful introspection"[109] while Bonnie Parsley comments that "rarely is an individual given to such total *introspection*. . . . [H]e is able to see the self delusion and denial of reality that had motivated his political life since the beginning."[110] One critic calls RS "Introspective, Insightful & Intellectually Honest. . . . His life story is as compelling as any you'll find."[111] Another affirms the sophistication of such efforts: "Horowitz's transformation is far too complex to be adequately described in a short review."[112] Confirming a relationship between reflexivity and the civil-religious line that Horowitz straddles, R. Coleman finally notes that "his gradual move to the Right is tested and validated with intimate *reflection* and revelation."[113]

Other critics have been less supportive. One reviewer writes that "though he was a red-diaper baby and a Marxist himself, Horowitz asks the reader to believe that at virtually every step of his political life he entertained profound doubts about the beliefs and methods of those around him."[114] Another finds that "Horowitz's intense and lengthy introspections are sometimes a little repetitive."[115] Leonard Bushkoff relates, too, that Horowitz frames his experience in terms of a tiring, "endless introspection."[116] Jeff Coulter says that the story "is often intensely self-critical, and the honesty of many of its pages is quite striking."[117] He asks why Horowitz fails to discuss the sins of the Right, however, omitting a litany of events that could qualify the author's claims. These include findings that genuine democracy has not really emerged in countries where Communism has been rolled back, former secretary of state Robert McNamara's confessions over policy toward Vietnam being a criminal act, and contradictions inherent in the United States's support for murderous Third World governments, among other issues.[118]

I would add that Horowitz's reflexivity has a stopping point. Reflexivity merges with the linear conversion form to present readers with only one political turn from which Horowitz interprets ensuing events. We might question how deliberative the claims to reflexivity are in the autobiography's totality. Horowitz asserts that his conversion involved a period of deliberation but also that his political understandings are now firm, contradicting the endlessly reflexive standard that Horowitz asserts.

To be clear, I do not mean to downplay the virtues of self-reflection and criticism. My aim has been to highlight the use of reflexivity as an epistemological weapon in Horowitz's turn to conservatism. This analysis concurs with Lynch that "a reflexive analysis must be entrusted to *an uncertain fate*" since "there are no guarantees of success" or "inherent advantages" in simply being reflexive.[119] The problem is that under the conversion form, reflexivity has a *certain* fate. Simply being able to turn and have second thoughts does not mean that conclusive knowledge has been attained. The extent to which the self is implicated in this process signals a self-sealing reflexivity of absolute conclusions, not a journey of continuing, informed debate.

Ultimately, *RS* uses a political mode of thought analogous to inductive approaches to religion. Religion scholar Wade Clark Roof has meticulously documented how "a reflexive spiritual style" or a "self-directed approach to cultivating spiritual sensitivity and religious consciousness" now marks many Americans' religious orientations.[120] Following the expanding pluralisms and uncertainties of late modernity, such practices often emphasize "self-understanding and self-reflexivity" so much that "the current religious situation in the United States is characterized not so much by a loss of faith as a qualitative shift from unquestioned belief to a more open, questing mood."[121] Horowitz grounds his rhetoric in this approach but speaks a language of openness that remains anything but open.

In this vein, a second, related rhetorical resource informs Horowitz's conversion narrative. Horowitz uses literal and metaphorical frames of youth and adulthood in his rhetoric, knitting together a story about the relationship between himself and his father with the story of his journey to a mature, reflexive worldview.[122] In essence, conversion narratives can interact with a rhetoric of maturity to conflate biological with political development.

Crossing Personal with Political Development: Maturity

A maturity metaphor works with the conversion narrative, with the political transformation framed as an experiential matter of "growing up." Horowitz describes Communism, radicalism, and the New Left and its many allies with terms such as "children" and structures the autobiography chronologically with "growth" and "family" themes throughout.[123] Horowitz's father becomes increasingly "infantile" in his Marxist beliefs, while Horowitz finally "grows up" as a conservative. The author characterizes leftists as incomplete and immature—for example, New Left leader Robert Scheer, who is described as an "*unfinished* human being."[124] Horowitz tells one of the leaders of the anarchist Yippie movement, "[Y]ou never grew up."[125] Leftist "children" should be neither seen nor heard. Children lack an ability to know themselves, wallowing in a world of naïve, often egotistical, perceptions: "Socialism was not only a childish wish, but a wish for childhood itself."[126] With deliberative implications, *RS* advocates that the politics of the Left and the Right should hence be viewed in generational terms of developmental maturation.

Conversion reinforces the maturity resource. Between old and new lives, Horowitz connects the political journey to his personal development as a human being. In chapter headings such as "Coming of Age," he makes bodily growth a part of the journey to conservatism.[127] Biological and political development merge, so much that literal and metaphorical allusions to each are often indistinguishable across the book's 446 pages. Growth is a common metaphor in public discourse, referring to physical and mental development,[128] functioning in Horowitz's case to appropriate terms such as "progress" and "progressive" from the left.[129] The term "progress" also has historical connections to conversion, as in John Bunyan's conversion classic *The Pilgrim's Progress*.[130] By shifting between biological and political meanings of maturity, *RS* frames leftists as in a state of arrested development. One of the book's major concerns is with the future of youth, an appeal that connects biological development with one's political views, so that one's beliefs can be seen as either dissonant or accordant with human nature. This makes progress more a matter of "growing up and getting with the predetermined program" than creating political meaning with others.

Since one of the author's larger projects is to critique universities, reflexivity and maturity interact to replace scholarly with experiential authority. Horowitz once told a student who questioned his conclusions about the propagandistic intentions of university professors, "[Y]ou do not have the mental capacity to understand."[131] Not yet mature enough in his or her biological and political development to think again, the student's questions go unconsidered. Horowitz considers one's a priori status as a human being *before* his or her arguments, dismissing the latter under the attributions of the former. In this rhetoric, the 1960s was thus not about issues such as gender roles; it was about childish actions such as bra-burning.

Wayne Booth calls this "motivism," where "if you can find a class interest or a sexual drive or a kinship interest or a childhood trauma—you have explained away whatever 'surface reasons' anyone offers for his belief or actions."[132] In framing the Left in childhood terms, *RS* offers less of a deliberative encounter than a motivist discharge of others' political actions.

The conversion narrative is also about literal children as a rhetorical resource. In the book's first few pages, Horowitz cites Irving Kristol, who observed that the barbarian danger for every generation is to its kids, whose main challenge is to become civilized.[133] Every person has come from a family somewhere, so Horowitz crafts a broad-ranging appeal to the needs of parents and communities. The book concludes with a line supporting his parenting skills and the rightness of the larger political vision: "[M]y children: I had done this right."[134] Since conservative appeals about children generally find favor with the public,[135] Horowitz targets parents and adults concerned about future generations, becoming an authority on youth who flirt with leftist interests.[136]

A journey to the right connects a new, mature life with a rhetoric for future generations. One of Horowitz's former wives desired to be at home with their children, which his former political colleagues frowned upon.[137] In having a third child, he disassociates with his father, who chastises him for breaking the Marxist mold; kids were seen as obstructing the revolution's goals.[138] At times, Horowitz even enlists his mother as a doubting Thomas–type character, stating that she once told one of his former wives that "the

Left was wrong about how to raise children."[139] Of note is how the conversion form makes support for progeny an exclusive characteristic of the Right. This vision is enforced at both a larger political level (the picture that Horowitz paints of liberals/radicals writ large) and from a personal level (Horowitz's father). Horowitz even states that not having kids is itself a way to be a child.[140] Combining the conversion form with connotations of arrested development communicates that one cannot be for a Left that is against the very advancement of humanity.

As with reflexivity, there is also a parallel between maturity and antiabortion rhetoric. Randall Lake finds that appeals to childhood innocence are a common feature of conservative discourse. Often used in conservative rhetoric, deontological ethics (or theories of moral obligation) exemplify the communicative approach that one would use with a child, asserting fixed, pre-symbolic conclusions in public communication.[141] Similarly, Horowitz uses the maturity device to minimize the deliberative capacities of others.

From a rhetorical perspective, the point of using the child/adult device is to make the narrative seem natural and inevitable and to dismiss the counter-narrative to this natural and inevitable process by construing those who did not convert as abnormal. This explains why Horowitz devotes so much time to telling readers that others had "second thoughts"; he positions himself as a unique political convert but also creates the impression that there was a mass exodus to the right, so that those who did not make the leap are simply stubborn exceptions to a rule.

Some key figures supplement the child/adult device. Horowitz's political conversion occurred alongside his friend Peter Collier, with whom he coauthored several popular books on the Rockefeller, Kennedy, and Ford family dynasties. The co-conversion relays that the author is not out on a limb with his conservative turn. Since the two cowrote *Destructive Generation* as a challenge to the "adolescent posture[s]" of the 1960s,[142] maturity becomes more than an idiosyncratic claim. Citing Arthur Koestler, Horowitz also describes this friendship as a kind of mutual goading toward conservative truth, arguing coauthors see "a father figure in the other."[143] Despite Horowitz's fractured relationship with his own father, the political conversion enables another father-like friend to set him back on the path to maturity and normality.

Other characters normalize contrasts between living as a child and an adult and add confessional, civil-religious overtones to the political switch. Several years after their political conversions, Collier states that Horowitz had a developmental disability during his Marxist phase. Playing the father figure, he had to yell at Horowitz once to carry out the same procedure as a therapist bringing an autistic child back to reality.[144] As a Marxist, Horowitz is not just a child but an abnormal child, impervious to the demands of growing up. The analogy of a therapist pulling the child out of this phase of stunted growth uses a psychological frame to diagnose the problems resulting from the 1960s (a device explored further below in this chapter). Enlisting Collier as a sidekick to the conversion shows that, as in religious spheres, confessing to others about one's former actions becomes more than a lifestyle choice; in Horowitz's rhetoric, it is a path to the right-minded development required of every human being.[145]

The father character underscores these maturity claims. The child/adult device switches the typical son/father relationship, as a synecdoche for radical/liberal intransigence, compared with conservative openness. Marxism gave Horowitz's father an attitude of absolute certainty.[146] His father's stubbornness and angst as a Marxist was an adolescent cry for attention.[147] The author's father embodies the argument: radicals/liberals forge forward with unwarranted certainties that keep them in an arrested state. Horowitz contrasts this with his new political paradigm that tolerates deviance, debate, and broad ideological viewpoints.[148] Horowitz also details how his father's public image was very different from his private anguish.[149] Horowitz describes his father as seemingly heroic but "childlike and beaten."[150] This public/private split presents his father and the Left as half-characters, underscoring Horowitz's holistic accomplishment as a political convert.

Paradoxically, while appealing to a need for conversion (i.e., grand change), *RS*'s rhetoric solidifies human nature in a way that communicates that little individual or social change is possible. Horowitz comments on the irreducible nature of his childrens' character.[151] He describes the "immutable state of our nature"[152] and opposes progressives as wrong in thinking that evil is simply a lack of understanding.[153] In classifying people as either youth or adults, *RS* reduces human knowledge and action to fixed individualistic orientations in which interlocutors can do little. The external events of the world may act as a check and counter to one's orientation but mostly present one with a choice to get in line with reality rather than debate a different course of action. Strong contrasts between death and life that, as mentioned, figure prominently in conversion narratives[154] support such emphases. Horowitz relates that the loss of his friend at what he believes were the hands of the Black Panthers confirms that her murder was connected to a worldview they had absorbed from their "mother's milk."[155] This discourse alternates between biological and political development, positioning the latter concept in terms of the former.

Similar to reflexivity, maturity discourse claims both continuity and change. The author reminisces that Robert Scheer used to ascribe an "innocence" to Horowitz.[156] He also refers to the "virginal quality" he had in his early life.[157] A contradiction emerges between how others are accountable and not innocent for their previous acts and the purity that Horowitz attributes to himself in his early life and as a Marxist. Oppositely, for instance, *RS* takes great pains to describe how there is an ongoing "myth of innocence" about Tom Hayden and many young 1960s political activists as idealistic youth.[158] One implication is that, just as there are bad kids and good kids, while Horowitz was a captive of the Left, he was so uninformed as to be less accountable for previous, detestable acts. We find here an effort to communicate both "I have changed" and "I never changed," locating the blame for generational mistakes more squarely upon other 1960s advocates and allowing Horowitz to answer charges of political expedience and opportunism with consistency claims.

Although Horowitz claims to be agnostic,[159] admonitions about maturity often take on a biblical quality, highlighting the implicit civil-religious strategy at work across the text. In one passage, he explains that he had reached a point where he neeeed to grow up and *"put away childish things* and to . . . live with passion, love wisely, and know oneself."[160] The Judeo-Christian Bible is replete with references to and advice toward children.[161] Horowitz repeats the biblical verse from 1 Cor. 13:11 (without attribution) in the line: "[W]hen I was a child, I spake as a child, I understood as a child, I thought as a child: but when I became a man, I *put away childish things*."[162] The title of the book, *Radical Son*, itself echoes the Father-Son relationship at the center of the New Testament, including the "prodigal son" story.[163] In one section, he further intones a double meaning between his first name, David, and the biblical figure David.[164]

Political converts can claim no faith (and that liberals/radicals are religious) while still using a language of faith. Horowitz says as much throughout the book: that he needed to write his life's events in order to make sense of it all, a task that he describes as religious in nature.[165] Horowitz plays both sides of the fence in coding his message to secular and religious audiences, or what David Domke and Kevin Coe call a double-messaged "God strategy."[166] This strategy also helps Horowitz reinforce his point about reflexivity.

This is no Pauline conversion experience. Horowitz implies that his political turn is a decision both rationally thought through and well-informed by experience rather than the result of a childish, blind leap of faith. He advises the reader to "know oneself"—not to know "God," as in Chambers's case, but to become inductively self-conscious and epistemologically regenerated. Yet the conversion form and subtle religious allusions are retained throughout the narrative. Horowitz even remarks that in his post-conversion life, for the first time, "I felt a providence at work."[167] Using biblical and secular-psychological language, *RS* blends references to growing mature as a matter of transcendent principle with growing mature as a thinking, self-aware being.

Various critics have affirmed the maturity resource. One reviewer resonates with all three of the book's rhetorical devices in claiming that "the reviewers who discount this work are at best individuals with *growth stunted intellects* who wish to remain Peter Pans and *never grow up*. . . . I see that the Left is basically a huge *dysfunctional family*."[168] Bowman finds that Horowitz is to be praised for recovering from "a life spent with overgrown children."[169] Horowitz is authoritative and exceptional, as "it takes someone who is himself recovering from an epic case of arrested development really to understand the essentially infantile quality in the New Left. . . . [I]t is only he and not his fellow radicals who grows up."[170] Another reviewer confirms that "Radical Son is a powerful and moving book. In the deepest sense, it is a book about growing up, politically, intellectually, spiritually."[171] One critic states: "I will use it to continue teaching my children the Truth."[172] Dave Duffy, a fellow traveler from the political left to the right, finds it an inspirational book, especially in its "Rebirth of Individualism" and contrast between youthful innocence and the learned experience of adulthood.[173] Affirming a religious reception of the political conversion narrative (and thus the kind of civil-religious double-coding identified in the book), one Christian pastor writes that *RS* is "a very influential book for me. . . . If Horowitz is a 'radical' son, our Lord Jesus is a *Covenant* Son, and so are we all—sons & daughters."[174]

On the other hand, Justin Raimondo negates the maturity persona: "David Horowitz is such a big crybaby. . . . In other words: Wahhh! Wahhhh!"[175] Jeff Coulter finds that "to fetishize a reified conception of human nature is a standing flaw of conservative thought throughout the ages . . . which demeans the indefinitely creative and transformative powers of humanity,"[176] just as the "maturity journey" tends to narrow others' rhetorical capacities. Horowitz's development is toward determined, absolutist ends in which speech can do little.

In early twentieth-century "generational" discourse in the United States, some scholars have observed a point when many young people "introduced psychological notions of care and understanding to intergenerational relations."[177] Illuminating this historical pattern, political converts can combine their narratives with psychological, identity-focused experience to yield a third form of inductive rhetoric.

Extrapolating One's Self: Psychological Experience

With relevance to deliberative matters, Horowitz merges a language of psychological experience with the political conversion narrative. *RS* constructs a conversion from "structural" and "sociological" ways of thinking and acting to a new "individual" and "psychological" orientation to personal and political life. The 1960s and the Left are considered a disorder, and the author grounds his new knowledge in the experience of being "mugged by reality"[178] —so that unlike liberals, he has moved from the world of "ideas" and unreflective "abstractions" to inductive, "concrete living" and "worldly" concerns.

Just as the maturity device appropriates a language of "progress" from the left, psychological experience employs features of feminist rhetoric toward conservative aims. Feminists have promoted shifts from abstract thought toward more experiential bases of knowledge.[179] Much of the 1960s was about "experience," and autobiography is a medium well suited to such individualistic, narrative communication. As Horowitz notes, since "all the books I had written on my own were abstract and analytic, their style unsuited to the autobiographical task,"[180] the medium of choice reinforces a psychological rhetoric involving a conversion from an impersonal old life to a personal new one.[181]

From writing the Marxist *Free World Colossus* to biographies of the Rockefellers, Kennedys, and Fords, as well as conservative books such as *Dangerous Generation*, Horowitz retrospectively applies the psychological experience standard to all his writings. After toggling between abstract and concrete ways of writing,[182] he applies conversion language in stating that "finally, I had found a narrative voice capable of introspection, and realized that I had arrived at a point in my life where I felt a sense of completion in the themes that had shaped it."[183] The narrative voice and reflexive ability ("capable of introspection") are attributed to the bifurcated, directional "sense of completion" wrought by the conversion form. Like a new religious initiate, he feels lost at first but then finds his way. Dropping his former "Marxist filter" where "the narrative we constructed, and the psychological portraits we drew, were so much window dressing for the important message about the System," Horowitz converts to "the biographical enterprise."[184] These individualistic emphases may also explain why so many of these narratives have been told by left-to-right converts, since the Right is generally where local and libertarian language has more resonance.

The biographical voice itself becomes a powerful persona throughout the work. This voice urges the author to come to terms with the memory of his parents after their deaths—"the biographer insisted."[185] Horowitz relates that in his former writings, "I was too tentative in my authorial voice,"[186] but later in *RS* states that in writing his first biography, "the narrative voice was authoritative."[187] This move is both descriptive and persuasive, since Horowitz associates the shift to a biographical mode of writing with the view that individualism is best in public matters. Combining these personal claims with the conversion form permits little space for both sociological and biographical-narrative modes to work together; instead, they exist as sides of a dichotomy, charted between the past and present.

The story joins a rhetoric about experience with the language of popular psychology, so it is no coincidence that Horowitz's best-selling biographies of the Rockefellers, Kennedys, and Fords have been labeled "pathographies" by some, "because of their focus on social and emotional dysfunction."[188] In writing biographies, Horowitz admits, "I was not used to thinking in psychological terms."[189] But he increasingly finds utility in analyzing social life from this perspective, making attributions of others, such as the "rage rolling inside him came from psychological layers so deep that he himself had lost contact with them."[190] When his mother was dying, Horowitz explains that the worst part was watching her psychological deterioration.[191] He even labels his political conversion a "psychic fission."[192]

Psychological language bears on the convert's claims to see more truly and deeply into the nature of human activity. Horowitz views causes for problems like a clinical psychologist. Statements in the book often begin with the explanation, "at some deeper and more psychological level."[193] Originally he, his parents, and the political Left were in a state of "denial" over the true implications of their political convictions,[194] and after being unfaithful to his one of his former wives, Horowitz asserts that there was probably some psychological reason for his adultery.[195] Extending the disease metaphor, Horowitz, too, argues that "I had been given insight into the psychology behind such malignant [New Left] politics."[196]

Like Horowitz's rendering of the Left as childlike, this psychological rhetoric erases opponents' communicative abilities and absolves Horowitz from having had any control over actions from his previous life as a radical and liberal. The author attributes Marion Rockefeller's radicalism, for instance, to forces that were "more psychological than political."[197] *RS* attends less to the reasons for liberal and radical activities than the deep urges beyond communication that drive such efforts. Just as Podhoretz's conversion narrative reduces the Left's speech to primal biological impulses rather than freely chosen actions,[198] Horowitz's terms reduce others' messages to inflexible psychological motives and mere expressions of subconscious drives. Noting historical precedents for such language, Berger writes that "the translation of religion into psychological language has been very popular in America."[199] Like the other devices, the text links the abnormal psychology of the Left with fate but makes agency a quality of conservative conversions. Horowitz cites many conservative activists and everyday workers who were, for example, "self-made."[200]

Some scholarship finds that "a dominant feature of right-wing discourse concerning the 'culture wars' is the appropriation of liberal discourse for its own, contrary purposes," especially in antiabortion rhetoric, where "the purpose of debate is conversion."[201] In Horowitz's story, the purpose of debate is to extend conversion, and the purpose of conversion is not to debate—with a language of "choice" affording an opportunity to make only *right* choices. Horowitz explains that the tenants at Sunnyside, the Marxist community where he grew up, showed him that the people he knew were "helpless" and lacking in any ability to exert control over their lives.[202] On the other hand, as a political convert to conservatism, Horowitz begins to gain "control" over his own.[203] Despite statements focusing on the choices that people have in life, across the narrative it becomes apparent that choice can be found only on one side of the conversion divide.

Similar to the other resources, psychological experience interacts with the conversion form to fashion a civil-religious rhetoric that makes the Left fanatical. Among many examples, *RS* concludes that the Left treats as idolatry an idea that people can be gods and create utopias on earth.[204] Having its head in the heavens, the Left cannot possibly hope to address real human problems. Yet Horowitz subtly draws from religious texts and the conversion form to maintain a thin threshold of generalized faith across the narrative. In fact, as with *Breaking Ranks*, one problem that *RS* hopes to address is the opinion that "our second thoughts were a religious conversion—therefore irrational and dangerous."[205] Through civil-religious rhetoric, the author grounds his new political beliefs in down-to-earth terms while naming the Left a "political religion."[206] *RS* gets to have the best from both worlds, advancing and submerging religiosity throughout the narrative to make broad appeals.

Critically, an individual's direct, unmediated view of experience generates insights in an inductive political conversion. Converts play a special role in public affairs as people who have weathered the times; as the author asserts, "the secret of good judgment? Experience"[207]—just as experience led him to conservatism.[208] On the other hand, Horowitz once married a woman who was hostile toward experience.[209] Departing from Podhoretz's conversion rhetoric in which ideas are primary, experience dissociates mere ideas from reality. With the maturity theme, an exacting binary is drawn between naïve and mature, empirical thinking—attacking Marxists for their "ideas"[210] and for being "Platonists inhabiting a reality that was separate, and that could not be refuted by events."[211] Yet the Platonic charges are ironic, as the conversion form underscores Platonic themes through sentences in *RS* such as "I emerged from the shadows to the world of reality,"[212] employing "experience" in an equally evangelical fashion.

In turn, the experience-based rhetoric serves Horowitz's university project. Far from the minds of airy professors in the ivory tower, Horowitz claims a hardheaded, practical look at public affairs. Different from a typical religious conversion narrative, political transformation is cast in terms of discovering earth rather than the heavens. Horowitz's time as a Marxist had made him "unworldly,"[213] since Marxists forgo sensory experience in favor of ideas.[214] He faces the cold, hard facts of reality in an inductive manner, finding himself "constantly blindsided by events."[215] This language assumes that the world's events simply speak for themselves, requiring little interpretation. "Ideas" are so divorced from reality that they are variable and hence unproductive. Personal experience and earthly "reality," however, present themselves to human beings as simply factual.

Others are enlisted across the narrative to heighten the conversion form's dichotomy between experienced and inexperienced people. The author's previous orientation used to be future focused and intellectual, while one of his former wives was always centered on life, the present, and concrete, external events.[216] She makes the author increasingly aware of a world outside himself and of how harsh abstract arguments could feel,[217] justifying a turn to concrete, narrative terms. When he was seventeen, a girlfriend accuses Horowitz of being too obsessed with analyzing rather than living in experience.[218] As a result, Horowitz realizes that in his old life, "I was still innocent of any real experience."[219]

Here, again, Horowitz appropriates feminist discourses, implying that activists' idea that "the personal is political"[220] applies to conservatism. Feminist standpoint theorist Nancy Hartsock argues that Marxist political theories miss the material experiences of women's lives. While women's experiences tend to be concrete, men often live in far more abstract, Platonic worlds. Hartsock claims that this is partly due to differences in bodily experiences such as menstruation. Men tend to go about their lives more separated from the external world and others than women, for whom intimacy and connection are more familiar.[221]

The conversion narrative further employs a type of "consciousness-raising" rhetoric. Richard Gregg describes consciousness-raising as a "struggle for a resurrected self" that worked parallel to 1960s movements' activism.[222] In groups, it is a procedure for sharing personal experiences to establish "new psychological orientations for those involved" and to "create new political values."[223] As Karlyn Kohrs Campbell identifies, consciousness-raising is "dialogic and participatory" in a way that "speaks from personal experience to personal experience."[224] A critical difference between Horowitz's rhetoric and this kind of process is that consciousness-raising involves a collaborative journey between communicators. The conversion narrative promotes one's isolated arrival at preestablished truths, which are deep (i.e., reason is replaced by psychological impulses), directional rather than inquiry-based, and simply beyond human beings in interaction.

In Horowitz's case, the conversion narrative is a discovering of internal and external essences to be adhered to rather than the sharing and co-creation of political truths, which evade directional necessities and preordained results. A key problem, then, is that Horowitz offers a deductive, deontological politics in the guise of an inductive, experiential language. The use of experience-based language may be read as a way of engaging a wider audience for conservative appeals (and as a civil-religious strategy attempting to avoid fundamentalist or overly rationalist overtones), just as support for feminism has galvanized U.S. audiences in the past. Since 1980, women have voted more consistently for Democrats than for other candidates in presidential elections,[225] an issue to which *RS* may be responding. The appropriation of feminist language is akin to what Roland Barthes has described as second-order semiological systems. By hiding the ideological origins of key terms in public discourse—both where they came from and the reasons for their use—histories and voices that might have provided critical alternatives to present claims can become muted.[226]

Ultimately, the conversion form reconfigures 1960s rhetoric in cynical terms. By stripping the social and activist intentions of feminist and other language from its bases, *RS* crafts a rhetorical vision where possibilities for change are limited to psychological, individualistic boundaries that admit little access to or from others. As Horowitz argues, "it was no longer the world I had to change, but myself."[227] Ironically, Horowitz's newfound respect for experience, empirical reality, and the events of the external world are positioned with messages that put political engagement primarily within the self. At the same time, this rhetoric fails to account for the experiences of others, which do not necessarily need to be validated but might at least be addressed.

We know that Horowitz was instrumental in creating terms for the Right such as "compassionate conservatism." The use of liberal/radical language partially softens hard-edged conservative connotations. Conservatives are known for their support of harsh punishments for criminals, for example.[228] Using liberal/radical language can co-opt publics for whom the situational language of experience resonates. The prominence of concepts such as "generations" and "youth" in the history of U.S. public discourse relates to gender issues, as "both terms have been male discourses."[229] Through the conversion form and psycho-experiential resource, generational rhetoric can be framed in more feminine terms to create a broader appeal, while retaining traditionalist themes invoking masculine connotations.

Some *RS* reviews affirm the book's use of psychological rhetoric. Concerning this "introspective autobiography," one reviewer writes that "the book's candid explanation of the psychological roots of first communism and then the New Left are very enlightening."[230] Bernard Chapin, too, affirms the book as "a psychological study of the progressive mind."[231] A number of other responses confirm the realism asserted in Horowitz's rhetoric. Martin Asiner resonates with Horowitz's "raw human experience" and how he "survived and thrived to warn the current generation."[232] Praising *RS*'s inductive emphases, one reviewer finds it "a rare odyssey: Someone who rethinks their political beliefs from the ground up. . . . This is the most interesting political odyssey stor[y] since Whittaker Chambers' 'Witness.'"[233] One blogger writes that "when confronted by a reality he couldn't deny, Horowitz refused to retreat into the world of pretty ideas,"[234] while another states: "I say thank goodness for those all-too-few such as Horowitz who speak from a position of experience."[235]

One writer says that "Radical Son is full of harrowing personal detail . . . but the book's real importance lies not in its anecdotal revelations or even in its political message but in its embrace of a chastened realism, a modesty not personal but metaphysical."[236] Note how the "chastened realism" is confirmed by a "metaphysical" message, affirming the text's civil-religious overtones. Another reviewer asserts that "no book I have read in the last 20 years affected me more profoundly than did Horowitz's autobiography *Radical Son*, both in terms of helping to understand the destructiveness of the utopian impulse, and also in getting a perspective on the 60's and the Vietnam era."[237] Kent Worcester is more ambivalent: "at times, the rhetoric gets out of hand . . . certainly hyperbolic—but the book provides a useful corrective to overly idealistic treatments of the politics of the 1960s."[238]

Some reviews rebuke the author's device. Jonathan Yardley writes that the book is about "a self-administered therapeutic process that does not, on the evidence presented here, appear to have worked."[239] One reviewer argues that "this book is a Freudian analyst's dream" and "hilariously awful."[240] Tim Lieder asks, "[W]hy do most people talk psychology about Horowitz? Because his self-righteous idiocy is the same no matter what political stripe he wears."[241] Ultimately, by combining the conversion form with a rhetoric of psychology, individuality, biography, and experience, psychological experience puts little faith in reason and reasonability, future change, and, at base, communication.

CONCLUSION

One idea that has circulated in public is that, "If you're not a liberal when you're 25, you have no heart. If you're not a conservative by the time you're 35, you have no brain."[242] Stories like *Radical Son* attempt to strike a middle position between these lines, but ultimately in the service of one ideology. Numerous points can be drawn about Horowitz's messages.

First, the reflexivity resource and conversion form create a special epistemological ability for self-criticism and awareness that detach the convert from public reasoning and reasonability. Horowitz claims an ability to see into the true nature of things and know more than others, given his construction of a unique mental faculty. Relative to public deliberation, this revisionary ability begins and ends with the self, asserting one's righteous, linear path to self-validated truth. Overall, the conversion form and Horowitz's understanding of reflexivity involve a self-perfected rhetoric that bypasses human exchange as a route to knowledge and insight.

As a rhetoric of open-mindedness, reflexivity downplays the traditionally dogmatic attributes of the conversion form. A problem is that the political conversion narrative is fine with choice, so long as the *right* choice is made. Process values that may be ultimate values for liberals can be appropriated by conservatives; but when such values are located within deontological frameworks, they serve foregone conclusions.[243] The political conversion narrative similarly deals with a product/process issue in its construction of open-mindedness as good, so long as it leads to absolute political truth. Thus, while deliberation scholars such as Seyla Benhabib argue that deliberation creates a reflexive orientation that gives individuals an "enlarged mentality,"[244] *RS* features a type of reflexivity rhetoric that works toward opposite ends.

The appropriation of tolerant language has implications for public civility. Stephen Olbrys finds dangerous "the manipulation of the language of academic freedom to achieve singular ends," especially when advocates use claims to two-sided debate as a mask for advocacy and "pen themselves into their own tribe's enclaves and never test ideas and beliefs against alternatives."[245] My analysis suggests that converts embody two-sided debate but co-opt sides in a way that closes communicative space for deliberation and further learning. Some public reactions to *RS* imply that the political convert is, indeed, seen as embodying all sides of a public discussion.[246] On its surface, Horowitz's rhetoric asserts a reflexivity that speaks to the author's desire for fair deliberation. But examining how argument operates in Horowitz's attacks against the university system, Henry Farrell finds that he concocts

> a farrago of innuendoes, half-truths, and out-and-out lies in order to beat down those whom he sees as his political opponents. However, when he's attacked in the same terms as those he himself engages in, he's perfectly happy to appeal to academic norms of reasoned debate in order to accuse his accusers of themselves being politicized. . . . Because Horowitz is able to use the low standards of political debate, while demanding that his intellectual opponents adhere to the high ones of academic argument, he wins either way.[247]

I would add that Horowitz uses the conversion form to double-code his rhetoric in a totalizing manner. The political convert can be everything to everyone, using a language of tolerance and civility while employing an argument form with little deliberative space.

Under the conversion form, reflexivity becomes a directional journey and foregone conclusion. Horowitz's generational rhetoric seeks to absolve conservative politics in a way that forgoes the possibility of ending up in different places. This time-based rhetoric therefore creates a gradual vision for knowledge production; deliberative encounters can do little to produce knowledge; only knowledge inductively generated over the course of decades has lasting value.

This time-based assumption helps Horowitz deal with possible objections about political flip-flopping. Changing one's views, or "flip-flopping," can constitute a lack of political consistency and balance.[248] Paradoxically, Horowitz implies that as long as converts flop to the right side, these charges can be avoided. The conversion form's religious history and undertones also come in handy here, absolving one's political sins so that a grand change can be justified. Along with the double-coded, civil-religious discourse, the political convert's efforts can be interpreted as being at the center and the periphery of societal influence. Converts are framed as experienced leaders at the forefront of public affairs *and* marginalized, countercultural advocates.

Ultimately, the political convert's reflexivity has a stopping point. Horowitz weds reflexivity to the linear conversion form, presenting readers with only one political turn from which ensuing events are to be interpreted. The political conversion involved a period of deliberation, but the author's political understandings are now firm, which goes against the endlessly reflexive standard that the narrative asserts. The second thoughts rhetoric effaces the possibilities for "third thoughts" and more. "Second thoughts" communicates an open-mindedness that is ironically unidirectional, with readers asked to take only one self-reflective turn. Overall, being able to turn and have second thoughts does not mean that knowledge has been attained, that second thoughts are necessarily more reliable, or that some distinctive mark should be attributed to the convert.

Second, the conversion form and maturity resource interact to make political transformation an experiential, naturalized matter of "growing up" that is beyond deliberation. A rhetoric of growth toggles ambiguously between one's biological and political development, naturalizing the convert's choices as parallel to his or her development as a human being—so that one's beliefs can be seen as potentially dissonant or accordant with human nature. A deliberative problem is that the inductive conversion narrative looks to one's a priori status as a human being *before* his or her actual arguments, dismissing the latter under the attributions of the former. The child/adult device, in particular, makes one's political conversion seem normal and inevitable, with childhood terms offered less for deliberative encounter than as a motivist discharge of others' actions.

These maturity terms appeal to both the "strict parent" and "nurturant parent" frameworks that George Lakoff says lie at the heart of U.S. liberal and conservative worldviews.[249] Horowitz's maturity resource meets these metaphorical demands by presenting the political convert as an experienced adult who can put the nation's youth on the right path. This explains how and why Horowitz was the political activist to invent terms such as "compassionate conservatism" for the Republican movement, which simultaneously appeals to the strict traditionalist and nurturing care frames. The conversion form contributes to this double-coded rhetoric, with the convert straddling old and new paradigms in a way that transcends and incorporates both.

In drawing simple divides between children and adults, the conversion form tends to evade broader data and histories. Julia Vitullo-Martin critiques the selective history in *RS*, such as Horowitz's "odd ignorance of the civil rights movement." In its rush to cast the 1960s as a terrible decade, she claims that the book misses the

> public spiritedness of the early sixties and the interconnections among youngsters who volunteered in the Peace Corps and Vista, who trained in the liberal Protestant theological schools, who were active in the Catholic Left both in urban parishes across the country and in the rural South. Horowitz ignores the thousands of young Americans who thought there was some possibility of making a better world, and worked hard to do it.[250]

Others have also called Horowitz's memory about the 1960s into question.[251] As noted, Horowitz omits Watergate, Iran-Contra, and many other events that transpired between the 1960s and 1990s. These omissions complicate the narrative's claim to reflexivity.

Maturity and growth rhetoric appropriates concepts such as "progress" and "progressive" from the left toward absolutist ends. *RS* urges that progress is more a matter of growing up and getting with the predetermined program than much else. In this vision, drawing a dichotomy between old and new is more than a simple lifestyle choice; it is a path to the balanced, right-minded development required of every human being. In so doing, the political convert employs a curious paradox between change and continuity, using a rhetoric of conversion to establish political permanence.

Public deliberation involves a general adherence to the belief that the future can be changed through symbolic action,[252] but the conversion narrative creates a mature rhetoric that is anything but forward-looking. Horowitz says that human beings have no saving future that can change their nature.[253] Since we cannot save ourselves in any way, why bother trying to create change in the world? To the author, the inability of politics to reach utopia necessarily curbs future feats. Concurrently, since the opposite of growth is atrophy, death, and decay, others who hold contrary views are dead to the potential for rhetorical exchange. Without the possibility of being informed by other beliefs, values, and attitudes, the discourse crafts a vision for political resignation rather than engagement.

RS does make a valid point about the need for empirical testing in the service of future design. Past experience is typically given presumption in debate.[254] Compared with an unknown future, hindsight at least offers some knowledge and precedent for deliberation. A problem is that Horowitz uses the conversion form to dichotomize the Left and the Right on these matters—

liberals are concerned only with a fantasy future, while conservatives remain properly concerned with the lessons of the past[255]—when the two concerns are not mutually exclusive. Characterizing the Left as unconcerned with the past equally lacks fidelity. Much of the U.S. Left has concerned itself with centuries of bad policies regarding basic human rights on issues such as race,[256] looking back in order to progress forward.

Last, the conversion form and psychological experience rhetoric draw lines between an old, abstract sociological worldview and a new, concrete narrative orientation. The personal becomes a locus for public engagement, and the bifurcated conversion form permits little room for both sociological and biographical-narrative modes to work together. The psychological, therapeutic language deepens the individualistic political vision by buttressing the convert's claims to see more truly and deeply into the nature of human activity. At the same time, like Horowitz's rendering of the Left as childlike, the psychological rhetoric reduces opponents' actions to intransigent motives. Under these psychological layers, we are treated to, borrowing Kenneth Burke's terms, a "procession of solemn, humorless caricatures" and the "slap[ping] together of various oversimplified schemes that reduce human motives to a few drives or urges or itches."[257] These fateful attributions are deepened by a civil-religious rhetoric making the Left religious, while Horowitz continues to draw from religious texts and the conversion form to maintain a thin threshold of generalized faith across the narrative.

Psychological experience additionally appropriates some aspects of feminist rhetoric toward conservative purposes, particularly standpoint theories and the language of consciousness-raising. These terms can appeal to wider audiences and mask the conversion form's propagandistic emphases. Importantly, feminist language is divorced from its origins to serve a conservative cause that much feminist thought counters. Horowitz pulls from the resonance of these terms while occluding the feminist debates with which the terms are related. The conversion form tends not to place value upon the worth of communicative processes in coming to new political positions. In Horowitz's case, we have a conversion narrative that is a discovering of internal and external essences to be adhered to, rather than generative political argumentation that avoids preordained, directional necessities.

One important final comment is warranted regarding the autobiography's rhetorical strategies. We should be willing to give Horowitz the benefit of the doubt that he had a genuine change of heart based upon an examination of his earlier life experience. The deliberative problem with *RS* is that everybody can do that. Every person goes through processes of maturation—biologically, psychologically, and communicatively. But Horowitz's rhetoric constructs these developmental standards through a conversion experience so that they become necessarily aligned with political positions. In personal or psychological terms, just as everyone undergoes changes that result in certain political positions (since there is a need for *some* footing, judgment, and certainty in life), people cannot engage only in reflexivity by itself, in perpetuity. Citizens have to land somewhere in their beliefs, carving out spaces for political affirmation and assent. Horowitz conflates the process of coming to new beliefs with an end state, however. In this sense, what Horowitz means by deliberation is communication about or toward a conclusion that one has already reached, with anything other than that seen as outside the scope of inquiry. Most politically active, culturally aware 1960s activists were going through the same process and were reflexively evaluating their experience of the 1950s to arrive at a different place.[258] Yet Horowitz aligns this process singularly with conservatism, while attributing dogmatism to the Left.

Reflection and experience can certainly constitute good reasons in the public square, but they are not the only forms of knowledge. Part of maturity is seeing that one's experience is also idiosyncratic; this knowledge needs to be tested against larger truths in the world. *RS* puts little faith in the testing of discourses. It is largely a "self-made" story that deflects engagement with others outside one's own current perspective. Covering similar ground, Craig Martin finds that applying a distinction between one's experiences and broader institutional claims to truth often "allows individuals to take their own local values and local hermeneutic (embedded of course in local interests and local battles), project them onto the world or interpret the world in terms of them, and as such mistake their creation for reality itself."[259] In other words, communicators can become blind to how much they are using their personal experiences to cover for everyone else's. Likewise, Horowitz ends up caricaturing reflexivity, essentially saying, "I only remember those parts of my experience that lead me to where I am now, and I forget the other parts that complicate the picture."

By tracing the cumulative interactions between the narrative's rhetorical resources and the conversion form, I conclude that *RS* is a propagandistic text. Cotton Mather once remarked that *"we our selves are the commentary."*[260] There are perhaps few other communication strategies where fundamentalist selves and commentary come to align so closely as conversion rhetoric. Before moving to conclusions about what political conversion narratives contribute to our understandings of public discourse, it is worth pausing to consider a tale almost told. As a part of the same intertextual thread connecting Chambers, Podhoretz, and Horowitz, the next chapter covers a story that helps qualify our knowledge of the features and functions of political transformation rhetoric—in this case, by bypassing its seductions.

NOTES

1. Horowitz, *Radical Son*, 376.

2. See Scott Sherman, "David Horowitz's Long March," *Nation*, June 15, 2000, www.thenation.com/article/david-horowitzs-long-march/, par. 9. Outside Horowitz's press, other conservative authors have reflected *RS*'s second thoughts rhetoric. For example, conservative radio talk-show host Dennis Prager wrote a book called *Think a Second Time* (New York: HarperCollins, 1995).
3. Sanders Hicks, "Compassionate Communists and Cussing Conservatives," Sanders Hicks.com, www.sanderhicks.com/articles/horowitzint.html, 1.
4. Catherine Seipp, "Right Warrior," *National Review*, April 15, 2005, www.nationalreview.com/script/printpage.p?ref=/seipp/seipp200504150751.asp (no longer available), par. 15.
5. As one example, Sherman finds:

> Horowitz has stepped into a new role: Republican Party theoretician. His pamphlet "The Art of Political War: How Republicans Can Fight to Win" is causing a stir on the right: Thirty-five state Republican Party chairmen have endorsed it, the Heritage Foundation sent 2,300 copies to conservative activists and House majority whip Tom DeLay provided copies to every Republican Congressional officeholder, with a cover note praising its contents. On April 5, Senators Arlen Specter, Rick Santorum and Sam Brownback, plus a dozen members of the House, hosted a soiree for Horowitz in Washington, at which $40,000 was raised for his activities. (Sherman, "David Horowitz's Long March," par. 7).

6. Horowitz, *Radical Son*, 443.
7. Ibid., 411.
8. Ibid., 377. Horowitz was also convinced by public figures such as P. J. O'Rourke, Irving Kristol, and Nathan Glazer. Charlton Heston "was another second-thoughter." Ibid., 377, 429.
9. Ibid., 2. See also ibid., 401.
10. Daniel Berger, "The Whittaker Chambers of Our Time," Amazon.com, April 29, 2007, www.amazon.com/Radical-Son-Generational-David-Horowitz/product-reviews/0684840057/ref=dp_top_cm_cr_acr_txt?ie=UTF8&showViewpoints=1, par. 3.
11. Sean Hackbarth, "Journey from Left to Right," April 15, 2001, www.amazon.com/Radical-Son-Generational-David-Horowitz/product-reviews/0684840057/ref=dp_top_cm_cr_acr_txt?ie=UTF8&showViewpoints=1, par. 1.
12. David (Joel) Horowitz, *Biography Resource Center*.
13. David Horowitz, *The Free World Colossus: A Critique of American Foreign Policy in the Cold War* (New York: Hill & Wang, 1971).
14. Jack E. White, "A Real, Live Bigot," *Time*, August 22, 1999, www.time.com/time/magazine/article/0,9171,29787,00.html, par. 5.
15. "Interview with David Horowitz," *Chuck Baldwin Live*, 1997, www.chuckbaldwinlive.com/horowitz.html (no longer available).
16. Some of Horowitz's other books include: David Horowitz, *The Politics of Bad Faith: The Radical Assault on America's Future* (New York: Touchstone, 1998); *Hating Whitey: And Other Progressive Causes* (Dallas: Spence, 1999); *Uncivil Wars: The Controversy over Reparations for Slavery* (San Francisco: Encounter Books, 2001); *Left Illusions: An Intellectual Odyssey* (Dallas: Spence, 2003); *Unholy Alliance: Radical Islam and the American Left* (Washington, DC: Regnery, 2004); *The End of Time* (San Francisco: Encounter Books, 2005); and *Indoctrination U: The Left's War against Academic Freedom* (San Francisco: Encounter Books, 2007).
17. David Horowitz, *The Professors: The 101 Most Dangerous Academics in America* (Washington, DC: Regnery, 2006); idem, "In Defense of Intellectual Diversity," *Chronicle of Higher Education*, February 10, 2004.
18. Scott Jaschik, "Tattered Poster Child," *Inside Higher Education*, November 29, 2005; idem, "Retractions from David Horowitz," *Inside Higher Education*, January 11, 2006; David Horowitz, "Some of Our Facts Were Wrong: Our Point Was Right," *Front Page Magazine*, March 15, 2005; Nicholas Lemann, "On Balance: At the J-Schools: The Case against Ideological Engineering," *Columbia Journalism Review* 44 (2006): 16–17.

19. See Duncan Campbell, "Right Turn," *Guardian*, May 30, 2001; Jeff Jacoby, "Smear Victim Fights Back," *Boston Globe*, September 2, 1999; Alex S. Jones, "A Painful Irony: The Media's Moral Obligations," *Harvard International Journal of Press/Politics* 6 (2001): 3–7; Robert Stacey McCain, "Contrarian Controversy," *Insight on the News*, November 15, 1999.

20. John Gorenfeld, "Roger Ebert and Mohammed Atta, Partners in Crime," *Salon*, April 12, 2005, www.salon.com/2005/04/12/horowitz_database/.

21. Ibid., par. 8.

22. David Horowitz, "Can There Be a Decent Left? Michael Walzer's Second Thoughts," FrontPageMagazine.com, 2002, www.frontpagemag.com/Articles/Printable.asp?ID=1011, par. 1.

23. Peter Collier and David Horowitz, *Destructive Generation: Second Thoughts about the '60s* (New York: Free Press, 1989).

24. Philip Abbott, "A 'Long and Winding Road': Bill Clinton and the 1960s," *Rhetoric & Public Affairs* 9 (2006): 4.

25. Nicolaus Mills, "Scornful of the '60s," *Christian Science Monitor*, June 9, 1997, par. 1, 5.

26. Edward Morgan, *The 60s Experience: Hard Lessons about Modern America* (Philadelphia: Temple University Press, 1991), 9.

27. "Interview with David Horowitz," par. 60; Mills, "Scornful of the '60s," par. 9. In a study, Bernard von Bothmer finds that "between 1980 and 2004, liberals and conservatives used selective memories of separate portions of the 'The Sixties' (1960 to 1974) to gather voter support for candidates and justify policy positions." While "liberals evoked the positive associations of 'the good sixties' (1960–1963) . . . conservatives called up the specter of 'the bad sixties' (1964–1974)." Bernard von Bothmer, "Blaming 'The Sixties': The Political Use of an Era, 1980–2004" (PhD diss., Indiana University, 2007), abstract, par. 3.

28. Jason D. Roberts, "Disillusioned Radicals: The Intellectual Odyssey of Todd Gitlin, Ronald Radosh and David Horowitz" (PhD diss., George Washington University, 2007), 245.

29. Horowitz, *Radical Son*, 442. Linking conversion experiences and violence, William James once noted that "emotional occasions, especially violent ones, are extremely potent in precipitating mental arrangements." James, *The Varieties of Religious Experience*, 198.

30. "Interview with David Horowitz," par. 17.

31. Tandy McConnell, "Introduction," vol. 10 of *American Decades*, ed. Judith S. Baughman et al. (Detroit: Gale, 2001), par. 1.

32. Ibid., par. 7, 2–6.

33. Aristotle, *Rhetoric*, trans. W. Rhys Roberts (New York: Modern Library, 1954); Karl Mannheim, "The Problem of Generations," in *Essays on the Sociology of Knowledge*, ed. Paul Kecskemeti (London: Routledge and Kegan Paul, 1952).

34. G. Thomas Goodnight, "Generational Argument," in *Argumentation: Across the Lines of Discipline*, ed. Franz H. van Eemeren et al. (Dordrecht, Netherlands: Foris, 1986), 134.

35. Ibid., 141.

36. Glenn Wallach, *Obedient Sons: The Discourse of Youth and Generations in American Culture, 1630–1860* (Amherst: University of Massachusetts Press, 1997), 2.

37. Philip J. Greven, "Youth, Maturity, and Religious Conversion: A Note on the Ages of Converts in Andover, Massachusetts, 1711–1749," *Essex Institute Historical Collections* 108 (1972): 129; Stephen R. Grossbart, "Seeking the Divine Favor: Conversion and Church Admission in Eastern Connecticut, 1711–1832," *William and Mary Quarterly* 46 (1989): 730.

38. Horowitz, *Radical Son*, x.

39. Wallach, *Obedient Sons*, 7.

40. Ibid., 8.

41. Ibid., 12; emphasis in original.

42. George B. Forgie, "Father Past and Child Nation: The Romantic Imagination and the Origins of the American Civil War" (PhD diss., Stanford University, 1972), 153.

43. Wallach, *Obedient Sons*, 15, 13.

44. P. Berger, *The Heretical Imperative*, 172, 64.

45. Ibid., 128.

46. Robert N. Bellah et al., *Habits of the Heart: Individualism and Commitment in American Life* (Berkeley: University of California Press, 2008), 233.

47. Ibid., 235.

48. Out of 171 reviews of *RS* on Amazon.com, 71 percent gave it five stars. "Customer Reviews: Radical Son," www.amazon.com/Radical-Son-Generational-David-Horowitz/dp/0684840057/ref=sr_1_1?ie=UTF8&qid=1516075847&sr=8-1&keywords=radical+son. One reviewer, Bnewell, claims: "I will forever frame my vision of contemporary politics through the lens David so masterfully created." Another, Sane 54, asserts that "this is one of the most mind-altering things I've ever read. . . . [I]t makes utterly believable a thesis I would have formerly thought ridiculous." Similarly, reflecting the autobiography's conversion language, Knitwit says: "[T]hank you David for showing me the light at the end of the tunnel, instead of the tunnel at the end of the light." Falcoff argues that "*Radical Son* is the most remarkable testament of its kind since Whittaker Chambers's *Witness*, a book which it resembles in more ways than one." Breitenbach, too, claims that *RS* is a "sensitive and forthright autobiography of a Sixties radical who later came to have second thoughts about his political philosophy." Jerome R. Breitenbach, "Suggested and Nonsuggested Reading," September 13, 2005, under "Politics and Current Events," https://courseware.ee.calpoly.edu/emeritus/jbreiten/sugread.html, par. 6. Lewy praises Horowitz, who "bares these trials with Rousseau-like candor and fervor." Guenter Lewy, "*Radical Son*," *National Interest* 49 (1997), http://nationalinterest.org/bookreview/another-country-review-of-david-horowitzs-radical-son-a-journey-through-our-time-780, par. 3, 7. An academic finds that *RS* "is a sobering and moving account of America's cultural revolution from the moral high points to the sociopathic low points. . . . Students need an alternative to the triumphalist narrative of the Sixties, and this is one of the best." Mark Bauerlein, "An Anti-progressive Syllabus," *Inside Higher Ed*, July 5, 2007, www.insidehighered.com/views/2007/07/05/anti-progressive-syllabus, par. 16. A blogger writes that *RS* "really woke me up about my own upbringing and gave me a compatriot." Jonathan Adler, "When Michael Met David," *The Volokh Conspiracy*, December 7, 2006, under "liberty," par. 2 and "the rut," par. 1, www.volokh.com/posts/1165502003.shtml. To Olson, this is "a document of the first importance for understanding the legacy of '60s radicalism." Ray Olson, "*Radical Son: A Journey through Our Times*," *Booklist*, January 1, 1997, 813. Noting the generational theme, another reviewer says that it is "the foremost manual on how the 1960s generation completely destroyed this country." Alwayscowgirl, "Horowitz Was Right," Amazon.com, September 21, 2008, www.amazon.com/Radical-Son-Generational-David-Horowitz/product-reviews/0684840057/ref=dp_top_cm_cr_acr_txt?ie=UTF8&showViewpoints=1, par. 1. Comporting with Horowitz's university project, another review explains that "it is necessary reading for those who wish to understand how the extreme left operated in the Vietnam era AND how the extreme left is operating today. . . . The renascent New Left described by Horowitz above resides in the colleges and universities of the United States." RFLaird, "Archives," May 9, 2004, *Instapunk*, www.instapunk.com/archives/InstaPunkArchiveV2.php3?a=83 (no longer available). One critic urges: "[W]hatever mistakes he has made—or continues to make—in life, he committed few of them in the shape and ring of *Radical Son*'s very affecting paragraphs." Sanford Pinsker, "Still Crazy (or Fuming) after All These Years," *Georgia Review* 51 (1997): 358.

49. Julia Vitullo-Martin, "*Radical Son: A Journey through Our Times*," *Commonweal*, June 4, 2004, www.commonwealmagazine.org/radical-son; S. Hicks, "Compassionate Communists"; Jack Shafer, "David Horowitz: Sore Winner," *Slate*, June 5, 1997, www.slate.com/id/1000016.

50. See David M. Oshinsky, "*Radical Son: A Generational Odyssey*," *New Leader*, December 16, 1996, 5–8.

51. John Reilly, "World's Oldest Red Diaper Baby Tells All," *JohnReilly*, 1997, www.johnreilly.info/rsdh.htm (no longer available); Orrin Judd, "Orrin's All-Time Top Ten List—Non-Fiction/Conservative Thought," Brothersjudd, February 9, 2001, http://brothersjudd.com/index.cfm/fuseaction/reviews.detail/book_id/969/Witness.htm, par. 16.

52. Vitullo-Martin, "Radical Son," par. 7; Pinsker, "Still Crazy," 358; Robert D. Archer, "When You Get Down to It, Just Another Extremist," Amazon.com, January 7, 2009, www.amazon.com/Radical-Son-Generational-David-Horowitz/product-reviews/0684840057/

ref=dp_top_cm_cr _acr_ txt ?ie=UTF8&showViewpoints=1, par. 1; Brad Fuller, "Two Poles of Ideological Extremism," Amazon.com, January 1, 2000, www.amazon.com/Radical-Son-Generational-David-Horowitz/product-reviews/0684840057/ref=dp_top_cm_cr_acr_txt?ie=UTF8&showViewpoints=1, par. 1; Michael W. Lynch, "Capital Letters: Aging Radicals," *Reason*, July 2000, www.reason.com/news/show/27760.html, par. 5.

53. See, e.g., Burke, *Permanence and Change*; Golden, Berquist, and Coleman, "Secular and Religious Conversion"; Ch. Griffin, "The Rhetoric of Form in Conversion Narratives"; McGee, "Witnessing and *Ethos*"; Jasinski, *Sourcebook on Rhetoric*.

54. While I agree with scholars such as Thomas Benson that autobiography synthesizes the fragmentation of one's life experience, I do not think that it necessarily produces "a fully rhetorical action to which Being (and becoming), Knowing, and Doing contribute equally" (13). Horowitz's rhetoric places *knowing* above *being*—an epistemological trumping in his conversion account. Thomas W. Benson (1974), "Rhetoric and Autobiography."

55. Abercrombie, Hill, and Turner, *The Penguin Dictionary of Sociology*, 322. Showing a common concern for self-referentiality, see also A. Johnson, *The Blackwell Dictionary of Sociology*, 255.

56. Horowitz, *Radical Son*, 438.

57. Michael Lynch, "Against Reflexivity as an Academic Virtue and Source of Privileged Knowledge," *Theory, Culture, and Society* 17 (2000): 34.

58. Ibid., 26.

59. Ira Bruce Nadel, *Biography: Fiction, Fact, and Form* (New York: St. Martin's, 1984), 6.

60. Orrin Judd, "*Radical Son: A Generational Odyssey* (1997)," BrothersJudd, January 27, 2001, www.brothersjudd.com/index.cfm/fuseaction/reviews.detail/book_id/103, par. 1; emphasis added.

61. This proposition bears similarities to Burke's concept of "casuistic stretching." Burke, *Attitudes toward History*.

62. Horowitz, *Radical Son*, 273.

63. Horowitz even labels his experience as between "old" and "new" lives, in terms of breaking himself into two parts and going back and forth between these lives until he could no longer keep them consistent. Ibid., 289, 290.

64. Ibid., 400.
65. Ibid., 399; emphasis added.
66. Ibid., 164.
67. Ibid., 337.
68. Ibid., 45, 46.
69. Ibid., 71.
70. Ibid., 297.
71. Ibid., 387.
72. Ibid., 427; emphasis in original.
73. Ibid.
74. Ibid., 428.
75. Ibid., 370; emphasis in original.
76. Ibid., 302, 307, 306. Elsewhere in the narrative, Horowitz makes reflective attentiveness to history a sine qua non of his political conversion, arguing that the Left simply did not care for the past. Later, he draws the conclusion that progressives are concerned only with a fantasy future, as opposed to conservatism's proper reflections on the lessons of the past. Ibid., 337, 396.
77. Ibid., 400.
78. Ibid., 326.
79. Goodnight, "The Liberal and the Conservative Presumptions," 313.
80. Ibid., 323–24.
81. Horowitz, *Radical Son*, 425. See also ibid., 305.
82. R. Lake, "The Metaethical Framework of Anti-abortion Rhetoric," 494.
83. Ibid., 494, 496.
84. Horowitz, *Radical Son*, 44.
85. Ibid.

86. Ibid.
87. Ibid., 440.
88. On "cosmopolitan communication," see Pearce, *Communication and the Human Condition*, 167–206.
89. Horowitz, *Radical Son*, 44.
90. Michael Wallace, "Ronald Reagan and the Politics of History," *Tikkun* 2 (1987): 17.
91. See Fisher, "Narration as a Human Communication Paradigm," 8.
92. Branham, "The Role of the Convert in *Eclipse of Reason* and *The Silent Scream*," 418.
93. Horowitz, *Radical Son*, 374.
94. Ibid., 113, 396, 361.
95. Ibid., 381.
96. Ibid., 368.
97. Ibid., 407.
98. On the language of "counterculture," see Albert and Albert, eds., *The Sixties Papers*, 15–22.
99. Reilly, "World's Oldest," par. 17.
100. Oneida J. Meranto, "Commentary: The Third Wave of McCarthyism: Co-Opting the Language of Inclusivity," *New Political Science* 27 (2005): 230.
101. See Kosterlitz, "Bush's Left Right-Hand Men," 1304. See also Thomas Frank, *What's the Matter with Kansas?: How Conservatives Won the Heart of America* (New York: Metropolitan Books, 2004).
102. On standpoint theory, see Nancy Hartsock, "The Feminist Standpoint," in *Discovering Reality*, ed. Sandra Harding and Merrill B. Hintikka (London: D. Reidel, 1983), 283–310.
103. T. Bowell, "Feminist Standpoint Theory," *Internet Encyclopedia of Philosophy*, n.d., www.iep.utm.edu/fem-stan/, par. 1.
104. C. Caldwell, "Renegade," par. 15.
105. Sanford Pinsker, "Coming Clean about the Late Sixties," *Partisan Review* 65 (1998): 325, 326.
106. James Bowman, "*Radical Son*," *National Review*, March 24, 1997, 50.
107. Tendays Komyathy, "'Fusion and Unity—This Was the Cry of My Father's Communist Heart,' Writes Horowitz, 'His Unquenchable Longing to Belong,'" Amazon.com, July 5, 2008, www.amazon.com/Radical-Son-Generational-David-Horo witz/product-reviews/0684840057/ref=d4p_top_cm_cr_acr_txt?ie=UTF8&showView points=1, par. 1.
108. Monaldo, "*Radical Son*," par. 13; emphasis added.
109. John Walker, "Reading List: *Radical Son*," *Fourmilog*, March 16, 2007, www.fourmilab.ch/fourmilog/archives/2007–03/000821.html, par. 6.
110. Bonnie M. Parsley, "A Life Transformed by Truth," Amazon.com, November 12, 2007, www.amazon.com/Radical-Son-Generational-David-Horowitz/product-reviews/06 84840057/ref=dp_top_cm_cr_acr_txt?ie=UTF8&showViewpoints=1, par. 1.
111. Johnny "Uncle Johnny," "Introspective, Insightful & Intellectually Honest," par. 1.
112. Wes Wynne, "David Horowitz's *Radical Son: A Generational Odyssey*," www.contumacy.org/1BookRev.html (no longer available).
113. R. Coleman, "Coming Home," Amazon.com, October 22, 2004, www.amazon.com/Radical-Son-Generational-David-Horowitz/product-re-views0684840057ref=dp_top_cm_cr_acr_txt?ie
=UTF8&showViewpoints=1, par. 1; emphasis added.
114. Judd, "*Radical Son*," par. 5.
115. Elektrophyte, "Remarkable," Amazon.com, June 23, 2005, www.amazon.com/Radical-Son-Generational-David-Horowitz/product-reviews/0684840057/ref=dp_top_cm_cr_acr_txt?ie=UTF8&showViewpoints=1, par.1.
116. Leonard Bushkoff, "60s Radical Still Shuns Moderation," *Christian Science Monitor*, April 7, 1997, 13.
117. Jeff Coulter, "Why I Am *Not* a Right-Winger: A Response to David Horowitz," *New Political Science* 20 (1998): 97, 98; emphasis added.
118. Ibid., 99, 110.
119. Lynch, "Against Reflexivity," 42; emphasis added.

120. Wade Clark Roof, *Spiritual Marketplace: Baby Boomers and the Remaking of American Religion* (Princeton, NJ: Princeton University Press, 2002), 12.
121. Ibid., 9.
122. Horowitz, *Radical Son*, 440.
123. For example, Horowitz explains that his political growth involved acting more conservatively than his radical colleagues while he was a member of the New Left, since his family life kept him from being overly radical. Ibid., 171.
124. Ibid., 103; emphasis added.
125. Ibid., 410.
126. Ibid., 279.
127. Ibid., 33.
128. McGee, "Witnessing and *Ethos*."
129. For a brief history of progressives and terms of progress in politics, see William J. Kelleher, *Progressive Logic: Framing a Unified Field Theory of Values for Progressives* (La Canada, CA: Empathic Science Institute, 2005); William G. Anderson, "Progressivism: An Historiographical Essay," *History Teacher* 6 (1973): 427–52.
130. John Bunyan, *The Pilgrim's Progress*, ed. N. H. Keeble (New York: Oxford University Press, 1998).
131. Adam Jentleson, "Sen. Lamar Alexander David Horowitz," Center for American Progress, April 18, 2006, http://thinkprogress.org/2006/04/18/alexander-horowitz, par. 6.
132. Wayne Booth, *Modern Dogma and the Rhetoric of Assent* (Chicago: University of Chicago Press, 1974), 25.
133. Horowitz, *Radical Son*, 3.
134. Ibid., 444.
135. Ted G. Jelen, "Political Esperanto: Rhetorical Resources and Limitations of the Christian Right in the United States," *Sociology of Religion* 66 (2005): 303–21.
136. Horowitz, *Radical Son*, x.
137. Ibid., 118.
138. Ibid., 171.
139. Ibid., 45.
140. Ibid., 206.
141. R. Lake, "Order and Disorder in Anti-abortion Rhetoric." See also Jean Goodwin, "Three Faces of the Future," *Argumentation and Advocacy* 37 (2000): 75.
142. Horowitz, *Radical Son*, 381.
143. Ibid., 445.
144. Ibid., 191.
145. Ibid., 381.
146. Ibid., 18.
147. Ibid., 32; emphasis in original.
148. Ibid., 394–95.
149. Ibid., 25.
150. Ibid., 52.
151. Ibid., 396.
152. Ibid., 47.
153. Ibid., 59.
154. Finn, *From Death to Rebirth*, 254.
155. Ibid., 261.
156. Horowitz, *Radical Son*, 173.
157. Ibid., 80.
158. Ibid., 168.
159. Ibid., 414.
160. Ibid., 446; emphasis added.
161. "Children," Bible.com, n.d., www.bible.com/search/bible?page=1&q=children&version_id=1.
162. 1 Cor. 13:11 [KJV], *BibleHub*, n.d., http://bible.cc/1_corinthians/13-11.htm; emphasis added.

163. See "Luke 15:11–32" [KJV], Biblegateway.com, n.d., www.biblegateway.com/passage/?search=Luke%2015:11–32&version=KJV. In the autobiography's conclusion, Horowitz sits with memorabilia from his father and discovers, tellingly, "what turned out to be my father's posthumous gift of healing to his prodigal son." Horowitz, *Radical Son*, 435.

164. There is an allusion toward and citation of the Old Testament biblical figure of David provided at one point in the autobiography. Ibid., 33.

165. Ibid., 445.

166. See Domke and Coe, *The God Strategy*.

167. Horowitz, *Radical Son*, 432.

168. A Customer, "More Proof that 'Liberalism' Is So Much Let's Pretend," Amazon.com, August 31, 1999, www.amazon.com/Radical-Son-Generational-David-Horowitz/product-reviews/0684840057/ref=dp_top_cm_cr_acr_txt?ie=UTF8&showViewpoints=1, par. 1; emphasis added.

169. Bowman, "*Radical Son*," par. 1.

170. Ibid., par. 7, 9.

171. "Speaking of Sidney Blumenthal," *New Criterion* 15 (April 1997), www.newcriterion.com/issues/1997/4/speaking-of-sydney-blumenthal, par. 4.

172. Jenny M. Hatch, "I Have Come Full Circle," Amazon.com, December 23, 2003, www.amazon.com/Radical-Son-Generational-David-Horowitz/product-reviews/0684840057/ref=dp_top_cm_cr_acr_txt?ie=UTF8&showViewpoints=1.

173. Dave Duffy, "Confessions of a Former Liberal," *Backwoods Home Magazine*, 1998, www.backwoodshome.com/articles/duffy50.html, pars. 15, 1.

174. Paul Rosa, "Covenant Son," *New Prospect Church*, March 2, 2007, www.newprospectchurch.org/sermon1.html (no longer available).

175. Justin Raimondo, "David Horowitz, Crybaby," Antiwar.com, January 5, 2004, www.antiwar.com/blog/2004/01/05/david-horowitz-crybaby.

176. J. Coulter, "Why I Am *Not* a Right-Winger," 115.

177. Wallach, *Obedient Sons*, 154, 157.

178. Often quoted, Kristol once said that "a neoconservative is a liberal who has been mugged by reality." Kristol, *Reflections of a Neoconservative*, 75.

179. See, e.g., Karen A. Foss, Sonia K. Foss, and Cindy L. Griffin, *Feminist Rhetorical Theories* (Thousand Oaks, CA: Sage, 1999); Cindy L. Griffin, "Rhetoricizing Alienation: Mary Wollstonecraft and the Rhetorical Construction of Women's Oppression," *Quarterly Journal of Speech* 80 (1994): 293–312; Carol Hanisch, "The Personal Is Political," in *The "Second Wave" and Beyond*, 2006, http://scholar.alexanderstreet.com/pages/viewpage.action?pageId=2259 (no longer available); Bonnie J. Dow and Mari Boor Tonn, "'Feminine Style' and Political Judgment in the Rhetoric of Ann Richards," *Quarterly Journal of Speech* 79 (1993): 286–302.

180. Horowitz, *Radical Son*, 423. Horowitz further shares that his father frowned upon his biographies, thinking that his son should write books about the world economic crisis. Ibid., 285.

181. Ibid., 439, 270, 258.

182. Ibid., 216.

183. Ibid., 423.

184. Ibid., 316. See also ibid., 113.

185. Ibid., 435.

186. Ibid., 139.

187. Ibid., 317.

188. Randall Rothenberg, "Ad in Campus Papers Stokes Protest, but on Wrong Issue," *Advertising Age* 72 (2001): 26.

189. Horowitz, *Radical Son*, 282.

190. Ibid., 336.

191. Ibid., 371.

192. Ibid., 218.

193. Ibid., 50.

194. Ibid., 3, 11–12, 46, 254.

195. Ibid., 175.

196. Ibid., 335. *RS* was published in the 1990s, when President Clinton also used much therapeutic rhetoric. Abbott, "A 'Long and Winding Road,'" 7.
197. Horowitz, *Radical Son*, 212.
198. See Burke, "(Nonsymbolic) Motion"; K. Campbell, "The Ontological Foundations of Rhetorical Theory."
199. P. Berger, *The Heretical Imperative*, 105.
200. Horowitz, *Radical Son*, 394, 411.
201. Randall A. Lake and Barbara A. Pickering, "The Anti(Abortion) Public Sphere," in *Arguing Communication & Culture*, ed. G. Thomas Goodnight (Washington, DC: National Communication Association, 2001), 480, 481.
202. Horowitz, *Radical Son*, 39.
203. Ibid., 324.
204. Ibid., 415.
205. Ibid., 360.
206. Ibid., 44.
207. Ibid., 430.
208. Ibid., 429.
209. Ibid., 289.
210. Ibid., 87.
211. Ibid., 400.
212. I borrow from Plato's *Allegory of the Cave* in Book VII of *Republic* here. Plato, *Republic*, in *Plato: Complete Works*, ed. John M. Cooper, trans. G. M. A. Grube (Indianapolis, IN: Hackett, 1997), 1132–55.
213. Horowitz, *Radical Son*, 99.
214. Ibid., 88; emphasis added.
215. Ibid., 50.
216. Ibid., 170.
217. Ibid., 216, 204.
218. Ibid., 88; emphasis in original.
219. Ibid.
220. On the origin of the phrase "the personal is political" in relation to the 1960s (especially the feminist movement), see Hanisch, "The Personal Is Political."
221. Hartsock, "The Feminist Standpoint," 283–310.
222. Gregg, "The Ego-Function of the Rhetoric of Protest," 81.
223. James W. Chesebro, John F. Cragan, and Patricia W. McCullough, "The Small Group Technique of the Radical Revolutionary: A Synthetic Study of Consciousness Raising," *Communication Monographs* 40 (1973): 136, 137.
224. Karlyn Kohrs Campbell, "The Rhetoric of Women's Liberation: An Oxymoron," *Communication Studies* 2 (1999): 131.
225. Celinda Lake and Matt Price, "Snapshot: The Women's Vote, 2008," *Ms. Magazine*, Spring 2008, www.msmagazine.com/spring2008/reallyWant_celindaLake.asp.
226. Roland Barthes, *Mythologies*, trans. Annette Lavers (New York: Hill & Wang, 1972), 129–42.
227. Horowitz, *Radical Son*, 289.
228. George Lakoff, *Moral Politics: How Liberals and Conservatives Think* (Chicago: University of Chicago Press, 2002).
229. Wallach, *Obedient Sons*, 8.
230. A Customer, "An Extremely Perceptive and Well Written Book," Amazon.com, May 2, 1997, www.amazon.com/Radical-Son-Generational-David-Horowitz/product-reviews/0684 840057/ref=dp_top_cm_cr_acr_txt?ie=UTF8&showViewpoints=1, par.1.
231. Bernard Chapin, "Thank God for His Journey," Amazon.com, August 6, 2007, www.amazon.com/Radical-Son-Generational-David-Horowitz/product-reviews/06848 40057/ref=dp_top_cm_cr_acr_txt?ie=UTF8&showViewpoints=1, par. 4.
232. Martin Asiner, "Radical from Both Sides," Amazon.com, February 21, 2009, www.amazon.com/Radical-Son-Generational-David-Horowitz/product-reviews/0684840057/ ref=dp_top_cm_cr_acr_txt?ie=UTF8&showViewpoints=1, par. 2.

233. P. McGuinness, "A Genuinely Profound Autobiography," Amazon.com, July 11, 2004, www.amazon.com/Radical-Son-Generational-David-Horowitz/product-reviews/0684840057/ref=dp_top_cm_cr_acr_txt?ie=UTF8&showViewpoints=1, par. 1.

234. Neo-neocon, "More from *Radical Son*," http://neo-neocon.blogspot.com/2005/06/more-from-radical-son.html, par. 4.

235. Kenneth Sohl, "Out from Under the Rock," Amazon.com, March 20, 2006, www.amazon.com/Radical-Son-Generational-David-Horowitz/product-reviews/0684840057/ref=dp_top_cm_cr_acr_txt?ie=UTF8&showViewpoints=1, par. 1.

236. "Speaking of Sidney Blumenthal," par. 5.

237. "Horowitz—the End of Time," *Wizblog*, May 20, 2005, www.danwismar.com/archives/wizblog/003685.html.

238. Kent Worcester, "*Radical Son: A Journey through Our Times*," *Library Journal* 121 (1996): 108.

239. Jonathan Yardley, "Strife with Father," *Washington Post*, February 9, 1997, X03.

240. A Customer, "Hilariously Awful," Amazon.com, December 11, 1999, www.amazon.com/Radical-Son-Generational-David-Horowitz/product-reviews/0684840057/ref=dp_top_cm_cr_acr_txt?ie=UTF8&showViewpoints=1, par. 1.

241. Tim Lieder, "Hmm," Amazon.com, May 10, 2000, www.amazon.com/Radical-Son-Generational-David-Horowitz/product-reviews/0684840057/ref=dp_top_cm_cr_acr_txt?ie=UTF8&showViewpoints=1, par. 2.

242. James Tilley, "Political Generations and Partisanship in the UK, 1964–1997," *Journal of the Royal Statistical Society* 165 (2002): 121. Tilley incorrectly attributes this statement to Winston Churchill, as do many others. See "Quotes Falsely Attributed to Winston Churchill," *International Churchill Society*, n.d., www.winstonchurchill.org/resources/quotes/quotes-falsely-attributed/. Apparently, John Adams and Francois Guizot, among others, had a hand in the statement's origination. Fred Shapiro, "John Adams Said It First," Freakonomics, August 25, 2011, http://freakonomics.com/2011/08/25/john-adams-said-it-first/.

243. See R. Lake, "The Metaethical Framework"; idem, "Order and Disorder."

244. Seyla Benhabib, "Toward a Deliberative Model of Democratic Legitimacy," in *Democracy and Difference*, ed. idem (Princeton, NJ: Princeton University Press, 1996), 71, 72.

245. Stephen G. Olbrys, "*Dissoi Logoi*, Civic Friendship, and the Politics of Education," *Communication Education* 55 (2006): 358, 363, 367.

246. M. Capps, Jr., "Great Book for Understanding the Counter Culture," Amazon.com, December 7, 2004, www.amazon.com/Radical-Son-Generational-David-Horowitz/product-reviews/0684840057/ref=dp_top_cm_cr_acr_txt?ie=UTF8&showViewpoints=1, par.1.

247. Henry Farrell, "Why We Shouldn't Play Nice with David Horowitz: A Response to *What's Liberal about the Liberal Arts*," Crooked Timber, June 11, 2007, http://crookedtimber.org/2007/06/11/why-we-shouldn%e2%80%99t-play-nice-with-david-horowitz-a-response-to-what%e2%80%99s-liberal-about-the-liberal-arts/#more-5963 , par. 23.

248. Slain, "So . . . He Is a Flip Flopper?" Amazon.com, July 3, 2007, www.amazon.com/Radical-Son-Generational-David-Horowitz/product-reviews/0684840057/ref=dp_top_cm_cr_acr_txt?ie=UTF8&showViewpoints=1, par. 1.

249. George Lakoff, *Don't Think of an Elephant!* (White River Junction, VT: Chelsea Green, 2004).

250. Vitullo-Martin, "*Radical Son*," par. 8, 12.

251. Hicks finds that Chambers is selective about the Black Panthers' history—failing to mention that it was monitored by the FBI, speeding its organizational decline. S. Hicks, "Compassionate Communists," 1. Shafer takes issue with Horowitz's assertions about how "Democrats supported the Black Panthers and progressives funded them, and that the Panthers turned out to be murderous swine. This is *news*? It's the *conventional wisdom* . . . [that Horowitz] didn't go public with his suspicions about the Panthers until he co-wrote a March 1981 feature in New West magazine. That story came three years after New Times magazine printed its July 10, 1978, expose of the group." Shafer, "David Horowitz," par. 2–4; emphasis in original.

252. Asen, "Toward a Normative Conception of Difference in Public Deliberation."

253. Horowitz, *Radical Son*, 276; emphasis in original.

254. Thomas A. Hollihan and Kevin T. Baaske, *Arguments and Arguing* (Long Grove, IL: Waveland, 2005); Goodnight, "The Liberal and the Conservative Presumptions," 304–37.

255. See Horowitz, *Radical Son*, 396, 356, 360.

256. See Edw. Morgan, *The 60s Experience*.

257. Burke, *The Rhetoric of Religion*, 299.

258. See Edw. Morgan, *The 60s Experience*.

259. C. Martin, "Williams James in Late Capitalism," 186.

260. Cotton Mather, *Successive Generations: Remarks upon the Changes of a Dying World, Made by One Generation Passing Off and Another Generation Coming On* (Boston: B. Green, 1715), 1; emphasis in original.

Chapter Four

Political Conversion as Bypassed Seduction

Garry Wills's Confessions of a Conservative

There is an author who was on the path to telling a political conversion narrative like those of Chambers, Podhoretz, and Horowitz. He had been part of many of the same conservative social circles in the postwar years, was an early admirer of *Witness*, and had shifted his politics over time—but with some distinctive differences. That person is longtime journalist and scholar Garry Wills, whose prolific career covering political and religious issues has left an indelible mark on public affairs.

Wills's autobiographical work *Confessions of a Conservative* (hereafter, *CC*) bypasses the seductions of a political conversion narrative. As someone who would have had good reasons to tell a story of political transformation, Wills provides a fitting example of discourse that diverged from the other authors' tales, given its rhetorical features and functions. From the outset, Wills makes evident some of his reasons for resisting the types of moves seen in the preceding narratives:

> Once one defines oneself primarily in opposition to one other thing, the essential surrender is made. . . . The obsessed person longs for some Ahab showdown with his own white whale. He grows to resemble the cruel thing he opposes, becoming its antitype or photographic negative. . . . Obsession with an enemy almost always makes one's neighbors become the enemy.[1]

Given the attention that Wills has paid to these issues, in both content and form his book provides a perspective on the deliberative concerns that have been the focus of this book. Before moving to final conclusions about political conversion narratives, this chapter provides one alternative vantage point for discussing how to think about such stories, while raising normative expectations about what a more democratic discourse could look like in public culture.

One important qualification needs to be reiterated in this analysis. Wills's changes have, by many accounts, involved a move from the political right to the left on many issues. To repeat a point made in the introduction, the deliberative problems of conversion narratives should not be defined in terms of allegiances to particular political movements. It might be tempting to assume that because Wills seemingly moved leftward (and most political conversion narratives in the last seventy years of U.S. history appear to be conservative), anti-deliberative qualities essentially emerge from belonging to or affiliating with a political party. As will be shown, Wills complicates the picture of a linear political journey between old and new movements in a way that defies easily assigning him to an ideology.

This volume has also argued that the construction and evaluation of an author's deliberative vision is best ascertained through a focus on the author's discourse, rendering movement affiliation relevant but not determining. As also mentioned in the introduction, another case study of a right-to-left political conversion, *Blinded by the Right*, illustrated how its author constructed a story in anti-rhetorical, absolutist terms, making political identity a foregone conclusion, much like the three previous cases in this book.[2] Such textual moves can be equally performed on the left or on the right.

A brief overview of Wills's life and context will help draw attention to several themes showing how the author bypasses a political conversion narrative and presents an alternative, more deliberative story. I use Wills's story in this chapter less to offer an ideal example of political transformation rhetoric than to focus on some potential ways out of the thicket of concerns raised by the preceding conversion narratives. Wills also offers a view of what better understandings of rhetoric have to offer our public discourse more generally.

WILLS'S LIFE AND TIMES

Born in 1934, Garry Wills grew up immersed in Catholic culture and spent six years in a Jesuit seminary before beginning his career as a writer. Wills has been called "perhaps the most distinguished Catholic intellectual in America over the last fifty years."[3] He has been an avid follower of figures such as Saint Augustine, G. K. Chesterton, and Cardinal John Henry Newman, and has written more than forty books covering topics such as civil rights, religious doctrine, and presidential histories. His tomes *Nixon Ago-*

nistes and *Inventing America*, in particular, received critical acclaim for their detailed, revisionist histories of Richard Nixon and Thomas Jefferson.[4]

Wills has written for *Esquire* magazine and has been a college professor for many years, first at Johns Hopkins and then at Northwestern University. His countless honors include a host of fellowships, honorary degrees, and a 1993 Pulitzer Prize for *Lincoln at Gettysburg*.[5] The author describes his career as one of "outside looking in"—as primarily an "observer" rather than a participant in public life.[6] Although Wills describes himself in such terms, he has spent periods at the forefront of various political movements.[7] After his seminary years, Wills was hired by William F. Buckley's conservative publication *National Review*, where he spent a decade as a drama critic for the magazine while pursuing a doctorate in classics at Yale. Wills noted the many ex-leftists who worked at the magazine,[8] underscoring the continuity of Chambers's and others' experiences as political converts at the organization. Upon leaving the magazine, and despite avowals that he was still a legitimate (though reformed) conservative for a time, he was viewed by his former friends as a liberal or radical.[9]

The magazine subsequently attacked Wills in response to his critique of the police at the 1968 Chicago Democratic National Convention, through a "National Review cover [that] superimposed Wills's head on the body of the activist and Black Panther leader Huey Newton."[10] As discussed by Michael Mcdonald, the magazine even had a recurring section called "Wills Watch," which "existed to chronicle Wills's post–*National Review* activities in service to American liberalism."[11] Compared with the previous three authors, who had something to reap from their political conversions during the periods when their books were released, Wills stood to gain little from publishing his book in 1979. One *National Review* staffer later even told Wills that he was glad that the author had been unable to enjoy the success of the conservative movement from 1980 forward.[12]

I consider naming Wills as a liberal/radical or conservative less important than identifying how *CC*'s rhetorical features and functions open deliberative space for tentative political judgments. This chapter does not aim to create a definitive account of deliberative discourse about political transformation rhetoric, nor does it conceive of deliberative communication in terms of some exacting thresholds. The following instead explores how several themes and theories in Wills's text provide at least one entry point for discussing how messages of personal political change could be fashioned in a more deliberative way.

WILL'S'S DELIBERATIVE RHETORIC

Bypassing Ultimate Demands: Processes over Products

CC bypasses many features of typical conversion rhetoric through a preference for open decision-making *processes* over conclusive rhetorical *products*.[13] In two of the book's most telling lines, Wills states: "Approving a completed journey is not deciding on a course,"[14] articulating that citizens should remain wary of times and places where "conclusion for its own sake becomes the supreme norm" in public affairs.[15] This is not to say that conclusions and judgments are unnecessary but rather that they should remain tentative considerations among competing claims. The author forgoes a rhetoric of conclusive ends or dogmatisms whereby, as Edwin Black explains, "an audience is solicited to view its social character in terms of one prevailing and exclusionary set of perceptual values determinative of social allegiance."[16] Where conversion rhetoric tends to frame political discourse with a sense of linear, foreordained demands, Wills's text circumvents such moves by committing to ongoing and relatively open judgments in public matters.

In some ways, Wills escapes from the rhetorical trajectory set by *Witness*.[17] Where *Witness* sought to promote a political conversion of Manichaean dualism, Wills draws from Augustinian texts to counter these ideas. *CC* notes that one of Augustine's insights in leaving Manichean dualism was "Evil is not positive or self-existent. It is flawed good."[18] From a rhetorical perspective, Augustine attempted to reconfigure the either/or nature of a conversion, which, in Wills's analysis, can create divisions between good and evil that are too easy. At the very least, the framing of evil as a "flawed good" repositions the Christian tenet in less essential, binary terms.

In *CC*, dualistic problems result from group acts, not simply political "beliefs." Wills outlines that "the more precisely we define the nature of justice and truth and reality, the more we exclude from our fellowship those who disagree," particularly among political approaches that are firmly "dedicated to a proposition,"[19] or closed to the possibility that future messages or events could further guide one's understanding. Just as Neil Postman once argued that "fanaticism begins with our falling in love, so to speak, with certain sentences,"[20] Wills situates fanaticism as a rhetorical phenomenon. Reflecting on the potential dangers that group discourses can demand leads the author to warn against the many ways theocracies can be generated through words.[21]

In forming conclusions, Will notes that people become part of groups through habits, commitments, styles, and formal attachments rather than beliefs.[22] Collective pressures and persuasive practices are mutually implicated in conversion narratives, which ask human beings to adhere to habitual rhetorical patterns and follow commitments among group members. Shifting from a focus on rhetorical conclusions to the processes by which they are created, Wills bypasses the type of conversion narratives examined to this point by calling into view *how* people even reach such commitments in the first place.

By skirting a rhetoric of totalizing group demands, at issue are the ways in which one can be too "bold and deep in [a] theory of politics," tempting one to be "right 'too soon.'"[23] One of the tricky features of political conversion rhetoric has been that authors often focus on the gradual nature of their experiences. Yet such incremental change is offset by how deep and determined political positioning can become, no matter how long the conversion has taken. Wills's excursions into politics turn instead to what kind of deliberative processes are at stake in personal political changes; he notes, for example, that politicians should compromise to counteract the development of rigid opinions in a changing political environment.[24]

Some detachment from a time-based rhetoric of past, present, and future is necessary to break the conversion mold. Where the conversion pattern has enticed some of its practitioners to place an unswerving template on their personal and political experiences, in a critical passage Wills turns from a need for final discourses in public life. He says that many people see the future as an external, knowable target toward which their lives should aim, having started at some past point and developing outward in a linear trajectory; he argues that this target is illusory, however, and that what happens next holds numerous possibilities that come into being from toggling between many pasts and many potential futures.[25] This explains why so many political platforms and pledges end up overstating what they can actually know about the future. Hence, the best approach is to gain as much broad and deep knowledge about the past as possible, but to always move forward with tentative judgments, a commitment to continual inquiry, and a respect for the world's complexity and surprises.[26]

Wills sees the past as a reservoir for future actions but bypasses predeterminations about what those possible futures will bring by countering terms that fix what can be known. Chambers saw the future as determined and parallel to his own conversion experience. Wills constructs a more limited picture of what one can claim from past experience, warning against closed orientations to the many paths that future political events may take. Practical wisdom can be informed by past experience; but in his words, history is not a revelation on par with religious scripture.[27] The future is more in flux than communicators often acknowledge.[28] Conversion can be the kind of rhetorical weapon that excludes, segregates, or falls prey to "'isolationism' and [the] individualism of solipsism."[29] In this sense, conversion defines a mostly fictitious end point.

Wills's stress upon how much a narrative should continue to frame future experiences distinguishes his book from the others in this volume. Where the other cases tended to force connections between temporality and essence, Wills implies that there are no such necessities. Black has even noted how *Witness* goes awry in Chambers's "attempt to compensate by apocalyptic posturing for the discrepancy between his account of his youthful, witless commitment to Communism, and the condition of desolated heroism that his memoir coaxes the reader to assign him. *Witness* may work as parable, but it is unconvincing as tragedy."[30] Overall, narratives with tragic, determined features ask readers to inhabit a world of dualistic divisions that are problematic for politics.

CC further opposes a solidified rhetoric of conversion by emphasizing humans' creative capacities. To the author, human beings are like God when they exhibit their creativity qualities, just as God made the earth and heaven, we also must make each day anew.[31] It is worth noting the constitutive force that Wills applies to story making. He does not deny the existence of certain realities, truths, and, in this case, beginnings. But human action is seen as a continuous, selective process that makes and unmakes what we know of the past, present, and future.

This focus on processes partly follows from Wills's implicit theory of rhetoric. Identifying Augustine as a professional rhetorician, Wills writes that for the famous theologian, people should not just look to the future or past, but rather use both in a "mutually constitutive" dialectic that demonstrates "reciprocally generative acts of man's *verbum* and his self."[32] In this approach, time, identity, and language are each positioned as subject to rhetorical intervention, as generated through and affected by human beings' ability to create political and social worlds through speech.

CC thus remains wary of how individuals and groups can tie themselves up in linguistic knots, proposing that such complications can be equally amended through further discourse. The human self is itself "constituted" because memory is created.[33] Politics is about human creation, not the eternal reflections of traditional Greek forms.[34] These creations are not individualistic, since, in Wills's Trinitarian terms, "God *faced* God" and "God creates by acting on himself."[35] Looking to the past is as much a communal as a creative process, inviting a recognition that such processes occur prior to, and are demonstrably more important for public deliberation than any products of rhetorical actions.

The other three cases in this volume have demonstrated that conversion rhetoric often demands an adherence to internal or external essences as loci for human decision making. When political judgment is called for, Horowitz turned to attributions of the convert's deep, internal reflexivity to make decisions, while Chambers saw the convert's journey as reflective of dualistic universal battles that control human action from above. On the other hand,

Wills prioritizes human community (and attendant communicative processes) as one of the best checks and balances for truth-seeking and policy development. *CC* takes issue with individuals and groups whose practices avoid debate.[36] Similarly, in working through his own Catholic faith, Wills follows others such as Cardinal Newman, who let bishops govern but located religious claims "in the Christian community at large, not in the private revelation to Popes."[37] Relative to the conversion narrative, *CC*'s prioritizing of rhetorical processes over products also focuses a larger consideration about terms of redemption or convention in political affairs.

Redemption or Convention: Convenience Rhetoric

Glenn Tinder writes that political systems tend to pursue either a politics of redemption or of convenience.[38] In a politics of redemption, governments attempt to redeem their populations in the same way religions have historically enforced protocols among their members. In a politics of convenience, it is merely the job of government to maintain order in society so that many different interests and perspectives can flourish. A defining feature of *CC* concerns its comparable use of what Wills says is the purpose of politics: "to hold people together in peace, not to enunciate 'raw justice,'" so that "the nation should be a human convention."[39] For the sake of analysis, I use the terms "convenience" and "convention" interchangeably to describe a limited, socially created politics that seeks to work with every citizen's needs and expressions despite imperfections in practice. Wills clarifies that society would not be possible if every political argument were grounded in ultimate, virtuous claims; in fact, civil war would be a constant.[40] I find that such "convenientist" (Wills's term) discourse calls for more epistemological humility and accountability for one's rhetorical choices than those made by this book's other political converts, who tend to introduce inviolable, undebatable experiences into public affairs.

By dichotomizing experience between old and new lives at each turn, conversion rhetoric tends to polarize politics with more "redemptive" than "convenient" weighting. As mentioned earlier, it is the difference between a political outlook that largely sees others as evil rather than merely mistaken.[41] Outlining his political theory, Wills underscores that politics is not about destroying others, but giving the losing player or side a "rematch"; while parties may campaign in grandiose terms, at the end of the day they agree to "Apocalypse No."[42] In battles between the two Cold War superpowers, the author admonishes that cosmic demands have little place in politics, since the idea of convenience calls for compromises that brook militaristic forms of rhetoric seeking to eliminate other political systems.[43] Instead, drawing from Augustine's *City of God*,[44] he calls for a politics based on a far less eternal "transitory unity."[45] More than one's political beliefs, the degree of space admitted for political tussling and differing judgments is at issue—not simply a priori commitments that automatically exclude others from a civic community.

Analyzing Augustinian ideas, *CC* counters the redemptive directionality that conversion accounts can manifest. Wills partly outlines that an ends-focused, determined politics runs opposite to his Catholic faith, but it is additionally Augustine's unknowingness about other men's souls within this religious tradition that leads the author to skepticism over righteousness and certainty.[46] When this convenience rhetoric edges close to drawing divides between old and new lives, however, the author is quick to note how much he supports traditions and how his proclivity for conservatism remains, along with his general respect for the political system's continuities and coherence, which "surely are conservative values."[47]

In this vision, conservatism should be comfortable with what Cardinal Newman called "a certain assemblage of beliefs, convictions, rules, usages, traditions, proverbs, and principles" that can be drawn from in pursuing practical political wisdom.[48] Wills positions politics as a matter of variable human measures over divine dictate or inner sanction, yet he leaves room for human agency and passionate advocacy in stating that voices of moral courage and change are heroic, and that we must foster such light at every opportunity.[49] In this spirit, there is a wry liminality to the book's title, *Confessions of a Conservative*, which appears to draw from both Barry Goldwater's *Conscience of a Conservative* and Augustine's *Confessions*, demonstrating the very "assemblage" of beliefs that Wills finds useful for politics.

Communication scholar Dan Hahn notes that citizens use rhetorical forms to react to uncertain political circumstances, providing themselves with stable language structures that can unfortunately overclaim what is knowable in a situation.[50] Similarly, the conversion form may be used as a structure to direct life stories and policy positions, but Wills's convenience rhetoric leaves open more space for uncertainty and future change than the conversion form has tended to admit (at least in this volume's previous cases). Wills asserts continuity and change less to use one's life experiences as a political weapon than to preserve the limits of one's knowledge and continual need to work with information from past and present others.

CC opens deliberative space by configuring politics as about horizontal rather than vertical or top-down rule. The best political relations are seen as a kind of "brotherhood without a father."[51] In both domestic and international affairs, politics should "settle for less" than implementing absolute justice, instead aiming "for the modest goal of protecting our shared good things."[52] A rhetoric of convention would, by implication, proceed from reflections over one's whole political community first, considering the breadth of human experiences capable of being incorporated into political deliberation and decision making.

Where typical conversion narratives start from and end with one's own experience or commitment to an ideology as a basis for political knowledge, approaching the public arena with redemptive, vertical posturing, a convenience rhetoric underscores how one's claims need be considered as part of a wider circle of relationships. Such rhetoric leaves more room for the unexpected paradoxes, chance encounters, and turns and returns than one-way, redemptive political visions. As Wills writes, the foundation for reasoning and reasonability in a complex social world are complexities themselves and an acknowledgment of the messiness of even having freedoms to begin with.[53]

The redemption or convention distinction is not an argument for a strict separation between religion and politics; nor is it to say that the state should not create or enforce norms of justice. Reinforcing the process-based politics explored in the previous section, convenience rhetoric simply calls for a more limited, communal approach to constructing public judgments than the features of conversion narratives tend to promote.

Some critics called into question *CC*'s apparent contradictions between saying that there should be affirmative action for blacks and arguments that it is not the state's role to preserve justice—i.e., so that the criterion of a convenient state is put aside for Wills's own causes.[54] M. J. Sobran says that distinguishing between "mere" and "final" justice would have helped in this regard, with the former meaning better "civic relations" rather than "ultimate" rewards.[55] The division between "mere" and "final" is useful, but I would add that a communicative understanding of these distinctions can also incorporate agency and communal accountability to processes of judgment, instead of the deductive, self-evident, or idiosyncratic claims to knowing found in much political conversion rhetoric.

In the U.S. context, Wills ironically finds that disestablishment between church and state has helped religious groups and practices proliferate.[56] In other words, politics should always admit room for religion; but for their very own interests, religious communicators should be wary of becoming too dominant in the public square. An open, convenient deliberative environment is far more conducive to the promotion of faith viewpoints than applying redemptive discourses to political matters. In this way, politics should involve accommodation rather than revelation.[57]

In practice, redemptive political discourses run into additional quandaries. Reinhold Niebuhr once argued in *Moral Man and Immoral Society* that the more political power human beings attain, the less "moral" their choices tend to become. By virtue of the kinds of decisions that political leaders have to make—for example, going to war in a foreign country *or* leaving an afflicted population without help, power and morality necessarily share an inverse relationship.[58] Anything more than a circumspect approach to political decision making hence runs the risk of overreaching in its ethical claims. Avoiding the revelatory demands of the other political conversion narratives, Wills's rendering of how justified accommodations to the political environment could best take place provides one approach to the problem of moral overstatement in public affairs.

Decision Making and Difference: Endless Argumentation

Just as *CC* prioritizes open decision-making processes above conclusive rhetorical products, the text operates with an implicit theory of argumentation about how such processes might occur. Deflecting the unidirectional features of conversion narratives, the text approaches difference as a matter for responsive deliberation rather than redemptive battle. W. Barnett Pearce writes that scholars should evaluate different forms of communication as positive or negative, depending on how they deal with difference.[59] In this spirit, Wills puts forward a theory of decision making accounting for the need to work with others, however messy: "The constant adjustings and compromisings, pushings and shovings, takings and givings, settlements and half measures that are ridiculed in our politics are the signs of life reacting as a whole; making society responsive to a number of needs, so we can move and change together."[60] Where the imperfections of human debate might be cause for trying to perfect oneself toward what is more right, true, and permanent—along the lines of many conversion narratives—Wills's deliberative vision remains content with the partial, tentative goods that endless argumentation can provide.[61] In public culture, concepts dealing with dialectical forms of communication such as "controversy" often carry negative connotations.[62] Countering these trends, Wills situates the tentative workings of political give-and-take as positive forces worth pursuing.

Drawing again from Augustine's discussion of the earthly, sinful City of Man and the heavenly City of God, which Wills distinguishes from a third city—the political sphere—the author remarks that "the other two cities have both process and finality. Their members are pilgrims before they reach final citizenship. The third city has no final citizens. It has only process, not finality."[63] Wholly uncompromising positions that fail to recognize and deal with difference have to do their best to avoid the ongoing changes of the political world.

Amid these changes, the public realm requires judgments (even judgments that have life or death impacts), but such judgments should be recognized for their partial human characteristics.[64] Wills spotlights that the body politic requires some temporary unities; after all, even demons and devils have a minimum threshold of getting along to constitute a group, such that peaceful foundations tellingly apply to both the just and unjust.[65]

Terms like "best" and "evil" miss the point of a deliberative politics[66] where, as a result of necessary processes of adjustment and compromise, solipsistic or idiosyncratic candidates are generally weeded out. In effect, if politicians could not compromise the only thing they would represent would be themselves.[67] This language of "compromise built on compromises" and even trying to accommodate those who won't reciprocate bypasses typical conversion terminology, promoting forms of power built on "holding out, deliberating, [and] bargaining," as Wills says.[68] Against the conversion form's tendency to have one pick and stick with a "side," Wills says that it's no accident that most politicians are lawyers, since lawyers engage in mediation, negotiation, and other skills involving working for one side one day and another the next; "the neutral agent is not a friend of one side, and therefore no enemy to the other side."[69]

Decision making that attends to difference leads to election results that are an expression by many people not to impose themselves on others, in a way that almost always guarantees that those who win can't destroy their opponents.[70] This line of reasoning does not mean that citizens should approach politics with minimalist expectations. Wills instead invites awareness of how problematic insular forms of communication that brook no opposition, or that have their politics worked out for good, are for societies.

Wills makes a case for endless argument evident through other models. He remarks that conservative political philosopher Willmoore Kendall was always debating with himself, looking for assumptions, questions missed, and inquiring about his own conclusions with integrity.[71] This is a different approach to reflexivity from the one set forth by Horowitz, which had stopping points for rhetoric and argument. Affirming Kendall's civic identity, Wills says that finding time for reflection, study, and creating are integral to original thought.[72] According to Wills, this is a mode of thinking and communicating that got Kendall ousted from Yale's political science department and, eventually, *National Review*, where he had been a staple figure. Wills attributes Kendall's departure to editor William F. Buckley's squelching of debate and creation of a "theocratic" atmosphere at the magazine.[73] *CC*'s awareness of the tensions that difference brings to the public square supports an implicit theory of deliberation where testing and criticism remain forever incomplete, yet necessary.

Along with rhetorical forms such as the conversion narrative, a host of other forces in society make an endlessly argumentative approach to politics difficult. Wills covers how geographical single-party pressures bear on free-thinking individuals—for example, if a longstanding Republican moves to a place that's largely Democratic, the chances are high that that person will become a Democrat or at least stop voting Republican, which will in turn affect her or his children.[74] Peer pressures, professional values, and ideological allegiance can play a larger role in one's orientation to politics than rational arguments about policies.[75]

Because of these pressures, Wills sees politics as mostly about continuity, perhaps giving more praise to the status quo and what the electoral systems preserve than may be warranted. At a minimum, *CC* asks readers to think about how geography, identity, and one's social groups affect argumentative processes, broadening a theory of deliberation to account for limiting interpretive prejudices while offering the possibility of reflection and revision from such embeddedness.

In Wills's eyes, when politicians gather their supporters and repeat the same clichéd messages and simply give them what they want to hear, they foster a mediocre politics.[76] Civil society can thus provide one of the most promising venues for public debate. By taking his lobbying directly into the streets and public places, Martin Luther King, Jr. ultimately opened up debate where the electoral process had shut it down.[77] In other words, endless argumentation in the face of difference offers a more informed approach to advocacy than the dictates of structures such as the conversion form tend to offer. A final characteristic of *CC* focuses a critical question about conversion narratives: What might more deliberative forms of identity rhetoric look like?

Toward Many Political Selves: Expansive Identity Discourse

Operating with multiple political selves, Wills's identity rhetoric provides an alternative deliberative vision to the other cases. This is not to downplay the importance of identity choices, or the impact of factors leading to what Pierre Bourdieu has called a "habitus"[78] —or situated habits and predispositions. *CC* shows, rather, how individuals should remain attentive to communicative forms inviting fixed ideological positionalities. *CC* invites readers to consider a dialectical, active understanding of identity, using terms such as "flexible," "polymorphous," and "easy [to] access" to describe civic selves that are both open to the deliberative environment and capable of understanding the complications that rhetorics about political identity can create for oneself and others.[79]

Individuals cannot avoid processes of identity change. Wills outlines that knowledge is dynamic and always in progress, changing our sense of selves from day to day: "we are different people by the time we end a sentence from the ones who began it. To *move* to a conclusion is to change in the very act of concluding."[80] In this formulation, human identity is recursive rather than fixed or determined, at once always drawing from the past but also innovating upon it with each utterance about the self. Wills's identity rhetoric is primarily verb driven, avoiding the solidifying nouns or adjectives of conversion language, leading one reviewer to note that the author "is not, after all, seeking followers but *drawing* up his own intellectual inventory."[81] Ultimately, a more positive form of civic identity than that offered by conversion narratives is marked by movement, restiveness, and a tendency to want to let one's thinking journey in different directions.[82]

As a Catholic and a political writer, Wills affirms various roles in the text, yet brackets these identity claims as subject to continued communicative inquiry. In a section of the text where he may have easily slipped into a conversion narrative propagating a grand chasm between old and new lives, Wills instead relates that:

> But people *do* keep asking what one is; and while I do not want to fight for a term . . . I could make up a third name, a new one; but that hardly solves the problem. If I were to call myself a "convenientist," that would involve more explanation than conservatism itself. If I called myself "Augustinian," I must recognize that Augustine's thought labors under centuries of misapplication and misunderstanding. . . . There is a sense in which I could still call myself a distributist, as I did in 1957, but I would have to distinguish between my form of distributism and all others—there is no using a term simply in the complex world of our politics.[83]

In this passage, Wills does not make political identity a blank canvas on which any fleeting self might be painted. He plays with how messages about potential selves could create different futures in which there is little room for further talk of what identities might mean. One process-based term that defies political conversion in this regard is "explore." Wills says that he finds himself still exploring pieces of one philosophy on economics, another on political realism, and another on moderation.[84]

Yet identity terms still have to be negotiated effectively in an environment pressing for such labels. Wills cites one constant pressure, in particular: a demand that he confess to an identity as a conservative, an attribution that he says he often failed to live up to.[85] But he quickly turns to a larger consideration—that the idea of confession itself has many meanings in Augustinian thought.[86] As Wills underscores in another section, Augustine himself held multiple roles and had multiple conversions, and was a critic of both pagan and Christian superstitions.[87] In this spirit, *CC* highlights an ongoing tension between every human being's need to make rhetorical choices while not becoming a slave to them. Since people live in a world of tangled up language, they have to be especially wary of substituting slogans and explanations from leaders for dialectic, challenging thought; but they also need to use the terms that are available to open up the possibility of renewing or redefining words.[88] A recursive self is evident in both the defining processes and the defined products of human rhetoric.[89] More important, these conceptions make problematic identity claims to "authenticity." Discourse can be authentic only to the extent that it represents a useful term for the moment, not some immutable substance that positions identity as incapable of amendment or redefinition. Compared with conversion rhetoric, *CC* brackets and complicates attributions as important choices but always as among many others that could have been made.

Juxtaposed against Horowitz's reflexivity rhetoric, for instance, a more deliberative, democratic identity rhetoric would not commit to stopping points. Ironically, the growth espoused by conversion narratives withers at a point where political-identity decisions have reached a dead end. Wills underscores that "to have an identity is not to be fixed at one stage of learning; it is, rather, to have a capacity to integrate new experience within a self-correcting continuum. One is never more oneself than in the extension of the self. To cease extending is to begin decomposing, losing identity as a living unit."[90] In a media environment enamored with political typecasting, Wills bucks such trends by focusing on the kinds of rhetorical identity choices that can create an inflexible sense of selves. In this regard, conversion's reifying tendencies are sidestepped through commitments to continue self-creating.[91] No matter how embedded in a context one might be, generating alternative identity choices is made critical to the advancement of democratic societies.[92]

One productive way to foster more expansive identity rhetorics is to play with the ambiguities, contradictions, oppositions, and paradoxes that consistent identity claims tend to manifest. For example, according to Wills, everyone is a living contradiction in being both an elitist and not an elitist, with conservatives, for example, despising many elite professors but loving CEOs of companies and military leaders, and vice versa for liberals.[93] Additionally, everyone has both liberal and conservative tendencies, remembering the past with awe while looking toward the future with anticipation—just as innovation without tradition can be dangerous.[94] *CC* recognizes how commitments to some political-identity terms, although necessary, fold on more minute examination. Seeing how a claim to any one identity term such as "liberal" prevents one from perceiving all the ways that one is likely also not liberal bypasses conversion's emphasis on the unbridgeable differences between old and new lives.

R. Z. Sheppard finds that Wills "insists on rigorous and adventurous exploration of paradox and contradiction."[95] Another critic characterizes the author as "too much his own man with his own mind to fit into any pigeonhole. Just as it is not easy to classify his beloved Chesterton, so it is difficult to label Wills."[96] Others describe how *CC* affected their understandings of the author: "If the world is divided between those who think Alger Hiss despicably guilty and those who are certain he is admirably innocent, Wills can be counted on to come along and explain him as simultaneously guilty and admirable."[97] Another reviewer noted, as well, "whereas liberals are secularists, [Wills] is a Catholic. Similarly, he is viewed as a journalist in the academy and as an academic by journalists."[98] Overall, Wills's multiple identities and general approaches to rhetoric evidence an exceptional case when compared with other political conversion narratives.

CONCLUSION

Wayne Booth once remarked that "whatever imposes belief without personal engagement becomes inferior to whatever makes mutual exploration more likely. . . . The process of inquiry through discourse thus become more important than any possible conclusions, and whatever stultifies such fulfillment becomes demonstrably wrong."[99] By prioritizing rhetorical processes over products, conceptualizing a politics of human convention over redemption, creating grounds for endless argumentation, and promoting conditions for expansive identity rhetorics, *CC* bypasses the totalizing features of the other political conversion narratives, engaging a process discourse in both content and form.

One of the most important tasks for public policy has been to refine standards for public discourse and deliberation,[100] so this chapter has offered an alternative illustrating what more democratic forms of rhetoric could look like compared with stories using the conversion form. Connections between *CC*'s ideas and current debates covering reason and religion, public deliberation, and the possibilities for democratic discourses bring into view what Wills's text contributes to some larger issues at stake in political conversion narratives.

By examining four interrelated cases for their deliberative outlooks, this volume has focused on what I claim to be more or less propagandistic public discourse. Nicholas O'Shaughnessy finds that some classic elements of propaganda include Manichaean dualism, a quest to create enemies at every turn, and "the eliding of a complex world into a condensed and coherent and tightly defined framework."[101] For many of the aforementioned reasons, Wills's text could have easily slipped into such a structure. As some religious controversies have illustrated, a tendency to embellish conversion narratives with a "particular bent toward narrative one-upmanship" has presented problems for congregations[102]—and the temptation to heighten and dramatize one's "before" and "after" experiences to fit the conversion form's pressures presents an ongoing problem for public discourse.

Relative to this concern, a central debate in current scholarship regards the role of religion in political movements. In a dialogue with Pope Benedict XVI, Jürgen Habermas has been a proponent of the idea that religion provides both a powerful "motivation" and commitment to the "common good" among citizens in a way that legal rules cannot.[103] He finds that religious traditions can still thrive without "dogmatism," or "the coercion of people's consciences" in modern societies,[104] building on his earlier work proposing that "neither science nor art can inherit the mantle of religion; only a morality, set communicatively aflow and developed into a discourse ethics, can replace the authority of the sacred."[105] Michael Sandel has similarly commented that "a politics that brackets morality and religion too completely soon generates its own disenchantment. Where political discourse lacks moral resonance, the yearning for a public life of larger meaning finds undesirable expression."[106] In this vein, Wills's text resembles Habermas's twin concerns for involving religion in the public square while heeding dogmatisms, using religion as a motivator for both producing and critiquing politics.

As Wills's book illustrates, at stake is a theory of reflexivity prioritizing communicative processes and endless argumentation. Habermas finds that "as long as participants inhabit the same discursive universe, there is no hermeneutic impulse to reflect on otherwise self-evident, unarticulated background motivations."[107] I find that the question of whether discourse becomes dogmatic has less to do with assigning religiosity to messages than with the types of rhetorical forms that can lock individuals and groups into the "same discursive universe[s]," deflecting a rhetoric of inquiry. Although some indicators highlight that, for example, presidential candidates are becoming "more partisan, sectarian, and liturgical" in their public messages combining faith and politics,[108] the fact that faith is involved is less important than how religious discourse operates in the political realm.

Some Christian traditions manifest the tensions evident in political conversion rhetoric. In another book, Wills conducted an exhaustive survey of U.S. religious history, finding that continual strains between head and heart—or reason and emotion—have gone on for quite some time between Enlightenment-conditioned rational religion and experiential and mission-oriented Evangelicalism.[109] Chambers, Podhoretz, and Horowitz show that political conversion accounts have also been reflective of these tensions, working under various rational or experiential guises. Along these lines, Robert Glenn Howard finds that Martin Luther created a reformation that made both fundamentalism and pluralism possible, since Luther configured faith "beliefs" as "authorized by an individual experience of the divine," but with the effect that any actor or the state could now be challenged, opening space for all kinds of conflicting religious interpretations.[110] Compared with figures such as Erasmus, for whom God's words were to be studied and debated, Luther prioritized individual access to transcendent authority—effacing public deliberation from theological and political matters.[111]

In different ways, Chambers, Podhoretz, and Horowitz are more in Luther's camp while Wills's book can be positioned with Erasmus's. A rhetorical study of these four authors shows how a close reading of discursive features can provide entry points to deliberative theories.[112] Kristy Maddux finds that terms such as "evangelicalism, fundamentalism, and modernism can be defined as rhetorical styles rather than institutions, groups of people, or individual leaders."[113] In other words, communication criticism can unearth the rhetorical habits of particular texts, providing vantage points on how the tonal or structural choices of deliberators tend to fix positions. G. Thomas Goodnight also underscores how "at stake in any particular style, trend, or performance (that is in the rhetoric) of public engagement may be . . . the communicative practices invoked to articulate and enact a public sphere."[114] In creating the conditions for a politics in which all can participate, not all discourse forms are created equal. Empirical research has shown that narratives tend to reduce the ability of individuals to offer critiques and counterarguments.[115] So one implication is that deliberative theorists need to engage discourse forms aiming to silence rhetoric, especially redemptive speech with little concern for ongoing, innovative, and robust speech.

Through an extensive analysis of the ways in which figures such as Thomas Hobbes have undermined deliberative discourse in their political theories, Bryan Garsten asks scholars to examine "speech that aims to persuade [and] can engage our capacity for practical judgment," as distinguished from "efforts to avoid rhetorical controversy" that "tend to produce new and potentially more dogmatic forms of rhetoric."[116] He advises a deeper engagement with many of the tricky methods by which advocates can manifest "anti-rhetorical rhetoric[s]," such as calls to public reason that homogenize diverse expressions in the name of an overly demagogic joint perspective.[117] From this, Garsten crafts a definition of deliberation that "stimulates reflection or judgment by disrupting ordinary habits of response," as opposed to "universally acceptable procedures of argumentation."[118]

Wills's deliberative vision avoids the overly homogenizing emphases of rhetorical forms like conversion, making tentative identity claims without folding political processes into redemptive, singular, and powerful voices that have little interest in drawing out reflection and further judgments. A primary danger facing public deliberation is "the atavistic belief that identities can be maintained and secured only by eliminating difference and otherness."[119] As political conversion narratives highlight, rhetoric seeking to excise differences go far beyond religious spheres. Some studies even show that redemption and rebirth messages continue to permeate the U.S. government's missions.[120]

Deliberation scholar Seyla Benhabib asks, "[S]ince all identities . . . are riven by multiple, complex, and heterogeneous allegiances, does not the 'politics of presence' run the risk of reinforcing a form of identity-essentialism, a defunct metaphysics of group presences?"[121] It is toward this question that Wills's discourse is perhaps most distinguished from the other narratives. Conversion stories merge identities with movement claims, running the risk of introducing partially or fully metaphysical assertions (for reasons that can be either religious or self-induced) into a political arena that necessarily manifests more groups, allegiances, and, ultimately, proliferating rhetorics than essentialized discourses can contain. Wills affirms various identities as a contribution to the public sphere but positions identity as a matter for continual upkeep, subject to further education.

At the same time, *CC* is not a perfect text. In continuing efforts to work toward more deliberative theories of democracy, perfection should not be expected, in any case. The book could be faulted for being too undecided, too inaccessible to non-Catholics or others not sharing Wills's environ, or simply too distanced from many of the concrete political events happening during the time it was written. John Lee writes that Wills's book may even be seen as a call to political passivity, given the author's many affirmations of the electoral and political system.[122] As a well-to-do writer working at the top of his craft, Wills could also be seen as elitist. Critic Jack Beatty takes issue with Wills's implication that virtue should be equated with knowledge, pointing out that educated elites send populations into wars like Vietnam even when citizens are often against it.[123] Still, in circumstances that could well have prompted a political conversion narrative, Wills said no.

NOTES

1. Wills, *Confessions of a Conservative*, 59.
2. Waisanen, "Political Conversion as Intrapersonal Argument." As a former conservative journalist turned liberal media activist, David Brock uses the conversion form to document his political transformation. Similar to Horowitz, Brock attended the University of California at Berkeley, was inspired to become a conservative by the writings of Norman Podhoretz, and went on to become a writer for various conservative publications. Brock, *Blinded by the Right*, 5. Brock cites former leftists Irving Kristol and Ronald Reagan (two figures influenced by Chambers) as also having influenced his turn to conservatism. Conversely, in his journey out of conservatism, Brock admits that he searched for inspiration from others who had traversed the opposite path and found that Lee Atwater, the "Republican pitbull strategist," had "made telephone calls from his deathbed apologizing to those he had slandered." See David Brock, "Unliving a Lie," *Fast Company*, September 2004, 75. Appalled by the conservative smear campaigns that he was a part of in the 1990s, Brock turned from his former ways and created Media Matters for America, a watchdog organization for conservative media practices. Brock's political conversion narrative highlights that the author does not appear to be invested in revelatory, transcendent "truth" as a standard for his conversion, instead focusing on fixed "recovery" of self terms. That is, there is an equally foundational framing of inner validity in Brock's narrative that bears significant similarities to the first three cases in this volume. Brock presents readers with notions of a "real" self and "authenticity" in the public sphere—or a way to justify a "true" experience of recovery that, given the weight of evidence, forgoes public reasoning and reasonability. Waisanen, "Political Conversion as Intrapersonal Argument."
3. John L. Allen, "'Poped Out' Wills Seeks Broader Horizons," *National Catholic Reporter*, November 21, 2008, http://ncronline.org/news/people/poped-out-wills-seeks-broader-horizons, par. 2.
4. "Garry Wills," Contemporary Authors Online (Detroit: Gale Biography in Context, 2012).
5. Jack J. Cardoso, "Garry Wills," in *The Scribner Encyclopedia of American Lives Thematic Series*, ed. Arnold Markoe and Kenneth T. Jackson (New York: Gale Biography in Context, 2003), par. 12–13.
6. Garry Wills, *Outside Looking In: Adventures of an Observer* (New York: Viking, 2010).

7. As one critic notes, this started early, since "at a 1972 antiwar demonstration in Washington, Wills decide[d] to make a rare lurch from outsiderdom to activism, undergoing arrest." John Leo, "Wills's Testament," *Commonweal* 138 (2011): 22.
8. Wills, *Confessions of a Conservative*, 29. Wills editorializes further that the people who hated the New Deal and government regulation ended up loving the much grander form of the "warfare state." Ibid., 30.
9. Frank Gerrity, Review of *Confessions of a Conservative*, Best Sellers, 1979, 224.
10. Cardoso, "Garry Wills," par. 6.
11. Michael McDonald, "Wills Watching," *New Criterion*, June 2011, 74.
12. Wills, *Confessions of a Conservative*, 79.
13. For more on this distinction in public argumentation, see Daniel J. O'Keefe, "Two Concepts of Argument," *Journal of the American Forensic Association* 13 (1977): 121–28.
14. Wills, *Confessions of a Conservative*, 85.
15. Ibid., 112.
16. E. Black, *Rhetorical Questions*, 39.
17. When Wills worked for *National Review*, he was once assigned to review Chambers's *Cold Friday*. Wills relates that he had to go back and reread *Witness* again to corroborate the witty and delightful Chambers he knew in person from the pretentiousness he observed across Chambers's writings. Wills, *Confessions of a Conservative*, 50.
18. Ibid., 193.
19. Ibid., 201.
20. Postman, *Crazy Talk, Stupid Talk*, 107.
21. Wills, *Confessions of a Conservative*, 54.
22. Ibid., 112. Elsewhere, Wills helpfully explains that genre has to do with a text's external relationships, while form is about its internal mechanics. Ibid., 98.
23. Ibid., 180.
24. Ibid.
25. Ibid., 217.
26. Ibid.
27. Ibid., 197.
28. Ibid., 226–27.
29. Ibid., 59.
30. E. Black, *Rhetorical Questions*, 44–45.
31. Wills, *Confessions of a Conservative*, 231.
32. Ibid., 229. At the same time, Wills appears to be unsettling the type of "sacred canopies" described by others, such as Peter Berger. See Peter L. Berger, *The Sacred Canopy: Elements of a Sociological Theory of Religion* (Garden City, NY: Doubleday, 1967).
33. Wills, *Confessions of a Conservative*, 223–24; emphasis in original.
34. Ibid., 221.
35. Ibid; emphasis in original.
36. Ibid., 158.
37. Ibid., 68.
38. Glenn Tinder, *Political Thinking: The Perennial Questions* (New York: HarperCollins, 1995), 198–204.
39. Wills, *Confessions of a Conservative*, 58.
40. Ibid., 184, 187.
41. See Burke, *Attitudes toward History*.
42. Wills, *Confessions of a Conservative*, 116.
43. Ibid., 58.
44. Augustine, *The City of God*, trans. Marcus Dods (Peabody, MA: Hendrickson, 2009).
45. Wills, *Confessions of a Conservative*, 197. Some readers might find Wills's interpretation of Augustine as a "convenientist" surprising, since the historical figure is often assumed to be a Neoplatonist. In his reading, Wills clarifies that Augustine rebelled against both Plato and Aristotle and is not a Neoplatonist, particularly by looking at certain passages from the *City of God*. Ibid., 54.
46. Ibid., 210.

47. Ibid.
48. Ibid, 214.
49. Ibid.
50. Hahn writes that "politics, by its very nature, seldom deals in certainties; rather, it deals with actions today that will produce reactions tomorrow. It deals with hypotheses, speculations, and arguments about which actions among those possible for today will produce which reactions, desirable and undesirable, that are possible for tomorrow. Thus politics, inherently, is involved with rhetoric about the unknowable. How, then, do people come to believe so fervently that they do know? How do they become so positive that the newest flux of illegal immigrants will hurt the economy or that failure to build a certain weapon system will doom us to another war?" Dan Hahn, *Political Communication: Rhetoric, Government, and Citizens* (State College, PA: Strata, 2002), 74.
51. Wills, *Confessions of a Conservative*, 66. Wills says that his view is drawn from how Catholics tend to begin from the social structure of the family over individuals. This understanding of the family is not about patriarchy, however—mutual admiration and neighborly respect are the relations most worth pursuing. Ibid., 56–57.
52. Ibid., 207.
53. Ibid., 132, 130.
54. David Gordon, "Confusions of a Conservative," LewRockwell.com, November 18, 2005, www.lewrockwell.com/gordon/gordon14.html (no longer available).
55. M. J. Sobran, "Up to Liberalism," *National Review*, May 25, 1979, 686.
56. Garry Wills, *Head and Heart: American Christianities* (New York: Penguin, 2007).
57. Wills, *Confessions of a Conservative*, 199.
58. Reinhold Niebuhr, *Moral Man and Immoral Society* (Louisville: Westminster John Knox, 1960).
59. W. Barnett Pearce, *Making Social Worlds: A Communication Perspective* (Malden, MA: Blackwell, 2007).
60. Wills, *Confessions of a Conservative*, 214.
61. My reference to "endless argumentation" is akin to Burke's metaphor of "unending conversation." Burke, *The Philosophy of Literary Form*, 110–11.
62. G. Thomas Goodnight, "Controversy," in *Argument in Controversy*, ed. Donn W. Parson (Annandale, VA: Speech Communication Association, 1991), 1–13.
63. Wills, *Confessions of a Conservative*, 198.
64. Ibid., 119.
65. Ibid., 194.
66. Ibid., 114.
67. Ibid., 172.
68. Ibid., 173, 204, 174.
69. Ibid., 175.
70. Ibid., 113; emphasis in original.
71. Ibid., 23.
72. Ibid., 181.
73. Ibid., 24–25. Wills further refers to the many occasions where differences within the conservative coalition assembled at *National Review* were bypassed. Ibid., 13.
74. Ibid., 103.
75. Ibid., 104. In another part of the book, Wills castigates rational models of debate that fail to take into account how visceral political commitments can become, among other factors. Ibid., 163. Edwin Black has made similar comments: "The acquisition of a social identity, then, is not only the relatively simple matter of embracing a term or a set of terms. It is, also, the infinitely more complex act of assimilating whole networks of affiliation, value, and vocabulary." E. Black, *Rhetorical Questions*, 49–50.
76. Wills, *Confessions of a Conservative*, 183.
77. Ibid., 161.
78. Pierre Bourdieu, *Distinction: A Social Critique of the Judgment of Taste*, trans. Richard Nice, (Cambridge, MA: Harvard University Press, 1984).

79. Wills, *Confessions of a Conservative*, 176. In a different context, for an analysis of how deliberation and multiple political identities relate, see Waisanen, "Toward Robust Public Engagement."
80. Wills, *Confessions of a Conservative*, 222; emphasis in original.
81. Joseph Lelyveld, "Intellectual's Inventory," *New York Times*, July 15, 1979, www.nytimes.com/books/97/06/01/reviews/wills-confessions.html; emphasis added. Wills clarifies that "man begets himself in his act of knowledge," using Gerard Manley Hopkins's verb "to self" to describe such constitutive identity rhetoric. Wills, *Confessions of a Conservative*, 224.
82. Wills, *Confessions of a Conservative*, 230; emphasis added.
83. Ibid., 211–12.
84. Ibid., 215.
85. Ibid., 3.
86. Ibid. More often than not, Wills wrestles with terms that others have used to characterize him, apparently through attempts to make him into a political convert. After his book on Nixon came out he was surprised to learn that many did not consider him a conservative anymore, while he was also not a liberal given his critical approaches to electoral politics on the left. Despite these criticisms, Wills was called a liberal by *National Review* and a radical by William F. Buckley, but he clarifies that this was misleading (as most political attributions are), since he did not support the anti-elitist sentiments shared by radicals. Ibid., 121–22. One *CC* reviewer writes that Wills will always be claimed by others, regardless of what he either does or does not espouse about his political identity. Walter Karp, "The Constructs of a Conservative," *Harper's*, November 1979, 96.
87. Wills, *Confessions of a Conservative*, 190–91.
88. Ibid., 213.
89. Ibid., 230.
90. Ibid., 65.
91. Ibid., 230.
92. Ibid., 147–48.
93. Ibid., 65.
94. Ibid., 216; emphasis in original.
95. R. Z. Sheppard, "The Heart and Head of the Matter," *Time*, April 23, 1979, 86–87.
96. Paul K. Cuneo, review of *Confessions of a Conservative*, *America*, June 30, 1979, 540.
97. Werner J. Dannhauser, "Against the Center," *Commentary*, July 1979, 68.
98. Michael McDonald, "Wills Watching," *New Criterion*, June 2011, 76–77.
99. Booth, *Modern Dogma and the Rhetoric of Assent*, 137.
100. Giandomenico Majone, *Evidence, Argument, and Persuasion in the Policy Process* (New Haven, CT: Yale University Press, 1992).
101. Nicholas O'Shaughnessy, "The Death and Life of Propaganda," *Journal of Public Affairs* 9 (2010): 9–10.
102. "Bearing True Witness: Why We Are Tempted to Embellish Conversion Stories," *Christianity Today*, July 2010, 45.
103. Jürgen Habermas and Joseph Ratzinger, *The Dialectics of Secularization: On Reason and Religion*, trans. Brian McNeil (San Francisco: Ignatius, 2005), 22–23, 30. In other works, Habermas notes that "the ambition of philosophy's 'translation program' is, if you like, to rescue the profane significance of interpersonal and existential experiences that have so far only been adequately articulated in religious language." Jürgen Habermas, *Religion and Rationality: Essays on Reason, God, and Modernity* (Cambridge, MA: MIT Press, 2002), 164.
104. Habermas and Ratzinger, *The Dialectics of Secularization*, 43. Even Joseph Ratzinger (who became Pope Benedict XVI) writes that "there exist *pathologies in religion* that are extremely dangerous and that make it necessary to see the divine light of reason as a 'controlling organ.'. . . However, we have also seen in the course of our reflections that there are also *pathologies of reason*. . . . [I]t suffices here to think of the atomic bomb or of man as a 'product.'" In this understanding, religion and reason can correct each other's limitations. Ibid., 77–78; emphasis in original.

105. Jürgen Habermas, *The Theory of Communicative Action*, vol. 2, trans. Thomas McCarthy (Boston: Beacon, 1987), 92.

106. Michael J. Sandel, *Democracy's Discontent: America in Search of a Public Philosophy* (Cambridge, MA: Belknap, 1996), 322.

107. Habermas, *Religion and Rationality*, 155.

108. Brian Kaylor, "No Jack Kennedy: Mitt Romney's 'Faith in America' Speech and the Changing Religious-Political Environment," *Communication Studies* 62 (2011): 504.

109. Wills, *Head and Heart*.

110. This was far before *The Fundamentals* of the U.S. fundamentalist movement was written in 1910. Robert Glenn Howard, "The Double-Bind of the Protestant Reformation: The Birth of Fundamentalism and the Necessity of Pluralism," *Journal of Church and State* 47 (2005): 92.

111. Examining past or shared resources thus became irrelevant to working out one's theological interpretations; given this theory of public engagement, Luther unsurprisingly refused to meet Erasmus to discuss these issues. Ibid., 97, 101.

112. See Edward Schiappa, *Defining Reality: Definitions and the Politics of Meaning* (Carbondale: Southern Illinois University Press, 2003).

113. Kristy Maddux, "The Foursquare Gospel of Aimee Semple McPherson," *Rhetoric & Public Affairs* 14 (2011): 291.

114. G. Thomas Goodnight, "The Personal, Technical, and Public Spheres: A Note on 21st Century Critical Communication Inquiry," *Argumentation and Advocacy* 48 (2012): 261.

115. Jeff Niederdeppe, Michael A. Shapiro, and Norman Porticelli, "Attributions of Responsibility for Obesity: Narrative Communication Reduces Reactive Counterarguing among Liberals," *Human Communication Research* 37 (2011): 295.

116. Bryan Garsten, *Saving Persuasion: A Defense of Rhetoric and Judgment* (Cambridge, MA: Harvard University Press, 2006), 174–75.

117. Ibid., 181–82.

118. Ibid., 190, 196.

119. Seyla Benhabib, "Introduction: The Democratic Moment and the Problem of Difference," in *Democracy and Difference: Contesting the Boundaries of the Political*, ed. idem (Princeton, NJ: Princeton University Press, 1996), 4.

120. Jason A. Edwards, Joseph M. Valenzano, III, and Karla Stevenson, "The Peacekeeping Mission: Bringing Stability to a Chaotic Scene," *Communication Quarterly* 59 (2011): 351.

121. Benhabib, "Introduction," 10.

122. John Lee, review of *Confessions of a Conservative*, *Commonweal*, September 28, 1979, 536.

123. Jack Beatty, review of *Confessions of a Conservative*, *New Republic*, May 19, 1979, 38.

Chapter Five

Political Transformation in U.S. Politics

Isocrates once said that "the argument which is made by a man's life is of more weight than that which is furnished by words."[1] Threading together lives with words, in postwar U.S. politics advocates and movements have used a communication strategy with a long history—the conversion narrative. The presence of conversion stories in politics reveals their persistence as a persuasive form. Influencing top government figures, these stories have even been instrumental in the creation of public policies. My purpose has been to ascertain how public discourse might be broadened or constrained by the features and functions of political conversion stories. Exploring several prominent autobiographies led to a conclusion that political conversion narratives are largely propagandistic, anti-deliberative forms of rhetoric assuming various guises in public affairs.

Propaganda is most free to cast its spells in our lives when we lose sight of how rhetoric works. Indeed, Longinus once stated that "no [rhetorical] figure is more excellent than the one which is entirely hidden, so that it is no longer recognized as a figure."[2] Similarly, conversion texts model persuasive ideas and practices for audiences in tricky, unobvious ways. The features of conversion rhetoric tend to do such a comprehensive job of making one's politics a foregone conclusion that little space is left for human agency or argument. In other words, these texts challenge the very concept of deliberation through their respective methods of communication. A polarized and polarizing, extreme left to right rhetoric (and vice versa) tends to proceed from conversion stories,[3] explaining why there do not appear to be many stories in public affairs titled, for instance, "the political transformation of an ex-moderate."

Conversion narratives also speak to the workings of religious and secular discourses in modern societies. They negotiate the lines between church and state by using a traditionally powerful religious form while only providing general nods toward specific religious sentiments in the public arena. Public figures have double-coded their rhetoric in this manner in attempts to improve their images, justify a monumental identity change, and make their political work more effective. A number of implications follow from the body of work examined in the preceding chapters.

POLITICAL CONVERSION NARRATIVES AS PUBLIC ARGUMENTS

To develop an interlocking vocabulary and a set of criteria for dealing with conversion narratives and similar stories, I identified several themes emerging across this book's cases. By teasing out these rhetorical operations—and, as Wills's case suggests, some ways in which they might be bypassed—we learn how networks of converts can influence our public culture as well as the standards that can be used to evaluate these types of messages as public arguments.

Totalizing Interactional Rhetoric

The books of Chambers, Podhoretz, and Horowitz demonstrate that conversion narratives work with other rhetorical devices and resources in ways that have not yet been deeply explored. Conversion rhetoric merges with these textual devices to create discourses whose qualities can be considered greater than the sum of their parts. Morgan Marietta writes that "while it is an important normative point that all arguments reduce in the end to value justifications, it is an important empirical point that some arguments arrive there more quickly and immovably than others."[4] This book's cases highlight such examples of absolutist, immovable public arguments in varying guises. They ultimately use the structure of the conversion form to amplify other textual features toward totalizing ends.

Chambers uses the conversion form to reinforce conspiracy rhetoric, for example, putting his political conversion and the vast context of his life experience in the service of unsupported assertions. The sheer length of his story allows him to gloss over a wealth of needed detail in support of his conspiracy claims. In the end, the structured conversion experience gives authority to these random speculations, making the convert a bearer of special knowledge in a way that cannot be confirmed or argued against. Similarly, Podhoretz spends so much of his narrative criticizing his opponents' type of communication that he rarely addresses their actual complaints. The conversion narrative works with a civil persona that relieves the author of considering others' claims of injustice while providing support for his own conclusions. Horowitz further crosses conversion between an old and a new life with devices such as maturity to herald his adult authority while diverting the reader from his opponents' claims, dividing others' childish status from the convert's credibility.

The all-encompassing workings of political conversion discourses show how textual form and content can interact to create ideologies. Dan Hahn reminds us that rhetorical form is often overlooked as a persuasive commitment to "certain ways of thinking, of viewing the world . . . that are not necessarily implied by the substance of the discourse."[5] The conversion form directs content in particular ways and urges audiences to repeat its structure in their own rhetoric. This book has illustrated that figures also look to the evidence of their contexts, to the paths traveled by other converts, for forms to follow and adapt. On the other hand, that Garry Wills, who was implicated in the same social circles as the other three authors, managed to think through and avoid conversion rhetoric's absolutist pressures illustrates that breaks can be made in these networks of influence.

Political Conversion Types

Generally speaking, this book's first three case studies typified political conversions analogous to three modern modes of religious thought: deduction, reduction, and induction. Outside political spheres, religionists have themselves developed different strands of conversion rhetoric in denominational histories. David Hempton finds that varying conversion forms have played out within Christian practices, for instance: "Moravian conversion narratives, as befitted the roots of the tradition in late medieval piety, are more quietist and agonistic" than "Methodist conversions," which are "characterized by charismatic joy and spontaneous ecstasy."[6] The three general types of political conversion in this book's first three cases similarly emphasize the variety of forms and divergent methods of argument that these tales may take.

In colloquial terms, Chambers's deductive political conversion narrative is a wolf in wolf's clothing, asserting an overt transcendent vision that has little place for reason and reasonability in public discourse. Podhoretz's case, however, is a wolf in sheep's clothing. By asserting a public concern for intellectualism and public debate, his rhetoric would seem to make an important contribution to public discourse. But the narrative exhibits propagandistic qualities, even by its own standards, with Podhoretz elevating an onslaught of self-referential expertise unaccountable to others.[7]

By contrast, Horowitz's narrative is a wolf in ewe's clothing, co-opting feminist and standpoint rhetorics to serve his conservative cause. Like Podhoretz, Horowitz engages in seemingly deliberative terms like reflexivity. Yet when these terms are put in the service of a unidirectional conversion, the narrative's anti-deliberative qualities emerge more clearly. As such, although there are various modes that these narratives may take, each text ultimately asserts an a priori public vision that admits little place for new knowledge or others under its form, constructing concepts like reason and reflexivity under an anti-communicative framework.

In the three different modes of religious thought that the autobiographies parallel, each story has specific views about the relationship between reason and emotion, highlighting how differing contexts might constrain how conversion stories can be told. Between reason and emotion, Chambers lands far more on emotion's side. Podhoretz uses a dichotomy between reason and emotion in *Breaking Ranks* (*BR*) that mostly frames his conversion in terms of reason. Horowitz's turn to experience is very much an attempt to bridge this dichotomy, or transcend it, so that reason is not opposed to emotion. While Podhoretz distances himself from 1960s rhetoric, Horowitz uses it to make his case. Many movements of the 1960s were, sociologically speaking, efforts to recover the whole human person.[8] Feminists reacted to the split that gendered and compartmentalized public understandings of these phenomena—for example, that men operated in the realm of reason while women acted purely on emotion. There is a sense in which many student antiwar activists responded to this gendered dichotomy, too, as a division highlighting the technocratic realism and government expertise that originally gave the Vietnam War momentum.[9] Whether conscious about it or not, Horowitz in his conversion story appropriates some 1960s movement rhetoric to build the narrative's inductive guise in his 1990s context.

The degree to which Chambers and Horowitz use certain kinds of experience as evidence also appears to influence their choice of conversion types within their respective contexts. Chambers's story was told at a time when the generational issues that Horowitz identifies were not as current. Chambers also does not rely upon the psychological rhetoric of the self in the same way as Horowitz, instead fashioning a Manichaean form well suited to his Cold War environment. Political conversions can thus exhibit unique characteristics in responding to different situational demands.

Undermining Public Communication

Political conversion narratives tend to undermine public communication by locating knowledge deep inside or outside human beings. The authors' implicit theories of human communication elevate internal experiences or external motives to such a high degree that public communication processes are marginalized—a problem that Wills's book brings into even sharper focus. The autobiographies of Chambers, Podhoretz, and Horowitz place little faith in communication to effect political change, constructing valid decision making almost wholly in terms of inner personal experiences or outer spiritual forces. Robert Asen says that models of the public sphere should not assume "a subject with a fixed set of desires that cannot be modified through dialogue."[10] Political conversion narratives tend to assume fixed outcomes in advance and are more about discovering internal and external essences to be adhered to than the creation of tentative political truths.

Chambers attacks the use of one's intellect from a variety of angles. His autobiography is made part of a deterministic, divine master plan, and he uses nature as a rhetorical resource to transfigure the material world in terms of a dualistic spiritual realm making human speech unnecessary. Through a fateful vision promoting civic escapism, Chambers loses faith in human communication. By implying that intuition is superior to human reasoning, Chambers suggests that interlocutors best communicate with signs rather than symbols. In *Witness*, symbols exist solely to be aligned with "true" or "correct" courses of action. At the same time, one's self-sealed inner experience guides public affairs, as prefigured under transcendent realities.

In a much trickier way, Podhoretz undermines public communication by using the conversion form to cast high intellectual standards as axiomatic. Ideas exist as immutably prior to and beyond the variability of the political realm, so that reason becomes an expert-driven, technical concept to which only a special few have access. Podhoretz prioritizes reason to rein in participatory politics, asking citizens to defer to those who have the time to think about political issues rather than those who act impulsively. *BR* necessitates an association between intellectualism and the telling of the convert tale, tying reason to the authenticity of one's confession—so much that presentations of genuineness become more important than one's reasons. At critical points in *BR* where we might expect the author to stop attacking others and discuss their views, little discussion ensues. Just as Dave Tell finds that modern, secular practices of "confession" often forgo a faith in rhetoric, illustrating how for many communicators, "the depths of the self are too personal and too real to be adequately disclosed through the conventions of speech,"[11] the conversion form forgoes much of the intellectual reasoning that the narrative expects.

More about independently finding one's way from wrong to right universal criteria than collaboratively creating standards for the public good, Podhoretz narrows conceptions of human rhetoric, castigating a variety of practices—such as the diatribe—in favor of strict civility in all matters. The reductive conversion form works to reduce the messages of Podhoretz's opponents to a paradoxical form of public expression: characterizing others as recklessly expressive as well as mute, effectively incapacitating others as undeveloped persons who are yet to become civil advocates who can be taken seriously (a framing that the author shares with Horowitz, although the latter takes the resource to a whole other level). Podhoretz further narrows deliberative space by arguing that attitude without content is bad and that dissenters who think that they know the truth are also bad—either way, only the convert comes out a winner.

Rather than engage in reasoning with others, Horowitz asks his readers to turn exclusively inward for insights about public affairs. *Radical Son*'s (*RS*) conversion structure and Horowitz's understanding of reflexivity reflect a self-focused rhetoric that skirts public reason as a route to knowledge, instead taking issue with others for failing to look inside themselves. Horowitz's maturity rhetoric is anything but forward-looking, however. Public deliberation involves a general understanding that the future can be changed through speech. But *RS*'s psychological language and reduction of opponents' actions to an apolitical status—that is, as guided by deeply intransigent motives akin to biological diseases rather than reasoned opinions—forgoes such change. This psychologizing links an abnormal psychology of the Left to "fate," while proposing that a conservative conversion involves a newfound agency. The narrative's attributions of one's reflexive ability or inability are deliberatively crippling, with the author maintaining that there is little point in dealing with the reasons of others who lack reflexivity.

American individualism has long threatened public discourse.[12] *RS* promotes individualism by asserting that the purpose of debate is a conversion in which politics begins and ends with one's experience. From his work on religious activism, Jason Bivins concludes that "if one thing is central to the vitality of a democracy, it is that the contest over the issues and decisions of import to its citizens be continuous."[13] Political conversions work to prevent this kind of endless argumentation. In these stories, experience and reality present themselves to human beings as simply factual and unmediated and therefore beyond the reach of public reason and reasonability.

In the end, political conversion narratives fail to account for the experiences of others, which do not necessarily need to be validated but might at least be addressed. Chambers characterizes left-wing intellectuals as shrieking birds (via its use of nature rhetoric), Podhoretz reduces leftists to mere shouters, and Horowitz reduces the same figures' actions to simple psychological impulses. The individual, narrative, and psychological life experiences of others who hold contrary views are outside each conversion story's scope. Without the possibility of being informed by others, the texts ultimately implicate social and political resignation.

We should be willing to give each author the benefit of the doubt that he had a genuine change of heart, based on an examination of his earlier life experiences. However, a problem with political conversion stories is that they tend to align these developmental standards with political positions. Each autobiography conflates the process of coming to new beliefs with a developmental end state, so that what Chambers, Podhoretz, and Horowitz mean by deliberation is a conclusion that one has already reached. In both biology and thinking, one has fully developed so that no further growth or learning about politics is necessary.

While reflection and experience can certainly constitute good reasons in the public square, they are not the only forms of knowledge. Part of maturity is seeing that one's experience is also idiosyncratic, so that this knowledge needs to be tested against the larger, diverse social and material truths of the world. Each narrative essentially asserts: "I remember only those parts of my experience that lead me to where I am now, and I forget the other parts that complicate the picture." Wills, on the other hand, widens political space through a text emphasizing rhetorical processes, human conventions, endless argumentation, and expansive identity rhetorics. If, as Thomas Farrell writes, "a rhetorical culture is an institutional formation in which motives of competing parties are intelligible, audiences available, expressions reciprocal, norms translatable, and silences noticeable,"[14] the way that people envision communication becomes critical to establishing the very conditions for public deliberation.

Civil-Religious Persuasion

Political conversion stories are double-coded messages that negotiate church–state tensions. They give advocates a way to communicate in an evangelical fashion without bearing the costs that overt religious expression can carry in public. As mentioned, the authors use a conversion form that has been historically resonant with religious and secular audiences, making general nods toward faith beliefs to maintain a slight threshold of religious commitment while submerging specific religious content[15]—which many U.S. audiences find ill fitting for political discourse.[16] Political conversion narratives can thus function as forms of "invisible religion,"[17] promoting civil-religious behaviors fit for the U.S. context.[18]

While Chambers, Podhoretz, and Horowitz share a civil-religious strategy, the degree to which faith is advanced or submerged in each analysis varies. Chambers is the most explicit about his Christianity but still constructs a quasi-religious tale that is more about a generalized Manichaean universe, of good and God, rather than the articulation of specific tenets of the Christian faith. His prefiguring rhetoric additionally associates the progressive revelation characterized in the Old and New Testaments with a political-religious conversion. Podhoretz maintains a respect for "first and last things" in his narrative but does not go beyond this thin description to advance his intellectualism and non-fanaticism. Horowitz remains an agnostic in his faith but embeds religious messages throughout his conversion tale, such as references to New Testament verses and biblical figures. Despite the different degrees of civic or religious rhetoric, each author plays both sides of the civil-religious fence.

Curiously, Chambers, Podhoretz, and Horowitz compare their former paradigms to a false religion (and, in Chambers's case, the use of one's mind to a false religion) and their former colleagues to religious fanatics. The authors imply that any bad connotations about religion are entirely on their opponents. Podhoretz even uses "conversion" in a pejorative sense to talk about the change undertaken by his opponents while he advances his own political conversion. The writers claim a minimal threshold of religiosity to appeal to religious audiences but also frame their opponents as faith-driven fanatics in order not to appear *too* religious in their politics.

Via this strategy, converts can be everything to everyone. The authors infer that whatever religion the political convert still holds to involves true religious beliefs. The conversion narrative's directionality and realism bear upon these beliefs by forcing divides between true or false religion/politics. Chambers, for instance, uses the conversion form to dichotomize political issues into an ambiguously religious and nonreligious framework, promoting developments such as the contemporary religious Right. Wills should not be considered the panacea to all the problems of conversion stories. Inasmuch as he sought a politics of convention over redemption, however, he was also the most explicit in discussing his own faith and the potential role of religion in the public square. Compared with the other writers, Wills tended to put his cards on the table more often than not in these matters.

Overall, the case studies teach us about the quiet power of religion in public life. To reiterate, a conclusion that these are civil-religious narratives is not intended to invoke a framework of legal determinism, where such accounts might be seen to follow strictly from founding documents or legal doctrines such as the disestablishment clause. It is to argue that such narratives are the outgrowth of a whole panoply of cultural performances in American history (of which founding texts and legal doctrines are certainly a part), where communicators have attempted to meet official and unofficial, paradoxical expectations over the roles of church and state in public discourse.

Consistency and Change

One of the more curious results from this project has been how, across the first three case studies, political converts paradoxically testify to both immense change and consistency in their public transformation. Wills also testifies to both consistency and change but largely to play with the ambiguities, contradictions, and paradoxes that such claims tend to manifest rather than as a natural, linear outgrowth of a principled and consistent past life. Looking back at their lives, converts perceive the end as already written at the beginning. Chambers, in particular, argues that his conversion was already prefigured in many of his past actions. Prefiguring creates a double pardon for the convert's life, so that one can communicate that he or she never changed but also underwent a grand change. Similarly, Podhoretz uses the conversion form to tidy up contradictions and flatten out inconsistencies or inconveniences in his story.[19] Horowitz's maturity and growth rhetoric further advocate that his political development was toward known ends. Hence, while political conversion autobiographies tend to assert a rhetoric of variability, the deeper conversion structure defines this variation in terms of change to only one option. This conversion strategy evades choice or innovation by asserting one's conversion to a "new" life as a foregone conclusion—evidencing a complex, prefigured rhetoric of new choices. If the future is known in this way, there is little point in deliberating about it.

On one level, this type of discourse highlights another double-coding strategy. The conversion form frames the authors as experienced leaders at the forefront of public affairs, as well as marginalized, countercultural advocates.[20] Political conversion is one means by which "counter publicity" (or elite claims to oppression that co-opt the messages of socioeconomically disadvantaged groups) can be created.[21]

On another level, political converts maintain both consistency and change to deal with audience objections about political transformation. In U.S. culture, being "consistent" is a valued quality,[22] and changing one's views, or "flip-flopping," is often seen as evidence of self-interest or being unprincipled.[23] Chambers, Podhoretz, and Horowitz imply that as long as converts flop to the right side they should avoid these charges, and the conversion form's religious undertones are recruited in this effort—absolving one's political sins so that a grand change can be justified in the public sphere. Some claim that conservative victories in U.S. politics have been partly due to the movement's narrative victories,[24] and conversion stories have likely contributed to this trend by constructing a totalizing structure incorporating both consistency and change.

Converts ultimately gain by embodying both sides of a political argument. As discussed, Horowitz's maturity terms appeal to both the "strict parent" and "nurturant parent" frameworks that lie at the heart of U.S. liberal and conservative worldviews.[25] Horowitz's use of both paradigms helps explain why he was the political activist to invent terms such as "compassionate conservatism" for Republicans, which simultaneously appeals to strict and nurturing frames. The bifurcated conversion form contributes to the formation of such double-coded rhetoric by straddling yet transcending old and new political languages to create a discourse incorporating both, while still serving a single political cause.

The larger the political chasm one crosses, the larger the potential for public praise or scorn. It can be risky when former supporters of a party, politician, or issue write a book providing alternative points of view, examples of which are not hard to find.[26] In such situations, the political conversion narrative offers an opportunity to maintain consistency and change but, as this book's cases illustrate, typically at the price of asserting a certain type of polarized and polarizing rhetoric in public affairs.

Complex Bifurcated Appeals

The first three cases in this book revealed other paradoxical demands: asserting a complex, quantitative onslaught of various types of experience into politics, while also advancing reductionist, bifurcated discourses chaining out from the conversion form. Chambers's dualism promotes what I term a "complex dichotomy," where dogmatic arguments appear more intricate than warranted. At each turn, Chambers draws stark black and white divides reflecting the binaries of his conversion from an old to a new conservative Christian life, the political battle between East versus West, and, more largely, a Manichaean battle between good and evil. Given Chambers's approximately 800-page journey, a lot of these black and white arguments about the nature of reality appear as complex, well-reasoned positions.

Podhoretz crafts a complex conversion tale by creating an impression that his messages avoid the simple binary conclusions attributed to his former colleagues' practices. Following the conversion form's bifurcating emphases, though, Podhoretz strains to classify any and all human agency that the political Left may evince as blindness and ignorance. Horowitz, too, uses the conversion form to dichotomize the Left and the Right on these matters across a series of divides between the old and the new, the concrete and the abstract, and conservative wisdom in the past versus what he perceives as liberal utopias about the future.

As a bifurcated experience between two poles of existence, the conversion form is therefore particularly amenable to the U.S. political context, which has almost always been based on a two-party system of government. As a type of rhetoric reinforcing this divide, conversion narratives tend to foreclose third and more options. The conversion form's dogmatic tendencies might also be seen as contributing to an "us versus them" culture war mentality that has informed much public discourse in the postwar period. By largely reducing the universe to two options at each turn, political converts miss opportunities to invent and compromise in ways that do not fit within the parameters of the bifurcating mold, as Wills's tale brings into focus. In other words, conversion's dichotomizing features and functions leave little space for matters of degree. One's personal and political choices are either in or out, meaning that further reflection, doubt, struggle, or interaction beyond the divides remain unnecessary. In conversion narratives, communication is not a driver of human experience but a means of aligning with or diverting from inner or cosmic realities that care little for human effort, will, or deliberation.

Conversion as a Special Faculty

Conversion is more than an "experience" that one may publicly claim. It allows individuals to survey and know their political environment better than others. In this volume's first three cases, conversion becomes a special faculty used to generate authority in politics. In *Witness*, Chambers suggests that he has direct access to unmediated truths as a result of his political-religious experience. Podhoretz is the most explicit, in naming the form of reasoning that each case study invokes "autocase history"—or the drawing of conclusions about one's political environment from the evidence of personal experience. *BR* endows this experience with a godlike, intuitive faculty to know more than others. The author's accuracy rhetoric, in particular, does more than describe the reality of events; it allows the political convert to make precise attributions of others' motives, such as other intellectuals' desire for attention and influence beyond other considerations.

In the vast, gradual turn from an old to a new life, this faculty ultimately makes political generalizations appear less like generalizations. In the context of other narrative features, such as the frequent use of medical metaphors, authors like Podhoretz rhetorically extinguish (rather than deliberate with) the "fevers" and "plagues" of others' political beliefs. Nowhere does this special faculty become clearer than in Horowitz's use of reflexivity, which he constructs as a special epistemological ability for self-criticism and awareness completely unavailable to those on the opposing side. Reflexivity allows Horowitz to see into the true nature of things and know more than others, building authority as a guide to the times. Relative to public deliberation, this revisionary ability begins and ends with the convert, becoming a resource for asserting one's righteous, directionally laden path to self-validated truth.

In each of these cases, readers are rarely treated to any insight on how the authors know others' chief motives beyond the point that, because they were themselves on the other side of the political divide once, they have the authority to know about others' present motives and interests. The conversion form is hence used as a way to know more than one can know, involving a new intuitive ability to judge the political world without broader data.

In argumentative terms, these political conversion autobiographies tend to engage in hasty generalizations, an insight that became apparent in many reviewers' objections to the books. One critic argued that Horowitz "has no right whatsoever to project his own particular lifetime's angst on to a worldwide movement in order to discredit millions of decent people who sought a better, more just world."[27] Another wrote that the author "inexplicably seems to believe that the history of counterrevolutionary thought begins with him."[28] One reviewer even writes of both Chambers and Horowitz that "the two had a flair for the dramatic, equating their life stories with the rise or fall of Western civilization."[29]

Conversion as a special projective faculty raises a further contextual problem. Attwood finds that "those who have experienced an event and bear witness to it have come to be regarded as the most authentic bearers of truth about the past, indeed as the embodiment of history," often replacing professional historians as arbiters of record. The goal of witnessing about the past has especially shifted from "the *acquisition* of *historical knowledge*" to "the *transmission* of *pasts* to future generations in a way that creates a sense of a strong transgenerational link between the faces and voices of witnesses and those who listen to them."[30] As a rhetorical form, conversion blurs autobiographical testimony with history by not simply transmitting *a* past but, in propagandistic fashion, *the* past.[31]

Fixed Time and Identity

Scholars have drawn attention to a possibility that the directionality in convert tales may be troublesome for public communication.[32] Across the first three case studies, time and identity worked together in this fashion. Political conversion stories possess essentializing qualities, propagating that humans act out history's scripts in a predestined fashion. Chambers uses flash-forwarding techniques to tell readers that providence has been at work in his life. Podhoretz creates a picture of the world where universal ideas exist prior to and independently of anyone's variable political thoughts. Horowitz spends so much of the narrative discussing his unidirectional conversion and Second Thoughts Project that he ignores the potential for third thoughts or even fourth thoughts to enter the picture. *RS* asserts that the political conversion involved a period of revision but that Horowitz's political understandings are now firm, undermining the endlessly reflexive standard that the narrative asserts. On the other hand, Wills's book does not fall prey to a bounded sense of time or a fixed understanding of political identity, offering the possibility that alternate beginnings or senses of self might be forwarded through creative communication.

Following the directional conversion pattern, the first three authors in this project assume that only knowledge that has stood the test of time is valuable in public affairs. Podhoretz communicated "I'm a complex thinker" by telling readers that his political conversion was no quick decision. Through the conversion form, gradual reasoning is fit to political contexts where publics might expect leaders to engage in gradual, reasoned judgments.[33] Yet time-based, directional emphases make such discourse a foregone conclusion, one in which deep, fundamental identity change moves from a bifurcated wrong to a right in politics. Here conversion's temporal metaphor (change from an *old* to a *new* life) crosses with the directional metaphor of politics (change from *left* to *right*, or vice versa) to reinforce an accurate, essential political identity. The conversion narrative makes the directional journey to the right about "rightness," but an issue of revisability arises—as argumentation itself is set within a lengthy, storied framework, the possibility for public amendment appears diminished.

A deliberative problem is that political conversion narratives are fine with choice, so long as the *right* choice is made. A parallel product/process issue exists in how these stories construct open-mindedness as good, so long as it leads to Truth, a problem that Wills's discourse avoids. The traditionally dogmatic attributes of the conversion form fashion a rhetoric of open-mindedness glossing over the discourse's intolerance. The narratives further fix time and identity through youth/adult devices, especially through Horowitz's generational advocacy and Chambers's and Podhoretz's appeals to parenting their children. Chambers and Podhoretz bookend their narratives with letters to their children, just as Horowitz often uses letters between his father and himself throughout *RS*.[34]

The public letter device has historical precedent. Benjamin Franklin's autobiography begins with a public letter to his son.[35] There are also connections between the development of autobiography and different stages of biological growth. Patricia Spacks finds that autobiographies in the eighteenth, nineteenth, and twentieth centuries emphasized different periods of life—maturity, childhood, and adolescence, respectively[36]—themes with which the first three case studies work. Chambers urges his children to get in line with a transfigured, foreordained universal reality. Podhoretz and Horowitz parallel biological development with political development, so that one's beliefs can be seen as dissonant or accordant with human nature. Horowitz, in particular, says that his conversion was from a condition of non-reflexivity (childish naïveté) to a redemptive condition of reflexivity (adult reflection). In each case, the stories bring together biology and directionality, with history moving to vindicate each author's politics in a way that circumvents the possibility of ending up in different places.

Although deliberation scholars such as David Ryfe find that stories can be connected to efforts at successful deliberation and meaningful civic values, the features and functions of particular types of stories thus matter for public communication.[37] Laura Black argues that some narrative types can inform deliberative encounters, including "transformation stories" that are characterized by "mixed, contradictory, or changing emotions" of "personal and social transformation."[38] These stories can help an individual entertain doubts through the mutual exploration of political topics. At least in this book's cases, however, political conversion narratives are a type of transformation story working toward an opposite purpose.

In this regard, other political practices bear similarities to political conversion stories. Richard Crosby writes about the modern drive to sign "oaths" in U.S. politics:

> Whereas traditional political argument in the democratic tradition meant to create openings for action, oath rhetoric is circumscriptive. It locks individual identity within a hermetically sealed ideological system. Those who refuse the oaths are treated as apostates who have no place within the system. The result is a political culture based on the affirmation of allegiance rather than the deliberation over and creation of policy.[39]

In the same way, conversion experiences can reduce the possibility for open and robust public discourse through directional and self-sealing performances.

Autobiographical Thinking

The autobiographical medium itself affords Chambers, Podhoretz, and Horowitz the opportunity to combine the conversion form with a wealth of detail that reinforces the anti-deliberative aspects of their stories. In short, the deliberative problem is not with autobiography but the way in which autobiography serves and is served by conversion. In Chambers's case, information about nature in the autobiography reinforces the authenticity of the conversion narrative, grounding his abstract political-religious dualism in concrete detail—and making the conversion journey appear a part of the natural progression of his transfigured universe. Each of these choices contributes to an overall picture of public deliberation, as Chambers infers that there is little malleability or hope in the development of future policies.

For Podhoretz, the autobiographical medium plays an important part in constituting conversion and accuracy. As a red herring, the sheer depth and breadth of detail afforded in the narrative thwarts attention from how *BR* has little evidence and few citations for many of its political conclusions and sometimes makes misleading claims. These problems become more acute, given Podhoretz's implication that converts have a precise and proportionate sense of where particular issues hit the mark or go awry, especially on topics such as U.S. race relations. The lack of citations in *Witness* (except for references to such figures as Dante and Shakespeare) and the lack of sources in *RS* follow from each author's use of conversion as a special faculty.[40] There is little need to go to other sources or others' experiences when one's epistemological vision single-handedly does away with the rest of the world.

In Horowitz's case, the conversion form and psychological experience rhetoric draw lines between an old, abstract sociological worldview and a new, concrete psychological-narrative orientation that limits attention to others' experiences as a route to political knowledge. Both Chambers and Horowitz state that their political conversions were partly wrapped up with a move to more autobiographical modes of writing. It is noteworthy that, in *Witness*, Chambers says that he had to learn to write a new and "unnatural" journalistic form,[41] a point that Horowitz used and adapted in his story.

The divide between sociological and psychological-narrative writing gives us insight into why so many conservatives seem to have written political conversion autobiographies. Autobiography is a form well suited to nonstructural, individualist, narrative ways of thinking, providing a powerful medium for the convert's persona. At least from this volume's cases, political conversion tends to create little room for sociological and biographical-narrative modes to work together. Ironically, Martha Watson finds that authors who construct grand personal mythologies through autobiography may actually make their lives inaccessible and hard to emulate.[42]

Autobiography authenticates knowledge forms such as testimony and experience, which, in these cases, amplify the propagandistic qualities of conversion stories. Gabrielle Spiegel writes that testimony provides "the promise of a certain emotional and gestural vividness—a vividness strongly reinforced by the customarily oral form of its delivery—that operates to transform into a virtually transparent form of transmission."[43] Although testimonies can make important contributions to public discourse, as a form of evidence they can appear unmediated and free from persuasion. Stories are particularly impervious to statistical modes of reasoning, as formulaic structures where "an image of a single child can stir the world while millions can go hungry unnoticed."[44] Autobiographical testimonies, experiences, or stories are not necessarily bad forms of reasoning, but they can circumvent other forms of reasoning under the conversion form's influence.

The contemporary applications of this kind of discourse are far-reaching. Adam Curtis finds that neoconservatives have used a number of deceptive political campaigns with similar techniques: constructing "reality out of fragments of evidence," regarding the "USSR in the 70s" and "Iraq and the weapons of mass destruction [in the 2000s]. They took fragments and knitted them together and they did it with such force because they believed it was important."[45] This technique need not be limited to those on the right, of course, and conversion narratives demonstrate a variety of methods that authors of any ideology could employ to leverage autobiographical rhetoric toward movement claims.

Between Identities and Movements

Conversion narratives are nexus points between identities and movements. In election contexts, Robert Huckfeldt, Paul Johnson, and John Sprague find:

> The conversion of any single individual to a particular candidate's cause is not only important in terms of a single vote or a single unit of social influence. It is also important in terms of the enhancement and attenuation effects that it creates throughout the networks of relationships within which the individual is imbedded, quite literally transforming entire patterns of social influence.[46]

Far from being isolated texts, this volume's cases show how conversion narratives are as much "we" as "I" experiences.[47] Political conversions draw from others' stories and are cited across the public realm as support for individuals' claims to belong to one movement or another. They carry authority for many convinced that someone's having made a grand, life-altering switch in political paradigm or party affiliation provides conclusive proof for devaluing other perspectives. Additionally, conversion narratives are highly effective ways to stage a rhetorical "comeback" within and between movements.

There has been little development of the role that political converts play within social movements.[48] As others have noted, the deliberation literature also needs a better "theory of citizenship that focuses on identity."[49] Political conversion narratives are performances that speak to both areas. Empirical evidence suggests that citizens are often motivated to deliberate by opportunities to perform "identity and identification," rather than for strictly instrumental or other reasons.[50] Anthony Giddens argues that, in late modernity, a person's identity is bound up with "keeping a narrative going,"[51] which may be one reason that citizens feel a need to tell and retell stories of conversion within movements. Opportunities for these types of "expressive rationality" are "relevant in late modernity where civic engagement has changed along lines of increasing reflexivity and individualization."[52] Overall, political conversion narratives provide examples of expressive rationality embedded within networks of influence.[53]

Much about the U.S. conservative movement's formation can be gleaned from these tales. *Witness*'s dualistic emphases were critical to the development of Cold War language influencing Presidents Reagan and Nixon. Podhoretz's intellectual conversion carried influence among politicians and policy makers and was central to the neoconservative movement's creation. Horowitz draws inspiration from and cites both *Witness* and *BR* in his autobiography, but goes much further by marketing an entire industry of networked political conversions. This rhetoric of transformation, "party-switching," and being a "turncoat" continue to inform public culture. As mentioned, Zell Miller, a longtime Democratic senator, stood before the public at the Republican National Convention in 2004 and proclaimed his support for conservative president Bush. Miller never announced that he had switched parties, nor did he write an autobiography evidencing his fundamental change, but there are clearly elements to his performance that carry rhetorical weight—demonstrating how the influence of Chambers, Podhoretz, and Horowitz continue to find traction in politics, since "life informs and is informed by stories."[54] The power of political conversion partly arises from communal calls to repeat performances, just like religious conversions where "endlessly repeated stories about how our ancestors had been converted were the very substance of our lives, the daily confirmation that who we were made ultimate sense."[55] And as Walter Fisher notes, stories do more than simply order human experience; they bid audiences to come dwell in them.[56]

The choice to use this communication strategy has much to do with nods toward transcendence in political conversions to the right. In recent decades, the Right has traditionally been the place where faith appeals are made and carry impact, particularly in the development of conservatism after World War II.[57] Historical conversion discourse often worked with "Truth" as a possibility, especially in the classical world, where Platonic conceptions of reality were guided by the gradual or immediate casting off of old illusions for new, otherworldly certainties.[58] As Wills's story shows, religious beliefs and concerns for truth can and should be a part of public discourse. From a deliberative viewpoint, however, the extent to which advocates use such truths to open or close space for further rhetoric within and outside their movements is certainly worth underscoring.

Conversion's Contradictions

These narratives manifest a number of contradictions that have emerged between their theory and practice. Chambers's post-*Witness* shifts in belief and attitude highlight a tension between the stringent positions in his book (e.g., dualism) and experienced disagreements within his own movement. This contradiction would perhaps be greater had *Witness* been written in more recent history, as other fundamentalist forms of discourse have emerged in politics with which Chambers might be less supportive.[59] Podhoretz engages in performative contradictions, such as the belief that others should not use Nazi analogies (while he employs his own) and *BR*'s passionate case for a cause, engaging in the very kind of advocacy for which it critiques others. The fairness of Podhoretz's metaphorical choices in characterizing the Left is questionable, as are the clustering of others under ad hominem characterizations, which would appear to lack the accurate, critical nuance that Podhoretz so often asserts as an essential deliberative criterion.

BR's intellectual guise leads to a deliberative contradiction at the center of these objections: Podhoretz positions rationalistic discussions of public policy within a political conversion narrative—reserving an exclusive right to make "aesthetic judgments" in the public sphere. Morality is not offered to leftists in the same way that Podhoretz performs these criteria for the Right, only drawing boundaries for the convert's idealism in political affairs. *RS*, too, exhibits tensions in making others accountable for their previous acts, while Horowitz attributes purity to himself in his early life and as a Marxist. In the same way, the autobiography asserts that a reflexivity in line with one's immutable nature is best, making human communication conform to a directional pattern that downplays the potential for further political choices.

The tensions exhibited in performing political conversion narratives ultimately illustrate the difficulties of maintaining dogmatism in the public sphere. Authors are forced into making paradoxical claims that show little awareness for the pressures wrought by their use of the totalizing conversion form in a contingent political terrain. There is always a potential to be too fanatical or to misconstrue one's opponents or issues in public debate. In this regard, the conversion experience that the first three authors call for is insufficient for a viable politics; it does not always guarantee the right outcomes and, as the end of Chambers's life suggests, is not necessarily the way toward political progress.[60] On the other hand, Wills's story provides insight into how these contradictions can be interrogated through a rhetoric that commits to, but is not bound by, political identity choices—with a focus on political commitments as ongoing processes over and above the reified weapon conversion stories can so easily become.

THE FUTURE OF POLITICAL CONVERSION

Although the four autobiographies in this book had a unity justifying their study as a trajectory of rhetoric, many other autobiographies and political conversion accounts are out there, so I am not claiming to universalize these findings. To examine the issues that conversion texts raise for public discourse, this volume focused on the trees rather than the forest. To extend the scope of inquiry about political conversion, one promising avenue could include narratives that focus on identity politics and race and ethnicity (such as former Bush administration official Linda Chavez's *An Unlikely Conservative*) or post–September 11, 2001, political conversions (such as Joshua Key's *The Deserter's Tale*).

A larger sample of autobiographies and stories of political conversion or party-switchers could be amenable to statistical analyses covering identity changes. Indeed, there are already some data in political science about these larger dynamics. From an aggregate perspective, for instance, "about one-third of the 16 United States representatives who switched [political parties] since 1980 lost the next election for either their House seat or another office. Others, however, have become influential and admired members of their new party."[61] Senator Arlen Specter and Congressman Michael Forbes, who both changed from Republican to Democrat, only to be ousted in their next election campaigns, exemplify such trends.[62]

In this project, some generalizability was sacrificed for the unique and interrelated contributions of the authors and autobiographies examined. Yet these narratives' intertextuality and anti-deliberative qualities show that there may be some generic qualities to political conversion narratives as a whole. The autobiographies were also all by relatively elite public writers, forgoing nonelite accounts that could further illuminate the contours of this type of communication. Since each case study was in book form, a question remains about what political conversion narratives look like in other types of media, such as television, radio, or on the internet.

Comparative political conversion narratives may also provide a rich source of material for analysis. Are there other countries or places where these types of tales are told to justify and navigate one's political worldview or policy choices?[63] To this point, scholars have found that conversion narratives are mostly a Western phenomenon. D. Bruce Hindmarsh writes that Protestant missionaries had a difficult time implementing their religious conversion forms in non-Western societies, where the notion of "sin" was less a part of the historical context.[64] Donald Lopez notes how "belief" is a Christianized notion unavailable in many Eastern religious practices. As a historical development, "belief" was fashioned as an assent to propositions, dividing subjects in ways unfamiliar to many non-Western societies.[65] Ultimately, the religious conversion form is "a distinctive confluence of cultural circumstances in the eighteenth-century English-speaking world."[66]

At the same time, the conversion narratives covered in this book were all by individuals who make a living as writers, and writing opens up possibilities for conversion that other modes of communication may preclude. Gerald Peters argues that "it is no coincidence that [the Christian apostle] Paul was a writer. Conversion of the kind that he undergoes depends on the ability to make oneself into a subject through one's writing, and to be able to sustain this image of the self through the production of permanent traces."[67] The conversion form's bifurcating tendencies between old and new lives advance these divisions in Western contexts. But with globalization and the adaptation of Western forms in other societies, political conversion narratives may have found their ways into other cultures across the world.

Some may object that the argument that political conversion narratives are propagandistic raises a question about whether these stories should be written at all. Surely these stories make some contributions to public discourse, such as giving us critical details about ex-Communist experiences. Should a book like *Witness* even have been introduced into public life? An answer to this question partly depends on how the story is taken up and how an author wants the story to be received. We can appreciate these stories as simply autobiographical and as one among many testimonies and individual experiences in the civic realm. Yet it is another matter to look at their persuasive features as expanding or constricting deliberative space.

Relatedly, it may be asked whether conversion forms in religious discourses are anti-deliberative. Wills's *Confessions of a Conservative* partially helps us find a way through this question by focusing the dogmatic language qualities at issue with these kinds of narratives, rather than any religious or nonreligious designation that might be attributed to them. Wills's tale uses religion a lot, especially in drawing upon Augustinian texts to explore political positions. At the same time, spheres of private religious faith would appear to suit conversion rhetoric better than more political contexts, since pluralism is generally less expected within many faith groups. In sacred spaces, one can be a Christian, Muslim, or Buddhist, among other choices, but not all of these at the same time (universalist congregations excluded). In political spaces, to avoid a war of all against all, one has to be more than any single religious identity can contain to find the kinds of compromises that Wills notes are necessary even to have a politics in the first place.

Transformation narratives invite readers into, as Wayne Booth notes, "a world infinitely truer, realer, than the one I will fall back into after listening,"[68] so there is danger in how citizens may perceive conversion's terms of ultimate allegiance (regardless of more secular or religious inflections) as bearing on political circumstances. Scholars have asked, "[W]hat happens to the promise of the totalizing narrative, what vicissitudes must it undergo, when the belief in a logocentric, metaphysical authority disappears?"[69] However metaphysical or not, it is doubtful whether the concept of conversion can be separated from such forms of authority, whether they are validated by externally religious or internally essential constructs. Peters finds that

> a mechanism [conversion] once connected to metaphysical verities has become enmeshed in the totalizing web of state or corporate power. Paradoxically, individuals who believe they are liberating themselves from external authority by confessing their individuality are only making themselves subject to the kind of authority they are trying to overcome.[70]

In other words, in a major irony, a form of communication most focused on asserting one's new political change is actually one of the least suited to political and ideological liberation. Many calls to conversion are simply pronouncements to "get with the program" rather than remain open to different political possibilities. Wills provides his readers with a way through this issue, urging us to commit to processes and identities that are, in effect, the most free to continue learning and growing.

Looking forward, a few final observations are in order. First, messages about political transformation and repositioning beckon more public accountability. Thomas Farrell says that "the very aim of rhetorical theory has always been to define and articulate a vision of what the highest potential of rhetorical practice might be."[71] Cold War rhetoric often had a harmful effect on public participation, as "deliberation became secondary to patriotism," spawning a culture of expertise and secrecy.[72] Political converts assert individualistic messages of change in the public sphere, using largely patriotic and monologic appeals that reinforce the status quo, often placing transcendent standards and personal experience at a discursive impasse in public affairs.[73] Public discourse can be constrained through forms of reasoning that individualize deliberation and judgment, "privilege expert over everyday knowledge," and bring brute necessities into contingent affairs.[74]

Second, religion and secularity are not discrete concepts. Addressing the long-debated question, "What is Athens to Jerusalem?"[75] authors of political conversion narratives position their messages in a liminal space between faith and politics. In the 1940s and 1950s, the use of civil religion escalated in the United States, reflecting tensions for religion's presence as well as absence in politics. The Constitution has no references to God, and Article VI, Section 3 states that "no religious test shall ever be required as qualification to any office or public trust under the United States."[76] Yet communicators persist in using transcendent appeals in the civic realm, often choosing to make their messages both civil and religious to negotiate these barriers. Political conversion stories reflect these larger trends, similar to other methods for using religiously inflected terms in politics.

President Clinton, for example, made national "rebirth" the central theme of both his inaugural speeches; additionally, the language of "faith" and family" is often used in politics as a double-coded signal that resonates with religious citizens and secular audiences alike.[77] In political contexts, such discourses exhibit elasticity and polysemy, straddling the church–state nexus by bringing a consuming order to one's experience while remaining faithful to the evolving nature of cultural and political disestablishment. Even activists such as Jerry Falwell and his followers build explicitly religious rhetorics that would seem to be the antithesis of many public figures' more implicit, civil-religious strategies. Susan Harding documents:

> Heterogeneity not homogeneity, hybridity not purity, fluidity not fixity, characterized [Falwell's] movement at every level. One's identity as a Bible-believing Christian was not narrowly defined or stationary; there were dozens of culturally distinct ways of being "born again," and more emerged every day. Nostalgia, mimesis, parody, pastiche, double-voicing, intertextuality, and deconstruction were all at work in the cultural texts of Bible believers.[78]

Religion and secularity may be mobilized by different individuals for varying purposes; but in practice, humans always evolve and adapt these messages in subtle ways.

Third, while political conversion can be performed across ideologies, the fact that these political transformations have mostly been from the left to the right in U.S. politics is of no small consequence. One study of presidential debates from 1976 to 2004 found that Republicans employed sacred rhetoric far more frequently and across a wider range of issues than Democrats, who have tended to focus on numbers and plans rather than "values." This has given Republicans an "absolutist advantage" in public discourse invoking "nonnegotiable convictions rather than reasoned consequences."[79] Empirical research further supports a "valorization effect," where audiences view leaders who use a priori, absolutist discourse as "more principled, virtuous, and determined than others," so that "Democrats are publicly committed to doing what is best, while Republicans are publicly committed to doing what is right."[80] Conservative victories during this period may be linked to the resonance of these types of principled messages. This book has highlighted how absolutist forms can be constructed in many different guises, with conversion stories often structuring nonnegotiable convictions in a manner that appears negotiable.

Fourth, political conversion narratives play a vital role in the maintenance of political paradigms. Political movements rely on these advocates to preach to their own, ritualistically reinforcing current party platforms. The work of speaking to and governing millions of citizens is difficult. Political converts provide vivid models for why voters should continue to support a political party. They personify counterarguments against the political opposition and are resources to draw from in gauging, disassembling, or co-opting adversaries. In an age of information overload, political converts act as quick heuristic cues to why the other side(s) should be discounted, as embodied evidence for the failure of other political causes.

Fifth, the personalization and tabloidization of politics that were heightened with the advent of radio, television, and other media can be related to the forms of communication in these autobiographies. Many scholars have argued that U.S. politics is becoming a less deliberative, celebrity-driven society where politics is increasingly focused on identity[81]—and these autobiographies parallel the rise of image-driven media ecologies. The very wrappings of these narratives in "book" form invites readers to see them as more authoritative than other types of media. Yet they largely perpetuate modern media norms for, as mentioned in the introduction, "the present, the unusual, the dramatic, simplicity, action, personalization, and results."[82] Studies show that political candidates' personal characteristics tend to influence citizens more than their policies.[83] These norms help us understand why Obama campaign volunteers were trained to tell conversion stories instead of guiding citizens through policy proposals,[84] and why we find these political tales throughout bookstores, reflecting broader trends in which conversion narratives play a part.

The circulation of political conversion through digital media further stands to amplify such rhetoric. One prominent conservative blogger made a *Los Angeles Times* headline for creating an online post titled "Ten Reasons I

Parted Ways with the Right," which generated controversy in the blogosphere.[85] Strategies like conversion can break through a cluttered media environment,[86] and recent studies in social media and online electioneering underscore a striking finding with relevance to the conversion narrative and deliberation: "We are potentially moving from swing states to *swing individuals*, employing savvy marketing professionals to attract these persuadables and mobilize these supporters with little semblance of the slow, messy deliberative practices enshrined in our democratic theories."[87]

In fact, the internet is now replete with stories of political conversion, such as Josh Passell's "My Friends Don't Know I'm a Conservative" in the *Boston Globe*, the *New Yorker*'s coverage of former Westboro Baptist Church member Megan Phelps-Roper finding a new life outside the religious and political movement, Jack Camwell's "Political Conversion: I Think I'm a Libertarian" on the author's blog, or many videos now being uploaded to YouTube, such as Gulbirk's "My Political 'Conversion.'"[88] If individual influences become more pronounced in new media spaces, conversion and similar rhetorical forms may play an even greater role in future elections and their aftermath.

Political conversion narratives are here to stay. Both historical and contemporary, stable yet evolving, they show little sign of exiting the political stage. Ultimately, the convergence of lives and words in conversion tales constitutes a powerful communication strategy. And so long as we find ourselves as targets of these and similar persuasive appeals, soberly identifying and disassembling the pretensions of such efforts will remain a critical task.

NOTES

1. Isocrates, *Antidosis*, trans. G. Norlin, Loeb Classical Library (Cambridge, MA: Harvard University Press, 1982), 279.

2. Quoted in Chaim Perelman and Lucille Olbrechts-Tyteca, *The New Rhetoric: A Treatise on Argumentation*, trans. John Wilkinson and Purcell Weaver (Notre Dame: University of Notre Dame Press, 1969), 171.

3. In this regard, Bushkoff's remarks about *Radical Son* are telling: "[B]ut the extreme leftist turned extreme rightist overlooks the essence of democracy: moderation, balance, toleration, a willingness to live and let live. Without these, democracy is impossible." Bushkoff, "60s Radical Still Shuns Moderation," 13.

4. Morgan Marietta, "The Absolutist Advantage: Sacred Rhetoric in Contemporary Presidential Debate," *Political Communication* 26 (2009): 391.

5. Hahn, *Political Communication*, 70.

6. David H. Hempton, "Enchantment and Disenchantment in the Evangelical Tradition," *Harvard Divinity Bulletin* 36 (2008): 44.

7. That is, Podhoretz deflects public reason by constructing a narrative between personal and technical reasoning. See G. Thomas Goodnight, "The Personal, Technical, and Public Spheres of Argument: A Speculative Inquiry into the Art of Public Deliberation," *Journal of the American Forensic Association* 18 (1981): 224–25. Steffensmeier and Schenck-Hamlin report that much of the deliberation literature shows that nonexperts argue in narrative terms while experts tend to use more traditional forms of deliberation, although in their study citizens

tended to use both. Timothy Steffensmeier and William Schenck-Hamlin, "Argument Quality in Public Deliberations," *Argumentation and Advocacy* 45 (2008): 22.

8. See Albert and Albert, eds., *The Sixties Papers*.

9. See Edw. Morgan, *The 60s Experience*.

10. Asen, "Toward a Normative Conception of Difference in Public Deliberation," 290.

11. Even a religionist such as Jimmy Swaggart unconsciously drew from secular traditions rather than a traditional Augustinian view of confession emphasizing public, political speech beyond the self's solipsism—in the same way that I find Wills uses Augustine. Swaggart's implicit rhetorical theory praises unreflective speech, deemphasizing language use in favor of natural, "simple effusion from the depths of self" and equating "inarticulateness and authenticity." Ultimately, "the more *human* Swaggart became, the less *politically accountable* he remained." Dave Tell, "Jimmy Swaggart's Secular Confession," *Rhetoric Society Quarterly* 39 (2009): 126, 137, 142. Political conversion rhetoric is also similar to civic epistemologies grounded in notions of "uncertainty" that tend to bypass deliberation. See Marcus Paroske, "Deliberating International Science Policy Controversies: Uncertainty and AIDS in South Africa," *Quarterly Journal of Speech* 95 (2009): 148–70.

12. See Bellah et al., *Habits of the Heart*, xvii; Robert Putnam, "Bowling Alone: America's Declining Social Capital," *Journal of Democracy* 6 (1995): 65–78.

13. Bivins, *The Fracture of Good Order*, 175.

14. Thomas B. Farrell, *Norms of Rhetorical Culture* (New Haven, CT: Yale University Press, 1993), 1.

15. This civil-religious rhetoric extends the framework developed in Domke and Coe, *The God Strategy*. These findings also speak to interdisciplinary research exploring secularization in modern societies. Chaves writes that secularization should not be understood as the decline of religion in the modern world but the "declining scope of religious authority" across society's institutional spheres. Mark Chaves, "Secularization as Declining Religious Authority," *Social Forces* 72 (1994): 749. Hamilton extends this view: "People look to political institutions and processes for justice and for better conditions, not to the Church or to the life hereafter. The state is expected to provide for those in need. The Church has lost its educational role and with it its ability to promote its message and itself. The role of the Church in defining moral standards has declined now [so] that parliaments and politicians increasingly concern themselves with such questions." Malcolm B. Hamilton, *The Sociology of Religion: Theoretical and Comparative Perspectives* (New York: Routledge, 1995), 173.

16. R. Hart and Pauley eds., *The Political Pulpit Revisited*.

17. Luckmann, *The Invisible Religion*. At the same time, religion in the United States has evolved toward "inwardness, subjectivity, the experiential, the expressive, [and] the spiritual," rather than public and communal causes. In effect, "the discourse on spiritual 'journeys' and 'growth' is now a province not just of theologians and journalists, but of ordinary people in cafes, coffee bars, and bookstores across the country." Roof, *Spiritual Marketplace*, 7.

18. Many societies have not developed civil religions to the same extent as the United States. A. Johnson, *The Blackwell Dictionary of Sociology*, 39.

19. For example, Podhoretz claims that his new political beliefs were actually more in line with what he previously believed, and finds much consistency between his long literary education and turn to conservatism. Podhoretz, *Breaking Ranks*, 172, 171.

20. This conclusion parallels Dorsey's finding that in modern American autobiographies, conversion experiences have "socializing function[s]" but often portray a "separateness" or mark of "estrangement," too. Dorsey, *Sacred Estrangement*, 10.

21. Asen, "Ideology, Materiality, and Counterpublicity."

22. Robert B. Cialdini, *Influence: Science and Practice*, 5th ed. (New York: Allyn & Bacon, 2008).

23. Slain, "So . . . He Is a Flip Flopper?" par. 1.

24. Robert C. Rowland and John M. Jones, "Recasting the American Dream and American Politics: Barack Obama's Keynote Address to the 2004 Democratic National Convention," *Quarterly Journal of Speech* 93 (2007): 427, 430.

25. See Lakoff, *Don't Think of an Elephant!*

26. Ben Smith, "Bush Backer Pens Pro-Obama Book," *Politico*, June 16, 2008, www.politico.com/news/stories/0608/11099.html.
27. J. Coulter, "Why I Am *Not* a Right-Winger," 113.
28. Stephen Schwartz, "The Curious Case of David Horowitz," *Los Angeles Times*, October 11, 1998, http://articles.latimes.com/1998/oct/11/books/bk-31283?pg=1, par. 4.
29. Jas. Roberts, "Disillusioned Radicals," 265.
30. Bain Attwood, "In the Age of Testimony: The Stolen Generations Narrative, 'Distance,' and Public History," *Public Culture* 20 (2008): 79, 86; emphasis in original.
31. See ibid., 89.
32. Branham, "The Role of the Convert," 418; Burke, *The Rhetoric of Religion*.
33. See also Fabj, "Intolerance, Forgiveness, and Promise in the Rhetoric of Conversion"; Spencer, "The Rhetoric of Malcolm Muggeridge's Gradual Christian Conversion." Popkin finds that "changes in voters' party identification are generally slow, often even glacial; but changes in their comparative assessments of how well parties handle different problems, or what groups the parties stand for, can be rapid." Popkin, *The Reasoning Voter*, 56. Griffin suggests that autobiographies are particularly fitting for studying gradual conversion, as there is much room for rhetoric to play a subtle role in conversions that occur over a period of time. Ch. Griffin, "The Rhetoric of Form in Conversion Narratives."
34. Chambers also frames his story around young people's reactions to his work, as when a young man came up to Chambers after the August 25 Hiss hearing and told him that his statements were meaningful to the younger generation. Chambers, *Witness*, 695. While Horowitz doesn't use the letter device from the start, he does focus the first few pages of *RS* on the young generation and their vulnerability to a world in flux. Horowitz structures his entire autobiography around the relationship between his father and himself and frequently provides admonitions to his children about their political futures. Podhoretz additionally sets his sight on youth, in calling Lillian Hellman's play *Scoundrel Time* silly and dangerous, especially for its possible impact on naïve youth. Podhoretz, *Breaking Ranks*, 318. Kimmage argues that Podhoretz shifted Chambers's emphasis away from "the intellectual as revolutionary or reformer or rebel" to "the intellectual as parent, passing wisdom on to an immature younger generation." Kimmage, "Whittaker Chambers's *Witness* and the Dilemma of Modern Conservatism," 961.
35. Benjamin Franklin, *Autobiography of Benjamin Franklin*, ed. Frank Woodworth Pine (New York: Henry Holt, 1916), 3.
36. Patricia Meyer Spacks, "Stages of Self: Notes on Autobiography and the Life Cycle," in *The American Autobiography: A Collection of Critical Essays*, ed. Albert E. Stone (Englewood Cliffs, NJ: Prentice Hall, 1981), 45, 54, 59.
37. David M. Ryfe, "Does Deliberative Democracy Work?" *Annual Review of Political Science* 8 (2005): 63.
38. Laura Black, "Deliberation, Difference, and the Story: How Storytelling Manages Identity and Conflict in Deliberative Groups" (PhD diss., University of Washington, 2006), 130.
39. Richard Benjamin Crosby, "Oath Rhetoric, Political Identity, and the Case of Jon Huntsman," *Argumentation and Advocacy* 49 (2013): 195.
40. One reviewer of *Radical Son* writes that "one thing about this book that agitated me was the complete lack of sources." Michael Rohm, "Interesting, but Horribly Flawed," Amazon.com, October 16, 2005, www.amazon.com/Radical-Son-Generational-David-Horowitz/product-reviews/0684840057/ref=dp_top_cm_cr_acr_txt?ie=UTF8&show Viewpoints=1, par. 1.
41. Chambers, *Witness*, 477.
42. Watson, *Lives of Their Own*, 112.
43. Gabrielle M. Spiegel, "Memory and History: Liturgical Time and Historical Time," *History and Theory* 41 (2002): 157.
44. John Durham Peters, "'The Only Proper Scale of Representation': The Politics of Statistics and Stories," *Political Communication* 18 (2001): 440, 439.
45. Koehler, "Neo-Fantasies and Ancient Myths: Adam Curtis on *The Power of Nightmares*."

46. Robert Huckfeldt, Paul E. Johnson, and John Sprague, *Political Disagreement: The Survival of Diverse Opinions within Communication Networks* (New York: Cambridge University Press, 2004), 121–22.

47. See also Booth, "The Rhetoric of Fundamentalist Conversion Stories," 393.

48. For a few examples, see Jasinski, *Sourcebook on Rhetoric*, 375–76; L. Griffin, "A Dramatistic Theory of the Rhetoric of Movements," 464; Bormann, Cragan, and Shields, "An Expansion of the Rhetorical Vision Component of the Symbolic Convergence Theory," 1–2; Charland, "Constitutive Rhetoric," 142.

49. Jakob Svensson, "Expressive Rationality: A Different Approach for Understanding Participation in Municipal Deliberative Practices," *Communication, Culture & Critique* 1 (2008): 213.

50. Ibid., 214. Svensson finds that "instrumental" and "communicative" visions of rationality fail to grasp citizens' motivations for public participation. In instrumental accounts of rationality, people communicate in pursuit of their own interests, performing cost/benefit analyses in public. In Habermas's communicative rationality, interpersonal discussion moves people beyond their subjectivities, coordinating interests and multiplying understandings in an ideal speech situation. Ibid., 214–15.

51. Anthony Giddens, *Modernity and Self-Identity* (Stanford, CA: Stanford University Press, 1991), 54. Brown also traces how a lifestyle and identity politics have become more important with the decline of the nation-state: "Since the collapse of a vital liberalism in the 1980s in the United States and elsewhere, the dominant conceptions of activist politics have been a left-wing pursuit of racial and sexual liberation and self-expression, and a right-wing advocacy of 'traditional values' and unregulated capitalism." Richard Harvey Brown, "Global Capitalism, National Sovereignty, and the Decline of Democratic Space," *Rhetoric & Public Affairs* 5 (2002): 353.

52. Svensson, "Expressive Rationality," 217.

53. This finding illustrates a point about rhetoric more generally: "[W]e are what we have consumed; we take in whatever takes us in, and we are forever altered." Booth, *Modern Dogma*, 166.

54. Guy A. M. Widdershoven, "The Story of Life: Hermeneutic Perspectives on the Relationship between Narrative and Life History," in *The Narrative Study of Lives*, ed. Ruthellen Josselson and Amia Lieblich (Newbury Park, CA: Sage, 1993), 2.

55. Booth, "The Rhetoric of Fundamentalist Conversion Stories," 368.

56. Fisher, "Narration as a Human Communication Paradigm," 6. Hardy also relates that "we dream in narrative, daydream in narrative, remember, anticipate, hope, despair, believe, doubt, plan, revise, criticize, construct, gossip, learn, hate and love by narrative." Barbara Hardy, "Towards a Poetics of Fiction: An Approach through Narrative," *Novel* 2 (1986): 5.

57. See Domke and Coe, *The God Strategy*.

58. See Plato, *Republic*, in *Plato: Complete Works*, ed. Cooper, trans. Grube, 1132–55.

59. Hyrum Lewis notes: "Chambers' theory looks particularly mistaken in the 21st century as the West finds itself at war not with a 'Godless' foe, but with groups whose very religion drives most of their animus toward the West. Would Chambers have taken the side of radical Islam in its war against the West because many of them hailed from premodern, god-centered societies? Probably not, and yet his theory would have allowed no other position." H. Lewis, "Sacralizing the Right," 121. It is hence ironic that another reviewer argues that Chambers's fight against Communism applies to a worldwide fight against Muslim jihadists who "want to impose their values and beliefs on everyone else by force, not debate." "Witness," *FirstPrinciples.US*, n.d., www.firstprinciples.us/sections/synopses/books.witness.asp (no longer available), par. 20–21.

60. One should not overlook the tensions experienced by religious converts, too. Hempton finds that many evangelical "disenchantment narratives" come from cognitive dissonance about the Christian scriptures, which have a lot of violence, judgment, and notions of eternal punishment in them. Many disenchanted Christians also struggle with the limiting of human agency in much evangelicalism. Hempton, "Enchantment and Disenchantment," 52–53.

61. Dan Balz and Chris Cillizza, "Sen. Arlen Specter Loses Pennsylvania Primary; Rand Paul Wins in Kentucky," *Washington Post*, May 19, 2010, www.washingtonpost.com/wp-dyn/

content/article/2010/05/18/AR2010051805561.html?hpid=topnews; Carl Hulse, "Risks of Switching Parties Are Clear," *New York Times*, January 3, 2010, www.nytimes.com/2010/01/03/us/politics/03cong.html?pagewanted=print, par. 5.

62. Hulse, "Risks of Switching Parties Are Clear." At the same time, I have defined political conversion narratives in terms of one's public assertion of or justification for changing from one political ideology to another. This definition precludes broader ways in which conversion may be conceived. For instance, when someone switches from a pro-choice to a pro-life position on abortion, without any change in political or party identification, a kind of conversion may still be said to have happened. If the term "conversion" were broadened further, other potential aspects of the phenomenon could also be targeted.

63. See, e.g., "Breaking Ranks: Andreas Papandreou, American Liberalism, and Neo-Conservatism," Woodrow Wilson International Center for Scholars, March 14, 2006, https://www.wilsoncenter.org/event/breaking-ranks-andreas-papandreou-american-liberalism-and-neo-conservatism.

64. D. Bruce Hindmarsh, *The Evangelical Conversion Narrative: Spiritual Autobiography in Early Modern England* (New York: Oxford University Press, 2005).

65. Donald S. Lopez, "Belief," in *Critical Terms for Religious Studies*, ed. Mark Taylor (Chicago: University of Chicago Press, 1998), 21–35.

66. Hempton, "Enchantment and Disenchantment," 45.

67. G. Peters, *The Mutilating God*, 128.

68. Booth, "The Rhetoric of Fundamentalist Conversion Stories," 386.

69. G. Peters, *The Mutilating God*, 162.

70. Ibid. Peters clarifies further: "Although society may be in the process of becoming more unified at the geopolitical level, it is also becoming more culturally and politically fragmented as various interpretive communities seek to attain their autonomy through the very totalizing strategies they repudiate at the more encompassing level. . . . Thus, in the name of cultural, sexual, or racial empowerment, the conversion narrative becomes the very means by which more complex, superior cultural unities become forestalled." Ibid.

71. T. Farrell, *Norms of Rhetorical Culture*, 3.

72. Thomas Kane, "Public Argument and Civil Society: The Cold War Legacy as a Barrier to Deliberative Politics," *Argumentation* 15 (2001): 112.

73. See also Palczewski, "Public Policy Argument and Survivor Testimony."

74. Elizabeth Britt, "Dangerous Deliberation: Subjective Probability and Rhetorical Democracy in the Jury Room," *Rhetoric Society Quarterly* 39 (2009): 103.

75. Quoted in Jeffrey Hart, "What Is the 'West,'" *Hoover Digest* 1 (2002), www.hoover.org/publications/digest/4484246.html (no longer available), par. 27.

76. In Domke and Coe, *The God Strategy*, 141.

77. Ibid., 59, 110.

78. Harding, *The Book of Jerry Falwell*, 274.

79. Marietta, "The Absolutist Advantage," 388.

80. Ibid., 388–89, 406.

81. See R. Davis and Owens, *New Media and American Politics*; Popkin, *The Reasoning Voter*.

82. Shinar, "The Peace Process in Cultural Conflict."

83. Kathryn M. Doherty and James G. Gimpel, "Candidate Character vs. the Economy in the 1992 Election," *Political Behavior* 19 (1997): 177–96; Carolyn L. Funk, "Bringing Candidates into Models of Candidate Evaluation," *Journal of Politics* 61 (1999): 700–20; P. Goren, "Character Weakness, Partisan Bias, and Presidential Evaluation," *American Journal of Political Science* 46 (2002): 627–41.

84. J. Hill, "Obama Basic Training," par. 7.

85. James Rainey, "Blogger Parts with the Right," *Los Angeles Times*, January 8, 2010, A2; Charles Johnson, "Ten Reasons I Parted Ways with the Right," *Little Green Footballs*, November 30, 2009, http://littlegreenfootballs.com/article/35243_Why_I_Parted_Ways_With_The_Right.

86. See Richard A. Lanham, *The Economics of Attention: Style and Substance in the Age of Information* (Chicago: University of Chicago Press, 2006).

87. David Karpf, "The Internet and American Political Campaigns," October 2013, www.cfinst.org/pdf/papers/08_Karpf_Technology.pdf, 7.

88. Adrian Chen, "Unfollow," *New Yorker*, November 23, 2015, www.newyorker.com/magazine/2015/11/23/conversion-via-twitter-westboro-baptist-church-megan-phelps-roper; Josh Passell, "My Friends Don't Know I'm a Conservative," *Boston Globe*, September 9, 2012, www.bostonglobe.com/magazine/2012/09/08/friends-don-know-conservative/6cZz78ANMMgs5uQeEnt6yI/story.html; Jack Camwell, "Political Conversion: I Think I'm a Libertarian," *Christian Fearing God-Man*, January 13, 2012, http://christianfearinggodman.blogspot.com/2012/01/political-conversion-i-think-im.html; Gulbirk, "My Political 'Conversion' (PART 1)," YouTube, February 25, 2012, www.youtube.com/watch?v=Y2M0VvKjLJ0 (no longer available).

Bibliography

1 Cor. 13:11. [KJV] BibleHub.com, n.d. http://bible.cc/1_corinthians/13–11.htm.
A Customer. "An Extremely Perceptive and Well Written Book." Amazon.com, May 2, 1997. www.amazon.com/Radical-Son-Generational-David-Horowitz/product-reviews/0684840057/ref=dp_top_cm_cr_acr_txt?ie=UTF8&showViewpoints=1.
A Customer. "Hilariously Awful." Amazon.com, December 11, 1999. www.amazon.com/Radical-Son-Generational-David-Horowitz/product-reviews/0684840057/ref=dp_top_cm_cr_acr_txt?ie=UTF8&showViewpoints=1.
A Customer. "More Proof that 'Liberalism' Is So Much Let's Pretend." Amazon.com, August 31, 1999. www.amazon.com/Radical-Son-Generational-David-Horowitz/product-reviews/0684840057/ref=dp_top_cm_cr_acr_txt?ie=UTF8 &showViewpoints=1.
Abbot, Porter H. "Autobiography, Autography, Fiction: Groundwork for a Taxonomy of Textual Categories." *New Literary History* 19 (1988): 597–615.
Abbott, Philip. "A 'Long and Winding Road': Bill Clinton and the 1960s." *Rhetoric & Public Affairs* 9 (2006): 1–20.
Abercrombie, Nicholas, Stephen Hill, and Bryan S. Turner. *The Penguin Dictionary of Sociology*. 5th ed. New York: Penguin Books, 2006.
Abrams, Nathan. "Stormin' Norman Strikes Back." *H-Net Reviews*, January 2001. www.h-net.org/reviews/showrev.php?id=4856.
"Accuracy." Dictionary.com, 2018. http://dictionary.reference.com/browse/accuracy.
Adler, Jonathan. "When Michael Met David." *The Volokh Conspiracy*, December 7, 2006. www.volokh.com/posts/1165502003.shtml.
Albert, Judith Clavir, and Stewart Edward Albert, eds. *The Sixties Papers: Documents of a Rebellious Decade*. New York: Praeger, 1984.
Allen, John L. "'Poped Out' Wills Seeks Broader Horizons." *National Catholic Reporter*, November 21, 2008. http://ncronline.org/news/people/poped-out-wills-seeks-broader-horizons.
Allen, Thomas B. *Declassified: 50 Top-Secret Documents That Changed History*. New York: Random House, 2008.
Alwayscowgirl. "Horowitz Was Right." Amazon.com, September 21, 2008. www.amazon.com/Radical-Son-Generational-David-Horowitz/product-reviews/0684840057/ref=dp_top_cm_cr_acr_txt?ie=UTF8&showViewpoints=1.
Anderson, Dana. *Identity's Strategy: Rhetorical Selves in Conversion*. Columbia: University of South Carolina Press, 2007.
Anderson, William G. "Progressivism: An Historiographical Essay." *History Teacher* 6 (1973): 427–52.
Annan, Noel. "An Editor and His Odyssey." *Times Literary Supplement*, April 25, 1980.

Archer, Robert D. "When You Get Down to It, Just Another Extremist." Amazon.com, January 7, 2009. www.amazon.com/Radical-Son-Generational-David-Horowitz/product-reviews/0684840057/ref=dp_top_cm_cr_acr_txt?ie=UTF8& showView points=1.
Arendt, Hannah. "The Ex-Communists." *Commonweal*, March 20, 1953.
Aristotle. *The City of God*. Translated by Marcus Dods. Peabody, MA: Hendrickson, 2009.
———. *Rhetoric*. Translated by W. Rhys Roberts. New York: Modern Library, 1954.
Aronoff, Yael S. "In Like a Lamb, Out Like a Lion: The Political Conversion of Jimmy Carter." *Political Science Quarterly* 121 (2006): 425–49.
Asen, Robert. "A Discourse Theory of Citizenship." *Quarterly Journal of Speech* 90 (2004): 189–211.
———. "Ideology, Materiality, and Counterpublicity: William E. Simon and the Rise of a Conservative Counterintelligensia." *Quarterly Journal of Speech* 95 (2009): 263–88.
———. "Toward a Normative Conception of Difference in Public Deliberation." In *Readings on Argumentation*, edited by Angela J. Aguayo and Timothy R. Steffensmeier, 281–96. State College, PA: Strata, 2008.
Asiner, Martin. "Radical from Both Sides." Amazon.com, February 21, 2009. www.amazon.com/Radical-Son-Generational-David-Horowitz/product-reviews/0684840057/ref=dp_top_cm_cr_acr_txt?ie=UTF8&showViewpoints=1.
Atkinson, James. *The Trial of Luther*. New York: Stein and Day, 1971.
Attwood, Bain. "In the Age of Testimony: The Stolen Generations Narrative, 'Distance,' and Public History." *Public Culture* 20 (2008): 75–95.
Augustine. *The City of God*. Translated by Marcus Dods. Peabody, MA: Hendrickson, 2009.
———. *Confessions*. Translated by R. S. Pine-Coffin. New York: Penguin Books, 1961.
"Awards: Presidential Medal of Freedom." *Facts on File World News Digest*, July 8, 2004. World News Digest.
Bacevich, Andrew J. Review of *The Norman Podhoretz Reader*, by Thomas L. Jeffers, ed. *Wilson Quarterly* 28 (2004): 127–28.
Badillo, Herman. *One Nation, One Standard: An Ex-Liberal on How Hispanics Can Succeed Just Like Other Immigrant Groups*. New York: Sentinel, 2006.
Bailey, David C. "Enacting Transformation: George W. Bush and the Pauline Conversion Narrative in *A Charge to Keep*." *Rhetoric & Public Affairs* 11 (2008): 215–41.
Baker, Hunter. "A Conservative-Libertarian Booklist for Spectator Readers." *American Spectator*, December 29, 2008. https://spectator.org/17061_conservative-libertarian-booklist-spectator-readers/.
Balz, Dan, and Chris Cillizza. "Sen. Arlen Specter Loses Pennsylvania Primary; Rand Paul Wins in Kentucky." *Washington Post*, May 19, 2010. www.washington post.com/wp-dyn/content/article/2010/05/18/AR2010051805561.html?hpid=top news.
Barnes, Fred. "Jon Voight, Whittaker Chambers Fan." *Weekly Standard*, September 3, 2007. www.weeklystandard.com/Content/Public/Articles/000/000/014/018 hyldo.asp.
Barth, Karl. "The Awakening to Conversion." In *Conversion: Perspectives on Personal and Social Transformation*, edited by Walter E. Conn, 35–49. Staten Island, NY: Alba House, 1978.
Barthes, Roland. *Mythologies*. Translated by Annette Lavers. New York: Hill & Wang, 1972.
Bartlett, Bruce. "Kristol Clear." *National Review*, June 26, 2002. http://old.nationalreview.com/nrof_bartlett/bartlett062602.asp (no longer available).
Bass, Jeffrey D. "The Appeal to Efficiency as Narrative Closure: Lyndon Johnson and the Dominican Crisis, 1965." *Southern Speech Communication Journal* 50 (1985): 103–20.
Bauerlein, Mark. "An Anti-progressive Syllabus." *Inside Higher Ed*, July 5, 2007. www.insidehighered.com/views/2007/07/05/anti-progressive-syllabus.
Baughman, Judith S., Victor Bondi, Richard Layman, Tandy McConnell, and Vincent Tompkins, eds. "Introduction." Vol. 6 of *American Decades*. Detroit: Gale, 2001.
———. "Introduction." Vol. 8 of *American Decades*. Detroit: Gale, 2001.
"Bearing True Witness: Why We Are Tempted to Embellish Conversion Stories." *Christianity Today*, July 2010, 45.
Beattie, Keith. *The Scar That Binds: American Culture and the Vietnam War*. New York: New York University Press, 1998.

Beatty, Jack. Review of *Confessions of a Conservative*. *New Republic*, May 19, 1979, 38.
Beichman, Arnold. "*Ex-Friends*." *Policy Review* 94 (1999): 82–88.
Bellah, Robert. "Civil Religion in America." *Daedalus* 1 (1967): 1–21.
Bellah, Robert N., Richard Madsen, William M. Sullivan, Ann Swidler, and Steven M. Tipton. *Habits of the Heart: Individualism and Commitment in American Life*. Berkeley: University of California Press, 2008.
Benhabib, Seyla. "Introduction: The Democratic Moment and the Problem of Difference." In *Democracy and Difference: Contesting the Boundaries of the Political*, edited by idem, 3–18. Princeton, NJ: Princeton University Press, 1996.
———. "Toward a Deliberative Model of Democratic Legitimacy." In *Democracy and Difference*, edited by idem, 67–94. Princeton, NJ: Princeton University Press, 1996.
Benson, Thomas W. "Rhetoric and Autobiography: The Case of Malcolm X." *Quarterly Journal of Speech* 60 (1974): 1–13.
Bercovitch, Sacvan. *The Puritan Origins of the American Self*. New Haven, CT: Yale University Press, 1975.
Berger, Daniel. "The Whittaker Chambers of Our Time." Amazon.com, April 29, 2007. www.amazon.com/Radical-Son-Generational-David-Horowitz/product-reviews/0684840057/ref=dp_top_cm_cr_acr_txt?ie=UTF8&showViewpoints=1.
Berger, Peter. *The Heretical Imperative: Contemporary Possibilities of Religious Affirmation*. New York: Anchor/Doubleday, 1979.
———. *The Sacred Canopy: Elements of a Sociological Theory of Religion*. Garden City, NY: Doubleday, 1967.
Birdsell, David S. "George W. Bush's Signing Statements: The Assault on Deliberation." *Rhetoric & Public Affairs* 10 (2007): 335–60.
Bivins, Jason C. *The Fracture of Good Order: Christian Antiliberalism and the Challenge to American Politics*. Chapel Hill: University of North Carolina Press, 2003.
Bizer, George Y., Shirel M. Kozak, and Leigh Ann Holterman. "The Persuasiveness of the Straw Man Rhetorical Technique." *Social Influence* 4 (2009): 216–30.
Bjerre-Poulsen, Niels. *Right Face: Organizing the American Conservative Movement 1945–65*. Copenhagen: Museum Tusculanum Press, 2002.
Black, Edwin. *Rhetorical Questions*. Chicago: University of Chicago Press, 1992.
———. "The Second Persona." *Quarterly Journal of Speech* 56 (1970): 109–19.
Black, Laura. "Deliberation, Difference, and the Story: How Storytelling Manages Identity and Conflict in Deliberative Groups." PhD diss., University of Washington, 2006.
———. "Deliberation, Storytelling, and Dialogic Moments." *Communication Theory* 18 (2008): 93–116.
Bliese, John R. E. "Richard Weaver and Piety towards Nature." *Modern Age* 47 (2007): 102–10.
Bloom, Alexander. *Prodigal Sons: The New York Intellectuals and Their World*. New York: Oxford University Press, 1986.
Bohman, James. *Public Deliberation: Pluralism, Complexity, and Democracy*. Cambridge, MA: MIT Press, 2000.
Bond, M. A. "The Political Conversion of Friedrich von Gentz." *European History Quarterly* 3 (1973): 1–12.
Booth, Wayne. *Modern Dogma and the Rhetoric of Assent*. Chicago: University of Chicago Press, 1974.
———. "The Rhetoric of Fundamentalist Conversion Stories." In *Fundamentalisms Comprehended*, edited by Martin E. Marty and R. Scott Appleby, 367–95. Chicago: University of Chicago Press, 1995.
———. *The Sacred Canopy: Elements of a Sociological Theory of Religion*. Garden City, NY: Anchor Books, 1969.
———. "The Scope of Rhetoric Today." In *The Prospect of Rhetoric: Report on the National Development Project*, edited by Lloyd F. Bitzer and Edwin Black, 93–114. Englewood Cliffs, NJ: Prentice Hall, 1971.
Bormann, Ernest G. *The Force of Fantasy: Restoring the American Dream*. 2nd ed. Carbondale: Southern Illinois University Press, 2001.

Bormann, Ernest G., John Cragan, and Donald Shields. "An Expansion of the Rhetorical Vision Component of the Symbolic Convergence Theory: The Cold War Paradigm Case." *Communication Monographs* 63 (1996): 1–28.
Bourdieu, Pierre. *Distinction: A Social Critique of the Judgment of Taste.* Translated by Richard Nice. Cambridge, MA: Harvard University Press, 1984.
Bowell, T. "Feminist Standpoint Theory." *Internet Encyclopedia of Philosophy*, n.d. www.iep.utm.edu/fem-stan/.
Bowling, Lawson H. "The New Party of Memory: Intellectual Origins of Neoconservatism, 1945–1960." PhD diss., Columbia University, 1990.
Bowman, James. "*Radical Son.*" *National Review*, March 24, 1997.
Branham, Robert J. "The Role of the Convert in *Eclipse of Reason* and *The Silent Scream.*" *Quarterly Journal of Speech* 77 (1991): 407–26.
"Breaking Ranks." *Atlantic Monthly*, November 1979.
"*Breaking Ranks*: Andreas Papandreou, American Liberalism, and Neo-Conservatism." Woodrow Wilson International Center for Scholars, March 14, 2006. https://www.wilsoncenter.org/event/breaking-ranks-andreas-papandreou-american-liberalism-and-neoconservatism.
Breit, Harvey. "Talk with Mr. Chambers." *New York Times*, May 25, 1952.
Breitenbach, Jerome R. "Suggested and Nonsuggested Reading." September 13, 2005. https://courseware.ee.calpoly.edu/emeritus/jbreiten/sugread.html
Brendan, Casper. Letter to the editor. *Time*, June 16, 1952.
Britt, Elizabeth. "Dangerous Deliberation: Subjective Probability and Rhetorical Democracy in the Jury Room." *Rhetoric Society Quarterly* 39 (2009): 103–23.
Brock, David. *Blinded by the Right: The Conscience of an Ex-Conservative.* New York: Three Rivers, 2002.
———. "Unliving a Lie." *Fast Company*, September 2004.
Brockriede, Wayne, and Douglas Ehninger. "Toulmin on Argument: An Interpretation and Application." *Quarterly Journal of Speech* 46 (1960): 44–53.
Brooks, David. "Stepping Out of the Tar Pit." *New York Times*, February 1, 2005.
Brouwer, Daniel C. "Communication as Counterpublic." In *Communication as . . . : Perspectives on Theory*, edited by Gregory J. Shepherd, Jeffrey St. John, and Ted Striphas, 195–208. Thousand Oaks, CA: Sage, 2006.
Brown, Richard Harvey. "Global Capitalism, National Sovereignty, and the Decline of Democratic Space." *Rhetoric & Public Affairs* 5 (2002): 347–57.
———. "Logics of Discovery as Narratives of Conversion: Rhetorics of Invention in Ethnography, Philosophy, and Astronomy." *Philosophy and Rhetoric* 27 (1994): 1–34.
———. *Toward a Democratic Science: Scientific Narration and Civic Communication.* New Haven, CT: Yale University Press, 1998.
Bruce, Elisabeth. *Autobiographical Acts: The Changing Situation of a Literary Genre.* London: Johns Hopkins University Press, 1976.
Bruce, Tammy. *The New American Revolution: Using the Power of the Individual to Save Our Nation from Extremists.* New York: HarperCollins, 2005.
Bruner, Jerome. *Acts of Meaning.* Cambridge, MA: Harvard University Press, 1990.
Buckley, William F., Jr. Foreword to *Witness*, by Whittaker Chambers. Washington, DC: Regnery, 1980.
Bunyan, John. *The Pilgrim's Progress.* Edited by N. H. Keeble. New York: Oxford University Press, 1998.
Bunzel, John H., ed. *Political Passages: Journeys of Change through Two Decades.* New York: Free Press, 1988.
Burke, Kenneth. *Attitudes toward History.* 3rd ed. Berkeley: University of California Press, 1984.
———. *A Grammar of Motives.* Berkeley: University of California Press, 1969.
———. "(Nonsymbolic) Motion/(Symbolic) Action." *Critical Inquiry* 4 (1978): 809–38.
———. *Permanence and Change.* Berkeley: University of California Press, 1984.
———. *The Philosophy of Literary Form.* 3rd ed. Berkeley: University of California Press, 1973.

———. *The Rhetoric of Religion*. Berkeley: University of California Press, 1970.
Burkhart, C. "Right Wing Conspiracy . . . ." *Christian Century*, 2002.
Burton, Jeff. "Witness." *Burtonia Blogs*, September 29, 2008. www.burtonia.com/blog/labels/Witness.html (no longer available).
Bushkoff, Leonard. "60s Radical Still Shuns Moderation." *Christian Science Monitor*, April 7, 1997.
Byers, Thomas B. "Hollywood." In *American Icons: An Encyclopedia of the People, Places, and Things That Have Shaped Our Culture*, edited by Dennis R. Hall and Susan G. Hall, 343–55. Santa Barbara, CA: Greenwood, 2006.
Byrne, Brian J. "Whittaker Chambers—Witness—Must Read. . . ." *Catholic Online Forum*, May 24, 2006. http://forum.catholic.org/viewtopic.php?f=35&t=39598&sid=5d49a55fbeaa7463f88dadcd8e09a751&p=532875 (no longer available).
Caldwell, Christopher. "Renegade." *Commentary*, June 1997, available in ProQuest database.
Caldwell, Patricia. *The Puritan Conversion Narrative*. Cambridge, MA: Harvard University Press, 1983.
Campbell, Duncan. "Right Turn." *Guardian*, May 30, 2001.
Campbell, Karlyn Kohrs. "An Exercise in the Rhetoric of Mythical America." In *Critiques of Contemporary Rhetoric*, edited by idem, 50–58. Belmont, CA: Wadsworth, 1972.
———. "The Ontological Foundations of Rhetorical Theory." *Philosophy and Rhetoric* 3 (1970): 97–108.
———. "The Rhetoric of Radical Black Nationalism: A Case Study in Self-Conscious Criticism." *Central States Speech Journal* 22 (1971): 151–60.
———. "The Rhetoric of Women's Liberation: An Oxymoron." *Communication Studies* 2 (1999): 125–37.
Camwell, Jack. "Political Conversion: I Think I'm a Libertarian." *Christian Fearing God-Man*, January 13, 2012. http://christianfearinggodman.blogspot.com/2012/01/political-conversion-i-think-im.html.
Capps, M., Jr. "Great Book for Understanding the Counter Culture." Amazon.com, December 7, 2004. www.amazon.com/Radical-Son-Generational-David-Horowitz/product-reviews/0684840057/ref=dp_top_cm_cr_acr_txt?ie=UTF8&showViewpoints=1.
Cardoso, Jack J. "Garry Wills." In *The Scribner Encyclopedia of American Lives Thematic Series*, edited by Arnold Markoe and Kenneth T. Jackson. New York: Gale Biography in Context, 2003.
Carlson, A. Cheree. "Gandhi and the Comic Frame: 'Ad Bellum Purificandum.'" *Quarterly Journal of Speech* 74 (1986): 310–22.
———. "Limitations on the Comic Frame: Some Witty American Women of the Nineteenth Century." *Quarterly Journal of Speech* 78 (1988): 16–32.
Carlyle, Thomas. *Sartor Resartus and Selected Prose*. New York: Holt, Rinehart and Winston, 1970.
Carolan, Matthew. "Chambers in the Morning." *National Review*, January 26, 1998.
Carriel, Perry. Letter to the editor. *Time*, June 16, 1952.
Cashill, Jack. "Conservatism for Dummies." *WorldNetDaily*, July 21, 2009. www.wnd.com/index.php?fa=PAGE.printable&pageId=102080.
Cathcart, Robert. "Movements: Confrontation as Rhetorical Form." *Southern Speech Journal* 43 (1978): 233–47.
Chambers, David. "Whittaker Chambers." www.whittakerchambers.org.
Chambers, Simone. "Deliberative Democratic Theory." *Annual Review of Political Science* 6 (2003): 307–26.
"Chambers, Whittaker." *United States Quarterly Book Review* 8 (1952): 232–33.
Chambers, Whittaker. *Cold Friday*. New York: Random House, 1964.
———. *Witness*. Washington, DC: Regnery, 1980 (first published in 1952).
"Chambers and His Critics." *Life*, June 9, 1952.
Chapin, Bernard. "Thank God for His Journey." Amazon.com, August 6, 2007. www.amazon.com/Radical-Son-Generational-David-Horowitz/product-reviews/0684840057/ref=dp_top_cm_cr_acr_txt?ie=UTF8&showViewpoints=1.

Charland, Maurice. "Constitutive Rhetoric: The Case of the Peuple Quebecois." *Quarterly Journal of Speech* 73 (1987): 133–50.
Chaves, Mark. "Secularization as Declining Religious Authority." *Social Forces* 72 (1994): 749–74.
Chavez, Linda. *An Unlikely Conservative: The Transformation of an Ex-Liberal (or How I Became the Most Hated Hispanic in America)*. New York: Basic Books, 2002.
Chen, Adrian. "Unfollow." *New Yorker*, November 23, 2015. www.newyorker.com/magazine/2015/11/23/conversion-via-twitter-westboro-baptist-church-megan-phelps-roper.
Chesebro, James W., John F. Cragan, and Patricia W. McCullough. "The Small Group Technique of the Radical Revolutionary: A Synthetic Study of Consciousness Raising." *Communication Monographs* 40 (1973): 136–46.
"Children." Bible.com, n.d., www.bible.com/search/bible?page=1&q=children&version_id=1.
Christiansen, Adrienne, and Jeremy Hanson. "Comedy as Cure for Tragedy: ACT UP and the Rhetoric of AIDS." *Quarterly Journal of Speech* 82 (1996): 157–70.
Cialdini, Robert B. *Influence: Science and Practice*. 5th ed. New York: Allyn & Bacon, 2008.
Clark, John A., John M. Bruce, John H. Kessel, and William G. Jacoby. "I'd Rather Switch than Fight: Lifelong Democrats and Converts to Republicanism among Campaign Activists." *American Journal of Political Science* 35 (1991): 577–97.
Clayton, Bruce. "Memoir as Social Criticism Rings with Passion." *Atlanta Journal-Constitution*, August 6, 2000.
Clinton, Bill. *My Life*. New York: Knopf, 2004.
Cogley, John. "*Witness*: Whittaker Chambers." *Commonweal*, May 23, 1952.
Coleman, R. "Coming Home." Amazon.com, October 22, 2004. www.amazon.com/Radical-Son-Generational-David-Horowitz/product-reviews/0684840057/ref=dp_top_cm_cr_acr_txt?ie=UTF8&showViewpoints=1.
Collier, Peter, and David Horowitz. *Destructive Generation: Second Thoughts about the '60s*. New York: Free Press, 1989.
Cooke, Maeve. "Five Arguments for Deliberative Democracy." *Political Studies* 48 (2000): 947–69.
Copernicus, Nicolas. *On the Revolutions [De Revolutionibus]*. Edited by Jerzy Dobrzycki. Translated by Edward Rosen. London: Macmillan, 1978.
Cormack, Patrick, ed. *Right Turn: Eight Men Who Changed Their Minds*. London: Leo Cooper, 1978.
Coulter, Ann. "Snuggle up with Ann Coulter's Top 10 Favorite Books." *Human Events*, November 29, 2005. http://humanevents.com/2005/11/29/snuggle-up-with-ann-coulters-top-10-favorite-books/.
Coulter, Jeff. "Why I Am *Not* a Right-Winger: A Response to David Horowitz." *New Political Science* 20 (1998): 97–115.
Cox, James M. *Recovering Literature's Lost Ground: Essays in American Autobiography*. Baton Rouge: Louisiana State University Press, 1989.
Cragen, John. "Rhetorical Strategy, A Dramatistic Interpretation and Application." *Central States Speech Journal* 26 (1975): 4–11.
Craig, Bruce. "Politics in the Pumpkin Patch." *Public Historian* 12 (1990): 9–24.
Craig, Jane Larkin. "Breaking Ranks: A Political Memoir." *Saturday Review*, October 27, 1979.
Creps, Earl G. "The Conspiracy Argument as Rhetorical Genre." PhD diss., Northwestern University, 1980.
Crist, Charlie, and Ellis Henican. *The Party's Over: How the Extreme Right Hijacked the GOP and I Became a Democrat.* New York: Dutton, 2014.
Crosby, Richard Benjamin. "Oath Rhetoric, Political Identity, and the Case of Jon Huntsman." *Argumentation and Advocacy* 49 (2013): 195–209.
Crosston, Matthew. "Neoconservative Democratization in Theory and Practice: Developing Democrats or Raising Radical Islamists." *International Politics* 46 (2009): 298–326.
Cuneo, Paul K. Review of *Confessions of a Conservative*. *America*, June 30, 1979, 540.
"Customer Reviews: *Radical Son*." Amazon.com. www.amazon.com/Radical-Son-Generational-David-Horowitz/dp/0684840057/ref=sr_1_1?ie=UTF8&qid=1516075847&sr=8-1&

keywords=radical+son.
"Customer Reviews: *Witness.*" Amazon.com. www.amazon.com/Witness-Cold-Classics-Whittaker-Chambers/dp/162157296X/ref=sr_1_2?ie=UTF8&qid=1516070151&sr=8-2& keywords=witness.
Dannhauser, Werner J. "Against the Center." *Commentary*, July 1979, 68.
Darsey, James. "A Conspiracy of Science." *Western Journal of Communication* 66 (2002): 469–91.
———. "Joe McCarthy's Fantastic Moment." *Communication Monographs* 62 (1995): 65–86.
Darwish, Nonie. *Now They Call Me Infidel: Why I Renounced Jihad for America, Israel, and the War on Terror*. New York: Sentinel, 2006.
"David (Joel) Horowitz." *Biography Resource Center*. Farmington Hills, MI: Gale, 2009.
Davis, Elmer. "History in Doublethink." *Saturday Review*, June 28, 1952.
Davis, Richard, and Diana Owens. *New Media and American Politics*. New York: Oxford University Press, 1998.
DC Dave. "PBS Lies for FDR over Allegations by Whittaker Chambers." DCDave.com, January 1, 2006. www.dcdave.com/article4/060129.htm.
Deaver, Michael K., ed. *Why I Am a Reagan Conservative*. New York: Harper, 2005.
Delany, Paul. *British Autobiography in the Seventeenth Century*. New York: Columbia University Press, 1969.
De Quincy, Thomas. *Confessions of an English Opium Eater*. New York: Penguin Books, 2003.
Descartes, René. *Discourse on Method and Meditations*. Translated by Lawrence Lafleur. Indianapolis, IN: Bobbs-Merrill, 1960.
de Toledano, Ralph. "The Imperatives of the Heart: A Friend Remembers Whittaker Chambers." *National Review*, August 1, 1986. www.nationalreview.com/article/219901/imperatives-heart-williumrex.
Deutscher, Isaac. *Heretics and Renegades*. New York: Bobbs-Merrill, 1957/1969.
Diamond, Glenn. "Norman Podhoretz and Jack Kerouac." *Los Angeles Times*, January 24, 1987.
Diggens, John P. *Up from Communism: Conservative Odysseys in American Intellectual Development*. New York: Columbia University Press, 1975/1994.
Doherty, Kathryn M., and James G. Gimpel. "Candidate Character vs. the Economy in the 1992 Election." *Political Behavior* 19 (1997): 177–96.
Domke, David, and Kevin Coe. *The God Strategy: How Religion Became a Weapon in America*. New York: Oxford University Press, 2008.
Donelson, Tom. "Whittaker Chambers: A Witness for a New Era." *Blogcritics Magazine*, September 10, 2004. http://blogcritics.org/archives/2004/09/10/124634.php (no longer available).
Dooley, Terence. *Innisken, 1912–1918: The Political Conversion of Bernard O'Rourke*. Dublin: Four Courts, 2004.
Dorsey, Peter A. *Sacred Estrangement: The Rhetoric of Conversion in Modern American Autobiography*. University Park: Pennsylvania State University Press, 1993.
Dos Passos, John. "Mr. Chambers's Descent into Hell." *Saturday Review*, May 24, 1952.
Dow, Bonnie J., and Mari Boor Tonn. "'Feminine Style' and Political Judgment in the Rhetoric of Ann Richards." *Quarterly Journal of Speech* 79 (1993): 286–302.
Downing, Francis. "Man Is the Measure of All History." *Commonweal*, February 29, 1952.
Doxtader, Erik W. "The Entwinement of Argument and Rhetoric: A Dialectical Reading of Habermas' Theory of Communicative Action." In *Readings on Argumentation*, edited by Angela J. Aguayo and Timothy R. Steffensmeier, 297–309. State College, PA: Strata, 2008.
Drew, Elizabeth. *The Corruption of American Politics: What Went Wrong and Why*. Woodstock, NY: Overlook, 2000.
Dryzek, John S. "Deliberative Democracy in Divided Societies: Alternatives to Agonism and Analgesia." *Political Theory* 33 (2005): 218–42.
Duffield, Marcus. "Amazing Autobiography of a Famous Ex-Communist." *New York Herald Tribune*, May 25, 1952.

Duffy, Dave. "Confessions of a Former Liberal." *Backwoods Home Magazine*, 1998. www.backwoodshome.com/articles/duffy50.html.
Duss, Matthew. "Giuliani's War Cabinet." *American Prospect*, September 25, 2007. www.prospect.org/cs/articles?article=giulianis_war_cabinet.
Eberstadt, Mary, ed. *Why I Turned Right: Leading Baby Boom Conservatives Chronicle Their Political Journeys.* New York: Threshold, 2007.
"Editors' Shop Talk." *Antioch Review* 12 (1952): 30.
Edwards, Jason A., Joseph M. Valenzano, III, and Karla Stevenson. "The Peacekeeping Mission: Bringing Stability to a Chaotic Scene." *Communication Quarterly* 59 (2011): 339–58.
Edwards, Lee. "Modern Tomes." *Policy Review* 84 (1997). www.hoover.org/research/modern-tomes.
———. "Whittaker Chambers: Man of Courage and Faith." Heritage.org, April 2, 2001. www.heritage.org/political-process/report/whittaker-chambers-man-courage-and-faith.
Edwards, Willard. "*Witness.*" *Chicago Daily Tribune*, May 25, 1952.
Elektrophyte. "Remarkable." Amazon.com, June 23, 2005. www.amazon.com/Radical-Son-Generational-David-Horowitz/product-reviews/0684840057/ref=dp_top_cm_cr_acr_txt?ie=UTF8&showViewpoints=1.
Eliot, T. S. *Christianity and Culture.* New York: Harcourt, Brace and World, 1949.
Epstein, Joseph. "Remaking It." *New York Times*, October 21, 1979. www.nytimes.com/books/99/02/21/specials/podhoretz-breaking.html.
Evans, Thomas W. *The Education of Ronald Reagan: The General Electric Years and the Untold Story of His Conversion to Conservatism.* New York: Columbia University Press, 2006.
Fabj, Valeria. "Intolerance, Forgiveness, and Promise in the Rhetoric of Conversion." *Quarterly Journal of Speech* 84 (1998): 190–208.
Farrell, Henry. "Why We Shouldn't Play Nice with David Horowitz: A Response to *What's Liberal about the Liberal Arts.*" *Crooked Timber*, June 11, 2007. http://crookedtimber.org/2007/06/11/why-we-shouldn%e2%80%99t-play-nice-with-david-horowitz-a-response-to-what%e2%80%99s-liberal-about-the-liberal-arts/#more-5963.
Farrell, Thomas B. *Norms of Rhetorical Culture.* New Haven, CT: Yale University Press, 1993.
Fenn, Richard K. "The Relevance of Bellah's 'Civil Religion' Thesis to a Theory of Secularization." *Social Science History* 1 (1977): 502–17.
Fenster, Mark. *Conspiracy Theories: Secrecy and Power in American Cultures.* Minneapolis: University of Minnesota Press, 1999.
Ferrero, Mario. "A Theory of Conversion to Exclusive Religious and Political Faiths." Paper presented at the annual conference of the European Public Choice Society, Durham, UK, March 31–April 3, 2005.
Finn, Thomas M. *From Death to Rebirth: Ritual and Conversion in Antiquity.* Mahwah, NJ: Paulist Press, 1997.
Fisher, Walter R. "Narration as a Human Communication Paradigm: The Case of Public Moral Argument." *Communication Monographs* 51 (1984): 1–22.
Fogarty, Robert S. "Editorial: Liberty and Security." *Antioch Review* 38 (1980): 3–4.
"Foreign Affairs Bestsellers." *Foreign Affairs* 87 (2008).
Forgie, George B. "Father Past and Child Nation: The Romantic Imagination and the Origins of the American Civil War." PhD diss., Stanford University, 1972.
Foss, Karen A., Sonia K. Foss, and Cindy L. Griffin. *Feminist Rhetorical Theories.* Thousand Oaks, CA: Sage, 1999.
Fox, F. Earle. "*Witness* by Whittaker Chambers." www.theroadtoemmaus.org/RdLb/21PbAr/Hst/US/ChmbrsWitnss.htm.
Fox, George. *The Journal of George Fox.* Richmond, IN: Friends United Press, 2006.
Frank, Thomas. *What's the Matter with Kansas?: How Conservatives Won the Heart of America.* New York: Metropolitan Books, 2004.
Frankel, Benjamin, ed. "Norman Podhoretz, American Editor, *Commentary*, 1960–." In *The Cold War, 1945–1991.* Farmington Hills, MI: Gale, 1992.
Franklin, Benjamin. *Autobiography of Benjamin Franklin.* Edited by Frank Woodworth Pine. New York: Henry Holt, 1916.

Freedman, Shalom. "He Heard the Sound of His Own Drummer." Amazon.com, October 10, 2007. www.amazon.com/Breaking-Ranks-Political-Memoir-Colophon/dp/0060908165.
Freud, Sigmund. *The Basic Writings of Sigmund Freud*. Translated and edited by A. A. Brill. New York: Random House, 1995.
Frohnen, Bruce, Jeremy Beer, and Jeffrey O. Nelson, eds. *American Conservatism: An Encyclopedia*. Wilmington, DE: ISI Books, 2006.
Fuller, Brad. "Two Poles of Ideological Extremism." Amazon.com, January 1, 2000. www.amazon.com/Radical-Son-Generational-David-Horowitz/product-reviews/0684840057/ref=dp_top_cm_cr_acr_txt?ie=UTF8&showViewpoints=1.
Funk, Carolyn L. "Bringing Candidates into Models of Candidate Evaluation." *Journal of Politics* 61 (1999): 700–720.
Galbraith, John Kenneth. "A Revisionist View." *New Republic*, March 28, 1970.
Gamson, William A. *Talking Politics*. New York: Cambridge University Press, 1992.
Gaouette, Nicole. "Middle East Peace." *CQ Researcher*, January 21, 2005.
"Garry Wills." Contemporary Authors Online. Detroit: Gale Biography in Context, 2012.
Garsten, Bryan. *Saving Persuasion: A Defense of Rhetoric and Judgment*. Cambridge, MA: Harvard University Press, 2006.
Gastil, John. *Political Communication and Deliberation*. Thousand Oaks, CA: Sage, 2008.
Gates, Henry Louis. "Frederick Douglass and the Language of the Self." In *Figures in Black: Words, Signs, and the "Racial" Self*, edited by idem, 98–124. New York: Oxford University Press, 1987.
Gay, James Thomas. "1948: The Alger Hiss Spy Case." *American History* 33 (1993): 26–35.
Genter, Robert. "Witnessing Whittaker Chambers: Communism, McCarthyism and the Confessional Self." *Intellectual History Review* 18 (2008): 243–58.
Gerrity, Frank. Review of *Confessions of a Conservative*. Best Sellers, 1979, 224.
Gerson, Mark. "Norman's Conquest." *Policy Review* 74 (1995). www.hoover.org/publications/policyreview/3564402.html (no longer available).
Giddens, Anthony. *Modernity and Self-Identity*. Stanford, CA: Stanford University Press, 1991.
Gill, Brendan. "Either/Or." *New Yorker*, May 24, 1952.
Goldberg, Bernard. *Crazies to the Left of Me, Wimps to the Right: How One Side Lost Its Mind and the Other Lost Its Nerve*. New York: HarperCollins, 2007.
Golden, James L., Goodwin F. Berquist, and William E. Coleman. "Secular and Religious Conversion." In *The Rhetoric of Western Thought*, 4th ed., edited by James L. Golden, Goodwin F. Berquist, and William E. Coleman, 565–586. Dubuque, IA: Kendall/Hunt, 1989.
Goodnight, G. Thomas. "Controversy." In *Argument in Controversy*, edited by Donn W. Parson, 1–13. Annandale, VA: Speech Communication Association, 1991.
———. "The Engagements of Communication: Jürgen Habermas on Discourse, Critical Reason, and Controversy." In *Perspectives on Philosophy of Communication*, edited by Pam Arneson, 91–110. West Lafayette, IN: Purdue University Press, 2007.
———. "Generational Argument." In *Argumentation: Across the Lines of Discipline*, edited by Franz H. van Eemeren, Rob Grootendorst, J. Anthony Blair, and Charles A. Willard. Dordrecht, Netherlands: Foris, 1986.
———. "The Liberal and the Conservative Presumptions: On Political Philosophy and the Foundation of Public Argument." In *Proceedings of the [First] Summer Conference on Argumentation*, edited by Jack Rhodes and Sara Newell, 304–37. Annandale, VA: Speech Communication Association, 1980.
———. "The Personal, Technical, and Public Spheres: A Note on 21st Century Critical Communication Inquiry." *Argumentation and Advocacy* 48 (2012): 258–267.
———. "The Personal, Technical, and Public Spheres of Argument: A Speculative Inquiry into the Art of Public Deliberation." *Journal of the American Forensic Association* 18 (1981): 224–25.
Goodnight, G. Thomas, and John Poulakos. "Conspiracy Rhetoric: From Pragmatism to Fantasy in Public Discourse." *Western Journal of Communication* 45 (1981): 299–316.
Goodwin, Jean. "Three Faces of the Future." *Argumentation and Advocacy* 37 (2000): 71–85.

Goody, Jack. *The Logic of Writing and the Organization of Society*. New York: Cambridge University Press, 1986.
Gooren, Henri. "Reassessing Conventional Approaches to Conversion: Toward a New Synthesis." *Journal for the Scientific Study of Religion* 46 (2007): 337–53.
Gordon, David. "Confusions of a Conservative." LewRockwell.com, November 18, 2005. www.lewrockwell.com/gordon/gordon14.html (no longer available).
Goren, P. "Character Weakness, Partisan Bias, and Presidential Evaluation." *American Journal of Political Science* 46 (2002): 627–41.
Gorenfeld, John. "Roger Ebert and Mohammed Atta, Partners in Crime." *Salon*, April 12, 2005. www.salon.com/2005/04/12/horowitz_database/.
Graham, William. *Beyond the Written Word: Oral Aspects of Scripture in the History of Tradition*. New York: Cambridge University Press, 1987.
Greenberg, David. "Zealots of Our Time." *American Prospect* 19 (2008): 38–41.
Gregg, Richard. "The Ego-Function of the Rhetoric of Protest." *Philosophy & Rhetoric* 4 (1971): 71–91.
Greven, Philip J. "Youth, Maturity, and Religious Conversion: A Note on the Ages of Converts in Andover, Massachusetts, 1711–1749." *Essex Institute Historical Collections* 108 (1972): 119–34.
Griffin, Charles. "'Movement as Motive': Self-Definition and Social Advocacy in Social Movement Autobiographies." *Western Journal of Communication* 64 (2000): 148–64.
———. "The Rhetoric of Form in Conversion Narratives." *Quarterly Journal of Speech* 76 (1990): 152–63.
Griffin, Cindy L. "Rhetoricizing Alienation: Mary Wollstonecraft and the Rhetorical Construction of Women's Oppression." *Quarterly Journal of Speech* 80 (1994): 293–312.
Griffin, Leland. "A Dramatistic Theory of the Rhetoric of Movements." In *Critical Responses to Kenneth Burke 1924–1962*, edited by William M. Rueckert, 456–78. Minneapolis: University of Minnesota Press, 1969.
———. "The Rhetorical Structure of the 'New Left' Movement: Part I." *Quarterly Journal of Speech* 50 (1964): 113–35.
Griffin, Robert S. "Political Paleontology." *Occidental Quarterly* 5 (2005). www.toqonline.com/archives/v5n2/TOQv5n2Griffin.pdf.
Gring-Pemble, Lisa M. "'Are We Now Going to Govern by Anecdote?': Rhetorical Constructions of Welfare Recipients in Congressional Hearings, Debates, and Legislation, 1992–1996." *Quarterly Journal of Speech* 87 (2001): 341–65.
Grossbart, Stephen R. "Seeking the Divine Favor: Conversion and Church Admission in Eastern Connecticut, 1711–1832." *William and Mary Quarterly* 46 (1989): 696–740.
Gulbirk. "My Political 'Conversion' (PART 1)." YouTube, February 25, 2012. www.youtube.com/watch?v=Y2M0VvKjLJ0 (no longer available).
Gustainis, Justin, and Dan Hahn. "While the Whole World Watched: Rhetorical Failures of the Anti-war Protest." *Communication Quarterly* 36 (1988): 203–16.
Habermas, Jürgen. *Between Facts and Norms: Contributions to a Discourse Theory of Law and Democracy*. Translated by William Rehg. Cambridge, MA: MIT Press, 1996.
———. *Religion and Rationality: Essays on Reason, God, and Modernity*. Cambridge, MA: MIT Press, 2002.
———. *The Theory of Communicative Action*. Vol. 2. Translated by Thomas McCarthy. Boston: Beacon, 1987.
Habermas, Jürgen, and Joseph Ratzinger. *The Dialectics of Secularization: On Reason and Religion*. Translated by Brian McNeil. San Francisco: Ignatius, 2005.
Hackbarth, Sean. "Journey from Left to Right." Amazon.com, April 15, 2001. www.amazon.com/Radical-Son-Generational-David-Horowitz/product-reviews/0684840057/ref=dp_top_cm_cr_acr_txt?ie=UTF8&showViewpoints=1.
Hahn, Dan. *Political Communication: Rhetoric, Government, and Citizens*. State College, PA: Strata, 2003.
Haiman, Franklyn. "The Rhetoric of the Streets: Some Legal and Ethical Considerations." *Quarterly Journal of Speech* 53 (1967): 99–114.

Bibliography

Halper, Stefan, and Jonathan Clarke. *America Alone: The Neo-Conservatives and the Global Order*. New York: Cambridge University Press, 2004.
Hamilton, Malcolm B. *The Sociology of Religion: Theoretical and Comparative Perspectives*. New York: Routledge, 1995.
Hanisch, Carol. "The Personal Is Political." In *The "Second Wave" and Beyond*, 2006. http://scholar.alexanderstreet.com/pages/viewpage.action?pageId=2259 (no longer available).
Harde, Roxanne. "'I Consoled My Heart': Conversion Rhetoric and Female Subjectivity in the Personal Narratives of Elizabeth Ashbridge and Abigail Bailey." *Legacy* 21 (2004): 156–71.
Harding, Susan F. *The Book of Jerry Falwell: Fundamentalist Language and Politics*. Princeton, NJ: Princeton University Press, 2000.
Hardy, Barbara. "Towards a Poetics of Fiction: An Approach through Narrative." *Novel* 2 (1986): 5–14.
Hart, Jeffrey. "What Is the 'West.'" *Hoover Digest* 1 (2002). www.hoover.org/publications/digest/4484246.html (no longer available).
Hart, Roderick P., and Suzanne Daughton. *Modern Rhetorical Criticism*. 3rd ed. Boston: Pearson, 2005.
Hart, Roderick P., and John L. Pauley, eds. *The Political Pulpit Revisited*. West Lafayette, IN: Purdue University Press, 2004.
Hartman, Kabi. "'What Made Me a Suffragette': The New Woman and the New(?) Conversion Narrative." *Women's History Review* 12 (2003): 35–50.
Hartsock, Nancy. "The Feminist Standpoint." In *Discovering Reality*, edited by Sandra Harding and Merrill B. Hintikka, 283–310. London: D. Reidel, 1983.
Hatch, Jenny M. "I Have Come Full Circle." Amazon.com, December 23, 2003. www.amazon.com/Radical-Son-Generational-David-Horowitz/product-reviews/0684840057/ref=dp_top_cm_cr_acr_txt?ie=UTF8&showViewpoints=1.
Hauser, Gerard A., and Chantal Benoit-Barne. "Reflections on Rhetoric, Deliberative Democracy, Civil Society, and Trust." *Rhetoric & Public Affairs* 5 (2002): 261–75.
Hausknecht, Murray. "Confession and Return." *Antioch Review* 14 (1954): 76–86.
Haynes, John. *In Denial: Historians, Communism and Espionage*. San Francisco: Encounter Books, 2003.
Hayward, Steven. "Desperately Seeking David." *Reason*, March 1997. www.reason.com/news/printer/30159.html.
Heilbrunn, Jacob. "Rank-Breakers: The Anatomy of an Industry." *World Affairs*, Spring 2008. www.worldaffairsjournal.org/2008%20-%20Spring/full-breaking-ranks.html.
Heirich, Max. "Change of Heart: A Test of Some Widely Held Theories about Religious Conversion." *American Sociology Review* 83 (1977): 653–80.
Hempton, David H. "Enchantment and Disenchantment in the Evangelical Tradition." *Harvard Divinity Bulletin* 36 (2008): 39–54.
Hendriks, Carolyn M. "Integrate Deliberation: Reconciling Civil Society's Dual Role in Deliberative Democracy." *Political Studies* 54 (2006): 486–508.
Hicks, Darrin. "The Promise of Deliberative Democracy." *Rhetoric & Public Affairs* 5 (2002): 223–60.
Hicks, Sanders. "Compassionate Communists and Cussing Conservatives." SandersHicks.com. www.sanderhicks.com/articles/horowitzint.html.
Hill, Forbes. "Conventional Wisdom—Traditional Form—the President's Message of November 3, 1969." *Quarterly Journal of Speech* 58 (1972): 373–86.
Hill, John. "Obama Basic Training." *Sacramento Bee*, January 31, 2008. www.sacbee.com/111/v-print/story/649427 (no longer available).
Hiltzik, Michael A. "Undoing the New Deal." *Los Angeles Times*, June 26, 2005. www.latimes.com/business/investing/la-tm-hiltzik26jun26,1,7141492.story.
Hindmarsh, D. Bruce. *The Evangelical Conversion Narrative: Spiritual Autobiography in Early Modern England*. New York: Oxford University Press, 2005.
Hiss, Alger. "The Lessons of the Richard Nixon Case." *New York Times*, January 9, 1986. www.nytimes.com/books/97/03/09/reviews/chambers-letters-nixon.html.
Hiss, Anthony. *View from Alger's Window: A Son's Memoir*. Westminster, MD: Vintage Books, 2000.

Hitchens, Christopher. "Born-Again Conformist." *New Statesman*, March 21, 1980.
———. Review of *Ex-Friends*, by Norman Podhoretz, *Harper's*, June 1999, 73–76.
Hofstadter, Richard. *Anti-intellectualism in American Life*. New York: Vintage Books, 1963.
———. *The Paranoid Style in American Politics and Other Essays*. Chicago: University of Chicago Press, 1979.
Hollander, Paul. "*Breaking Ranks: A Political Memoir*." *Contemporary Sociology* 10 (1981): 440–41.
Hollihan, Thomas. *Uncivil Wars: Political Campaigns in a Media Age*. New York: Bedford/St. Martin's, 2001.
Hollihan, Thomas A., and Kevin T. Baaske. *Arguments and Arguing*. Long Grove, IL: Waveland, 2005.
Hook, Sidney. "The Faiths of Whittaker Chambers." *New York Times*, May 12, 1952.
Horner, Charles. "Why Whittaker Chambers Was Wrong." *Commentary*, April 1990.
Horowitz, David. "Can There Be a Decent Left? Michael Walzer's Second Thoughts." FrontPageMagazine.com, 2002. www.frontpagemag.com/Articles/Printable.asp?ID=1011.
———. *The End of Time*. San Francisco: Encounter Books, 2005.
———. *The Free World Colossus: A Critique of American Foreign Policy in the Cold War*. New York: Hill & Wang, 1971.
———. *Hating Whitey: And Other Progressive Causes*. Dallas: Spence, 1999.
———. "In Defense of Intellectual Diversity." *Chronicle of Higher Education*, February 10, 2004.
———. *Indoctrination U: The Left's War against Academic Freedom*. San Francisco: Encounter Books, 2007.
———. *Left Illusions: An Intellectual Odyssey*. Dallas: Spence, 2003.
———. *The Politics of Bad Faith: The Radical Assault on America's Future*. New York: Touchstone, 1998.
———. *The Professors: The 101 Most Dangerous Academics in America*. Washington, DC: Regnery, 2006.
———. *Radical Son: A Generational Odyssey*. New York: Touchstone, 1997.
———. "Some of Our Facts Were Wrong: Our Point Was Right." *Front Page Magazine*, March 15, 2005.
———. *Uncivil Wars: The Controversy over Reparations for Slavery*. San Francisco: Encounter Books, 2001.
———. *Unholy Alliance: Radical Islam and the American Left*. Washington, DC: Regnery, 2004.
"Horowitz—the End of Time." *Wizblog*, May 20, 2005. www.danwismar.com/archives/wizblog/003685.html.
Horton, Carol A. *Race and the Making of American Liberalism*. New York: Oxford University Press, 2005.
Howard, Robert Glenn. "The Double-Bind of the Protestant Reformation: The Birth of Fundamentalism and the Necessity of Pluralism." *Journal of Church and State* 47 (2005): 91–108.
Howe, Irving. "God, Man, and Stalin." *Nation*, May 24, 1952.
Huckfeldt, Robert, Paul E. Johnson, and John Sprague. *Political Disagreement: The Survival of Diverse Opinions within Communication Networks*. New York: Cambridge University Press, 2004.
Hulse, Carl. "Risks of Switching Parties Are Clear." *New York Times*, January 3, 2010. www.nytimes.com/2010/01/03/us/politics/03cong.html?pagewanted=print.
Hutchinson, Paul. "The Works of God?" *Christian Century*, June 11, 1952.
Hyvarinen, Matti. "Rhetoric and Conversion in Student Politics." In *Interpreting the Political: New Methodologies*, edited by Terrell Carver and Matti Hyvarinen, 18–38. New York: Routledge, 1997.
Ingwerson, Marshall. "A Radical Speaks Out." *Christian Science Monitor*, December 3, 1979.
"Interview with David Horowitz." *Chuck Baldwin Live*, 1997. www.chuckbaldwinlive.com/horowitz.html (no longer available).
Isocrates. *Antidosis*. Translated by G. Norlin. Loeb Classical Library. Cambridge, MA: Harvard University Press, 1982.

Ivie, Robert L. "Rhetorical Deliberation and Democratic Politics in the Here and Now." *Rhetoric & Public Affairs* 5 (2002): 277–85.
Jacoby, Jeff. "Smear Victim Fights Back." *Boston Globe*, September 2, 1999.
Jacoby, Susan. *The Age of American Unreason*. New York: Vintage Books, 2009.
———. "Alger Hiss—a Case for Our Time." *Los Angeles Times*, March 22, 2009. http://articles.latimes.com/2009/mar/22/opinion/oe-jacoby22.
James, William. *The Varieties of Religious Experience*. New York: Longmans, Green, 1902.
Jamieson, Kathleen H. *Eloquence in an Electronic Age: The Transformation of Political Speechmaking*. New York: Oxford University Press, 1988.
Jaschik, Scott. "Retractions from David Horowitz." *Inside Higher Education*, January 11, 2006.
———. "Tattered Poster Child." *Inside Higher Education*, November 29, 2005.
Jasinski, James. *Sourcebook on Rhetoric*. Thousand Oaks, CA: Sage, 2001.
Jeffers, Thomas L. "Norman Podhoretz's Discourses on America." *Hudson Review* 54 (2001): 202–28.
Jelen, Ted G. "Political Esperanto: Rhetorical Resources and Limitations of the Christian Right in the United States." *Sociology of Religion* 66 (2005): 303–21.
Jensen, Richard J., and John C. Hammerback. "From Muslim to Mormon: Eldridge Cleaver's Rhetorical Crusade." *Communication Quarterly* 34 (1986): 24–40.
Jentleson, Adam. "Sen. Lamar Alexander David Horowitz." Center for American Progress, April 18, 2006, http://thinkprogress.org/2006/04/18/alexander-horowitz.
Johnny "Uncle Johnny." "Introspective, Insightful & Intellectually Honest." Amazon.com, February 9, 2007. www.amazon.com/Radical-Son-Generational-David-Horowitz/product-reviews/0684840057/ref=dp_top_cm_cr_acr_txt?ie=UTF8&showViewpoints=1.
Johnson, Allan G. *The Blackwell Dictionary of Sociology*. 2nd ed. Oxford: Blackwell, 2000.
Johnson, Charles. "Ten Reasons I Parted Ways with the Right." *Little Green Footballs*, November 30, 2009. http://littlegreenfootballs.com/article/35243_Why_I_Parted_Ways_With_The_Right.
Johnson, Paul. "Shock Troops." *Spectator*, February 9, 1980.
Jones, Alex S. "A Painful Irony: The Media's Moral Obligations." *Harvard International Journal of Press/Politics* 6 (2001): 3–7.
Judd, Orrin. "Orrin's All-Time Top Ten List—Non-Fiction / Conservative Thought." Brothers-Judd, February 9, 2001. http://brothersjudd.com/index.cfm/fuseaction/reviews.detail/book_id/969/Witness.htm.
———. "*Radical Son: A Generational Odyssey* (1997)." BrothersJudd, January 27, 2001. www.brothersjudd.com/index.cfm/fuseaction/reviews.detail/book_id/103.
Judis, John B. "Two Faces of Whittaker Chambers." *New Republic*, April 16, 1984.
Judt, Tony. "The Dualist." *New Republic*, April 14, 1997.
Kakutani, Michiko. "Of the Words of War and the War of Ideas." *New York Times*, October 26, 2007.
Kane, Thomas. "Public Argument and Civil Society: The Cold War Legacy as a Barrier to Deliberative Politics." *Argumentation* 15 (2001): 107–15.
Karp, Walter. "The Constructs of a Conservative." *Harper's*, November 1979, 96.
Karpf, David. "The Internet and American Political Campaigns." October 2013. www.cfinst.org/pdf/papers/08_Karpf_Technology.pdf.
Kaylor, Brian T. "My Take: Don't Be Fooled by Candidates' God Talk." CNN.com, September 14, 2011. http://religion.blogs.cnn.com/2011/09/14/my-take-dont-be-fooled-by-candidates-god-talk.
———. "No Jack Kennedy: Mitt Romney's 'Faith in America' Speech and the Changing Religious-Political Environment." *Communication Studies* 62 (2011): 491–507.
Kelleher, William J. *Progressive Logic: Framing a Unified Field Theory of Values for Progressives*. La Canada, CA: Empathic Science Institute, 2005.
Kellett, Peter M. "Communication in Accounts of Religious Conversion: An Interpretive Phenomenological Account." *Journal of Communication and Religion* 16 (1993): 71–81.
Kelley-Romano, Stephanie. "Trust No One: The Conspiracy Genre on American Television." *Southern Communication Journal* 73 (2008): 105–21.

Kengor, Paul. "The Intellectual Origins of Ronald Reagan's Faith." Heritage Lectures, February 25, 2004. www.heritage.org/political-process/report/the-intellectual-origins-ronald-reagans-faith.

Kesler, Charles R. "An American Original." *National Review*, March 8, 2004. www.nationalreview.com/books/kesler200403251147.asp (no longer available).

Key, Joshua. *The Deserter's Tale: The Story of an Ordinary Soldier Who Walked Away from the War in Iraq*. New York: Atlantic Monthly Press, 2007.

Killian, Mitchell, and Clyde Wilcox. "Party Switching: The Effect of Abortion Attitudes." Paper presented at the annual conference of the Midwest Political Science Association, Chicago, April 15–18, 2004.

Kimmage, Michael. "Whittaker Chambers's *Witness* and the Dilemma of Modern Conservatism." *Literature Compass* 3 (2006): 940–66.

Kincaid, Cliff. "AIM Report: What Would Whittaker Chambers Do?—August A." *Accuracy in Media*, August 2, 2007. www.aim.org/aim-report/aim-report-what-would-whittaker-chambers-do-august-a.

King, Andrew. "The Rhetoric of Power Maintenance: Elites at the Precipice." *Quarterly Journal of Speech* 62 (1976): 127–34.

Kirk, Russell. *The Conservative Mind: From Burke to Eliot*. 7th ed. Washington, DC: Regnery, 2001.

Kisseloff, Jeff. "The Alger Hiss Story." http://algerhiss.com/alger-hiss/we-remember-alger/working-for-and-with-alger-hiss-by-jeff-kisseloff/.

Klehr, Harvey E. *Secret World of American Communism: Documents from the Soviet Archives*. New Haven, CT: Yale University Press, 1998.

Klein, Marcus. Review of *Ex-Friends*, by Norman Podhoretz. *New Leader*, December 14, 1998.

Knight, Peter. *Conspiracy Culture: From the Kennedy Assassination to the "X-Files."* New York: Routledge, 2000.

Koehler, Robert. "Neo-Fantasies and Ancient Myths: Adam Curtis on *The Power of Nightmares*." *Cinema Scope* 23 (n.d.). www.cinema-scope.com/cs23/contents.htm (no longer available).

Koestler, Arthur, Ignazio Silone, Richard Wright, André Gide, Louis Fischer, and Stephen Spender. *The God That Failed*, edited by David H. Crossman. New York: Columbia University Press, 2001.

Komyathy, Tendays. "'Fusion and Unity—This Was the Cry of My Father's Communist Heart' Writes Horowitz, 'His Unquenchable Longing to Belong.'" Amazon.com, July 5, 2008. www.amazon.com/Radical-Son-Generational-David-Horowitz/product-reviews/0684840057/ref=d4p_top_cm_cr_acr_txt?ie=UTF8&showView points=1.

Kosterlitz, Julie. "Bush's Left Right-Hand Men." *National Journal* (May 5, 2002): 1296–1304.

Kramer, Hilton. "*Breaking Ranks: A Political Memoir* by Norman Podhoretz." *New Republic*, November 17, 1979.

Kreisler, Harry. "The Battle over Ideas: Conversation with Norman Podhoretz, Former Editor, *Commentary*." Institute of International Studies, University of California at Berkeley. http://globetrotter.berkeley.edu/conversations/Podhoretz/podhoretz-con2.html.

Krim, Seymour. "Commentary on Podhoretz." *Book World*, November 4, 1979.

Kristol, Irving. "An Autobiographical Memoir." In *Neoconservatism: The Autobiography of an Idea*, edited by idem, 3–40. New York: Free Press, 1995.

———. *Reflections of a Neoconservative*. New York: Basic Books, 1983.

Lake, Celinda, and Matt Price. "Snapshot: The Women's Vote, 2008." *Ms. Magazine*, Spring 2008. www.msmagazine.com/spring2008/reallyWant_celindaLake.asp.

Lake, Randall. "Enacting Red Power: The Consummatory Function in Native American Protest Rhetoric." *Quarterly Journal of Speech* 69 (1983): 127–42.

———. "The Metaethical Framework of Anti-abortion Rhetoric." *Signs* 11 (1986): 478–99.

———. "Order and Disorder in Anti-abortion Rhetoric: A Logological View." *Quarterly Journal of Speech* 70 (1984): 425–43.

Lake, Randall A., and Barbara A. Pickering. "The Anti(Abortion) Public Sphere." In *Arguing Communication & Culture*, edited by G. Thomas Goodnight, 479–86. Washington, DC: National Communication Association, 2001.

Lakoff, George. *Don't Think of an Elephant!* White River Junction, VT: Chelsea Green, 2004.

———. *Moral Politics: How Liberals and Conservatives Think*. Chicago: University of Chicago Press, 2002.

Langer, Lawrence L. *Holocaust Testimonies: The Ruins of Memory*. New Haven, CT: Yale University Press, 1991.

Langer, Susanne K. *Philosophy in a New Key*. 3rd ed., 1942; repr. Cambridge, MA: Harvard University Press, 1996.

Lanham, Richard A. *The Economics of Attention: Style and Substance in the Age of Information*. Chicago: University of Chicago Press, 2006.

Lawrence, Windy Y. "Debilitating Public Deliberation: Ronald Reagan's Use of the Conversation Metaphor." *Southern Communication Journal* 72 (2007): 37–54.

Lee, John. Review of *Confessions of a Conservative*, *Commonweal*, September 28, 1979, 536.

Lee, Michael. "The Conservative Canon and Its Uses." *Rhetoric & Public Affairs* 15 (2012): 1–39.

———. "Creating Conservatism: Postwar Words That Made a Movement." PhD diss., University of Minnesota, 2008.

———. *Creating Conservatism: Postwar Words That Made a Movement*. East Lansing: Michigan State University Press, 2014.

Lehmann-Haupt, Christopher. "Books of the Times." *New York Times*, October 24, 1979.

Lejeune, Philippe. *On Autobiography*. Edited by Paul John Eakin. Minneapolis: University of Minnesota Press, 1989.

Lekachman, Robert. "Mean to Me." *Nation*, November 10, 1979.

Lelyveld, Joseph. "Intellectual's Inventory." *New York Times*, July 15, 1979. www.nytimes.com/books/97/06/01/reviews/wills-confessions.html.

Lemann, Nicholas. "On Balance: At the J-Schools: The Case against Ideological Engineering." *Columbia Journalism Review* 44 (2006): 16–17.

———. Review of *Ex-Friends*, by Norman Podhoretz. *Washington Monthly*, January/February 1999.

Leo, John. "Wills's Testament." *Commonweal* 138 (2011): 22.

Leonard, John. Review of *Ex-Friends*, by Norman Podhoretz. *Nation*, March 22, 1999.

Leslie, Andrew, and Stephen O'Leary. "Rhizomic Rhetoric: Toward an Ecology of Institutional Argument." In *Argument in Controversy: Proceedings of the Seventh SCA/AFA Conference on Argumentation*, edited by Donn W. Parson, 64–72. Annandale, VA: Speech Communication Association, 1991.

Levin, David. "The Authority of *Witness* in 'Whittaker Chambers: A Biography.'" *Sewanee Review* 105 (1997): 600–608.

Levin, James. "*Breaking Ranks: A Political Memoir*." *Library Journal*, January 1, 1980.

Lewis, Hyrum. "Sacralizing the Right: William F. Buckley, Jr., Whittaker Chambers, Will Herberg and the Transformation of Intellectual Conservatism, 1945–1964." PhD diss., University of Southern California, 2009.

Lewis, William F. "Telling America's Story: Narrative Form and the Reagan Presidency." *Quarterly Journal of Speech* 73 (1987): 280–302.

Lewy, Guenter. "Radical Son." *National Interest* 49 (1997). http://nationalinterest.org/bookreview/another-country-review-of-david-horowitzs-radical-son-a-journey-through-our-time-780.

Lieder, Tim. "Hmm." Amazon.com, May 10, 2000. www.amazon.com/Radical-Son-Generational-David-Horowitz/product-reviews/0684840057/ref=dp_top_cm_cr_acr_txt?ie=UTF8&showViewpoints=1.

Lind, Michael. *Up from Conservatism: Why the Right Is Wrong for America*. New York: Free Press, 1996.

Lindemann, Albert S. "Podhoretz in Retirement: A Report on the Morality of Friendship." www.writing.upenn.edu/~afilreis/50s/podhoretz-review.html.

Linder, Doug. "The Trials of Alger Hiss." 2003 http://law2.umkc.edu/faculty/PROJECTS/FTRIALS/hiss/hissaccount.html.
Lipset, Seymour, and Earl Raab. *The Politics of Unreason: Right-Wing Extremism in America, 1790–1977*. Chicago: University of Chicago Press, 1978.
Lofland, John, and Norman Skonovd. "Patterns of Conversion." In *Of Gods and Men*, edited by E. Barker, 1–24. Macon, GA: Mercer University Press, 1983.
Lopez, Donald S. "Belief." In *Critical Terms for Religious Studies*, edited by Mark Taylor, 21–35. Chicago: University of Chicago Press, 1998.
Loschnigg, Martin. "Autobiography." In *Routledge Encyclopedia of Narrative Theory*, edited by David Herman, Manfred Jahn, and Marie-Laure Ryan, 34–36. New York: Routledge, 2008.
Luckmann, Thomas. *The Invisible Religion*. New York: Macmillan, 1967.
"Luke 15:11–32" [KJV]. Biblegateway.com, n.d. www.biblegateway.com/passage/?search=Luke%2015:11–32&version=KJV.
Luker, Kristin. *Abortion and the Politics of Motherhood*. Berkeley: University of California Press, 1984.
Lyman, Stanford M. "Gunnar Myrdal's *An American Dilemma* after a Half Century: Critics and Anticritics." *International Journal of Politics, Culture and Society* 12 (1998): 327–89.
Lynch, Michael. "Against Reflexivity as an Academic Virtue and Source of Privileged Knowledge." *Theory, Culture, and Society* 17 (2000): 26–54.
———. "Capital Letters: Aging Radicals." *Reason*, July 2000. www.reason.com/news/show/27760.html.
Mackintosh, Barry. "'Politics in the Pumpkin Patch': A Response." *Public Historian* 12 (1990): 53–56.
Maddux, Kristy. "The Foursquare Gospel of Aimee Semple McPherson." *Rhetoric & Public Affairs* 14 (2011): 291–326.
Mahoney, Daniel J. "Whittaker Chambers: Witness to the Crisis of the Modern Soul." *Intercollegiate Review* 37 (2002): 41–48.
Majone, Giandomenico. *Evidence, Argument, and Persuasion in the Policy Process*. New Haven, CT: Yale University Press, 1992.
Manheim, Jarol. *Strategy in Information and Influence Campaigns: How Policy Advocates, Insurgent Groups, Corporations, Governments and Others Get What They Want*. New York: Routledge, 2011.
Mannheim, Karl. "The Problem of Generations." In *Essays on the Sociology of Knowledge*, edited by Paul Kecskemeti, 276–322. London: Routledge and Kegan Paul, 1952.
Marietta, Morgan. "The Absolutist Advantage: Sacred Rhetoric in Contemporary Presidential Debate." *Political Communication* 26 (2009): 388–411.
Martin, Craig. "Williams James in Late Capitalism: Our Religion in the Status Quo." In *Religious Experience: A Reader*, edited by idem and Russell T. McCutcheon, 177–96. New York: Routledge, 2012.
Martin, Craig, and Russell T. McCutcheon, eds. *Religious Experience: A Reader*. New York: Routledge, 2012.
Martin, Kingsley. "The Witness." *New Statesman and Nation*, July 19, 1952.
Mather, Cotton. *Successive Generations: Remarks upon the Changes of a Dying World, Made by One Generation Passing Off and Another Generation Coming On*. Boston: B. Green, 1715.
Mattson, Kevin. "Do Americans Really Want Deliberative Democracy?" *Rhetoric & Public Affairs* 5 (2002): 327–29.
McCain, Robert Stacey. "Contrarian Controversy." *Insight on the News*, November 15, 1999.
McConnell, Tandy. "Introduction." Vol. 10 of *American Decades*, edited by Judith S. Baughman, Victor Bondi, Richard Layman, Tandy McConnell, and Vincent Tompkins. Detroit: Gale, 2001.
McCorvey, Norma. *Won by Love*. Nashville: Thomas Nelson, 1997.
McDonald, Lauren E. "The Rise of Conservative Think Tanks: The Debate over Ideas, Research and Strategy in Public Education Policy." PhD diss., City University of New York, 2008.

McDonald, Michael. "Wills Watching." *New Criterion*, June 2011, 74.
McGee, Brian R. "Witnessing and *Ethos*: The Evangelical Conversion of David Duke." *Western Journal of Communication* 62 (1998): 217–43.
McGuinness, P. "A Genuinely Profound Autobiography." Amazon.com, July 11, 2004. www.amazon.com/Radical-Son-Generational-David-Horowitz/product-reviews/0684840057/ref=dp_top_cm_cr_acr_txt?ie=UTF8&showViewpoints=1.
Mcgurn, William. "The Witness of Whittaker Chambers: A Bitter Hope." *Modern Age* 28 (1984): 203–7.
McLennan, David B. "Rhetoric and the Legitimation Process: The Rebirth of Charles Colson." *Journal of Communication and Religion* 19 (1996): 5–12.
McMillan, Craige. "Fanatical Secular Faith." *WorldNetDaily*, June 24, 1999. www.worldnetdaily.com/index.php?fa=PAGE.printable&pageId=5909.
Me364459. "Re: Most Overlooked Essential." *WorldNetDaily*, December 27, 2008. http://forums.wnd.com/index.php?pageId=262&pageNo=4 (no longer available).
Medhurst, Martin. "Forging a Civil Religious Construct for the Twenty-First Century." In *The Political Pulpit Revisited*, edited by Roderick Hart and John Pauley, 143–52. West Lafayette, IN: Purdue University Press, 2004.
———. "Resistance, Conservatism, and Theory Building: A Cautionary Note." *Western Journal of Speech Communication* 49 (1985): 103–15.
Medved, Michael. *Right Turns: Unconventional Lessons from a Controversial Life*. New York: Crown Forum, 2005.
Melucci, Alberto. *Challenging Codes: Collective Action in the Information Age*. New York: Cambridge University Press, 1996.
Meranto, Oneida J. "Commentary: The Third Wave of McCarthyism: Co-opting the Language of Inclusivity." *New Political Science* 27 (2005): 215–32.
Merton, Thomas. *The Seven Storey Mountain*. New York: Harcourt Brace, 1999.
Miller, James G., and Jessie L. Miller. "*Witness*." *University of Chicago Law Review* 2 (1953): 598–604.
Miller, John J. "The House of Chambers." *National Review*, August 27, 2007.
Miller, Merle. "Memoirs from Sanctuary." *New Republic*, May 26, 1952.
Mills, Nicolaus. "Scornful of the '60s." *Christian Science Monitor*, June 9, 1997.
Minow, Newton. "Some Legal Aspects of the Hiss Case." *Journal of Criminal Law and Criminology (1931–1951)* 40 (1949): 344–53.
Morgan, Edward. *The 60s Experience: Hard Lessons about Modern America*. Philadelphia: Temple University Press, 1991.
———. *Visible Saints: The History of a Puritan Idea*. New York: New York University Press, 1963.
Morris, Richard B. "Chambers's Litmus Paper Test." *Saturday Review*, May 24, 1952.
Mulcahy, Susan, ed. *Why I'm a Democrat*. Sausalito, CA: PoliPointPress, 2008.
Murphy, John. "Domesticating Dissent: The Kennedys and the Freedom Rides." *Communication Monographs* 59 (1992): 61–78.
Nadel, Ira Bruce. *Biography: Fiction, Fact, and Form*. New York: St. Martin's, 1984.
Nash, George. "Joining the Ranks: Commentary and American Conservatism." In *Commentary in American Life*, edited by Murray Friedman, 151–73. Philadelphia: Temple University Press, 2005.
Navasky, Victor. "Hiss in History." *Nation*, April 30, 2007.
Nelson, T. J. "*Witness*." August 16, 2003. http://brneurosci.org/reviews/witness.html (no longer available).
Neo-neocon. "More from *Radical Son*." http://neo-neocon.blogspot.com/2005/06/more-from-radical-son.html.
Neuchterlein, James. "This Time: Neoconservative Redux." *First Things* 66 (1996): 7–8.
Neuhaus, Richard John. "At the Origins of the Culture War." *First Things*, April 1, 2000.
———. "Liberalism without a Left, Conservatism without Delusions." *First Things* (December 1999). www.firstthings.com/article.php3?id_article=3242.
———. Newton, John. "Amazing Grace." In *500 Best-Loved Song Lyrics*. Edited by Ronald Herder. Mineola, NY: Dover, 1998.

Niebuhr, Reinhold. *Moral Man and Immoral Society.* Louisville: Westminster John Knox, 1960.
Niederdeppe, Jeff, Michael A. Shapiro, and Norman Porticelli. "Attributions of Responsibility for Obesity: Narrative Communication Reduces Reactive Counterarguing among Liberals." *Human Communication Research* 37 (2011): 295–323.
Nieli, Russell. "The Cry against Nineveh: Whittaker Chambers and Eric Voegelin on the Crisis of Western Modernity." *Modern Age* 31 (1987): 267–74.
Nixon, Richard M. "Lessons of the Alger Hiss Case." *New York Times*, January 8, 1986. www.nytimes.com/1986/01/08/opinion/lessons-of-the-alger-hiss-case.html.
———. "Plea for an Anti-Communist Faith." *Saturday Review*, May 24, 1952.
Nock, A. D. *Conversion: The Old and the New in Religion from Alexander the Great to Augustine of Hippo.* Baltimore: Johns Hopkins University Press, 1933/1998.
Noll, Mark A. *The Scandal of the Evangelical Mind.* Grand Rapids, MI: Wm. B. Eerdmans, 1994.
"Norman Podhoretz." *Biography Resource Center.* Farmington Hills, MI: Gale, 2009.
Novak, Robert D. Foreword to *Witness*, by Whittaker Chambers. Washington, DC: Regnery, 1980.
Oates, Wayne E. "Conversion: Sacred or Secular?" In *Conversion: Perspectives on Personal and Social Transformation*, edited by Walter E. Conn, 149–68. Staten Island, NY: Alba House, 1978.
O'Keefe, Daniel J. "Two Concepts of Argument." *Journal of the American Forensic Association* 13 (1977): 121–28.
Olasky, Marvin. "A Witness for the Ages." *Boundless*, 2000. www.boundless.org/2000/departments/pages/a0000363.html.
Olbrys, Stephen G. "*Dissoi Logoi*, Civic Friendship, and the Politics of Education." *Communication Education* 55 (2006): 353–69.
O'Leary, Stephen. "Apocalyptic Argument and the Anticipation of Catastrophe: The Prediction of Risk and the Risks of Prediction." *Argumentation* 11 (1997): 293–313.
———. *Arguing the Apocalypse: A Theory of Millennial Rhetoric.* New York: Oxford University Press, 1994.
Olmsted, Kathryn S. *Red Spy Queen: A Biography of Elizabeth Bentley.* Chapel Hill: University of North Carolina Press, 2002.
Olsen, Steve. *Why You May Be a Liberal (and Why That's Okay): The Political Conversion of a Utah Mormon Bishop.* Printed by author, 2007.
Olson, Ray. "*Radical Son: A Journey through Our Times.*" *Booklist*, January 1, 1997.
O'Neill, William L., and Kenneth T. Jackson, eds. "Podhoretz, Norman Harold." In *The Scribner Encyclopedia of American Lives Thematic Series: The 1960s.* Farmington Hills, MI: Gale, 2009.
"On the Witness Stand." *Time*, June 9, 1952. http://content.time.com/time/magazine/article/0,9171,806492,00.html.
Osborn, Michael. "Archetypal Metaphor in Rhetoric: The Light-Dark Family." *Quarterly Journal of Speech* 53 (1967): 115–26.
O'Shaughnessy, Nicholas. "The Death and Life of Propaganda." *Journal of Public Affairs* 9 (2010): 9–10.
Oshinsky, David M. "*Radical Son: A Generational Odyssey.*" *New Leader*, December 16, 1996, 5–8.
Packer, George. "Sir Vidia's Shadow." *Dissent* 46 (1999): 99–104.
Palczewski, Catherine Helen. "Argument in an Off Key: Playing with the Productive Limits of Argument." In *Arguing Communication and Culture*, edited by G. Thomas Goodnight, 1–23. Washington, DC: National Communication Association, 2002.
———. "Public Policy Argument and Survivor Testimony: Pro-Ordinance Conservatives, Confession, Mediation and Recuperation." In *Argument and the Postmodern Challenge: Proceedings of the Eighth SCA/AFA Conference on Argumentation*, edited by Raymie E. McKerrow, 461–67. Annandale, VA: Speech Communication Association, 1993.
Parker, Kathleen. "What They Don't Know Can Hurt Them." *Jewish World Review*, March 17, 2005. www.jewishworldreview.com/kathleen/parker1.asp.

Paroske, Marcus. "Deliberating International Science Policy Controversies: Uncertainty and AIDS in South Africa." *Quarterly Journal of Speech* 95 (2009): 148–70.
Parsley, Bonnie M. "A Life Transformed by Truth." Amazon.com, November 12, 2007. www.amazon.com/Radical-Son-Generational-David-Horowitz/product-reviews/0684840057/ref=dp_top_cm_cr_acr_txt?ie=UTF8&showViewpoints=1.
Passell, Josh. "My Friends Don't Know I'm a Conservative." *Boston Globe*, September 9, 2012. www.bostonglobe.com/magazine/2012/09/08/friends-don-know-conservative/6cZz78 ANMMgs5uQeEnt6yI/story.html.
Patterson, Thomas. *The Vanishing Voter: Public Involvement in an Age of Uncertainty*. New York: Alfred A. Knopf, 2002.
Pattison, E. Scott. Letter to the editor. *Time*, June 16, 1952.
Pearce, W. Barnett. *Communication and the Human Condition*. Carbondale: Southern Illinois University Press, 1989.
———. *Making Social Worlds: A Communication Perspective*. Malden, MA: Blackwell, 2007.
Peeples, Jennifer A. "Arguments for What No One Wants: The Narratives of Waste Storage Proponents." *Environmental Communication* 2 (2008): 40–58.
Perelman, Chaim, and Lucille Olbrechts-Tyteca. *The New Rhetoric: A Treatise on Argumentation*. Translated by John Wilkinson and Purcell Weaver. Notre Dame, IN: University of Notre Dame Press, 1969.
Perlstein, Rick. "Second Read." *Columbia Journalism Review* 6 (2004). http://cjrarchives.org/issues/2004/6/perlstein-tribe.asp (no longer available).
Perry, Rick. *Fed Up!: Our Fight to Save America from Washington*. New York: Little, Brown, 2010.
Peters, Gerald. *The Mutilating God: Authorship and Authority in the Narrative of Conversion*. Amherst: University of Massachusetts Press, 1993.
Peters, John Durham. "'The Only Proper Scale of Representation': The Politics of Statistics and Stories." *Political Communication* 18 (2001): 433–49.
Phillips, William. "In and Out of the Underground: The Confessions of Whittaker Chambers." *American Mercury*, June 1952.
Pickering, Barbara. "Women's Voices as Evidence: Personal Testimony Is Pro-Choice Films." *Argumentation and Advocacy* 40 (2003): 1–22.
Pinsker, Sanford. "Coming Clean about the Late Sixties." *Partisan Review* 65 (1998): 323–26.
———. Review of *Ex-Friends*. *Virginia Review Quarterly* 76 (2000): 183–88.
———. "Still Crazy (or Fuming) after All These Years." *Georgia Review* 51 (1997): 356–64.
Pipes, Daniel. *Conspiracy: How the Paranoid Style Flourishes and Where It Comes From*. New York: Free Press, 1997.
Plato. *Republic*. In *Plato: Complete Works*, edited by John M. Cooper, translated by G. M. A. Grube, 1132–55. Indianapolis, IN: Hackett, 1997.
Podhoretz, Norman. *Breaking Ranks*. New York: Harper & Row, 1979.
———. *Ex-Friends: Falling Out with Allen Ginsberg, Lionel and Diana Trilling, Lillian Hellman, Hannah Arendt, and Norman Mailer*. New York: Free Press, 1999.
———. *Making It*. New York: Harper & Row, 1967.
———. *My Love Affair with America: The Cautionary Tale of a Cheerful Conservative*. New York: Free Press, 2000.
———. "My Negro Problem—and Ours." *Commentary*, February 1963.
———. *The Prophets: Who They Were, What They Are*. New York: Free Press, 2002.
Poletta, Francesca. "'It Was Like a Fever . . .': Narrative and Identity in Social Protest." *Social Problems* 45 (1998): 137–59.
Popkin, Samuel. *The Reasoning Voter: Communication and Persuasion in Presidential Campaigns*. Chicago: University of Chicago Press, 1991.
Postman, Neil. *Crazy Talk, Stupid Talk: How We Defeat Ourselves by the Way We Talk, and What to Do about It*. New York: Delacorte, 1976.
Powell, Kimberly A. "The Association of Southern Women for the Prevention of Lynching: Strategies of a Movement in the Comic Frame." *Communication Quarterly* 43 (1995): 86–99.

Powell, Larry, and Eduardo Neiva. "The Pharisee Effect: When Religious Appeals in Politics Go Too Far." *Journal of Communication and Religion* 29 (2006): 70–102.
Powers, Richard Gid. "The Left He Left Behind." *New York Times*, February 16, 1997.
Prager, Dennis. *Think a Second Time.* New York: HarperCollins, 1995.
Prelutsky, Burt. *Conservatives Are from Mars, Liberals Are from San Francisco: 101 Reasons Why I'm Happy I Left the Left.* Nashville: Cumberland House, 2006.
Prescott, Orville. "Books of the Times." *New York Times*, May 22, 1952.
"Publican & Pharisee." *Time*, May 26, 1952. www.time.com/time/printout/0,8816,859675,00.html.
Putnam, Robert. "Bowling Alone: America's Declining Social Capital." *Journal of Democracy* 6 (1995): 65–78.
———. *Bowling Alone: America's Declining Social Capital.* New York: Simon & Schuster, 1995.
Pyle, Richard. "Author Suggests Alger Hiss Wasn't a Spy." *Washington Post*, April 6, 2007. www.washingtonpost.com/wp-dyn/content/article/2007/04/06/AR2007040600304.html.
"Quotes Falsely Attributed to Winston Churchill." *International Churchill Society*, n.d. www.winstonchurchill.org/resources/quotes/quotes-falsely-attributed/.
Radosh, Ronald. Review of *Perjury: The Hiss-Chambers Case*, by Allen Weinstein. *American Historical Review* 84 (1979): 586–87.
Rahv, Philip. "The Sense and Nonsense of Whittaker Chambers." *Partisan Review* (July–August 1952): 472–82.
Raimondo, Justin. "David Horowitz, Crybaby." Antiwar.com, January 5, 2004. www.antiwar.com/blog/2004/01/05/david-horowitz-crybaby.
Rainey, James. "Blogger Parts with the Right." *Los Angeles Times*, January 8, 2010.
Ransom, John Crowe. "Reconstructed but Unregenerate." In *I'll Take My Stand: The South and the Agrarian Tradition*, edited by Louis D. Rubin, Jr., 1–27. Baton Rouge: Louisiana State University Press, 2006. Orig. pub. 1930.
Raskin, Jonah. *American Scream: Allen Ginsberg.* Berkeley: University of California Press, 2004.
Reagan, Ronald. "Remarks at the Annual Convention of the National Association of Evangelicals." Columbus, OH, March 6, 1984.
———. "Remarks at the Annual Convention of the National Association of Evangelicals in Orlando, Florida," March 8, 1983. In *Conservatism in America since 1930: A Reader*, edited by Gregory L. Schneider, 341–61. New York: New York University Press, 2003.
Reagan, Ronald, and Richard Gibson Hubler. *Where's the Rest of Me?* New York: Duell, Sloan and Pearce, 1965.
Regnery, Alfred S. *Upstream: The Ascendance of American Conservatism.* New York: Simon & Schuster, 2008.
Reilly, John. "World's Oldest Red Diaper Baby Tells All." *JohnReilly*, 1997. www.johnreilly.info/rsdh.htm (no longer available).
Reis, Charles. Letter to the editor. *Time*, June 16, 1952.
ReleaseTheHounds. "Whittaker Chambers Bears 'Witness' to Bill Clinton's Protestations." *Free Republic*, October 3, 2006. www.freerepublic.com/focus/f-news/1712902/posts.
RFLaird. "Archives." *Instapunk*, May 9, 2004. www.instapunk.com/archives/InstaPunkArchiveV2.php3?a=83.
Richer, Matthew. "The Cry against Nineveh: A Centennial Tribute to Whittaker Chambers." *Modern Age* 43 (2001): 195–201.
———. "The Ongoing Campaign of Alger Hiss: The Sins of the Father." *Modern Age* 46 (2004): 307–16.
Roberts, Henry L. "Recent Books on International Relations." *Foreign Affairs* 31 (1952): 150–62.
Roberts, James C. "2002: A Banner Year for Conservative Books." *Human Events*, November 18, 2002.
Roberts, Jason D. "Disillusioned Radicals: The Intellectual Odyssey of Todd Gitlin, Ronald Radosh and David Horowitz." PhD diss., George Washington University, 2007.

Rohm, Michael. "Interesting, but Horribly Flawed." Amazon.com, October 16, 2005. www.amazon.com/Radical-Son-Generational-David-Horowitz/product-reviews/0684840057/ref=dp_top_cm_cr_acr_txt?ie=UTF8&showViewpoints=1.
Romano, John. "Making Politics Simple." *New Leader*, November 5, 1979.
Roof, Wade Clark. *Spiritual Marketplace: Baby Boomers and the Remaking of American Religion*. Princeton, NJ: Princeton University Press, 2002.
Rosa, Paul. "Covenant Son." *New Prospect Church*, March 2, 2007. www.newprospectchurch.org/sermon1.html (no longer available).
Rosin, Hanna. "Oedipus & Podhoretz." *New York Magazine*, December 29, 1997. http://nymag.com/nymetro/news/media/features/1968.
Rothbard, Murray N. "The Evil of Banality." *Inquiry*, December 10, 1979.
Rothenberg, Randall. "Ad in Campus Papers Stokes Protest, but on Wrong Issue." *Advertising Age* 72 (2001): 26.
Rousseau, Jean-Jacques. *The Confessions*. Translated by J. M. Cohen. New York: Penguin Books, 1953.
———. *Émile*. Translated by Barbara Foxley. London: Everyman, 2000.
———. *The Social Contract*. Translated by Donald A. Cress. Indianapolis, IN: Hackett, 1987.
Rowland, Robert C. "Narrative: Mode of Discourse or Paradigm?" *Communication Monographs* 56 (1987): 264–75.
Rowland, Robert C., and John M. Jones. "Recasting the American Dream and American Politics: Barack Obama's Keynote Address to the 2004 Democratic National Convention." *Quarterly Journal of Speech* 93 (2007): 425–48.
Ryfe, David M. "Does Deliberative Democracy Work?" *Annual Review of Political Science* 8 (2005): 49–71.
———. "Narrative and Deliberation in Small Group Forums." *Journal of Applied Communication Research* 34 (2006): 72–93.
Salemi, Joseph S. "The Witness Revisited: Whittaker Chambers and American Conservatism." *University Bookman* 46 (2008). www.kirkcenter.org/index.php/bookman/article/the-witness-revisited.
Salvador, Michael. "The Rhetorical Genesis of Ralph Nader: A Functional Exploration of Narrative and Argument in Public Address." *Southern Communication Journal* 59 (1994): 227–39.
Sandel, Michael J. *Democracy's Discontent: America in Search of a Public Philosophy*. Cambridge, MA: Belknap, 1996.
Saturday Review, May 24, 1952.
Saunders, Kyle L., and Alan I. Abramowitz. "Ideological Realignment and Active Partisans in the American Electorate." *American Politics Research* 32 (2004): 285–309.
Scherer, Matthew. "The Politics of Persuasion: Habit, Creativity, Conversion." PhD diss., Johns Hopkins University, 2006.
Schiappa, Edward. *Defining Reality: Definitions and the Politics of Meaning*. Carbondale: Southern Illinois University Press, 2003.
Schlesinger, Arthur, Jr. "Whittaker Chambers & His *Witness*." *Saturday Review*, May 24, 1952.
Schmidt, Maria. "The Hiss Dossier." *New Republic*, November 8, 1993.
Schudson, Michael. *The Good Citizen: A History of American Civic Life*. Cambridge, MA: Harvard University Press, 1998.
Schwartz, Stephen. "The Curious Case of David Horowitz." *Los Angeles Times*, October 11, 1998. http://articles.latimes.com/1998/oct/11/books/bk-31283?pg=1.
Schwartzberg, Hugh J. "Philosophy of Whittaker Chambers: A Study in Political Conversion." B.A. thesis, Harvard University, 1953.
Schwarze, Steven. "Environmental Melodrama." *Quarterly Journal of Speech* 92 (2006): 239–61.
Sciolino, Elaine. "G.O.P. Devotees Pay Honor to Whittaker Chambers." *New York Times*, July 10, 2001, www.nytimes.com/2001/07/10/us/gop-devotees-pay-honor-to-whittaker-chambers.html.
Scott, Janny. "Alger Hiss, 92, Central Figure in Long-Running Cold War Controversy." *New York Times*, November 16, 1996. www.nytimes.com/books/97/03/09/reviews/hiss-obit.html.

Scott, Joan W. "The Evidence of Experience." *Critical Inquiry* 17 (1991): 773–97.
Scott, Robert L., and Donald K. Smith. "The Rhetoric of Confrontation." *Quarterly Journal of Speech* 56 (1969): 1–11.
Seipp, Catherine. "Right Warrior." *National Review*, April 15, 2005. www.nationalreview.com/script/printpage.p?ref=/seipp/seipp200504150751.asp (no longer available).
Shafer, Jack. "David Horowitz: Sore Winner." *Slate*, June 5, 1997. www.slate.com/id/1000016.
Shaidle, Kathy. "Witness, Part Two." RelapsedCatholic.blogspot.com, September 18, 2005. http://relapsedcatholic.blogspot.com/2005/09/witness-part-two.html (no longer available).
Shapiro, Fred. "John Adams Said It First." Freakonomics, August 25, 2011. http://freakonomics.com/2011/08/25/john-adams-said-it-first/.
Shatz, Adam. "About Face." *New York Times*, January 20, 2002. www.nytimes.com/2002/01/20/magazine/about-face.html
Sheerin, John B. "Chambers Again." *Catholic World*, December 1952.
———. "Chambers Provokes the Reviewers." *Catholic World*, July 1952.
Sheppard, R. Z. "The Heart and Head of the Matter." *Time*, April 23, 1979, 86–87.
Sherman, Scott. "David Horowitz's Long March." *Nation*, June 15, 2000. www.thenation.com/article/david-horowitzs-long-march/.
Shinar, Dov. "The Peace Process in Cultural Conflict: The Role of the Media." *Conflict & Communication Online* 2 (2003): 1–10.
Shoebat, Walid. *Why I Left Jihad*. Top Executive Media, 2005.
Short, Brant. "Earth First! and the Rhetoric of Moral Confrontation." *Communication Studies* 42 (1991): 172–88.
Shulevitz, Judith. "Norman Podhoretz's Old-Time Religion." *New York Times Book Review*, November 3, 2002.
Simons, Herbert. "Requirements, Problems, and Strategies: A Theory of Persuasion for Social Movements." *Quarterly Journal of Speech* 56 (1970): 1–11.
"Site in Hiss-Chambers Case Now a Landmark." *New York Times*, May 18, 1988. http://query.nytimes.com/gst/fullpage.html?sec=travel&res=940DEEDA1339F93BA25756C0A96E948260.
Slain. "So . . . He Is a Flip Flopper?" Amazon.com, July 3, 2007. www.amazon.com/Radical-Son-Generational-David-Horowitz/product-reviews/0684840057/ref=dp_top_cm_cr_acr_txt?ie=UTF8&showViewpoints=1.
Sleeper, Jim. "Yankee Doodle Dandy: Making It in America while Breaking Ranks and Settling Scores." *Los Angeles Times*, July 2, 2000.
Smith, Ben. "Bush Backer Pens Pro-Obama Book." *Politico*, June 16, 2008. www.politico.com/news/stories/0608/11099.html.
Smith, John. "The Concept of Conversion." In *Conversion: Perspectives on Personal and Social Transformation*, edited by Walter E. Conn, 51–61. Staten Island, NY: Alba House, 1978.
Smith, Kimberly K. *The Dominion of Voice: Riot, Reason, and Romance in Antebellum America*. Lawrence: University Press of Kansas, 1999.
Snow, David A., and Richard Machalek. "The Convert as a Social Type." *Sociological Theory* 1 (1983): 259–89.
Sobran, M. J. "Up to Liberalism." *National Review*, May 25, 1979, 686.
Sohl, Kenneth. "Out from Under the Rock." Amazon.com, March 20, 2006. www.amazon.com/Radical-Son-Generational-David-Horowitz/product-reviews/0684840057/ref=dp_top_cm_cr_acr_txt?ie=UTF8&showViewpoints=1.
Solomon, Martha M. "Autobiographies as Rhetorical Narratives: Elizabeth Cady Stanton and Anna Howard Shaw as 'New Women.'" *Communication Studies* 42 (1991): 354–70.
Spalding, Matthew, and A. Beichman. "The Cold War's Magnificent Seven." *Policy Review* 59 (1992): 44–55.
Spacks, Patricia Meyer. "Stages of Self: Notes on Autobiography and the Life Cycle." In *The American Autobiography: A Collection of Critical Essays*, edited by Albert E. Stone, 44–60. Englewood Cliffs, NJ: Prentice Hall, 1981.
"Speaking of Sidney Blumenthal." *New Criterion* 15 (April 1997). www.newcriterion.com/issues/1997/4/speaking-of-sydney-blumenthal.

Spencer, Gregory. "The Rhetoric of Malcolm Muggeridge's Gradual Christian Conversion." *Journal of Communication and Religion* 18 (1995): 55–64.
Spengemann, William C. *The Forms of Autobiography: Episodes in the History of a Literary Genre.* New Haven, CT: Yale University Press, 1980.
Spiegel, Gabrielle M. "Memory and History: Liturgical Time and Historical Time." *History and Theory* 41 (2002): 149–62.
Steffensmeier, Timothy, and William Schenck-Hamlin. "Argument Quality in Public Deliberations." *Argumentation and Advocacy* 45 (2008): 21–36.
Stein, Harry. *How I Accidentally Joined the Vast Right-Wing Conspiracy (and Found Inner Peace).* New York: Perennial, 2000.
Steinberg, Stephen. "Nathan Glazer and the Assassination of Affirmative Action." *New Politics* 9 (2003). http://nova.wpunj.edu/newpolitics/issue35/Steinberg35.htm.
Stember, Sol. "The Lessons of the Richard Nixon Case." *New York Times*, January 21, 1986. www.nytimes.com/books/97/03/09/reviews/chambers-letters-nixon.html.
Stern, Ken. *Republican Like Me: How I Left the Liberal Bubble and Learned to Love the Right.* New York: HarperCollins, 2017.
Stokes, Harold Phelps. "Whittaker Chambers's Story." *Yale Review* (Autumn 1952): 123–26.
Strachey, John. "The Absolutists." *Nation*, October 4, 1952.
Stromer-Galley, Jennifer, and Peter Muhlberger. "Agreement and Disagreement in Group Deliberation: Effects on Deliberation Satisfaction, Future Engagement, and Decision Legitimacy." *Political Communication* 26 (2009): 173–92.
Sundquist, Eric J. "*Witness* Recalled." *Commentary*, December 1988.
Sunstein, Cass. "Deliberative Trouble? Why Groups Go to Extremes." *Yale Law Journal* 110 (2000): 71–119.
Svensson, Jakob. "Expressive Rationality: A Different Approach for Understanding Participation in Municipal Deliberative Practices." *Communication, Culture & Critique* 1 (2008): 203–21.
Swan, Patrick. "Preface." In *Alger Hiss, Whittaker Chambers, and the Schism in the American Soul*, edited by idem, xi–xxiii. Wilmington, DE: ISI Books, 2003.
Szamuely, Helen. "Reputations—21: Whittaker Chambers." *Salisbury Review*, n.d. http://salisburyreview.co.uk/index.php?option=com_content&view=article&id=680:reputations-21-whittaker-chambers&catid=47:autumn2008&Itemid=28 (no longer available).
Talisse, Robert, and Scott F. Aikin. "Two Forms of the Straw Man." *Argumentation* 20 (2006): 345–52.
Tanenhaus, Sam. *Whittaker Chambers: A Biography.* New York: Random House, 1997.
———. "Witness for the Truth." *National Review*, February 15, 1993.
Taylor, Charles. *Modern Social Imaginaries.* Durham, NC: Duke University Press, 2004.
Taylor, R. S. "*Witness*." *Library Journal*, May 15, 1952.
Tell, Dave. "Jimmy Swaggart's Secular Confession." *Rhetoric Society Quarterly* 39 (2009): 124–46.
———. "The 'Shocking Story' of Emmett Till and the Politics of Public Confession." *Quarterly Journal of Speech* 94 (2008): 156–78.
Thandeka. "The Cost of Whiteness." *Afrocentric News*, 1999. www.afrocentricnews.com/html/cost_of_whiteness.html.
Thompson, Craig. "The Whittaker Chambers I Know." *Saturday Evening Post*, November 15, 1952.
Thompson, Keith. *Leaving the Left: Moments in the News That Made Me Ashamed to Be a Liberal.* New York: Penguin, 2006.
Tilley, James. "Political Generations and Partisanship in the UK, 1964–1997." *Journal of the Royal Statistical Society* 165 (2002): 121–35.
Tinder, Glenn. *Political Thinking: The Perennial Questions.* New York: HarperCollins, 1995.
Tobin, Jonathan. "The Children of 'Commentary.'" *Jewish World Review*, February 24, 2004. www.jewishworldreview.com/0204/tobin_2004_02_24.php3?printer_friendly.
Tomes, Robert R. *Apocalypse Then: American Intellectuals and the Vietnam War.* New York: New York University Press, 1998.

Tonn, Mari Boor. "Taking Conversation, Dialogue, and Therapy Public." *Rhetoric & Public Affairs* 8 (2005): 405–30.
Toulmin, Stephen E. *The Uses of Argument*. New York: Cambridge University Press, 2003.
Travisano, Richard. "Alienation and Conversion as Qualitatively Different Transformations." In *Social Psychology through Symbolic Interaction*, edited by G. P. Stone and H. Faberman, 594–606. Waltham, MA: Ginn-Blaisdell, 1970.
"True Whit." *Jeremayakovka*, April 1, 2007. http://jeremayakovka.typepad.com/jeremayakovka/2007/04/true_whit_part_.html (no longer available).
U.S. Bureau of the Census. Current Population Reports, Series P-60, No. 133, *Characteristics of the Population below the Poverty Level: 1980*. Washington, DC: U.S. Government Printing Office, 1982.
Van Den Haag, Ernest. "Breaking Bones." *National Review*, February 8, 1980.
Vitullo-Martin, Julia. *"Radical Son: A Journey through Our Times." Commonweal*, June 4, 2004. www.commonwealmagazine.org/radical-son.
von Bothmer, Bernard. "Blaming 'The Sixties': The Political Use of an Era, 1980–2004." PhD diss., Indiana University, 2007.
Waisanen, Don. "Political Conversion as Intrapersonal Argument: Self-Dissociation in David Brock's *Blinded by the Right*." *Argumentation and Advocacy* 47 (2011): 228–45.
———. "Toward Robust Public Engagement: The Value of Deliberative Discourse for Civil Communication." *Rhetoric & Public Affairs* 17 (2014): 287–322.
Walker, John. "Reading List: *Radical Son*." *Fourmilog*, March 16, 2007. www.fourmilab.ch/fourmilog/archives/2007-03/000821.html.
Wallace, Michael. "Ronald Reagan and the Politics of History." *Tikkun* 2 (1987): 13–18, 127–31.
Wallach, Glenn. *Obedient Sons: The Discourse of Youth and Generations in American Culture, 1630–1860*. Amherst: University of Massachusetts Press, 1997.
Walsh, James F., Jr. "Rhetoric in the Conversion of Maoist Insurgency Cadres and the Emotional Component of Conversion in Radical Social Movements: III." *World Communication* 19 (1990): 1–19.
Walsh, Katherine Cramer. *Talking about Race: Community Dialogues and the Politics of Difference*. Chicago: University of Chicago Press, 2007.
Warner, Edwin. "Radical Retreat." *Time*, October 29, 1979. www.time.com/time/printout/0,8816,917005,00.html.
Warner, Michael. "Publics and Counterpublics." *Public Culture* 14 (2002): 49–90.
Warner, R. Stephen. "Work in Progress toward a New Paradigm for the Sociological Study of Religion in the United States." *American Journal of Sociology* 98 (1993): 1044–93.
Watson, Martha. *Lives of Their Own: Rhetorical Dimensions in Autobiographies of Women Activists*. Columbia: University of South Carolina Press, 1999.
Watts, Jerry. *Amiri Baraka*. New York: New York University, 2001.
Weaver, Richard M. *Ideas Have Consequences*. Chicago: University of Chicago Press, 1948.
———. "The Southern Tradition." In *The Southern Essays of Richard M. Weaver*, edited by George M. Curtis, III, and James J. Thompson, Jr., 220–21. Indianapolis, IN: Liberty Fund, 1987.
———. "Up from Liberalism." In *Life without Prejudice and Other Essays*, edited by Richard M. Weaver, 129–55. Chicago: Regnery, 1965.
Weber, Max. *Max Weber: The Theory of Social and Economic Organization*. Translated by A. M. Henderson and Talcott Parsons. New York: Free Press, 1947.
———. *The Protestant Ethic and the Spirit of Capitalism*. Translated by Talcott Parsons. New York: Scribners, 1930.
Weidner, John. "For When You Understand What You See, You Will No Longer Be Children." *Random Jottings*, February 11, 2007. www.randomjottings.net/archives/002713.html.
Weinberger, Caspar Willard. *"Witness." San Francisco Chronicle*, May 18, 1952.
Weinstein, Allen. *Perjury: The Hiss-Chambers Case*. New York: Alfred A. Knopf, 1978.
Wessler, Hartmut. "Investigating Deliberativeness Comparatively." *Political Communication* 25 (2008): 1–22.
West, Rebecca. "Whittaker Chambers." *Atlantic Monthly*, June 1952.

"What Do Quakers Believe?" Quaker Information Center, November 4, 2009. www.quakerinfo.org/quakerism/beliefs.html.

White, G. Edward. *Alger Hiss's Looking-Glass Wars*. New York: Oxford University Press, 2004.

White, Jack E. "A Real, Live Bigot." *Time*, August 22, 1999. www.time.com/time/magazine/article/0,9171,29787,00.html.

Whitfield, Stephen. *The Culture of the Cold War*. Baltimore: Johns Hopkins University Press, 1991.

"Whittaker Chambers." *Booklist* 48 (1952): 319–20.

"Whittaker Chambers." www.myspace.com/whittakerchambers.

"Whittaker Chambers, American Journalist, Witness in the Alger Hiss Spy Case." In *The Cold War, 1945–1991*, edited by Benjamin Frankel. Farmington Hills, MI: Gale, 1992. http://galenet.galegroup.com/servlet/BioRC.

"Whittaker Chambers Today." www.facebook.com/group.php?gid=30271279599&ref= mf (no longer available).

Whittemore, Reed. "*Witness.*" *Furioso*, Summer 1952.

Widdershoven, Guy A. M. "The Story of Life: Hermeneutic Perspectives on the Relationship between Narrative and Life History." In *The Narrative Study of Lives*, edited by Ruthellen Josselson and Amia Lieblich, 1–20. Newbury Park, CA: Sage, 1993.

Will, George F. "Whittaker Chambers: Up a Winding Staircase." *National Review*, December 31, 1985.

Willard, Charles. "The Creation of Publics: Notes on Goodnight's Historical Relativity." In *Readings on Argumentation*, edited by Angela J. Aguayo and Timothy R. Steffensmeier, 266–81. State College, PA: Strata, 2008.

Williams, Huntington. *Rousseau and Romantic Autobiography*. London: Oxford University Press, 1983.

Williamson, Bishop. "Liberalism Is a Killer." July 7, 2003. www.leofec.com/bishopwilliamson/288.html.

Williamson, Chilton, Jr. *The Conservative Bookshelf*. New York: Citadel, 2005.

Wills, Garry. *Confessions of a Conservative*. Garden City, NY: Doubleday, 1979.

———. *Head and Heart: American Christianities*. New York: Penguin, 2007.

———. *Outside Looking In: Adventures of an Observer*. New York: Viking, 2010.

Wilson, John F., and Donald L. Drakeman. *Church and State in American History*. New York: MJF Books, 2003.

Wimberley, Ronald C., and James A. Christiansen. "Civil Religion and Church and State." *Sociological Quarterly* 21 (1980): 35–40.

Wimberley, Ronald C., and William H. Swatos, Jr. "Civil Religion." In *Encyclopedia of Religion and Social Science*, edited by William H. Swatos, Jr., 94–96. Walnut Creek, CA: Altamira, 1998.

Windt, Theodore Otto, Jr. "Administrative Rhetoric: An Undemocratic Response to Protest." *Communication Quarterly* 30 (1982): 245–50.

———. "The Diatribe: Last Resort for Protest." *Quarterly Journal of Speech* 58 (1972): 1–14.

Wisse, Ruth R. "The Jewishness of *Commentary*." In *Commentary in American Life*, edited by Murray Friedman, 52–73. Philadelphia: Temple University Press, 2005.

———. "The Maturing of *Commentary* and of the Jewish Intellectual." *Jewish Social Studies* 3 (1997): 29–41.

"*Witness.*" *Current History*, July 1952.

"*Witness.*" *Bull Virginia Kirkus' Bookshop Service*, April 1, 1952.

"*Witness.*" *FirstPrinciples.US*, n.d. www.firstprinciples.us/sections/synopses/books.witness.asp (no longer available).

Wolfe, Bertram. *A Life in Two Centuries*. New York: Stein and Day, 1981.

Worcester, Kent. "*Radical Son: A Journey through Our Times.*" *Library Journal* 121 (1996): 108.

Wright, Charles Alan. "A Long Work of Fiction." *Saturday Review*, May 24, 1952.

Wynne, Wes. "David Horowitz's *Radical Son: A Generational Odyssey*." www.contumacy.org/1BookRev.html (no longer available).

Yancey, Philip. "The Death of a Red and the Birth of a Soul." *Christianity Today*, March 11, 1991.

Yardley, Jonathan. "Strife with Father." *Washington Post*, February 9, 1997.

Young, Iris M. "Communication and the Other." In *Democracy and Difference: Contesting the Boundaries of the Political*, edited by Seyla Benhabib, 120–35. Princeton, NJ: Princeton University Press, 1996.

Young, Marilyn J., Michael K. Launer, and Curtis C. Austin. "The Need for Evaluative Criteria: Conspiracy Argument Revisited." *Argumentation and Advocacy* 26 (1990): 89–107.

Zarefsky, David. "Civil Rights and Civil Conflict: Presidential Communication in Crisis." *Central States Speech Journal* 34 (1983): 59–66.

———. "Conspiracy Argument in the Lincoln-Douglass Debates." *Journal of the American Forensic Association* 21 (1984): 63–75.

Index

abortion: advocacy for, 2, 9, 35n122; documentaries of, 15; pro-lifers for, 18
Abrams, Nathan, 116n177–117n178
activism: for autobiographies, 19; celebrity advocacy in, 122; in religion, 16–17; retreat from, 85. *See also* feminism
ad hominem/ad expressivism, 96
Aikin, Scott, 103
Albert, Judith, 107
Albert, Stewart, 107
American Communist Party, 45–46
American Idol, 20
anarchism, 13
Annan, Noel, 98, 105
anthropology, 14
antiabortion, 2, 35n122
anti-intellectualism, 49–53, 65–66
Arendt, Hannah, 56, 64, 79n169
Army, U.S., 40
Asen, Robert, 7, 87, 185
Augustine (saint), 11–12, 18–19, 162, 166; in *CC*, 168; on religion, 171–172; Wills on, 177n45
authors: claims of, 198; consistency in, 188–190; on deliberation, 186–187; family of, 193; on Podhoretz, 85. *See also* Chambers, Whittaker; Horowitz, David; Podhoretz, Norman; Wills, Garry
autobiographies: for activism, 19; black power, 19; common themes of, 19–20; deliberative criteria of, 43; development of, 33n105; feminist, 19; generalizability in, 199; on identity changes, 198; political, 2, 18–22; self in, 33n105; for socialization, 33n105; social movement, 19; subject in, 33n105; thinking for, 194–195
autocase method, 99

Bailey, David, 14
Barclay, Robert, 52
Barth, Karl, 31n80, 43–44
Beatty, Jack, 176
Bellah, Robert, 16
Benhabib, Seyla, 175
Bentley, Elizabeth, 41
Berger, Peter, 20, 74n58, 138
Berle, Adolf, 41, 46
Berquist, Goodwin F., 4
bifurcated appeals, 190, 192–193
Bjerre-Poulsen, Niels, 81n245
Black, Edwin, 14, 22, 178n75
Black, Laura, 193
Black Panthers, 33n103, 121, 126, 134, 156n251
Booth, Wayne, 10, 106–107, 132, 173, 200
Bormann, Ernest, 47, 112n47
Bowman, James, 129
Breaking Ranks (*BR*) (Podhoretz), 19, 21–22; accuracy in, 98–105, 107–108; as anti-rhetorical text, 108; criticism of,

235

111n36–112n37; as deliberation, 86–87; expression in, 93–98; focus of, 86; footnotes in, 96; intellectualism in, 86, 87, 105; moral advocacy in, 103–104; motivation for, 85; as narrative, 83–108; propagandistic discourse in, 105; Protestantism in, 86; on public policy on, 92; resources in, 86–87; reviews of, 98, 104–105, 113n60; rhetoric of, 24; straw man fallacy in, 102–103, 108; themes of, 93
Breit, Harvey, 79n173
Brock, David, 2, 18, 176n2
Brooks, David, 40
Brouwer, Daniel, 8
Brown, Jerry, 15
Brown, Richard Harvey, 32n101, 206n51
Bruner, Jerome, 33n105
Buckley, William F., 21, 40, 41, 87, 169
Bultmann, Rudolph, 86
Bunyan, John, 132
Burke, Kenneth, 10, 23, 61–62
Bush, George W., 2, 40, 119; campaign biography of, 14–15; Pauline conversion and, 34n117
Bushkoff, Leonard, 130

Caldwell, Christopher, 129
Campbell, Karlyn Kohrs, 140
Camwell, Jack, 203
Carmichael, Stokely, 96
Carter, Jimmy, 15
case studies, 4, 17–18
CC. See *Confessions of a Conservative*
Central Intelligence Agency (CIA), 41–42
Chamberlain, John, 40
Chambers, Whittaker, 3, 18, 19, 19–22; on anti-intellectualism, 49–53; approach of, 44; as authority, 44, 45; Bjerre-Poulsen on, 81n245; Breit on, 79n173; charges against, 55; childhood of, 60; Christianity of, 45; claims of, 46–49; on Cold War, 39; as Communist, 39, 40–41, 44, 45, 75n73; on conspiracies, 46–47, 182; on converts, 53–54, 75n71; criticism of, 53, 56–58; death of, 41; deliberations of, 43–44; doubts in, 64; Downing on, 71n55; early career of, 61; epistemology of, 51; on espionage, 44; experience of, 24; Facebook on, 70n33; on faith, 50, 185; family of, 42, 51, 54; Frankel on, 68n2; on future, 163; Genter on, 68n4, 77n113, 80n217; on God, 62; on Hiss, 54; Hiss on, 75n83; Hook on, 79n172; Horowitz on, 120; impact of, 39–40, 65; inconsistencies of, 70n42; journey of, 54, 66, 190; Lee on, 71n47; Lewis on, 77n117; life of, 40–42; on media, 55; on modernity, 49; motivation of, 42, 65–68, 205n34; on mysticism, 77n119; on nature, 58–62; Nixon on, 68n6; perjury of, 42; personal life of, 45–46; Presidential Medal of Freedom for, 39–40; pressures on, 55; as providential, 64; Rahv on, 79n180; Reagan on, 40, 56; on reason, 52; religion and, 41, 49–50, 54, 55, 187–188; resources of, 44–53; reviews on, 71n55–74n58; self-reflection of, 61; on Stalin, 77n129; Strachey on, 79n179; support of, 197; testimony of, 39–40, 41; on theology, 50; at *Time*, 52; transformation of, 63; vision of, 51–52; Weinstein on, 69n25; Wills on, 177n17; world view of, 57–58; Wright on, 76n90. *See also* Hiss-Chambers trials
Chapin, Bernard, 141
Charland, Maurice, 12
Chaves, Mark, 204n15
Chomsky, Noam, 96–97, 105
Christianity, 9; in ancient Rome, 18–19; Catholic rituals, 12; of Chambers, 45; Communism compared to, 63; in Greek philosophy, 9–10; Protestantism, 43; traditions of, 174
CIA. *See* Central Intelligence Agency
citizenship, 6, 27n39
civic engagement, 9
civic resignation, 67
civil religion: challenges of, 16–17; discourses of, 6; expressions of, 17; favoring, 23–24; persuasion of, 187–188; in politics, 35n130; rhetoric of, 23, 204n15; Rousseau and, 35n130; strategy of, 3–4, 16, 17; use of, 201
civil rights, 5–6
Clark, Ramsey, 91
Clayton, Bruce, 98

Clinton, Bill, 2, 201
Coe, Kevin, 135
Cold War, 24, 200–201; anxieties about, 42; Chambers on, 39; domino theory of, 3, 39; dualism and, 54; in prefiguring, 64
Coleman, William E., 4
Collier, Peter, 121, 128, 133
Colson, Charles, 15
Columbia University, 40
comic deliberative vision, 97
comic frame, 97, 114n116
Commentary, 84–85, 99, 100, 110n17
communication, 3; all-encompassing, 9; anti-deliberative, 23; criticism in, 175; to development, 94; forms of, 4; interactive processes of, 7–8; mass, 14; media and, 5; motivation of, 190; Podhoretz and, 84, 185; practice of, 9; public, 184–187; purpose of, 58; in religion, 10–11, 20; technology for, 5; theories of, 43, 114n98, 184–185
Communism, 5–6, 19–20, 21; Chambers in, 39, 40–41, 44, 45; Christianity compared to, 63; conspiracy theories in, 44–45; control of, 60, 125–126; fighting, 42; against intellectualism, 50; murders in, 48; Podhoretz on, 88; "sleeper apparatus" in, 47; threat of, 45; in U.S., 46. *See also* American Communist Party
Confessions (Augustine), 11–12, 13, 18–19
The Confessions (Rousseau), 1
Confessions of a Conservative (CC) (Wills), 22; argumentation in, 168–170; Augustine for, 162, 168; criticism of, 176; deliberative rhetoric of, 162–173; dualism in, 162; features of, 161, 162; on God, 164; on identity discourse, 170–173; on judgments, 168–169; language of, 200; as narrative, 159–176; oppositions in, 164; perspective of, 159–160; on politics, 165–166; on public life, 163; reviews of, 172–173; rhetoric of, 24–25
conservatism, U.S., 18, 56, 101, 166, 196; characteristics of, 141; Horowitz on, 129; metaethical commitment, 127; model for, 84; values of, 125; after World War II, 197. *See also* Republican Party
conspiracy theories, 44–47, 65
Constitution, U.S., 6, 201
contradictions, 197–198
Copernicus, Nicolas, 1
Coulter, Ann, 40
Coulter, Jeff, 130, 136
Craig, Jane Larkin, 113n60
Crist, Charlie, 2
Crosby, Richard, 194
Crosston, Matthew, 108n2
culture, 4, 34n116
current events, 62–63
Curtis, Adam, 106, 195

deconstructivism, 33n105
definition, 9–10
deliberation: Asen on, 7; authors on, 186–187; *BR* as, 86–87; goal of, 7–8; public, 7, 145; public expression, 95–96; *RS* as, 122–123; types of, 67
democracy: deliberative, 9; functioning of, 7; genuine, 130; Western, 19
Democrat Party, 2, 18, 201–202
Van Den Haag, Ernest, 93, 104
Descartes, René, 1, 12–13, 32n101
Destructive Generation (Collier and Horowitz), 121, 128, 133
Diamond, Glenn, 104
discourse: church-state, 4, 6–7, 16; of civil religion, 6; generational, 136; identity, 170–173; propagandistic, 105; religious, 182; secular, 10, 15, 182. *See also* public discourse
Domke, David, 135
Dorsey, Peter A., 34n112
Dos Passos, John, 62, 76n98
Downing, Francis, 71n55
dualism: challenges of, 57–58; Cold War and, 54; complex dichotomy, 66; as concept, 53–64; impact of, 56; Manichaean, 53; nature and, 58; opposition to, 56–57; parameters of, 55
Duke, David, 34n120
Durkheim, Émile, 16

elections, 5, 14, 16
Emancipation Proclamation, 19

Enlightenment, 87
ethnography, 32n101
Ex-Friends (Podhoretz), 116n177–117n178
experiential discourse, 35n128

Fabj, Valeria, 15
Facebook, 70n33
faith: battle between, 54; Chambers on, 50; reason and, 52; in rhetorical action, 52; traditions of, 90–91; uses of, 17
Falwell, Jerry, 17
Farrell, Henry, 143
Farrell, Thomas, 200–201
feminism, 13, 19, 140–141
Fenster, Mark, 74n61
film, 36n155
Finn, Thomas, 10
Fisher, Walter, 128, 197
Forbes, Michael, 198
foreign policy, 42
Frankel, Benjamin, 68n2
Free World Colossus (Horowitz), 137
The Free World Colossus (Horowitz), 120
French Revolution, 18–19
Freud, Sigmund, 1
future, 198–203

Garsten, Bryan, 175
Genter, Robert, 62, 68n4, 77n113, 80n217
Gerson, Mark, 88–89
Giddens, Anthony, 196
globalization, 199
God, 62, 123, 135, 164
The God That Failed (Koestler), 19
Goldman, Emma, 13
Goldwater, Barry, 166
Goodnight, Thomas G., 78n139, 122, 175
Goody, Jack, 34n116
Gooren, Henri, 31n77
Graham, William, 34n116
Greek philosophy, 9–10
Gregg, Richard, 140

Habermas, Jürgen, 5, 8, 173–174, 179n103–180n105
Hahn, Dan, 166, 178n50, 183
Harding, Susan, 17, 201
Hardy, Barbara, 206n56

Harstock, Nancy, 140
Hausknecht, Murray, 62
Hayden, Tom, 134–135
Heilbrunn, Jacob, 20, 36n143
Hellman, Lillian, 96
Hempton, David, 183, 206n60
Heterodoxy, 128
Hicks, Darren, 43, 156n251
Hill, Anita, 2
Hindmarsh, D. Bruce, 199
Hiss, Albert, 21, 41, 172; Chambers and, 54, 75n83; Richer on, 70n32; on testifying, 70n27
Hiss-Chambers trials, 41–43
history: patterns of, 6; persuasive appeals in, 11–14; premodern, 10; Western, 1
Hitchens, Christopher, 98, 105
Hobbes, Thomas, 175
Hollander, Paul, 98, 104
Hook, Sidney, 48, 79n172
Horner, Charles, 79n170
Horowitz, David, 2, 19, 20, 21–22, 119; on censorship, 126; on Chambers, 120; choices of, 128; on conservatism, 129; development and, 132, 136; disability of, 133–134; doubts of, 128, 145; education of, 120; family of, 131, 132–134, 138; on flip-flopping, 144; on generations, 132; on God, 135; innocence of, 134; journey of, 131–132; as knowing, 124; on Left, 125; life of, 120–122; as Marxist, 133–135; motivation of, 122; on Podhoretz, 120; on psychological experience, 136–142; on purity, 198; on racism, 121; on reflexivity, 124–131, 186; relationships of, 139–140; religion and, 135, 187–188; rhetoric of, 24, 129; second thoughts of, 133, 144; self-reflection of, 137; Teach Freedom Award for, 120; as unworldly, 139
House Un-American Activities Committee, 41
Howard, Robert Glenn, 174
Howe, Irving, 57
Huckfeldt, Robert, 195–196
Hulse, Carl, 207n62
human convention, 24–25
human rights, 48. *See also* civil rights

identity change, 23, 24, 198
impeachment, 2
Imus, Don, 40
innovation, 30n72
intellectualism, 50, 87–93; Communism against, 50; disservice to, 96; as resource, 105–106. *See also* anti-intellectualism
Isocrates, 181

Jacobsen, Arvid, 63
Jacoby, Susan, 42
James, William, 10
Jasinkski, James, 28n44
Johnson, Lyndon, 112n43
Johnson, Paul, 195–196
Judaism, 9, 10, 102
Judd, Orrin, 125
Judeo-Christian Bible, 135
judgments, 23–25
Judis, John, 43
Judt, Tony, 57

Kaylor, Brian, 4
Kendall, Willmoore, 169
Kerry, Bob, 40
Kesler, Charles R., 110n21
Killian, Mitchell, 36n144
Kimmage, Michael, 39
King, Martin Luther, Jr., 170
King, Rodney, 121–122
Koestler, Arthur, 19, 133
Kramer, Hilton, 97–98
Kristol, Irving, 87, 109n3, 132
Ku Klux Klan, 34n120

Lake, Randall, 35n122, 60, 133
Lakoff, George, 144
Lee, John, 176
Lee, Michael, 18, 39, 71n47
Lehmann-Haupt, Christopher, 104
Lekachman, Robert, 98
Leonard, John, 104
Lewis, Hyrum, 77n113, 206n59
liberalism, 21, 104
Lieder, Tim, 142
Lipset, Seymour, 19
literacy, 34n116
Locke, John, 13

Lofland, John, 20
Longinus (saint), 181
Lopez, Donald, 199
Luckman, Thomas, 23, 204n17
Luther, Martin, 174
Lynch, Michael, 124

Mafia, 15
Mahoney, Daniel, 53
Making It (Podhoretz), 99, 100, 109n9
Manichaean rhetoric, 65, 92
March of Reason, 87–93
Marietta, Morgan, 182
Martin, Craig, 11, 17, 147
Martin, Kingsley, 57
Marxism, 2, 46, 119, 133–135
materialism, 49
Mather, Cotton, 147
McCarthyism, 41, 42
McCutcheon, Russell, 11
Mcdonald, Michael, 161
McMillan, Craige, 56
McNamara, Robert, 130
Medhurst, Martin, 36n144
media: Chambers on, 55; communication and, 5; impact of, 7–8, 202–203; reasonability in, 5; reasoning in, 5–7; rise of, 5; values of, 5
medical metaphors, 89–90
Meranto, Oneida, 129
Mill, John Stuart, 13
Miller, Merle, 53
Miller, Zell, 2, 196–197
Mills, C. Wright, 98
Mills, Nicolaus, 121
Modernism, 49
Monaldo, Frank, 129
Moral Man and Immoral Society (Niebuhr), 167–168
Morris, Richard B., 75n74
motives, 34n120
motivism, 132
movements: 1960s, 83, 93–95, 96, 97, 100, 102, 108, 121; comeback between, 196; goals of, 28n44; identities and, 195–197; sexual minority, 98; social, 97

narratives: *BR* as, 83–108; *CC* as, 159–176; challenges of, 23–24; choices in, 193; comparison of, 183–184; impact of, 8; personal, 11–12; public amendment to, 193; of reasoning, 8; *RS* as, 119–147; subset of, 8; time and identity in, 192–194; *Witness* as, 39–68
Nash, George, 113n63
National Public Radio, 2
National Review, 40, 41, 99, 169
National Security Agency (NSA), 41–42
nature: Chambers on, 58–62; conversion and, 59; dualism and, 58; human action in, 60; metaphors on, 59–61; order of, 61; as reasoning, 61; in *Witness*, 58–62, 66
neoconservatism, 3, 83, 88, 89, 109n3
The Neoconservative Vision (Gerson), 88–89
Neuhaus, Richard John, 98
New Deal, 55
New Left, 83, 131, 136
Newman, Cardinal, 166
Newton, John, 1
New York Times, 40, 41–42, 128
Niebuhr, Reinhold, 46–47, 167–168
Nieli, Russell, 53
Nixon, Richard, 39, 68n6
Nixon administration, 15
Nock, A. D., 10, 30n73
Noll, Mark, 11
Novak, Robert, 40
NSA. *See* National Security Agency
Nye Committee, 76n105–77n106

Obama, Barack, 2, 202
Olasky, Marvin, 53
Olbrys, Stephen, 143
O'Leary, Stephen, 35n123
O'Shaughnessy, Nicholas, 173

Pagan, 10
Palczewski, Catherine, 8
Parsley, Bonnie, 130
The Party's Over: How the Extreme Right Hijacked the GOP and I Became a Democrat (Crist), 2
Passell, Josh, 203
pathographies, 137–138

Pauline conversion, 14, 31n87–32n88, 34n117
Perjury (Weinstein), 41
perservatism, 30n72
personal transformation, 2
persuasion theory, 51
persuasive appeal, 9–17
Peters, Gerald, 9, 34n116, 199, 200, 207n70
Pharisee effect, 27n41
Phelps-Roper, Megan, 203
The Pilgrim's Progress (Bunyan), 132
Pinsker, Sanford, 129
Podhoretz, Norman, 19, 20, 21–22; on anti-Semitism, 116n158; arguments of, 101; associations of, 95; as author, 85; beliefs of, 87; career of, 83; claims of, 106; communication and, 84, 182–183, 185; on Communism, 88; complexity for, 94; criticism of, 92, 93–94, 98, 109n4; deliberative vision of, 93; on dissent, 95; education of, 84; enemies of, 94–95; on environment, 91; expression use of, 97, 107; fairness of, 197; family of, 85, 86; Horowitz on, 120; on human agency, 190; inspiration for, 86; on intellectualism, 86, 87; journey of, 89; on Left, 102; life of, 84–85; methods of, 98; motivation of, 115n139; on movements, 89; praises from, 101; predictions of, 111n35; on public discourse, 84; on public policy, 106; on public reason, 203n7–204n8; public revelation of, 83; on radicalism, 90, 91–92, 93; reductive conversion of, 91; on religion, 187–188; religion of, 101–102; resources of, 87–108; respect of, 113n55; rhetoric of, 24, 106; on *Time*, 112n45; transformation of, 106; vision of, 107
policy: discussions on, 9; public, 92, 173; views of, 2. *See also* foreign policy
political development, 131–136
political parties, 17–18. *See also* Democrat Party; Republican Party
political transformations, 9–10
politics: authority in, 191–192; *CC* on, 165–166; celebrities in, 5; civil religion in, 35n132; confessional rhetorics in,

11; contemporary, 14–15; culture of, 4; decline in, 5; of human convention, 24–25; identity, 198; Italian, 15; modernity in, 14; personalization of, 202; postwar, 3, 181; reasoning in, 5–7; religion compared to, 6, 20; religion in, 4; self-disclosure in, 19; special faculty of, 191; support for, 202; transformation in, 19; U.S., 3; Wills in, 163

Popkin, Samuel, 5, 205n33

Postman, Neil, 105, 162

prefiguring: in Cold War, 64; definition of, 62; uses of, 63–64; in *Witness*, 62–64, 66

Presidential Medal of Freedom, 85

print culture, 18

The Professors (Horowitz), 121

progress, 13

propaganda, 181

The Prophets: Who They Were, What They Are (Podhoretz), 113n63

psychological-narrative writing, 195

public accountability, 200–201

public affairs, 4

public civility, 143

public debates, 8–9, 67, 182–198

public decision making, 8

public discourse: arguments, 8; case studies for, 25; concern for, 9; contributions to, 3, 199; criteria for, 24; leftists on, 94; Podhoretz on, 84; reason in, 201; reduction of, 194; strategic, 3; study of, 20; truth in, 197; *Witness* on, 40

public figures, 23

The Public Interest, 99

public reason, 203n7–204n8

public reorientation, 11

public square, 187

public storytelling, 7–9

public values, 6

Puritans, 12–13

Quakerism, 21, 52

Raab, Earl, 30n72

racism, 100–101, 121, 194

radical change, 30n73

radicalism, 100

Radical Son: A Generational Odyssey (RS) (Horowitz), 19; approach of, 131; criticism of, 130; debate in, 138–139; as deliberation, 122–123; on future, 145–146; generational focus in, 122–123; goal of, 142, 147; on human nature, 134; impact of, 119–120; maturity journey in, 136, 183; motivation of, 183–184; as narrative, 119–147; on progress, 145; resources in, 24, 123–142; reviews of, 123, 135–136, 141–142; strategies of, 146–147; vision of, 141

Rahv, Philip, 57, 61, 79n180

Raimondo, Justin, 136

Ratzinger, Joseph, 179n103–180n105

Rawls, John, 13

Reagan, Ronald, 8–9, 21, 40, 56, 83

reasoning: experience for, 8; narrative modes of, 8; nature as, 61; standards of, 87, 88

redemption, 24

reductive conversion form, 107

reflexivity, 124–131

Reformation, 12

Reilly, John, 128–129

religion, 1–2, 5–6, 7; activism in, 16–17; associations of, 37n166; Augustine on, 171; authority in, 20–21; Chambers and, 41, 49–50, 54, 55, 187–188; church, 34n116; communication in, 10–11, 20; conversion in, 9–10; discourses of, 182; Horowitz and, 135, 187–188; Podhoretz and, 101–102, 187–188; in politics, 4; politics compared to, 6, 20; prophetic, 10; in public life, 188; rational forms of, 20; sacred spaces in, 200; secularity and, 201; support from, 14; symbolism of, 16; thought in, 20–21; transformation within, 4; in U.S., 16; of Wills, 165, 171. *See also* civil religion; God

religionists, 6

Republican Like Me: How I Left the Liberal Bubble and Learned to Love the Right (Stern), 2

Republican Party, 2, 18, 119–120, 201–202

Republican Party National Convention
 (1966), 120
Republican Party National Convention
 (2004), 2
resources: of Chambers, 44–53; conspiracy
 as, 65; intellectualism as, 105–106;
 maturity as, 131–136, 144–145;
 reflexivity as, 124–131, 142–143; in
 RS, 123–142
revivalism, 123
rhetoric: apocalyptic, 62; confessional, 15,
 35n128; confrontational movement,
 93–94; conspiracy, 182–183;
 convenience, 165–168; generational,
 122, 126, 143–144; of Horowitz, 24,
 129; human knowledge, 126–127;
 inner-directed, 127; interactional,
 182–183; of maturity, 131–136;
 psychological experience, 136–142,
 146; reflexive, 127–128; Wills on, 164
Richer, Matthew, 70n32
Roberts, Henry, 53
Rockefeller, Marion, 138
Roe v. Wade, 2
Romano, John, 104, 112n37
Roof, Wade Clark, 131
Rothbard, Murray, 104–105
Rousseau, Jean-Jacques, 1, 13, 16, 18–19,
 35n130, 90–91
*RS. See Radical Son: A Generational
 Odyssey*
Rusher, William, 40
Ryfe, David, 193

Scheer, Robert, 131, 134
Scherer, Matthew, 32n102–33n103
Schlesinger, Arthur, 57
scholarships, 138; debate in, 173; focus of,
 10; interdisciplinary, 7; twentieth-
 century, 10
science, 1–2, 32n101, 91
scientific enlightenment, 13
Scott, Robert, 94
Second Thoughts Books, 119, 126, 192
self-definition, 19
self-plagiarizing, 100
self-reflection, 130
Sheerin, John, 53
Sheppard, R. Z., 172–173

Sherman, Scott, 148n5
Skonovd, Norman, 20
slaves, 13–14
Smith, Donald, 94
Sobran, M. J., 167
social advocacy, 19
social imaginary, 37n168
socialization, 33n105
social programs, 129
social trends, 18
society, 20
sociological writing, 195
sociology, 16, 20
Sontag, Susan, 92
Soviet Union, 48, 121–122
Specter, Arlen, 198
Spiegel, Gabrielle, 195
Spinoza, Baruch, 61–62
Sprague, John, 195–196
Stalin, Joseph, 77n129
Stanton, Elizabeth Cady, 13
Stern, Ken, 2
Strachey, John, 79n179
strategy: civil-religious, 3–4, 16, 17; for
 future, 17–25; of public figures, 23;
 rhetorical, 3; of *Witness*, 43–44
Students for Democratic Society, 95
Sunnyside, 138–139
Sunstein, Cass, 7
Supreme Court, U.S., 2, 6
Svensson, Jakob, 206n50
Swaggart, Jimmy, 204n11

Talisse, Robert, 103
Tanenhaus, Sam, 67
Taylor, Charles, 22, 37n168
Tell, Dave, 15, 35n128, 185
testimony, 9
theology, 50
Thomas, Clarence, 2
Time, 40, 52, 67, 112n45
Tinder, Glenn, 165
de Toledano, Ralph, 52
totalitarianism, 19, 110n17
traditionalist fundamentalism, 90
traditions, 17, 173–174, 174
transformation: in politics, 19; role of, 14;
 sense of, 11; social, 34n112
trends, 71n47

Trump, Donald, 2

Unitarianism, 16, 35n130
United States (U.S.): alliance of, 83; Communism in, 46; confessional form in, 35n128; disestablishment clause of, 23–24; espionage in, 44; faith in, 11; generational discourse in, 136; individualism in, 122, 186; modern conservatism in, 39; politics of, 3; postwar, 18, 68; power in, 67; racism in, 194; religion in, 16; trends in, 1–2; Wills on, 167. *See also* conservatism
University of California in Berkeley, 97

Vietnam War, 15, 20, 21, 83, 95
Vitullo-Martin, Julia, 145
Voight, Jon, 40
voting, 5

Walker, John, 130
Wallace, Michael, 128
Ware group committee, 46
Warner, Edwin, 111n36
Watson, Martha, 195
Weaver, Richard, 58–59
Weber, Max, 21
Weidner, John, 53
Weinstein, Allen, 41, 69n25
Wilcox, Clyde, 36n144
Will, George, 40
Willard, Charles, 8
Williamson, Bishop, 56
Wills, Garry, 22; as activist, 177n7; alliances of, 24–25; on Augustine, 177n45–177n46; career of, 159; on Chambers, 177n17; on community, 164–165; on contradictions, 198; direction of, 160; on family, 178n51; image of, 179n86; life of, 160–161; motivation of, 164, 200; in politics, 163; on pressures, 169–170, 183; on reasoning, 167, 169; religion of, 165, 171; on rhetoric, 164; on self, 172; on U.S., 167; vision of, 175
Witness (Chambers), 3, 18, 19, 21–22; conspiracy and, 44–49, 49; controversy over, 41; as deliberation, 43–44; Dos Passos on, 76n98; dualism in, 66; impact of, 39–40; journey in, 62; language of, 60; motivation for, 65–68; as narrative, 39–68; nature in, 58–62, 66; outcomes of, 68; prefiguring in, 62–64; in public discourse, 40, 67; reviews on, 48, 55, 64, 67, 75n75, 77n108; rhetoric of, 24, 42; role of, 40; second persona of, 43; strategy of, 43–44; structure of, 39, 53; success of, 42; *Time* on, 67; truth of, 43; vision of, 65–66, 183; worldview of, 66–67
women, 13, 140. *See also* feminism
Women's Social and Political Union, 13
Worcester, Kent, 142
World War II, 19, 42; conservatism, U.S. after, 197; impact of, 49; Judaism and, 102
Wright, Charles Alan, 76n90

Yancey, Philip, 64
Yardley, Jonathan, 142

About the Author

Don Waisanen is an associate professor in the Baruch College, CUNY Marxe School of Public and International Affairs, where he teaches courses and workshops in public communication—including executive speech training, communication strategy, and seminars on leadership and improvisation. All his research projects seek to understand how communication works to promote or hinder the force of citizens' voices. Previously, Don was a Coro Fellow and worked in broadcast journalism, as a speechwriter, and on political campaigns. He is the founder of Communication Upward, an adjunct lecturer at Columbia University, and he received a Ph.D. in communication from the University of Southern California's Annenberg School.